“There are probably few Churches in England which have passed through such vicissitudes as that of Greyfriars, Reading, and whenever its story comes to be told in detail, it will certainly be an interesting one.”

- William Ravenscroft, F.S.A., 1905

“For he who does not know the long story behind the privileges and treasures he inherits is in danger of taking them for granted, and, failing to appreciate them intelligently, he may not preserve them for posterity.”

- F. Gordon Spriggs 1963
in “History of the Church of Greyfriars Reading”

The east end dais

Contents:

Introduction: 700 years of history vii

1. The Grey Friars: 1233 to 1538 1
2. Dissolution and Disposal: 1538 to 1542 17
3. The Guildhall: 1542 to 1578 23
4. The Hospital/Poor House: 1578 to 1614 27
5. The House of Correction: 1614 to 1642 31
6. A Soldiers' Barracks: 1642 to 1643 43
7. The House of Correction, then Bridewell: 1644 to 1862 47
8. Rev. W. W. Phelps: The Restorer of Greyfriars 65
9. The Restoration: 1862 to 1863 75
10. Re-consecration: December 1863 85
11. Shadwell Morley Barkworth, the first Vicar: 1863 to 1874 91
12. Seymour Henry Soole: Vicar 1874 to 1905 113
13. Hugh Edmund Boultbee: Vicar 1905 to 1915 153
14. William Augustus Doherty: Vicar 1916 to 1924 171
15. John Clifford Rundle: Vicar 1924 to 1947 185
16. John Knott Page: Vicar 1947 to 1968 207
17. James Knox Spence: Vicar 1968 to 1978 233
18. Peter Norwell Downham: Vicar 1979 to 1995 253
19. Jonathan Anthony De Burgh Wilmot: Vicar from 1995 277

Epilogue 314
Acknowledgements 315
Endnotes and Sources 317

1311-2011

greyfriars church

700 years

Introduction

700 years of History

Greyfriars Church has a much more varied history than most other English parish Churches. It can probably boast several unique features in all, but its crowning glory is that it is the most complete Franciscan foundation in England that is still in use as a Church today. Unsurprisingly it is a Grade I listed building.

In 2011 Greyfriars celebrated 700 years since the completion of the Friary Church, and in December 2013 it celebrates 150 years as a Church of England parish Church. From the sixteenth to the nineteenth centuries there was a total of 325 years – almost half of its life – when the building was not used for religious purposes. This period stretched from the Dissolution of the Monasteries under Henry VIII until the Victorian era and the rapid expansion of Reading, which required more Churches to serve the growing population.

The stages of the life of the building can be briefly stated: initially a late thirteenth/early fourteenth century Friary with its Church; following its dissolution in 1538, the Friary Church became in turn the town Guildhall, a Poor House or Hospital, and then a House of Correction, or prison – later known as a Bridewell. Along the way it was also taken over for a short while as a garrison in the Civil War. Much of its site was taken up by housing by the nineteenth century. There was even a public house attached to it, fronting onto Friar Street. Then, in 1863, it was restored to Church use and began and has continued with a strong Evangelical tradition.

This history is not just the story of the Greyfriars Church buildings and land. As I have worked through the story of the last 700 years, using as far as possible contemporary sources, it has also been my aim to try to bring the experience of the people associated with Greyfriars and something of their story to life.

I have kept most of the original spelling in quoted sources, occasionally adding clarification where I thought that it might be needed. This has led to the interesting variety of names for the Church: Grey Friars' Church, Grey Friars Church, Greyfriars' Church, as well as the present day version Greyfriars Church. I did, however, draw the line at Grey Friar's Church and have therefore moved the apostrophe whenever that version appeared!

The west wall, west window, north and south walls and most of the columns are original 14th century stone

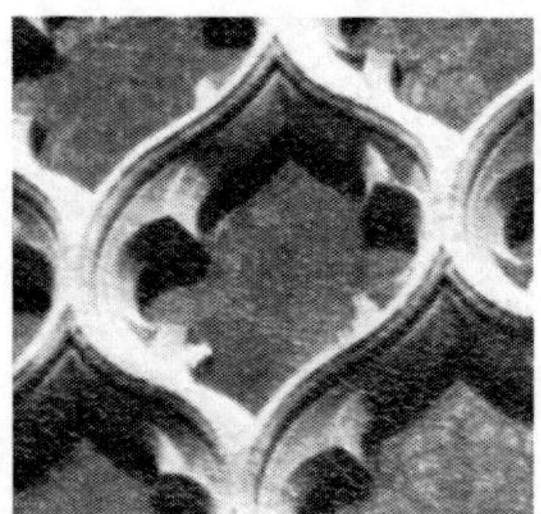

Detail of the fine tracery of the west window (viewed from outside)

Chapter 1

The Grey Friars: 1233 to 1538

Opinions differ as to the date when the Friars Minors, being those who followed the recently established rule of Francis of Assisi, actually arrived in England. It depends whether the original sources, who date the event in the fourth year after the coronation of King Henry III, meant the first such coronation date of 1216 when Henry was 10 years old, or the 1220 second coronation date.

Francis had obtained Pope Innocent III's sanction to the formation of his *Ordo Fratrum Minorum*, the Order of the Friars Minors, on 16th April 1209. The Order rapidly increased in number and very quickly spread across Europe and into Africa and Asia. Francis died on 3rd October 1226 and he was pronounced a saint by Pope Gregory IX less than two years later.

The leader of the mission to England, Agnellus of Pisa, had been hand-picked by Francis himself in 1219 following the Second General Chapter of the Order. Francis commissioned Agnellus to go to England, constituting him as "Minister Provincial of England." Francis wrote:

> I Brother Francis of Assisi, Minister General, command you Brother Agnellus of Pisa, in virtue of obedience, to go to England, and there do the Office of Minister Provincial. Farewell. In the year 1219.[1]

The earliest and latest possible dates of arrival in England given in the various Franciscan annals are 3rd May 1220[2] and 10th September 1224[3]. Although the date is uncertain, authorities agree that this first group of four clerics and five lay brothers landed at Dover and lost no time in reporting to the King and gaining his blessing. Their first House at Oxford was quickly established. Many more Franciscan arrivals over time bolstered their mission to England. It is a measure of their success that after about 30 years from their first arrival in England the Friars Minors had established almost 50 Houses with a total of over 1200 brethren. They went on to build in total some sixty-four churches, of which just fifteen remain to greater or lesser degree.

Unfortunately, nothing is known of the individual friars who came to Reading in 1233 with the intention of staying and ministering to the poor of the town. Their first task was to go to see the Abbot of Reading Abbey.

Having been founded by Henry I in 1121, by 1233 Reading Abbey was already over a hundred years old – although it had taken until about 1164 for the building work to be completed. The monks followed the Benedictine order and the House was both rich and influential. The Abbey was the main landowner of the area, with the Abbot as Lord of the Manor, and it dominated the town and its three churches – St. Giles, St. Laurence and St. Mary.

The friars, in their grey habits, presented themselves to the 11th Abbot, Adam de Lathbury, requesting to be allowed to settle near the town.

The friars had prepared the way beforehand. According to a contemporary source, they arrived at Reading Abbey with letters from both King Henry III and Pope Gregory IX, which instructed the abbot to allow them to live in the town. Not only with such powerful backing but also "through much insistence they obtained a place to live near the bridge of Reading from the reluctant abbot."[4]

The abbot's reluctance showed itself both by the location he decided upon and the constraints that he included. The deed covering the grant was dated at Reading on 14th July 1233:

> Enrolment of a deed, whereby the abbot and convent of Reading grant to the friars minors land in the culture, called Vastern, adjoining the high road, measuring thirty-three perches in length and twenty-three in breadth, that they may there build and dwell, so long as they have no property; and the friars minors agree that if at any time they have property or aught of their own, the abbot and convent may eject them from the said land without contradiction or appeal; and that they will never require any other dwelling place on the lands of the abbey or endeavour to enlarge their house, upon the same penalty; nor will they ever require any support from the said abbot and convent, save what is freely given to them, upon the same penalty; nor will they bury in their grave-yard at Reading any bodies but those of friars minors without special licence of the abbot and convent, upon the same penalty; nor shall they take any offerings, legacies or tithes due to the abbot and convent, upon the same penalty; but if the abbot and convent expel them on any other ground than those above recited, the king shall cause the said friars minors to possess the said land, so that they shall hold of his grace what they held of the grace of the abbot and convent; but if ever the said friars minors abandon their said habitation, the land and all the buildings thereon shall revert to the said abbot and convent; of all which a chirograph has been made and the part remaining

> with the abbot and convent sealed with the common seal of the minors in England, and with the seal of the King and with the seals of the Archbishop of York, and the bishops of Winchester, Coventry, and Worcester.[5]

The word "culture" was usually used in the Middle Ages to denote a cultivated piece of land. Since the land "called Vastern" was undoubtedly better described as marshy wasteland, this could be considered as something of a misnomer.

The medieval word "chirograph" might also need an explanation. This was a document written in duplicate on a single piece of parchment. The word *chirographum* was written across the middle and then the parchment was cut through, often with a wavy or serrated cut. Each party would posses a copy of the document, which could be verified as genuine by fitting the original pieces together.

The land that was granted to these first Grey Friars was on the right hand side of the road that passed over the Thames at the Caversham Bridge, about half a mile from the town. There was certainly a bridge over the Thames at this time as a record from just two years before mentions the "Chapel of St. Anne on the bridge at Reading over the Thames."[6]

The size of the plot granted by Reading Abbey was recorded as 33 perches by 23 perches. A Royal Ordinance of 1270 (Edward I) entitled "Assize of Weights and Measures" defined a perch as a quarter of a chain, which is 16½ feet. However, earlier in the century the perch varied in size up to 24 feet, often depending on the value of the ground being measured. In fact, the perch has led a very uncertain life over the centuries; in the 16th century, a perch was defined, for example, rather quaintly but imprecisely, as the total length of the left feet of the first 16 men to leave Church on a Sunday morning!

It is therefore difficult to be certain of the actual size of the land granted. Taking 16½ feet for a perch, the lengths convert to approximately 180 yards by 125 yards, or just less than 5 acres in area. If the Abbey used the more generous 24 feet to a perch, then the area would have been about 10 acres.

The development of the first Reading House of Grey Friars can be traced from the records of gifts made by King Henry III:

May 1234	Henry granted that "the Friars Minors of Rading" (Reading) may "without hindrance or chiminage [a toll for passing through a forest] be able to remove timber from the forest of Windles [Windsor] until the feast of St. Michael this year for their buildings."[7]

June 1234	The King commanded Gileberto de Everle to provide seventy oaks from the forest of "Penbergh" (Pamber) for the rafters of the Church.[8]
August 1237	Simon de Lewknor, Sheriff of Berkshire, was instructed to "cause the chapel of the Friars Minors at Rading to be wainscoted."[9]
April 1238	The King granted three oaks for the friars to make choir stalls.[10]
August 1239	The King directed Hugh le Despenser, Sheriff of Berkshire, to "cause the stalls of the Friars Minors at Rading in their Church to be completed and two altars to be made in the chapel."[11] In the following February, the sum paid to Despenser for this work was noted in the records: 12 marks 9 shillings and 2 pennies – that is, between £8 and £9.[12]
August 1239	Hugh le Despenser was commanded by Henry to build a dormitory and a chapter house for the Brothers "at the pond." In addition, the Church was to have an altar board "painted and starred with gold."[13]
October 1239	The King ordered the Sheriff of Berkshire to "cause to be bought 52 ells of russet to make tunics for the use of the twelve Friars Minors at Rading, to wit 11d an ell at the most."[14] Russet was a coarse woollen cloth that was dyed either a grey or a brown shade. Since the Franciscans were "Grey Friars," the former seems more likely; however, the early Friars Minors dressed in either grey or medium brown. (The modern Franciscan habit is dark brown.) An ell was defined as the length of a man's arm. It is easy to visualise how a tailor measured out the required number of ells by using his own arm as the measuring stick.
1241	A two storey privy chamber was built. This toilet block would have been built over running water – most probably the Portman Brook, but this is speculation on my part. A record in December that year notes that the Sheriff of Berkshire was to be paid back the 50 marks (about £33) spent on the works, plus 100 shillings (£5) for clothing the friars that year.[15]
May 1244	The refectory was enlarged; its walls and roof were raised, three more large windows were put in the roof to light the hall, and the roof well shingled. A "proper pulpit" was provided in the refectory, from which readings from the Bible and from lives of saints were given at meal times.[16]

May 1244	The King granted the friars 4 logs from Windsor Forest for fuel.[17] They either did not collect or did not receive these four logs, as two months later there was a counter writ changing the gift of 4 logs to brushwood to the value of 5 marks (just over £3).[18]
February 1246	Alan de Farnham, the new Sheriff of Berkshire, was commanded to "make for the friars minors in Rading a fireplace in their infirmary." In addition, he was to make "a wall outside the infirmary extending to their privy chambers."[19]
February 1246	The King granted the friars 40 shillings (£2) "for the fabric of their Church out of the amercements [fines] of the eyre [circuit court] of Robert Passelewe and his fellows, the last justices itinerant in the county for pleas in the forest."[20]
June 1247	The friars were granted a further 4 oak trunks from the "Forest of Penberch" (Pamber) by the King's command to Henry de Farley, the Warden of Windsor Forest.[21]
June 1257	The King granted the Friary 5 oak trunks from Windsor Forest.[22] The friars again only received (or collected) part of the gift. In the following summer the King issued an instruction to Godfrey de Lyston, the new Warden of Windsor Forest, telling him to let the friars have three oak trunks, as they had only had two to date of the five promised.[23]
March 1259	The friars were granted six oaks from Windsor Forest in order to re-shingle the Church roof.[24] However, due to the untimely death of the Warden, Henry de Farley, the friars did not receive this gift. A record of the following year instructs Thomas Gresley, the "Justice of the Forests this side of the Trent," to ensure that the friars received their six oaks.[25]

After Henry's son Edward I succeeded to the throne in 1272, there is a record from 1280 showing that Edward granted to the Friary three oak trunks for fuel from Pamber Forest.[26]

The Friary had been on the site at Vastern for a little over 50 years by 1285. However, it was far from being entirely suitable. The main problem was that the land was low lying and marshy. As the Archbishop of Canterbury, John Peckham, wrote in a letter to the Minister General of the Order of Friars Minors, Brother Allot:

> The friars at Reading, compelled by the monks who had the chief authority there, had accepted a marshy situation, out of the town, very subject to floods; that, in the time of an inundation, they were obliged to quit the place, or to remain there in great danger; and that in winter the distance from the town made it very inconvenient for them to procure necessaries.[27]

John Peckham was himself a Franciscan, who had become Archbishop in January 1279. He held a Provincial Council at Reading Abbey in July that year and it was possibly at this point that he became acquainted with the problems faced by the Friary. In 1282 he wrote to the Abbot at Reading Abbey, Robert of Burgate, requesting that the friars be allowed to enlarge their site. However, it was three years later that Robert of Burgate finally granted the friars more land to enable them to move to higher ground.

The deed that allowed the friars this additional land – where the Church now stands – was dated the 7th before the kalends of June in the year 1285. As the kalends of June is 1st June, the 7th day before it is 25th May 1285 and so the history of Greyfriars on its current site can be dated from then.

This extension to the Friary grounds measured 16½ perches by 16 perches, adding about a third again in area to the original site. It was a welcome addition to the Friary's land as it was far superior to the marshy living quarters they had had to date. It also joined on to the extreme north west of the town in an area that was long known as Town End and described in the deed as:

> upon a piece of ground between the house of Sir Stephen the chaplain, the rector of the Church of Sulham, on the east and the sandy ditch on the west, and extending from the common way called 'New Street' to the end of the piece of ground, the use whereof the Friars have hitherto had and have and shall have henceforth of the abbot and convent's grace, saving the conditions specified below.[28]

This new deed of settlement was careful to repeat the stringent conditions imposed 52 years earlier. The deed was sealed with the seals of the Abbot (Robert of Burgate), of the Minister General of the Friars Minors (Brother Allot), of the Archbishop of Canterbury (John Peckham) and of the King (Edward I).

In 1288 the Friary land was increased by a bequest from Robert Fulco of Reading, one of the King's most trusted men.[29] This land adjoined the Friary in New Street (which in the course of time became known as Friar Street, after the Friary). This extension of their land does not seem to be within either the letter or the spirit of the deed of settlement with the Abbey, but it does not seem to have caused any problem for the Friary.

This second site took longer to complete than the first. Henry de Lacy, 3rd Earl of Lincoln, gave the friars 56 oaks for the building work – almost certainly for the roof – from his wood in "Asherigge," probably Ashridge, near Wokingham. Since this was within the bounds of the King's Forest of Windsor, royal permission was needed. On 11th January 1303, Edward wrote from Odiham to John de London, Constable of Windsor Castle and Keeper of the King's Forest there, giving the "Order to permit the friars minors at Redyng to fell and carry whither they wish fifty-six oaks fit for timber in the wood of Henry de Lacy, earl of Lincoln, at Asherigge, which is within the bounds of the king's forest of Windsor, as the earl has given them the said oaks."[30] I wonder how long it took for the friars to travel backwards and forwards to "Asherigge" wood to cut down and then transport 56 oaks back to Reading!

Among some 14th century documents from Reading is the will of Alan de Bannebury, dated 4th November 1311.[31] The majority of his estate was to go to his wife Christine and daughter Margery, with his hat shop being left to one of his executors. Among smaller bequests is one of 5 shillings for the Friars Minors of Reading. The Latin phrase used is *opera fratrum minorum*, which has been variously translated as "to the work" or "to the building" or "for the use" of the Grey Friars. It is possible that this bequest was to assist in the building works, implying that the works were not yet complete, or possibly coming to completion, at this date.

1311 has generally been taken therefore as the date at which the new Friary was finished, while recognising that the actual date is not known. Given that this represents 26 years after the deed of settlement for the new location the work could certainly be expected to have finished by this point, especially since the first Friary took about 7 years to complete. Personally, however, I think an earlier date, in or soon after 1303 when the building was roofed, is more likely for the Church to have been completed.

In the 1726 work "Collectanea Anglo-Minoritica, or A Collection of the Antiquities of the English Franciscans," written by the Franciscan historian Anthony Parkinson, the writer sums up the available knowledge of the Friary in Reading by saying "Here was a famous Convent of Franciscans... But I cannot learn who was founder here, what was the Title of the House, or that it had any Endowment of Lands; and therefore presume the Friars here subsisted wholly upon alms." It is sometimes said, though with no corroboration in early documents, that the House was dedicated to St. James.[32]

The lands were large enough to include areas for the friars to grow plants and vegetables and no doubt to have an orchard or two. There was at least one pond and most probably the Portman Brook ran through or alongside the site. The whole Friary was therefore of an impressive size, although it could not compare with the Abbey's 30 acres, or with the size and splendour of the Abbey itself.

The new Friary Church was, however, a remarkable building. The diagram below, adapted from F. Gordon Spriggs' History[33], shows the extent of the original building still present in the Church (the darker sections), with a conjectural shape and length of the whole Friary Church. It was unlikely to have had transepts as it is thought that they did not feature in Franciscan Church building of the time. There was a bell turret, at least by the sixteenth century, in either a tower or a steeple. A feature of many Franciscan Churches was a "walking place," a walk way through from the street between the nave and quire to the rest of the Friary grounds. It is therefore quite possible that Greyfriars had this feature too.

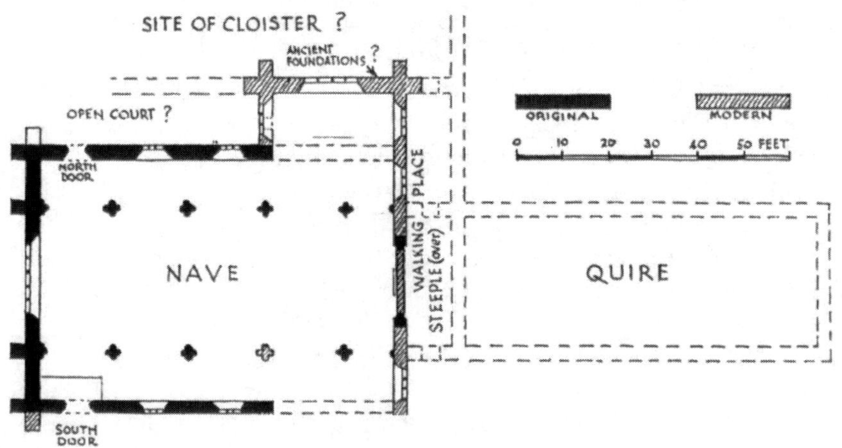

The style of architecture of the Friary Church is known now as "Decorated" or "Decorated Gothic." The key element of Decorated style is the fine tracery of the windows and this can be seen in the beautiful west window of the Church (see pages viii and 16). Although this window was restored in the 1862 – 1863 works, it remained faithful to the original style. An archaeological review in 1846 stated: "The west window is by far the finest part of the whole edifice and even now, worn and dilapidated as it is, presents a beautiful appearance. The tracery is of a flowing character, simple but elegant..."[34] Originally, it contained stained glass as some traces of this were discovered in the 19th century restoration.

Separating the aisles from the nave, a series of four pillars on each side create five arches, the most easterly arch being much narrower than the others as can be seen on the following photograph.

View to the north transept from the nave

The photograph below shows one of the original 14th century "head-stops" on the west end of the southern set of arches. Almost all of these head-stops had to be replaced in the 1862 – 1863 restoration.

Original 14th century head-stop on the west wall

The aisle windows, two to each side (north and south), show similarities to the west window, though with three lights instead of five and not arched.

Exterior of an aisle window, south side

The friars followed the Franciscan Rule of 1223, the third produced by Francis and the one still in use today. It begins: “The rule and life of the lesser brothers is this: To observe the holy gospel of our Lord Jesus Christ, living in obedience without anything of our own, and in chastity.”

After a year of probation, a new brother had to promise to follow the rule for the rest of his life, with no possibility of changing his mind – for “no one who puts his hand to the plough and then looks back is fit for the kingdom of God.”

The friars were to serve God in poverty and humility, “as pilgrims and strangers in the world,” and not be quarrelsome or critical of others. Rather they should conduct themselves at all times peacefully and gently, with an unassuming spirit. They were to be out in the world, helping the poor and those in ill health, the vulnerable and the downtrodden.

Original Mason's Mark
High up on the west window (not visible from the ground)
Photograph and sketch by F. Gordon Spriggs

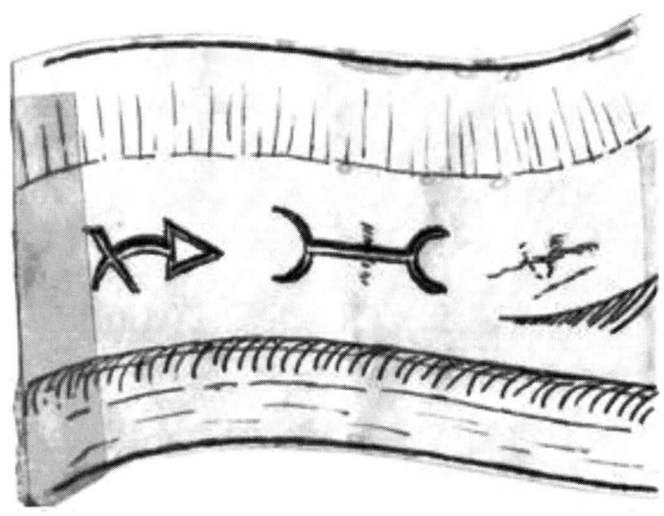

The Grey Friars were known as Preaching Friars. No brother (frère, from which we derive friar) could preach until he had been examined and approved by the Minister General of the Order. In their preaching their words should be "studied and chaste, useful and edifying to the people." The friars were also to be brief "because the Lord kept his words brief when he was on earth."

They were to keep the Divine Offices: matins, lauds, prime, terce, sext, none, vespers and compline, all according to the prescribed rites. They were to fast from All Saints to Christmas, during Lent and on Fridays. Their clothing was to be inexpensive – they were allowed two tunics, but only one of them was to have a hood. The friars were also to "avoid suspicious meetings or conversations with women," including the solemn injunction that they must not enter convents of nuns.[35]

The first friar whose name is known from the records is that of Warner, who is identified as the "Warden of the Franciscans at Reading." In 1320 Warner received from the Bishop of Salisbury, Roger de Mortival, a licence to hear confessions.[36]

By the end of the fourteenth century, there were some sixty Franciscan Houses, organised into seven "Custodies." The Reading House was in the Oxford Custody, according to a listing by Bartholomew of Pisa in 1399: "Oxford-Custody had eight Convents: viz 1. Oxford. 2. Reading. 3. Bedford. 4. Stanford. 5. Nottingham. 6. Northampton. 7. Leicester. 8. Grantham."[37]

The first friar from the Reading House to become known for his learning was John Lathbery, or Latterbury, of Reading. He flourished in the latter part of the fourteenth century, dying in 1406. He was a Doctor of Divinity of Oxford and became widely known for his deeply spiritual life and great understanding of the Bible. Leland wrote of his "manifold learning both sacred and profane; for he delved into the secrets of natural things and was a finished philosopher; he excelled also in the knowledge of theological learning."[38]

The next friar we know by name connected with the Friary in Reading was the most renowned English Franciscan of his day, variously called William Boteler or Butler. As Doctor and Professor at Oxford, he was considered "the chief Flower of their University."[39] He was chosen to be Minister General for the English Province around 1408. He wrote several learned books that were of great influence on the Church at the time, including "Determinatio," which argued for burning all copies of the English translation of the Scriptures. His belief was that if they were read by people who were not sufficiently qualified to understand them, it would lead to great error in the Church. He resigned his position as Minister General in 1410 and it was probably in that year that he retired to the Friary at Reading. Although there was a move to re-elect him as Minister General three years later, it is likely that he stayed in retirement and lived out his days quietly in Reading. In all probability he was buried in the Quire of the Friary, but this is conjecture.

The Friary continued to be the recipient of bequests. By a will of September 1461, proved in January 1462, John Hale of Reading bequeathed 3s 4d (a sixth of £1) to the Friary.[40] The relatively large gift of £10 5s 3d was made to the Friary in the will of John Leche, also known as John A'Larder, dated in London on 10th June 1477 and proved on 14th July in the same year.[41] John A'Larder's name lived on in Reading for a long time as he also endowed almshouses immediately to the west of St. Mary's Church.

In 1492, Brother William, Warden of the Grey Friars of Reading, wrote a letter to Katherine Goddarde of Bucklebury and her son William. In response to a gift she had sent and her evident devotion both to God and to the Franciscan House, the Warden received her "into the suffrages [prayers] of our Order" both during her lifetime and after her death. He further assured her that she and her son would be given "full participation in all the masses, suffrages, sermons, fastings and other good works" that the friars would carry out. Upon receiving the knowledge of her or her son's death – and the letter being produced – then "all shall be done for [them] that is customary to do for one of our own deceased brothers."[42]

This Warden, Brother William, was almost certainly the William Wursley of the Franciscans, Reading, who had been ordained deacon three years previously by Thomas Langton, Bishop of Salisbury, on Ember Saturday 19th December 1489 in Ramsbury Church, 30 miles west of Reading.[43]

In his will of 12th November 1493 the wealthy Reading clothier Henry Kelsall bequeathed "to the ffriers Minours there, xx s."[44] He gave the same amount (20s, or £1) to the churches of St. Laurence, St. Mary and St. Giles – although the Cathedral Church at Salisbury only merited 1s. Notably, he gave nothing to the Abbey. Towards the end of his will he lists gifts to another 31 local churches, each of 6s 8d (£$^1/_3$).

Margaret Twyniho (or Twyneo) was buried in the Friary, most probably in the Quire. Margaret was the widow of William Twyniho, who was seneschal of the Bishop of Salisbury's estates in Dorset from 1491.

William and Margaret are named as the patrons of Sulham in documents from 1486 and 1488.[45]

In a will that was dated in 1500 and proved in Lambeth on 3rd March in the following year, Margaret instructed that her body be buried in the chapel of St. Francis in the Grey Friars in Reading, "as nye the toumbe whiche I have made ove my fade and moder as can conveniently be thought."[46] In 1728 a coffin was found, in the area that would have been the Friary Quire, containing the bones of a woman, as will be described later. It is possible that these remains were of Margaret Twyniho.

In the inventories of St. Laurence's Church for 1531 – 1532 there is an entry describing the costs associated with the repair and re-binding of the Church books. A friar called Peter, almost certainly the Friary's Warden Peter Schefford (also known as Peter Lawrence), is mentioned as receiving payment for work done in "wryttyng & notyng" in the books – a skill that was comparatively rare in those times.[47]

The entry is (in part):

Payd for iij buk skynes ij stag skynes & viij shepe skynes	xviij s	vj d
Payd for xxi rede skynes	vij s	
Payd for glew		xij d
Payd to ffrere Peter for wryttyng & notyng the new grayle & for the Vellam therto	xlvj s	viij d

There is a listing of four manuscripts found in the possession of Greyfriars when John Leland visited about this time. Leland was made Keeper of King Henry VIII's Libraries in 1530 and from 1533 he travelled around the country, as the monasteries were being suppressed, inspecting their libraries and adding to the King's Libraries from their contents. During his travels, from 1533 to 1536, he kept thorough notes of all he found. This information was published much later, in 1715, in six volumes by Thomas Hearne. Leland wrote:

> Radingiae apud Franciscanos [Reading at the House of the Franciscans]:
> Beda de naturis bestiarum;
> Alexander Necham super Marcianum Cappellam;
> Alexandri Necham Mythologicon;
> Joannis Waleys commentarii super Mythologicon Fulgentii.[48]

Most of the Libraries described had many more manuscripts than this, but Franciscan Houses were not rich foundations. In Leland's lists there are several others that have just a handful of manuscripts, like Reading.

The Warden, Peter Schefford, appears as one of the witnesses to the will of Richard Bedowe, Vicar of St. Laurence's Church, dated 15th November 1533. In the will Bedowe bequeathed "to the freers mynours in Reading aforsaid xl s,"[49] that is £2.

Two years later, in the will of William Watts, dated 1st July 1535 and proved at Lambeth on 13th November the same year, the "ffriars Minours" received 6s 8d, the same amount that he bequeathed to each of the other Reading Churches.[50]

From about the same time, a letter survives from the "Warden of the Grey Friars at Reading to John Husee" at the "Lyon in Southwark, beyond London Bridge."[51] Husee was variously described as solicitor for, agent of, or servant of Arthur Plantagenet, 1st (and only) Lord Lisle, uncle of the king.

Sending Husee a gift of a pair of Reading knives, together with the offer of a bed at the Friary when next he should be in Reading, the Warden asked Husee to remind Lord Lisle that he owed money to the Friary. If Husee paid the bearer of the letter for the masses that had been said, then the relevant certificate would be handed over. The Warden also asked that Lord Lisle be reminded that he was behind in his payments for the masses for Lord Dudley (first husband of Lord Lisle's first wife Elizabeth, who had been executed by Henry VIII in 1510). For those masses, the Warden had sent the certificate via an intermediary, but had not received "the reward." Since Elizabeth had died by this point, one wonders whether there was much chance of the Warden receiving the overdue fees.

This was not the end of the dispute. Although it may relate to a later set of masses, about a year later Husee wrote to Lord Lisle that, although the Warden of the Grey Friars at Reading has not yet sent the certificate for "the other half of the masses," he had no doubt that it would arrive soon.[52] A fortnight later, Husee wrote to Lord Lisle, passing on a letter from the Warden, in which the latter refused to hand over the certificate without payment.[53] Time was about to run out for resolving the dispute. The first phase of the life of Greyfriars was coming to a close as, in 1538, all Franciscan Houses were suppressed.

The west window

(A drawing by Gordon Spriggs based on this photograph was used as the cover of Greyfriars News from July 1971 until February 1984)

Chapter 2

Dissolution and Disposal: 1538 to 1542

Dr. John London was a "royal commissioner for the visitation of the monasteries." This meant that he fulfilled, from 1538 to 1540, Henry VIII's desire to suppress and then dissolve the monasteries and other religious establishments throughout the land. Dr. London had been a Fellow and then Warden of New College, Oxford. He became noted for his single-minded zeal in closing the monasteries and acquiring goods and estates for the King. Perhaps unsurprisingly, in the words of David Knowles, Dr. London "is not a prepossessing figure and he seems to have made few friends."[1]

In August 1538, Dr. London arrived in Reading in order to suppress the Franciscan Friary. Most probably, he first met with the Warden, Peter Schefford, and then declared the King's intention to close the Friary and eject the brothers.

The whole Friary covered, according to Dr. London, about 20 acres. In the Church there was "little plate and jewels," with "windows decked with grey friars" – presumably in the stained glass windows. In the grounds were three "pretty lodgings": one for the Warden, a second for "Mr. Ogle, the King's servant," and a third kept by "an old lady called my Lady Saint Jane." The rest of the grounds included trees, an orchard and a pond. Dr. London also identified a "great trough" of lead at the well, a similar trough in the kitchen and the lead that covered the bell turret as valuable items.[2]

The twelve friars, whose names are all known from the final submission document, were mostly old men. Unlike monks, who were granted a pension by the King when they were removed from their monasteries, friars were turned out virtually penniless since they had made a vow to remain in poverty on joining the Franciscan order. Perhaps because of this harsh situation and in light of their age, Dr. London took the unusual step of writing to Thomas Cromwell to plead on behalf of the Warden and friars:

> And a frynde of myne, the warden of Grey Fryers in Reding, hathe also desyred me to be an humble sutar for hym and hys brothern, that they may with your lordeschip's favour also chaunge ther garmentes with ther papisticall manner of lyvinges. The most partt of them are very agede men, and be nott of strength to go moch abrode for ther lyvinges, wherefor ther desyr ys that yt myght please your lordeschippe to be a mediator unto the kinges grace for them that they might during ther lyves enjoy their chambres and orcharde, and they wolde assuredly pray unto almightie Godde long to preserve the kinges grace and your lordeschippe to hys most blessyd pleasure.[3]

It was a vain hope that Henry VIII would allow the men to remain living on the Friary land, since the King expected to make a considerable profit from selling off not only whatever moveable goods there might be but also the land itself. Indeed, within a fortnight, the Warden and friars had had to sign the standard "Act of Surrender" and within three days more they had been evicted from the Friary. It is worth quoting the document of surrender, dated 13th September 1538,[4] in full:

> The surrender of the House of Gray-friars, in Reding:
>
> Forasmuch as we do now consider, as well by dayly experience, as by example and doctrine of divers well learned persons, which have heretofore professed diverse sorts of pretended religions, that the very true way to perfection and to please God is ministered unto us sincerely and sufficiently by the most wholesome doctrine of Christ, his Evangelists and Apostolis, and after declared by the Holy Fathers in the primitive Church of Christ, and doth not consist in the traditions and inventions of man's witt, in wering of a grey, black, white or any other colored garment, cloke, frock or coate, in garding ourselves upon our outward garments with gurdells full of knotts, or in like peculiar manner of papisticall ceremonies; sequestering ourselves from the uniform, laudable, and conformable manner of liveing of all Christian men, used many yeares from the beginning of Christ's religion. Perceiving, also, that as well the high estates of this realme as the common people doe noote in us, and daylye doth laye unto our charges, the detestable cryme of hypocrisy, dissimulation and superstition, which draweth their benevolence and supportation from us, whereby we have been in tymes past in manner only sustained: We therefore the warden and convent of the house called commonly Grey-Fryers of Reding, considering that we may be the true servants of God, as well in a secular habit as in a fryer's coate, and knowing and well considering the miserable state we stand in, being fully determined in ourselves to leave all such papisticall and strange fashions of lyveing, with the garments appertaining to the same, with all our mutuall and free assents and consents, doe most humblye in this behalfe

> submitt ourselves and every one of us, our house and place wee dwell in, and all our buildings, ornaments, utensells, juells, tyths, commodities, and all our things, whatsoever they be pertaining to the same, and by these presents doe surrender the same, and yeilde them up into the hands and disposition of our most noble sovereign Lord the King's Majestie; most humbly beseeching the same, freely and without any charge, in consideration of our extreme poverties, to grant unto every one of us, his letters under writeing and his Grace's seal, to change our said habitts, and to take such manner of living, as honest seculer priests be preferred unto. And wee all shall ffaithfully pray unto Almighty God, long to preserve his most noble Grace. In witness of all the premisses and every part of the same, we have subscribed our names unto these presents, and have put to our common and conventual seal unto the same, the XIII day of ye month of September, and in the XXX yeare of the raigne of our sovereigne lord Henry the VIII.
>
> Petrum Schefford, Guardianum, S.T.B
> Egidium Coventre, S.T.B
>
> | | |
> |---|---|
> | Henricum Allen | Petrum Stanch |
> | Nicolaum Martin | Robertum Lambert |
> | Joh'em Newarke | Will'um Tudbodis |
> | Joh'em Gruer | Joh'em Rosell |
> | Ric'um Leyrston | Will'um Thompson[5] |

The initials S.T.B. after the first two names in the list stand for the *Sacrae Theologiae Baccalaureus* or Bachelor of Sacred Theology, showing that two at least of the twelve were well educated men. Possibly because of their relative standing, while nothing more is known of the other ten men than they were cast out of the Friary in normal clothes, the two at the top of the list appear again in the official record – as inmates of the Tower of London towards the end of the following year, as described below.

On the following day, a Saturday, the twelve men prepared to leave the Friary, changing "their coats." Dr. London wrote to Cromwell: "of friars they be noted here honest men." The letter concludes "On Monday I will pay their debts to victuallers and rid the house of them all."[6] One wonders if they were allowed to worship for one final time in the Friary Church on Sunday 15th September 1538. It would be 325 years before the next service of worship took place in the building.

The Mayor of Reading, Richard Turner, approached Dr. London and requested that the Church building be granted to the town for its Guildhall. Turner explained that the hall that they were using was very small and its location upon the river Kennet was not suitable for the "mynystracion of justice," due to the constant noise from the washer women's "batildores" (a wooden utensil for beating clothes) which interrupted and disturbed their meetings. Dr. London therefore wrote again to Cromwell:

> I besek your gudde lordeschippe to admytt me a power [poor] sutar for thees honest men of Redinge. They have a fayer towne and many gudde occupiers in ytt, butt they lacke that howse necessary, of the wiche, for the mynystracion of justice, they have most nede of. Ther towne hall ys a very small howse, and stondith upon the ryver, wher ys the commyn wassching place of the most partt of the towne, and in the cession dayes and other cowrt dayes ther ys such betyng with batildores as oon man can nott here another nor the quest here the chardg gevyng.
>
> The body of the Church of the Grey Fryers, wiche ys solyd with lath and lyme, wold be a very commodiose rowme for them. And now I have rydde all the fasschen of that Church in parcleses [screens], ymages, and awlters, it wolde make a gudly towne hall. The mayer of that towne, Mr. Richard Turner, is a very honest gentill person, with many other honest men, hathe expressyd unto me ther gref in thys behalf, and have desyred me to be an humble sutar unto your lordeschippe for the same, if it shulde be solde. The wallys besyd the coyne stonys be butt chalk and flynt, and the coveryng butt tile. And if it please the kinges grace to bestow that howse upon any of hys servantes, he may spare the body of the churche, wiche stondith next the strete, very well, and yt have rowme sufficient for a great man.
>
> Your most bounden oratour and servant,
> John London.[7]

On the next day, before leaving Reading for Aylesbury's Friary, Dr. London wrote a final letter to Lord Cromwell regarding Greyfriars:

> In my most humble maner I have me commendyd unto your gudde lordeschippe, with my assured prayer and service, I have sent upp to your lordeschippe the surrender of Grey Fryers of Reding with their plate suche as yt ys. I have inwardly defacyd the churche and dorter; the resydew of the howse I have left hole till I know your farther pleasur, and clerly dispacchyd all the fryers owt of the doores in ther seculer apparell, and have geven to every oon of theym mony in ther purcys, and have clerly payd ther dettes. Thys ys a town of moch power people, and they fell to steling so fast in every corner of the howse, that I have been fayne to tary a hole wek here to sett every thing in dew order and have and schall receyve to the kinges grace use I trust above £40 ... Att Reding, xviij Septembris.[8]

His work completed, Dr. London left Reading soon after. However, he did return less than five years later under quite different conditions. He fell out of favour at court after Cromwell's death and was convicted of perjury, then stripped of all his titles and position. He was then made to ride through Reading facing the horse's tail and put in the pillory with a notice declaring his crime on his forehead. After having to do the same in Newbury and Windsor, he was imprisoned in The Fleet, where he died in 1543.[9]

Greyfriars passed to the King's ownership, awaiting his disposal. Meanwhile, elsewhere in the town, the Abbey was suppressed and the last Abbot, Hugh Cook of Faringdon, was executed as a traitor to the crown near the Abbey gateway on 14th November 1539. At the same time, the former Warden of Greyfriars, Peter Lawrence/Schefford and fellow former friar (and probably Sub-Warden) Giles Coventry were imprisoned in the Tower of London.[10] The charge was treason. They were a part of a small group identified by name who had denied the King's supremacy in spiritual matters:

> When these traitors were arraigned, though they had confessed before and written with their own hands that they had committed treason, yet they endeavoured to justify themselves, and John Oynyon denied his crime... This protest he continued to the gallows... and he and his companions with the ropes about their necks confessed that they had committed high treason.[11]

These companions most probably included the ex-Warden and Sub-Warden of Greyfriars.

On 5th February 1540, Henry granted the Greyfriars site for a fee of £30, plus an annual rent of 6s 8d, to one of the grooms of his chamber, Robert Stanshawe. The grant went into great detail:

> ...all that house and site of a house once belonging to the Minor Brothers commonly called les Grey-Friars of Reading, in our county of Berk then dissolved. And all the burial places, and all the houses, buildings, orchards, orts, gardens, lands, tenements, trees, woods, pools, vineyards, and all the other hereditaments whatsoever with all and singular appurtenances thereof within the site enclosure and precinct and walls and ditches of the said house of the formerly existing Minor Brothers. And all wall, ditches, waters, pools and enclosures of the said site enclosure and precincts of the said house of the said former Minor Brothers and lying around them and adjacent to the same and the site enclosure and precinct of that house including and containing all by estimation six acres so fully and completely as the late Warden or Minister and Body of the said house of the former Minor Brothers or any of their predecessors in right of that house at any time before the dissolution of the

> same house had held or ought to have held, enjoyed all and singular, the same premises or any parcel of them and as fully and completely and in so full manner and form as they all and singular devolved or ought to have devolved into our hands by reason and pretext of the dissolution of the said house of the former Minor Brothers or by reason or pretext of any act of parliament or in any way whatever and then were or ought to have been in our hands...[12]

Legal terminology seems convoluted to the layman! Interestingly, the land described by Dr. London as being about twenty acres is here estimated as six.

However, the King had reserved to himself the Church building itself – the body and side aisles, together with access from the road. On 24th April 1542, Henry granted Reading a new Charter, the first after the fall of Reading Abbey, by which was set up a completely new governance for the town. In the Charter, Henry granted the Greyfriars Church building to the town of Reading to use as a Guildhall.

The Charter set out the grant:

> ... which body and side aisles of the Church together with a competent and sufficient road to the same are of the clear annual value of five pence and no more. Know ye that we of our special grace have granted and by these presents for us our heirs and successors grant to the said Mayor and Burgesses of Reading aforesaid and their successors for ever the body and side aisles of the said Church and one competent and sufficient road to the same.[13]

The charge was to be the hundredth part of one knight's fee (16d, possibly an initial payment) and an annual peppercorn rent of one halfpenny, payable on the feast of St. Michael the Archangel (29th September). The Mayor and Burgesses were then "at their own expense, [to] make and construct or cause to be made and constructed from the same a sufficient house there commonly called Le Gyldhawle for the said town."

Chapter 3

The Guildhall: 1542 to 1578

It is difficult to know exactly when the Mayor, Burgesses and Aldermen moved from the old Guild or Yield Hall site to the new Hall at Greyfriars, as the record simply continues to call their meeting place the "Gilda Aula." The move had certainly taken place by 1544 for in that year the old Guildhall was let to Richard Turner (by now former Mayor) for a term of 40 years, together with the neighbouring property, at an annual rent of 33s. 4d.[1]

There was no doubt a lot of work to do to convert the Church building to its new use, but this may not have taken many weeks after the Charter's date. The grant was entered into the Reading Corporation records:

> Item that the seid Mayour and Burgeses for ever shall have and enyoye to them and their successours the body and syde Iles of the Churche of the late Hous called the Grey Freres in Redyng aforseid and a competent and sufficient wey to the same, by the rent by the yere of one obolus for all maner of services, to th'entent to make therof a Gylde Hall for the seid borough, for ever to be and contynowe.[2]

An obolus was a small coin, standing here for the half penny rent.

In the period between the 1542 Charter of Henry VIII and the 1560 Charter of Elizabeth, the full meetings of the Mayor and Burgesses occurred four times a year, "every Imbryng Fryday." "Imbryng," or Ember, stood for the four seasonal periods of fasting following the first Sunday of Lent, Whitsunday, Holy Cross Day (14th September) and St. Lucia's Day (13th December). Perhaps because the Friday was one of the three fast days, in 1547 it was decided to move the meetings to the Monday of the "Imbryng weke."[3] This innovation did not last long, however, and from the December meeting of the following year the meetings again took place on Fridays.[4]

At this time, the Guildhall was in debt – quite possibly from the cost of the works to convert it from a Church. Several measures were undertaken, including taking out loans from the Wardens of St. Laurence's Church. In the meeting of 19th December 1547, the Mayor, Robert Bowyer, agreed to reduce his annual fee from £10 to 10 marks (£6 13s 4d, a 33% pay cut) – and it was decided that future Mayors would also be paid at that rate, until the debt was discharged.[5]

A record of 1552 assigns the "charge and dewtie" of the various officers of the Hall, from the Mayor downwards. Last on the list, the sergeants were given the task of cleaning and preparing the Hall for meetings: "Item that they shall be redy to dresse the Yeld Hall at all busynes ther to be had, and shall kepe the Yeldhall clene."[6]

Two years later, it was agreed that all newly elected Burgesses should pay a fee of 20 shillings (£1) "towards the mayntenaunce of the seid Hall." References to the Guildhall owing money had stopped by this point and so it is likely that the debts had been paid by this time. Further funds were to be raised by fining any of their number who did not arrive at their meetings "in his gowne decently" the sum of 20d. The Burgesses were also to process, two by two, accompanying the Mayor back to his house after each meeting – or pay a fine of 4d.[7]

The Mayor and Burgesses did not only raise money for the maintenance of the Hall. In 1554 they resolved that, whenever possible, each member and former member of the Guildhall should include in his will a bequest to the Hall, either 10 shillings for former Mayors, or 5 shillings for Burgesses. These funds were then to be used for former Burgesses who had fallen on hard times, who "in ther age and latter days... fall in decay and of them selves not hable to lyve without the good helpe and devocion of others."[8] In accordance with this, some years later, Thomas Aldworth, three times Mayor of Reading (1551–2, 1557–8 and 1571–2), stated in his will:

> In the name of God, Amen, the forthe daye of Januarye anno 1576, and in the xix^th yeare of the raigne of our soveraigne ladye Elizabeth by the grace of God Quene of Englande, Fraunce and Irelande, defendor of the faithe, &ce. I Thomas Aldworthe of Reading in the County of Berks Clothier, knowing I am naturallie borne to dye and pass from this mutuall worlde and transitory liefe, mynding to put as well in order as well of my landes, tenementes and hereditamentes as of my goodes and chattelles, to th'entent thear shalbe no striefe for the same after my deathe, doe make and ordayne this my present testament and conteyning herin my laste will in manner and fourme following...

> Item I geve to the towne halle tenne shillings in money to be paid within three monthes after my decease...[9]

This was just one of many bequests in the wealthy Thomas Aldworth's very long last will and testament.

The Friary land and buildings acquired by Robert Stanshawe in 1540 passed on at his death in 1551 to a succession of others. Listed in Coates's History are William Webb and Wolfstan Dixey in 1576/7, then John Carleton in 1614/5. About 1640 at least part of the land belonged to Tanfield Vachel. Both Vachel and Stanshawe are commemorated in roads off Greyfriars Road on land that formed part of the original Friary. In the 18th century, part of the land was bought by a Joseph Haycock, an apothecary, and became known as "Haycock's Friars." [10] His widow is noted as living there in 1747.[11]

In 1615 the Corporation debated the exciting event of the visit of the Queen, Anne of Denmark, Consort of King James I, as she passed through Reading on her way to Bath. She was to stay one night and plans were agreed that she should stay at the "Fryers." Although this is uncertain, this could well be one of the original Friary houses taken by Robert Stanshawe in 1540 and, in 1615, recently purchased by John Carleton. Alternatively, it could be a relatively newly built house on the former Friary land. Either way, the royal visitor was to stay in what had been part of Greyfriars.[12]

Earlier, in 1560, Queen Elizabeth had presented the Town of Reading with a new Charter. As part of this Charter, Elizabeth repeated her father Henry's grant to the Borough enabling the Mayor and Burgesses to continue to use Greyfriars as the Guildhall. Importantly, they were also empowered to:

> give grant alienate convey in fee or exchange or yield up the aforesaid body and side Iles of the said late Church and the way aforesaid belonging to the same to any person or persons whatever according to their own will and pleasure or to convert alter or dispose of them to any other use the letters aforesaid patent of our Father aforesaid or any condition specified in the same or any other thing cause or matter whatever to the contrary in any wise notwithstanding.[13]

This enabled the Mayor and Burgesses in due course to re-locate the Guildhall again, while putting Greyfriars to an altogether different use.

The Friary: Detail from John Speed's Map of Reading c1611

[The small Church opposite was
St. Edmund's Chapel,
founded in 1204]

Chapter 4

The Hospital/Poor House: 1578 to 1614

By 1578 the Mayor and Burgesses of the Borough had been using Greyfriars as their Guildhall for about 35 or 36 years. In that year they decided to move to the old Abbey "Hospitium," next to St. Laurence's Church.

Still standing, the Hospitium of St. John was the guest hall of the Abbey's dormitory for visitors. A considerable time before the dissolution, the building had been converted to the site of the grammar school (in time to become called Reading School), which explains why this particular building was not destroyed along with the rest of the Abbey in 1539. The corporation had an upper floor installed in the building. Leaving the lower part to the school, they took over the upper part for their new town hall.

Meanwhile, Greyfriars was converted into what can variously be described as a Hospital, Poor House or, to use a later term, Workhouse, for the three parishes of the town. The name "Hospital" may mislead; although the care for the poor would have included improving their health, the institution was not what we would call a hospital with a mission to care for the sick.

The problem of the poor had been growing over the preceding 50 years. One cause was the removal of the monasteries, which had made it their business to care for the poor. There were economic factors too, with a growing population and especially with changes to land use and land ownership. Among the general public there was a growing fear of migrant paupers becoming a burden on other parishes. Legislation was passed throughout the Tudor period to attempt to control the problem, but it was during Elizabeth's reign that the greatest changes were enacted.

In 1576 the "Act For Setting The Poor On Work" was passed. This legislation required stocks of materials – flax, hemp and wool, for example – to be provided and premises maintained in order to employ the able-bodied poor. It is likely that it was the Borough's response to this legislation that led to Greyfriars being set up as a Poor House two years later.

In the first year accounts it stated that there were 14 elderly persons and 21 children being looked after in the Hospital. Finance for the maintenance of the premises and the inmates came from a combination of private gifts and the proceeds of the work that the poor had to undertake. For example, in the final quarter of 1578 income from the sale of the work done in the Hospital was £12 8s 8d.[1]

In 1580 the Hospital received a donation of £40 to buy land from the will of Walter Bye. He was a wealthy man, by trade a fuller and employing at least twenty workers. His father-in-law, Richard Watlington, is remembered by a brass plaque in St. Mary's Church, recording that he was four times Mayor of Reading. Walter Bye, although never Mayor, was one of the Secondary Burgesses of the Town from 1570 to 1579.[2]

Three more private donations to the Hospital are known to us.[3] Robert Bowyer, who just a few years previously (in 1570 – 1) had served a fourth term as Mayor of Reading, gave some land worth an annual sum of £4.

In order to fund the sinking of a well, Mrs. Lendall, widow of Mayor William Lendall, a dyer, bequeathed the Hospital the sum of £5.

The third gift to the Hospital was of £3, given by Mrs. Hewet, who was the daughter of another Mayor of Reading – John Webbe, first named as a fuller, then clothier, who served as Mayor in 1579 – 80.

The Hospital was managed by a succession of overseers, appointed annually. One of them, William Green, was subjected to a law suit as a result of seizing a horse in lieu of debts:

> At this daye it was graunted and agreed that Willyam Greene should be paid all his costes and charges whiche he had expended In the sute brought against him by Mr. Danvers of the Fryers, for distreyninge his horse in the last yeare when Willyam Greene was one of the overseers of the poore; and that the said Willyam Greene should be defended in all thinges concerninge the same sute; and after wardes. Mr. Danvers dyed before the sute was ended.[4]

On 18th December 1590, the Corporation, under the leadership of Mayor Edward Butler, put forward a proposal to convert part of the Hospital into a House of Correction:

> At this daye it is fullye agreed by the whole Company that theire howse, commonlye called the Hospitall, or the most parte thereof, shalbe imployed and converted to a house of correction, as well for the settinge of the poore people

> to worke, being able to worke for their reliefes, and for the settinge of idle persons to worke therein, as also for the punnishinge and correctinge of idle and vagrant persons and that there shalbe a stocke provided therefore and officers and overseers necessarye and convenient for that intent, accordinge to the fourme of the statute in that case provided.[5]

It is clear from the Corporation Records that, although this change was intended, it was not actually carried out as much the same resolution was made over twenty years later.

In 1601 "An Act for the Relief of the Poor"[6] was passed, which substantially altered the provision for the relief of "the deserving poor." By the Act, a compulsory poor rate levy was made on every parish. The Churchwardens and a small number of local householders were to be sworn in as Overseers of the Poor each year. As in the 1576 Act, they were to purchase "a convenient Stock of Flax, Hemp, Wool, Thread, Iron and other necessary Ware and Stuff" to "set the Poor on Work." Any able-bodied pauper who would not carry out this work would be committed to a House of Correction, a type of prison.

The Act made it clear that the responsibility for keeping the "impotent" poor lay first and foremost with their parents and grandparents, or with their children, and specified a fine of 20s (£1) per month to be levied on all who were in a position to support them but who failed to do so. The parish should provide a poor house, if it were able to, for those "poor, old, blind, lame and impotent" who could not be looked after by relatives.

The Overseers had the power to bind children as Apprentices, where they believed the parents unable to support them, until the age of 24 (for a male) or 20 (for a female – or on her marriage if earlier).

By 1610 the Hospital had been put under the management of one man, appointed by the Corporation. At the meeting of 1st September that year it was noted: "At this daye it was agreed that John Dawson shall have 40s (£2) per annum, duringe the tyme he shall contynue the charge of the hospitall, and doe that office and service there to the good likinge of this Companye, and noe longer, beginninge at Michaelmas next."[7]

In that year there was a very good illustration of how the Hospital was funded. Former Mayor Thomas Deane (Mayor of Reading in 1599 – 1600 and in 1608 – 9) made a gift of £10 per year in order to fund two poor men and three poor children. He nominated John Kinfeild and Richard Avord as the first men to benefit. The gift allowed each man 12d per week and each child 8d.[8] The sum of these payments comes to 8 shillings more than the

£10, so it would be interesting to know how the shortfall was covered! When each beneficiary was able to leave the Hospital and take their place back in society – or, alternatively, when one died – they were replaced by another nominated by Mr. Deane and, after his death, by the Corporation. For example, in 1623, John Benyvent "was named and apoynted to have the roome and place that Willyam Hudson did hold of the guift of Mr. Deane in the hospitall, and the allowaunce of xij d per weeke."[9]

There is an account from 1614 showing that the total amount received for the Hospital was £53 16s 4d, with expenses of £13 7s 10d on beds, £20 on repairs and £20 for the stock of hemp.[10] In the same year, Reading Corporation, under Mayor Robert Reve, again decided that they should convert some of the Hospital into a House of Correction:

> At this daye the said Mayor and Burgesses were assembled at the Guildhall, and uppon good consideracions for the better governement of the sturdye, idle and disorderly persones, from tyme to tyme arisinge within the said boroughe, whiche cause and move muche trouble to the officers, yt was concluded and agreed that parte of their house, called the Hospitall, shalbe applyed and used for a house of correction; and for the better establishinge and contynuaunce thereof a convenyent stocke shall forthwith be raised of th'inhabitantes within the said boroughe by taxacion.[11]

The date of that decision is given in the Reading Records as 1st March 1613. However, until the Gregorian Reforms were finally accepted by the Westminster parliament in 1752, the year's number changed at 25th March, so that the day following 24th March 1613 was 25th March 1614. Dates from 1st January to 24th March therefore show what we would now consider to be the wrong year. Generally dates are corrected to show the year change at 1st January to avoid confusion and misunderstanding and are corrected to this "historical" or "new style" throughout this book. The date of the decision to convert part of the Hospital into a House of Correction should therefore be 1st March 1614.

Chapter 5

The House of Correction: 1614 to 1642

Having resolved twice – first in December 1590 and then in March 1614 – to create a House of Correction, there was a third resolution at the next meeting of the Corporation on Good Friday 22nd April 1614:

> At this daye alsoe there was present, with the said Mayor and Burgesses in the Guildhall, Sir Frauncis Knollis, Mr. Frauncis Moore and Mr. Edward Clerke, Justices of Peace in the said countye, and inhabitinge within the said boroughe, and of, by and with all their consentes and agreament, advise and direccions, it was then and there agreed that for the settinge to worke of such rogues, vagabondes, sturdye and unruly persones as from tyme to tyme should arise and be within the said boroughe, a house of correccion should be established, supported and contynued within the said boroughe; and that a stocke or some of £50 to provide hempe, flaxe and other necessarye stuffe and implementes for the settinge them to worke should be fourthwith had and raised of th'inhabitauntes within the said boroughe by taxacion; and that there shalbe six honest men, videlicet, 2 out of eache parrishe named, whiche shalbe presente masters and governours thereof, and soe yerely to be named for that purpose; and that there shalbe a sufficient man apoynted to use the said stocke and to sett the people to worke, which shalbe commytted thither.[1]

Following this third resolution in April 1614, the required actions were finally taken and the House of Correction was set up. However, it was probably not until October 1614 that Greyfriars actually operated as the House of Correction, for it is on the 30th of that month that the Corporation Records name the first six governors or overseers of the House, two each from the ancient parishes of St. Mary's, St. Laurence's and St. Giles'. These first six governors were: Robert Bent, Robert Knight, Jerome Pocock, John Symes, George Thorne and Richard Winche.[2] By 1618, the number of governors had fallen to three, being the Senior Cofferer (or

Treasurer of the Corporation) and the two Constables, all of whom were elected annually.

In May 1616, Christopher Turner paid £5 towards the furnishing of the House of Correction "with thinges necessarie," being the sum bequeathed by his father Richard, who had died sometime between 23rd February and 8th April. Richard Turner had been Mayor of Reading in 1585 – 6, 1594 – 5 and 1612 – 3.[3]

For at least forty years, Greyfriars operated as both a Hospital and a House of Correction. In both 1615 and 1616 the Overseers nominated by the Corporation were identified as officials of both the Hospital and the House of Correction.[4] As late as 1646 references to both the Hospital and the House of Correction name the same man in charge.[5] A record of 1652 speaks of Robert Westmerland's new lease of a house "opposite the Hospitall att the upper end of Frier Streete,"[6] although this may just be due to the name living on in memory.

These two roles of Hospital and House of Correction mirrored the Elizabethan view of the deserving and the undeserving poor. Those who were "deserving" – the children and the aged – were to be looked after and if possible restored to society able to look after themselves or to be looked after by relatives. This was the role of the Hospital. The House of Correction was the punishment for those who were considered "undeserving": beggars who were able bodied ("sturdie beggars" as they were known); those who were poor and destitute because they would not, rather than could not, find work; those "rogues" and "vagabonds" who seemed to have chosen the life rather than put in a hard day's labour.

At Easter 1615 there was a long statement drawn up defining the operation of the House of Correction, which was included in and extended by a record of the Berkshire Quarter Sessions of the Peace of April 1620.[7] Any "rogues and sturdie beggars" who were apprehended in the hundreds of Cookham, Bray, Reading and Theale were to be committed to the Reading House of Correction.

Several separate schedules then followed, dealing with different aspects of the running of the House of Correction.

The "Master or Governor" of the House of Correction was to serve for a term of seven years – as long as the Justices of the Peace remained content with his services – at a salary of £40 per annum. To assist him it was agreed to appoint a Marshall, on a wage of £5 per annum paid quarterly, and raised by tax on the various parishes that would benefit from his services.

The House of Correction was only to receive into custody those whom the Justices of the Peace or the Mayor had sent by warrant. This should not include any child below twelve years of age, adult over sixty, or woman "apparantlie with childe." No one with a damaged hand was to be committed to the House since they could not be "put to work." The House was not to receive anyone who had any apparent sickness or disease.

The Master or Governor of the House was expressly forbidden to accept any money from the "rogues and vagabonds," or from others on their behalf, with a view to improving their lodging, or sparing their work or punishment.

All inmates of the House had to work, to gain payment so that they could in turn pay for their own clothing, food and drink, and whatever raw materials they were to use in their work. However, the Master or Governor would keep for himself any money earned above the daily ascribed maximum allowed: men 4d, women 3d and children 2d.

Men and women were to be housed separately and all were to be safely under lock and bolt.

The Justices defined at some length the tools and materials that should be provided within the House of Correction, giving a good idea of the type of work that was carried out there by the "rogue, vagabond, idle, wandering and disorderlie person in his custodie":

> They shall have in a readynesse from tyme to tyme severall and distinct tooles and instruments to worke with and severall stuffes and thinges to worke both for men and women that shalbe comitted to them, as namely for men stockcards and woll, hempe from thread, quernes to grinde corne, wedges, beetles, hatchetts and axes to clean wood and the like, for weomen needles, threads, wheeles, reeles, wooll, hempe, yarne and the like.

The next schedule deals with the rules governing the whipping of those in his custody. Each was to be whipped just once. This was to be done only on a Friday afternoon at the Borough whipping post and then only in the presence of any two of: the Vicar of St. Laurence's Church, a Constable (who was an elected officer of the Corporation and from 1618 also an Overseer of the House of Correction), a "Tythyngman," or a "Bayliffe" of the town. These officers had it in their power to either mitigate the punishment, should they find the offenders to be mild or penitent, or to increase it for "sturdie and notorious roagues." A note in the "Reading Records" in 1624 states "13s 4d shalbe paid out of the House of Correccion to William Hill and his partener for money laid out for whipping rogues."[8]

The remaining schedules dealt with repeat offenders – "incorrigible rogues." Several categories of such miscreants were listed: those who had been committed to the House twice or more; those who had attempted (unsuccessfully or otherwise) to escape; those who had lied about their parish of origin or about their name; those who had conspired with other prisoners against the Governor; those who had already been branded from previous felonies. Such offenders were to be sent to the gaol rather than the House of Correction and would ultimately face execution as a felon if they did not reform.

A second document of similar date (April 1620) set out to define exactly what was meant, in law, by the category of disorderly persons, who along with the rogues, sturdy beggars, vagabonds and idlers, were to be sent to the House of Correction.[9] The list was substantial and included:

- the reputed fathers of illegitimate children;
- persons usually drunk, whether in alehouses or elsewhere;
- those who sit drinking at the time of divine service;
- those who play unlawful games at the time of divine service;
- poachers who use dogs or nets to take deer or pheasants;
- those who shoot with guns at pigeons on the dovecots, in the fields or elsewhere;
- those who set traps or nets for fish in rivers or ponds;
- those who hunt in warrens by night or upon the Sabbath day;
- blasphemers of the Word of God;
- servants or apprentices that steal their Master's goods (unless it is serious enough to be a felony);
- servants or apprentices who conspire with others to defraud their Master;
- servants or apprentices who assault or beat either their Master or Mistress;
- those who break or tear off wood from hedges;
- those who rob orchards;
- those who beat, assault or ill use constables or other officers in the execution of their duty.

These, the document declares, are disorderly persons and so may be sent to the House of Correction, whipped (once only) and discharged "without pasport."

Following John Dawson, who "had charge" of the Hospital in 1610 and was re-employed by the Corporation for at least the following year, the first Governor of the combined House of Correction and Hospital was John Ballard.

Unfortunately the only record that survives about John Ballard is not a good one. In an undated document addressed to "The Right Worshipfull Mr. Maior, and the Hospitall Burgesses of the Towne and burrough of Readinge and to William Hill Constable of the same" an unrelated complaint is made about several dissolute women in the town and then a complaint is made specifically about John Ballard:

> May it also please you to be further [advised] that the keeper of the house of correccion (Ballard by name) intertayneth poore men's children, other men's servauntes, both by daye and by nighte, suffering them to be there typling and spending their money untill they be drunken, which was not soe in John Dawson's time. [10]

By January 1623 John Ballard was no longer in charge of the House of Correction. The post was offered to John Remnant, who was given three weeks to decide if he wanted to take the post. John Ballard presented his accounts to the Corporation on the same date: with £34 wages and £4 allowed as expense against bills, he remained in debt to the Corporation to the tune of £2 as he had been advanced £40 of stock for the House. The Corporation were concerned that at this change over there may not be enough stock to keep the prisoners working and earning money, and so they paid for £2 of hemp to be given to John Remnant "until further consideracion be taken." [11]

Just less than three weeks later, John Remnant agreed to take on the liability for paying for the stock and the job as Governor:

> At this daye John Remnaunt answered this Company that having the stocke and those favours John Ballard had, with £8 wages and his charges to the assize and sessions, to hold 7 yeres, provided uppon 3 monethes warning to pay the stocke and to geve over, &c.

John Remnant, Steven Remnant and Robert Wickyns were "bound for the stocke,"[12] bearing the liability of paying the Corporation back from profits made at the House of Correction or making up the sum themselves if necessary. The first instalment of the stock, worth £10, was purchased by the Corporation and handed over to John Remnant at the end of April.[13]

The Hospital/House of Correction was often in need of repairs. In 1620, the large sum of £24 9s 2d was spent but unfortunately the record does not specify what part of the building was repaired.[14] Four years later there was a long list of works to be carried out over the following four months or so:

> Then it was bargayned and agreed by Robert Westmerland, in this manner, viz:— Robert Westmerland shall from hencefourth be the bricklayer and workman for the towne, he usinge himself well in that kynd and doeinge their worke reasonably, &c.
>
> And to begyn withall, he shall before Bartholomewe next amend and poynt the Hospitall all over in the roofe, and goodwief Dawson's house, where need is; and he shall amend the gable endes with bricke or tyle; and he amend the pavinge of the flower where the myll standes; and he shall amend and make uppe the wall at the goeinge into the Ospitall, at widowe Dawson's house, on both sides the postes of the doore; and he is to provide and fynd all manner of stuffe (excepting carpenter's worke and tymber) and of hart, lath and nayles, and where the tyles are great tyles there he shall use and lay great tyles; and for the doeinge thereof he shalbe paid £8 in this manner, £4 at the beginninge of the work and £4 at th'end of the worke.[15]

John Dawson, who had been in charge of the Hospital around 1610, had died in August 1621[16] and his widow had remained in the house which formed the entry to the Hospital/House of Correction. She would not be the last widow whom the Corporation found it difficult to move! The Corporation finally removed her in March 1625, upon agreement that she be paid 12d a week from the charitable funds.[17]

The repairs continued. Shortly after completing the previous works, Robert Westmerland was called upon again to take down and rebuild the chimney in the House of Correction, in order to cure it of its smoking. If he could manage it before All Saints day, then "for his paynes he shalbe paid when the worke is done £4 10s in money."[18]

The necessary work of the Hospital/House of Correction was taking its toll on the Corporation funds and so, inevitably, they had to raise special taxes in order to cover costs of repairs, equipment and wages. In 1624 the Corporation agreed that "a taxe shalbe made of the better sorte of the inhabitantes to raise £20 for the house of correccion."[19] In the following year, the Mayor, William Maulthus, proposed a scheme, which was agreed by the burgesses:

> At this daye (for the releivinge certen impotent, aged, sicke and needye persones, and for provision to be had to place some of them in the hospitall) it

> was agreed that a taxe shalbe made in the towne to raise the some of £14 not chargeinge any man to or with the taxe that payeth lesse than 3d per weeke, but every man that payeth 3d and upwardes, to be forthwith levyed... And for the apparellinge of those poore to be placed in the hospitall, it is agreed that the Overseers in eache parishe shall raise weekly by their bookes.
>
> | | |
> |---|---|
> | St. Laurence parishe weekly | 12d |
> | St. Mary's parishe | 12d |
> | St Giles' parishe | 8d.[20] |

On the same day, the Corporation also wanted the parish beadles to ensure that the streets were policed:

> The Bedells shall survey the streetes and take uppe all the beggars and bringe them before the next Magistrate, and he to send them to the House of Correccion by the Bedles and officers to be assistent.

In 1624 Henry Tubbs was appointed to assist John Remnant in keeping the House of Correction, to be paid 2s per week or just over £5 per annum.[21] This was the start of a very long association between Henry Tubbs and the House of Correction, lasting for at least 30 years. John Remnant was replaced as the Governor of the House of Correction/Hospital in 1625 by the third appointee: William Clayton and Margaret[22], his wife. From later entries it would seem that while he took charge of the House of Correction, she ran the Hospital.

> Agreed with William Clayton and his wief concerninge the House of Correccion or Hospitall. They shall have the house and howsinge that Widowe Dawson held at will of this Company rent free, and to be discharged agayne uppon 3 monethes warninge. And withall they shall have provided six boarded bedsteedes to be standerdes in that house. And for their wages they have £4 per annum paid quarterly; provided alwayes that they shall receave and take into their charge, keepe and sett to their worke all the boyes, wenches and chareweomen that shalbe sent unto them by the Mayour or his Brethren, or Overseers of the poore for the tyme being, able to worke, without any allowance to be had for any of them and shall alsoe at their own chardges fynd all those, whiche be able to worke, meate, drinke, apparell, lodgeinge and washinge in the house, soe long as they contynue there, and shall alsoe provide [spinning] wheeles, cardes, beddes and bedding at their owne chardges. And also they shall receave and take into their keepeinge all young poore children of the towne, not able to gett their livinges, havinge reasonable allowance as well for their apparell as towardes their feeding, untill, &c., by the Overseers of each parishe, &c.[23]

The opportunity arose in April 1625 to increase the amount of land around the House of Correction. John Saunders agreed to lease to the Corporation a garden plot, next to the street and adjoining the House of Correction, for ten years, upon payment by the Corporation of 30s half yearly. As part of the agreement, the Corporation were to make the wall higher on the north-west side of the garden. If at the end of the ten years Mr. Saunders did not wish to renew the lease, then the cost of restoring the wall to its original condition and height would fall to him.[24] It seems that the Corporation knew how to drive a hard bargain! From the description, this was probably the area of the current Nursery and grounds.

Having raised taxes in March 1625, the Corporation Records itemised how the money had been spent. Originally the taxes were for clothing the poor, but it seems that repairs were again the order of the day. On Friday 10th June 1625:

> At this daye Mr. Mayour [William Maulthus] made it knowne to the Company how and in what manner that sum of £20 levyed and had of th'inhabitantes, and that some of £10 lent by the Cofferers for and towardes the providinge thinges necessarye to sett poore children to worke in the hospitall was bestowed, and to whome, vizt. £30.

To Richard Breddes for tymber, boardes, stuffe and workmanshippe	£17		
To Robert Westmerland for stuffe & worke, as by bill appeareth	£5		
To John Browne the smyth for yron worke	£3	10s	5d
To John Davys, glasier, for glasse	£3	5s	
Not to be had upon the colleccion		6s	10d
Some	£29	2s	3d
Soe rest in hand		17s	9d
In toto	£30		

> Whiche 17s 9d was apoynted to be paid towardes the buylding of a porche at the Ospitall door, the charge of buylding not exceedinge 40s. Mr. Mayour paid 4s of that money to Goodwief Clayton for keepinge a boy 13 weekes. Memorandum, more to the plomer for worke and soder at the hospitall, 4s 6d.[25]

There were several payments to "Goodwief Clayton" for looking after poor children. The going rate became 14d a week for each child. The aim was that the work produced by each child would provide this sum, but the Corporation undertook to make up the balance if the children's work did not raise the sum needed.[26] However, this did not satisfy Mrs. Clayton, who continued to bargain with the Corporation for improved terms. In 1626 the parties came to an agreement:

> At this daye it was agayne agreed to satisfy Goodwief Clayton's request concerninge the Hospitall... She shall have her dwellinge as before she had her allowaunce out of the house of £4 per annum more, out of the charitable uses £4 per annum and their workes made uppe 16d a piecc every weeke by eache parishe for their owne children...
>
> 23° Aprilis, postea. it was soe agreed and accepted of by William Clayton and his wief before the Companye.[27]

Since the Mayor and Head Burgesses had power to hear legal cases and to commit various categories of law breakers to the House of Correction, many instances are described in the pages of the Reading Records. Some have only one line devoted to them while others have several witness testimonies transcribed. At this date it is rare for the duration of the committal to House of Correction to be identified – perhaps each inmate faced another hearing before being released rather than having their term set at the beginning.

In the ten years 1626 to 1635, for example, there are 40 committals recorded to the House of Correction, 29 of those being male and 11 female. The main charges were for vagrancy/begging (9 male, 4 female) and for theft (10 male, 1 female), with fathering an illegitimate child being the next most common (6 – all male, of course!). By way of illustration I have selected the following six incidents that cover the range of charges made in this ten year span.

In 1628 Clement Smyth, "a man able to work," abandoned his family and ran away from Reading, knowing that they would have to be looked after by the parish of St. Mary's in his absence. Some while later, he was apprehended and was committed to the House of Correction. He clearly had a forgiving wife for she petitioned for his release. Upon his promise to "allowe his wief 5s a weeke out of his labour hence forwardes," and re-paying the Overseer of the Poor the 12d per week his family received in his absence, he was discharged from the House of Correction "for this tyme."[28]

Theft from Sir Thomas Vachel of 3 turkeys, 5 hens and a cock over a six week period in 1629 was tracked down to a Reading blacksmith, John Barnes. In cross-examination Barnes admitted the thefts and that he had sold the hens for the sum of 35d, had left the cock in the keeping of one William Augustyne and the three turkeys at the home of John Clifforde –

the Cliffordes indeed had also purchased 3 of the hens. Barnes was committed to the House of Correction.[29]

Perhaps the most unusual charge was that of being "idle." In 1630 a Welshman, Edward Evans, a tailor by trade, arrived in the town and stayed at an "Inn called the Crowne" in the company of a woman he had met on the highway. When brought before the Mayor and Burgesses he "further saith he is nowe travellinge into his countrye idelye." He was forthwith sent to the House of Correction. Being idle was akin to vagrancy.[30]

Richard Cawfeild, a Yorkshire man who had recently landed in Cornwall from a "man of warr," was committed for vagrancy. He was caught in Reading town wearing a stolen smock, which had been missed from the hedge of a garden in Sandhurst. It emerged that another man had stolen the smock together with two lockram shirts, then had pawned one of the shirts for food and worn the other. He fell in with Cawfeild on the road and let him have the smock. While Cawfeild went to the House of Correction for vagrancy, the other man was sent to gaol for his theft.[31]

Periodically in the Record, the Corporation summoned all the victuallers to appear before them so that they could then ensure no illegal making or selling of beer was occurring. Having previously been fined 20s (£1) for selling beer without a licence, William Grumwell was caught again – and this time he was committed to the House of Correction.[32]

The final category is well illustrated by the story of Robert Jones, a "feltmaker." Alice Allen, spinster, brought forward the complaint that Jones "had her companye and knowledge of her bodye the Mondaye senight before Ladye-daye last, at night." He had promised to marry her at that time, but since then banns had been called in Church for him to marry her sister Anne. Alice was by this time about two months pregnant. Robert denied that he was the father of Alice's child, but Anne promptly said that she would not marry him "but doth and will ever renounce him." Judgement went against Jones and he was committed to the House of Correction. Normally, as well as serving time in the House, the father would also be instructed to pay between 8d and 12d per week for the child until they were 12 years of age, although this particular record does not supply those details. Instead, the following month Jones was bailed for the sum of £20 to appear before the Quarter Sessions in January 1635.[33]

William Clayton and his wife had been resident at and in charge of the House of Correction and Hospital for nine years by 1634. In March that year, William found himself before the Mayor, Robert Maulthus, and the Head Burgesses to answer for "divers misdemeanours whereof he was accused." Since Clayton "could not finde sufficient sureties for his good behaviour, [he] was therefore committed to the Gaole." [34] It took until August to provide a replacement, with the appointment of Henry Tubb to be the "sole Keeper of the House of Correction and Governour of men and weomen comitted thither by the Towne or Countrye." [35]

With William Clayton no longer in charge of the House of Correction, his family would have had just three months from the end of March to quit the premises. However, there was something of a problem removing "Goodwief Clayton," for over six months later the Record states:

> At this daye goodwief Clayton was willed to provide to dwell ellswhere and to remove awaye her goodes and to spend her provision betwixt this and Michaellmas-daye at the furthest. And that in the meane tyme she doe noe hurt, but order all thinges well, &c.[36]

This gave her just under three weeks to remove herself and her belongings. However, this was not the end of the Clayton family troubles in 1634. On the last day of the year, their son Edward was committed to the House of Correction for allegedly fathering a child with Suzan Dan while she was a prisoner in the House. Edward had been baptised at St. Laurence's in April 1616[37] and so was most probably just 18 years of age at this point. The Record states:

> The order made by the said Maiour and Justices, touching the keepinge of the bastard female childe begotten of the bodye of Suzan Dan, spinster, in the House of Correccion, the said Justices uppon examynacion of the matter founde Edward Clayton to be the reputed father, and that he from hencefourth shall paye to the Overseers of the poore of St. Marie's parishe, in Readinge, 12d every weeke, and the said Suzan 6d every weeke for the keepinge of the said bastard childe, the said paymentes to contynue untill the bastard childe be 12 yeares of age. And the said Edward Clayton shall for his offence be committed to the House of Correccion and the 12d to be paid weekly out of that whiche he shall gett by his labour in the said house, untill he put in securitye to performe this order of his parte to be performed.[38]

When Henry Tubb took over the running of the House of Correction and Hospital in 1634, an agreement was drawn up that identified both the confidence that the Corporation felt in him and the obligations he was to carry out. For example, he was to house men and women separately – a condition that the Mayor and Company were required to inspect. In addition, he was not allowed to keep a horse in order to grind at the mill: perhaps this would make life too easy for the inmates.[39]

Mrs. Clayton had to leave before Michaelmas Day, but she possibly left earlier as there is a document dated 1st September 1634 concerning work done on the Keeper's house:

> Then I Robert Westmerland received and had of John Saunders Esq by the appointment of the Maior and Burgesses of the towne of Readinge for the digging, making and finishing the house and office, vault and tunnel for the House of Correction in Readinge the sume of Tenn Pounds of lawfull money of England. x li [£10]
> Robert Westmerland[40]

At whatever date Mrs. Clayton did finally move out of the Keeper's House, Henry Tubb, his wife and their children (at least three by late 1634) would have moved in as soon as possible. Very sadly, Mary Tubb died in childbirth in July 1642, while the unfortunate baby, named Henry like his father, also died two weeks later.[41]

While poor Henry Tubb was suffering loss in his private life, the life of the country around him was going through terrible times too. It is difficult to say exactly when the Civil War started – January 1642 when King Charles fled London? When the King raised the Royal Standard in Nottingham on 22nd August? Or the first pitched battle, at Edgehill on 23rd October 1642?

It is easier to date when the Civil War came to Reading: 25th June 1642, when Henry Marten, MP for the County and subsequently one of the regicides, held a muster in the town for his Parliamentary forces.

Chapter 6

A Soldiers' Barracks: 1642 to 1643

Sir Henry Marten held Reading for the Parliament from June 1642. After the indecisive battle of Edgehill in Warwickshire on 23rd October, King Charles set up his headquarters at Oxford and Royalist cavalry under the King's nephew, Prince Rupert, were thought to be heading for Reading. With no defences, Marten decided to withdraw and took his militia to London.

On or just after 3rd November, King Charles himself arrived in Reading. He stayed for much of the month of November and made arrangements to turn the town into a Royalist garrison. The King placed Sir Arthur Aston in charge of the town, about whom a fellow Royalist (Sir Edward Hyde, 1st Earl of Clarendon) said that he "had the fortune to be very much esteemed where he was not known, and very much detested where he was."

The town was then made ready for a siege, with earthworks thrown up on all sides except where the several rivers and waterways provided natural barriers. Greyfriars formed part of the perimeter wall, at the north-west corner of the hastily thrown up defences.

Reading became a garrison of over 2000 foot soldiers and about 300 cavalry, all to be housed by a town with population of about 5000 inhabitants. This large body of military personnel were quartered in all possible places around the town, including in the House of Correction and the Oracle, this latter being the house of industry founded in 1628 by John Kendrick's bequest. Reading School became the arsenal.

Part of the book of accounts survives for the House of Correction over this period. It sums up the period with the paragraph:

> In ye year 1642 ye kings Army tooke uppe their Winter Quarters in this Towne of Reading where was made a Garrison for them and likewise they kept a Garrison there in the yeare 1643, In such years ye said house of correction was made a court of guards by ye soldiers whoe did ruinate and pull downe a great parte of ye said house, which house was after warde repayred att the charges of

> the Mayour Aldermen and Burgesses of Readinge whoe expended in and about ye reparaccon of ye same ye sume of £35 4s 6d.[1]

The Corporation had to fund both Aston's £7 per week salary and a massive £2000 "loan" to the King by March 1643. All those soldiers had to be fed too. Many of the wealthy families were on the road to ruin.

On Sunday 16th April 1643 the parliamentary forces under the Earl of Essex opened artillery fire upon the town, beginning the Siege of Reading. Thankfully, the Greyfriars building was not damaged, although St. Giles' steeple was not so lucky. The siege ended on Thursday 27th April when the Royalist Garrison, having surrendered, was allowed to leave from "Friars Gate" heading towards Caversham Bridge "with flying colours." Parliamentary forces took over Reading. This change of occupying force did not alter the situation for Greyfriars, though, which continued to be used as a barracks.

Parliamentary forces continued to occupy Reading until September 1643. Reading was then evacuated as part of the Parliamentary withdrawal to London following the First Battle of Newbury. Within a few days, a Royalist army under Sir Jacob Astley entered the town. This occupying force was even larger than Aston's, being approximately 3500 men. This occupation continued throughout the winter of 1643 to 1644.

Following another visit by the King, orders were given to break down the defences and abandon the Royalist occupation of the town in May 1644. By the 20th of that month, the Earl of Essex was back, holding the town for Parliament, with a comparatively small force. Parliamentary forces then held the town until the end of the Civil War.

Whether with Roundheads or Cavaliers in charge, the town suffered badly. The Corporation was repeatedly required to loan money – another £2000 in 1643 alone, then £500 per week for a month in the latter part of the same year – with no prospect of any return. All trade stopped as no-one would venture out on the roads. There was also much plundering of shops and homes by both armies. In his preface to Volume Four of "Reading Records," J. M. Guilding wrote that during the Civil War "the position of the Inhabitants was one of unexampled suffering" and of the state of the town after the siege:

> The Cloth Trade, which had already showed signs of decay, was now entirely gone. This cessation of trade, and the heavy exactions levied by both the contending parties, inflicted ruinous loss on the Town. Its population was seriously diminished, and until the present [nineteenth] century it never

> recovered the position it had once occupied as one of the chief centres of manufacturing industry in ... England.[2]

The House of Correction was in a ruined state by the end of 1643. Possibly it was also used by the Royalist garrison from late September 1643 to May 1644, but this is uncertain. The soldiers might have left it, but it was in no fit state to be used as a prison.

However, there is evidence that the Hospital, at least, continued to be in use throughout the time of occupation. There is a "noate" written by Henry Tubb, requesting payment for taking care of two women in the Hospitall:

> Ann Bennet was sent to ye Hospitall ye 24th of Ffebruary 1642 [1643 New Style] and dyed ye 18th of Sept 1643 w[hic]h is... 30 weeks w[hic]h come[s] to in money £2 12s 9d."
>
> "Goody Bayly was sent last to the Hospitall this 6th day of March 1642 [1643 New Style] and continued there until the 25th of March 1644... w[hic]h cometh to £4 16s 3d... And shee did remaine from the 25th day of March 1644 until the 23th (sic) May w[hic]h is eight weeks w[hic]h more cometh to £0 14s 9d.[3]

Both of these women would therefore have been in the Hospital during the Siege of Reading in April 1643.

The Bridewell in the 19th century

Chapter 7

The House of Correction, then Bridewell: 1644 to 1862

The House of Correction stood in need of repair until the late 1640s. In July 1646, the Mayor, George Wooldridge, "moved the Company to have the House of Correccion repaired and some new particions made therein for safe keeping and punishing of disorderly persons."[1]

Following this resolution, Henry Tubb, who had been appointed in charge of the House of Correction in August 1634, was asked by the Corporation to "view and consider what convenient roomes are needfull to be made againe in the House of Correccion"[2] with the help of some carpenters. He was instructed to report his findings back to the Company.

However, even by July 1647 the House of Correction was not fully repaired. For the first time, the Corporation appointed two men to be jointly in charge of the House:

> This daye Henry Tubb and Willyam Wooddes were appointed to be Keepers of the House of Correccion (within this Borough) for the Countie of Berks, & for the arreares due from the countie to the Keepers of the said House of Correccion during, &c., it is agreed [they] shalbe equally shared betweene the said Henry Tubb & Willyam Woodes, when the same or any parte thereof shalbe paid. Henry Tubb is appointed to have one chamber in the said House for his owne private use and Willyam Woodes to have two chambers, and both of them, the said Henry Tubb and Willyam Woodes, to have equally the managing of the mill in the said house. Willyam Woodes agreed to paye to the said Henry Tubb the one halfe of such monyes as the said Henry Tubb shall make appeare he hath expended about the reparacions of the said mill.
>
> Agreed that a certificate (concerninge the want of repaire of the House of Correccion) should be forthwith made, desiring those whom itt may concerne that the arreares due to this Corporacion for the said house may be satisfyed that soe the said house maye be repayred.[3]

In order to obtain the arrears from the County, Henry Tubbs and William Woode submitted an official request to the Sessions of the Peace at

Reading, which sat in January 1648. Prior to the Civil War, the County had paid £31 annually towards the maintenance of the House of Correction, but nothing had been received for five years: "And by meanes of the non payment of this said arreares the said house is fallen into decay and verie ruynous. The pet[itione]rs therefore most humblie praye that such order may be given for the payment of the said arrears as in your wos[hi]pps wisdomes shall seeme meete. And your pet[itione]rs shall dailie praye &c."

On the lower half of the petition document the decision is recorded:

> Daniel Blagrave.
> At the Sessions of the Peace at Reading in the County of Berkshire January 1647 [1648 New Style], Upon the peticion of Henry Tubb and Willyam Woode keepers of the house of Correccon att Readinge, it is ordered that the treasurers shall paye the arreares of rent due to the said house for two yeres last past and noe more, which is the time itt hath [been] last used as a house of Correction by this Countie, upon receipte of w[hi]ch money the house is to be repaired by them...[4]

Due to the state of the County finances, all that could be managed were payments of £15 per year for the next few years. In spite of Daniel Blagrave's decision above to pay Tubb and Woode for the previous two years' arrears, the Treasurer in fact only paid them £15.[5]

Greyfriars almost certainly lost the Hospital/Poor House part of its role when it was repaired after the Civil War. There is only other one reference to it as a Hospital after 1644: in May 1646 the Corporation "alsoe ordered that Mr. John Tench shall pay the £3 10s unto Henry Tubb, for his charges in releivinge Bailey's wife when shee was in the hospitall."[6] However, this could easily relate to the old debt of 1644 mentioned above (see page 45 for reference to "Goody Bayly").

By the early years of the 18th century, the land immediately to the east and north of Greyfriars had been acquired by Joseph Haycock (or Heycock), an apothecary from Reading. He purchased the land in August 1722 from the heirs of John Dalby Esq., at which time the area was known as the "Fryers Ground."[7] The back kitchen of Mr. Haycock's house was built up against the east wall of the House of Correction. The land became known as Haycock's Friars from this point, throughout the 18th century and even into the 19th. It was still in the Haycock family when Charles Coates wrote his History of Reading in 1802,[8] being sold soon after – in mid-November 1805 – by another Joseph Haycock, a Gentleman from Leicester.

Coates describes an incident from private correspondence which I have been unable to corroborate from another source. It relates to the discovery of a coffin on Haycock's land that might possibly have contained the remains of Margaret Twyniho, who had died in 1500 or 1501 (see page 14). Coates thought that it was "very probable" that the remains were hers. As we do not know how many burials there were in the Quire nor of those how many were of women, it is hard to judge how likely these remains actually were of Margaret Twyniho. The account, which is clearly contemporary with the finding, was as follows:

> On Thursday Oct. 17th, 1728, in the evening, was found in Mr. Heycock's fryars, about a yard from the middle of the foundation of the east end of the Bridewell, and scarce a yard under ground, a coffin of Freestone, six feet eight inches long from the outside to the outside, the stone being two inches and a quarter thick; it is likewise two feet three inches over, in the widest part, which is at the head; one foot five inches at the feet, and it is one foot two inches deep on the outside. The bones which are small, are thought to be a woman's, and are in it, and not quite rotten. It appears to have had no lid to it; but they found abundance of tiles before they came to it, which makes me think it was arched over with tiles.[9]

As shown by the quotation above, the House of Correction became known as the Bridewell by the 18th century. The name 'bridewell' is no longer in current use and deserves a brief explanation. The derivation of the word is from St. Bride's Well, near St. Bride's Church on Fleet Street, London. There was originally a Bridewell Palace on the site, which was a residence of King Henry VIII. Henry's son Edward VI gave the palace to the City of London for a poor house, hospital and prison. The name Bridewell was then used for prisons throughout London and beyond.

It is unlikely that the Greyfriars Bridewell was ever a pleasant place to be. With no heating, it must always have been cold and damp – although generally, of course, people had to cope with a much harsher environment than most of us are used to in the 21st century! The winters must have been particularly hard to bear. For people sentenced to spend more than a few days there, it was a difficult environment to endure. It is surprising that there were relatively few deaths in the parish records. In the last 40 years of the 18th century, for example, there were just 5, all buried at St. Laurence's Church: Benjamin Cook in January 1764; John Shelton and Richard Gallway on the same day in April 1768; Robert Arlett in October 1786; John Primmer in April 1789[10]. In January 1789 there was nearly a sixth name added to the list of deaths, as Martha Martin attempted to hang herself in the Bridewell and very nearly succeeded.[11]

There is a description of the Bridewell at this time, given by the renowned prison inspector and reformer John Howard. He visited the Bridewell on 1st January 1776 and wrote:

> ... the town Bridewell. It was formerly a church, and is a spacious room, with four small dark huts on one side for night-rooms. The county pays rent to the corporation. It is dirty and out of repair. Women and men are together in the day-time. No court; no water; allowance to felons, three-pence a day; and to petty offenders, two five-farthing loaves each every Sunday, and one every week-day.[12]

John Howard noted that there were 6 prisoners in the Bridewell that day. He took care also to record the Keeper's salary: £18 from the County; £2 from the town; half the profit of the prisoners' work; an allowance of £2 per year to buy straw for the cells. He also noted that, while there was a board with the prohibition for prisoners to have spirituous liquors, the Keeper was licensed for beer.

In 1782 Parliament passed an "Act For the Amending and Rendering More Effectual the Laws... relative to Houses of Correction."[13] In response the Midsummer Berkshire Sessions of the Peace that year appointed three Justices of the Peace – James Patey, Penyston Powney and the Rev. Henry Wilder – as the law required, to inspect the conditions in Reading Bridewell.[14] The intentions of the legislation were to ensure that all such Houses were able to punish with Hard Labour and to require separate accommodation for prisoners according to the nature of the crimes committed. The inspectors would not have been too impressed that Joseph Clack, the Keeper of the Bridewell in 1782, had had to advertise a couple of months earlier to ask if anyone knew the whereabouts of John Strickland, who had absconded from his master's service, and for whom Clack was offering the large reward of 10 guineas.[15]

The three inspectors in fact produced two reports on the Bridewell. In the following January they reported that "in its present state of building [Reading Bridewell] is by no means calculated to fulfil the purposes of the act of parliament, but that the same must be greatly enlarged and rebuilt." Three months later, their second report recommended that "refractory prisoners" needed to be kept in close confinement, that male and female prisoners should be separated and that the materials for work should be provided.[16]

Only two years later, complaints about the terrible state of the Reading Bridewell spurred the Berkshire Sessions on to build a new Bridewell near the Forbury – then a short distance outside the inhabited part of the town. It was completed by September 1786. From this date the Bridewell at Greyfriars was used only for Borough prisoners, rather than both Borough and County.

To cope with an increasing prison population, the cramped gaol on Castle Street was replaced in 1793 by a new building adjoining the new Bridewell on part of the Forbury and old Abbey ruins site.[17] The former gaol site was later used to build the new Episcopal Chapel of St. Mary, Castle Street, which opened in 1798. The new County Gaol and Bridewell lasted for just over fifty years and were replaced on the same site by the current buildings, which opened in 1844.

At this time, in addition to the Borough Bridewell at Greyfriars, there were some smaller town "lock ups." The Compter, near St. Laurence's Church, had three cells and was part of a public house. There was also a cell over the Compter gateway by St. Laurence's Church which was mainly used as a debtors' prison. Lastly, the "Hole" was a small cell, also near St. Laurence's, at the east end of the Piazza, which was used mainly for the custody of offenders taken during the night.

In the latter part of the 18th century, the roof of the nave of the Bridewell was removed. This was probably in 1786, as on Wednesday 27th September that year the prisoners had to be evacuated to safety – into the newly completed Bridewell near the Forbury. The Reading Mercury reported that "The decayed state of our Bridewell [renders] it exceedingly dangerous to the prisoners confined therein, particularly during the late high winds."[18] Removing the roof exposed the exercise yard to the elements, although it would also have improved the access to fresh air for the prisoners! The nave roof remained off until the restoration in 1862 – 3.

By December 1786 the Bridewell was back in use, with four men committed there to await trial for "assaulting, beating and dangerously wounding" William Taplin. The men had believed that Taplin was the author of an article in the newspaper in support of the abolition of the practice, each St. Thomas's day, of baiting two bulls in Market Place.[19]

Many of the people committed to the Bridewell were there either to await their case being heard, or as debtors. However, not everyone was happy to see out their time patiently! For example, the Bridewell Keeper in March 1791, John Shaylor, had inserted the following notice in the Reading Mercury:

> ESCAPED from JUSTICE: ROBERT BEESLEY, who broke out of Reading Bridewell in the night of the 29th instant: He is about five feet five inches high, 24 or 25 years of age, pale complexion, and wears his own black hair rather long; is a native of Reading, and is by trade a weaver; ... Whoever will apprehend the said Robert Beesley, and bring him to the keeper of the Borough Bridewell, shall receive of him FIVE GUINEAS reward.[20]

Beesley had been committed to the Bridewell on 19th January 1791 for stealing 28 fowls from Michael Blount, Esq, of Mapledurham, together with an accomplice.[21] The size of the reward offered for his recapture was about half John Shaylor's annual salary. In late April, the advert was repeated more widely[22] implying that Beesley probably made good his escape from justice.

On 6th May 1789 the Borough agreed a Lease for the "Alehouse adjoining the Bridewell... for 4 score years at £5 per annum." This public house must have been on the site for some time as within a year of the Lease, in April 1790, "leave [was] given to John Shaylor to inhabit the new Bridewell House until Michaelmas next that the public house may be rebuilt." This rebuilt public house was the "Pigeons," which remained attached to the Bridewell until it was knocked down in 1862 at the Church's restoration.[23]

In total, as a House of Correction and then a Bridewell, nearly 250 years of Greyfriars' history was spent as a prison. In almost all of the histories of Reading and of Greyfriars Church, it is stated that the Bridewell closed in 1844, at the time when the new County Gaol opened, leaving the Greyfriars site derelict for almost twenty years. In fact, the Bridewell was in use until March 1862, with the restoration work on the Church beginning just a month later on Monday 21st April.

At the end of 1801, James Neild, a prison reformer following in John Howard's footsteps, visited the Bridewell. He wrote, in a letter to the Gentleman's Magazine, in February 1802:

> The town Bridewell at Reading is built out of the ruins of an old Church; the keeper, John Shaylor, lives in the public house adjoining; salary £10. Prisoners on December 13th 1801: three. Neither the Act nor the preservation of health, nor the clauses against spirituous liquors, were hung up. No water accessible to the prisoners. This gaoler is one of the old school, rough, rude, and ignorant. He positively refused me admittance; luckily the Mayor was at home, and he gave me an order.[24]

In February 1806 Laurence Austwick, wine merchant, Alderman and past and future Mayor of Reading (1803–4 and 1812–13) purchased the land immediately to the east and north of the Bridewell. The area was a patchwork involving at least fifteen households, who were all tenants or under-tenants, in the main, of Joseph Hill of Savile Row in London. The Bridewell Keeper, John Shaylor, was one of them:

> ... and all those gardens containing by estimation 20p[erches] more or less in the tenure or occupation of John Shaylor and all that yard with the pigsties and appurtenances thereunto belonging containing by estimation 18p[erches] more or less in the tenure or occupation of the said John Shaylor...[25]

The land covered some 15 to 20 acres and cost Austwick the very large sum of £3000. In 1808, Austwick had five houses on the land pulled down and "erected a Capital Messuage or Dwelling house for his own residence and also removed or altered the internal division fences of the said pieces of land or gardens." He also built a stable, a coach house and various undefined outhouses. The whole was completed by "yards, gardens, lawns and pleasure grounds."

According to one account, this construction entailed pulling down the Greyfriars Chancel so that a servants' office and kitchen could be built there.[26] When the Church was restored in 1863, the Chancel Arch was clearly defined in the Church's rebuilt east end in the hope that one day the chancel could also be restored. The footings of the original chancel were found in an exploratory dig in the then Vicarage garden in the 1960s.[27] However, it is quite likely that the chancel had been removed much earlier than 1808 and possibly even when the land belonged to Robert Stanshawe in the mid 16th century. Certainly by the time the land belonged to Mr. Haycock in the early 18th century, his building abutted the east wall and so the chancel was unlikely still to have been there.

The Austwick house, which in time became first Greyfriars House and then, after 1905, Greyfriars Vicarage, has often been thought of as designed by the famous architect Sir John Soane. In fact, although Soane produced three different designs for a house for Austwick, none was actually built. The likelihood is that the designs were for a house for Austwick in a different location in Reading – the frontage in the Soane drawings being much narrower than the space available for 64 Friar Street. There is a letter in the papers in the Soane Museum in London asking Austwick to settle the costs of £78 15s for work dated 1st March to 11th

May 1796 for these designs, ten years before Austwick purchased the land next to the Bridewell. The letter ends: "Mr. Soane presents compliments to Mr. Austwick and sends him the above account, which he presumes has escaped Mr. Austwick's memory." The letter is dated 8th August 1811.[28]

The actual house built in 1808 was very loosely based on elements of the Soane plans. Unfortunately the architect's name is not known.

In 1810, Reading resident John Man published anonymously the book "The Stranger in Reading," purporting to be a series of letters by a traveller conveying their first impressions of visiting Reading. In the second of the letters he described in detail a visit to the town Bridewell. He gave the dimensions of the prison as 80 feet by 54 feet, this being the original body and side aisles of the Church "of the grey friars." The body of the Church was divided into two wards, separating the male and female prisoners, and the nave roof had been removed to prevent its collapse. This open central area, although paved with bricks, was damp and covered over with green growth and was used for an exercise yard for the prisoners.

The north aisle had been converted into cells for the prisoners, opening into the body of the Church. Beyond the line of the building to the north, there had recently been erected three solitary cells, 14 feet by 6 feet, connected to the Church by doors in the original walls. These solitary cells also had a small court, about 7 feet square. When the cell door was closed, neither light nor air could enter into them. The only furniture in each cell was a bed of straw.

He concluded his survey: "In these holes the wretched sufferer is compelled to linger... on the scanty prison allowance of bread and water, without a bed to lie on, and even deprived of fire in the coldest months of winter." He was undoubtedly not exaggerating when he finished with the statement that "they will probably carry with them the seeds of disorders that may render their future days full of pain and misery."[29]

In the picture on page 46 the view looks west towards the great window – clearly bricked up to the height of the tracery, no doubt to prevent escape that way. The overnight cells are on the right, between the Church columns and the north wall of the Church. To the left is the door to the Keeper's yard and house. I imagine that the shed-like structure is the earth closet toilet. The partition, which Man said separated men from women, later separated the main prison from the debtors' ward. From the picture it can be seen that it was located in the middle of the second set of arches, counting from the west window.

John Shaylor had died by 1811, as his widow's death is recorded in the Reading Mercury: "Thursday se'nnight died, after a lingering illness which she bore with Christian fortitude, Mrs. Shaylor, widow of the late Mr. Shaylor, many years keeper of the town Bridewell."[30]

The Bridewell Keeper during at least the period 1816 to 1821 was William Paradise. The role of the Bridewell Keeper not only included keeping the gaol, but also at times administering physical punishments. William S. Darter, Reading Alderman, Magistrate and later Mayor, in his "Reminiscences of Reading by an Octogenarian," wrote of one such incident he had personally witnessed and had been horrified by, which involved Paradise about the year 1816. An unemployed labourer had stolen a loaf of bread from Turner's bakery on Castle Street. Having been caught and duly tried, he was sentenced to be publicly whipped "at the cart's tail" from the Bridewell to his home on Silver Street. Stripped to the waist and followed by a huge crowd, the man had his back cut to shreds by Paradise's whipping by the time he reached his home. The man died of his injuries soon after.[31]

In 1825 Alderman Darter visited the Bridewell. William Paradise had almost certainly been replaced by John Warburton, a Police Officer, as Keeper by this point. Darter's visit began with an inspection of the Keeper's House, which consisted of four rooms: a sitting room and kitchen, with two bedrooms above, with no garden. He noted that in the Bridewell the best of the cells were set aside for the debtors, but he believed "even those were unfit for human beings to sleep in." The partitioning was partly made of wood and had been covered with graffiti by the prisoners. The whole structure of internal partitions struck him as frail.[32]

In a Town Council meeting in May 1838, the Mayor, Richard Billing, reported that the Bridewell was in a very dilapidated state and in his view was unfit to be used as a prison. He stated that the Bridewell should either be repaired or be replaced. The Council then decided upon a third option: to form a committee to consider what should be done. The Mayor and six of the Council were chosen.[33]

A report from the Council Finance Committee in December 1838 recommended that the Bridewell Keeper's salary should increase from £30 to £40 per annum and that of the matron from £10 to 10 guineas. The report went on to say that the increase was "in consequence of the increased duties of late."[34] Unfortunately, it does not say what these extra duties were.

A sketch of Greyfriars
From "Reading Past and Present," 1839
by William Fletcher

The Bridewell Keeper from 1832 to 1859 was John Readings.[35] Having been a cordwainer, or shoemaker, in Friar Street until his late forties, this was a second career, taken up soon after he lost his second wife.[36]

In the national census taken on the night of 6th June 1841[37] John Readings had with him in the Keeper's House three of his children, all now adults: his son Henry, also a cordwainer by trade (later he became a policeman); his daughter Elizabeth who is described as Matron of the Bridewell; and his married daughter Mary Ann James.

On that night, there were four prisoners in the Bridewell:

John Claydon, aged 40, a debtor, and a brewer by trade;
Charles Dredge, aged 25, a hawker (or street seller);
Sarah Burton, aged 45, a widow;
Henry Harden, aged 15, another hawker.

This was not Charles Dredge's last Bridewell sentence. In January of the following year he was convicted of assaulting his wife and fined 20s plus costs. In default of payment, he was committed to the Bridewell for one month.[38]

The pages of the Reading Mercury continued to carry many stories of those sent to the Bridewell. The most frequent crimes committed were assault, being drunk and disorderly, begging and theft. Many convictions were followed by a fine, which upon default by the prisoner meant that they served a time in the Bridewell. Although there were great variations, on the whole a fine of 5 shillings led to a 7 day imprisonment, 10s to 14 days and 20s (£1) to a month.

For example, Ann Rollins was convicted of causing an obstruction on Castle Street in September 1844 and fined 10s. As she could not pay, she served 14 days in the Bridewell. [39] She was discharged on Tuesday 1st October and within a few hours had assaulted a constable in Silver Street due to her drunken state. She was fined 40s (£2) and 7s costs, which she was unable to pay.[40] She could have considered herself fortunate in then only being sent to the Bridewell for one month – as pro rata she deserved two!

During 1846, begging became the most frequent cause of incarceration in the Bridewell, usually for less than 7 days. One woman – a frequent offender identified as "the most notorious" Sarah Goddard – was sentenced to 14 days.[41]

Sometimes it is hard to see why the particular sentences were given. Two boys, William Goodman and Richard Major, stole 6d worth of gooseberries from the garden of William Chesterman in June 1844. Following their guilty plea they were sentenced to 7 days' hard labour in the Borough Bridewell.[42] Compare this with the case in August 1845 of another boy, Henry Snow, aged about 14, who assaulted another lad with a knife, causing a wound. Snow was fined £1 8s 6d, with 11s 6d costs, which he could not pay. He was then committed to the Bridewell for just three days. He might have expected two months for that sum![43]

On Saturday 24th June 1843, a boy named Timothy Frankum was brought before the magistrates accused of stealing five tame rabbits from Mr. E. Brown of 116 Castle Street. He was remanded for further examination, due to take place on the following Monday. However, that evening, shortly before 8 o'clock, he made good his escape from the Bridewell. He had been locked in the exercise yard by Mr. Readings at about 7pm. He had then managed to climb up the walls and onto the roof tiles of a neighbouring house and somehow found his way down to the ground and disappeared.[44]

There was a sequel to this particular story. Frankum was apprehended some months later and was brought before the magistrate again in March of the following year.[45] No-one came forward to press charges and so Frankum was remanded for five days and then discharged. As he left the dock he was apprehended again by the police, who served a warrant for his arrest for trespass in pursuit of game. This time his received a sentence of two months' hard labour.

Interestingly, a very similar occurrence happened just over a year later with another lad – Daniel Greetham – who had been caught stealing rabbits. Perhaps he was an associate of Timothy Frankum! This time, however, although Greetham managed to scale the walls and get back down to street level in Friar Street, a resident captured him and took him back to the Bridewell. For the attempted escape Greetham was given 14 days' hard labour.[46]

In the 1851 national census[47], John Readings was given the grander title of Governor of the Borough Gaol. The address of the Keeper's house is given as 67 Friar Street. In 64 Friar Street, which was to become the Vicarage in time, was the family of Francis Slocombe, a Solicitor. The "Pigeons" public house, at 65 Friar Street, was run by Charlotte King, a 56 year old innkeeper.

The census shows John Readings, aged 67, living with his unmarried daughter Jane, aged 27, who is described as the Matron of the Borough Gaol. They also have John's grandson Thomas James, aged 6, living with them.

That night, 30th March 1851, the Bridewell had three prisoners:

> George Smith, aged 22, unmarried, a Day Labourer;
> Joseph Adams, aged 16, unmarried, a Day Labourer;
> Sarah Brooker, aged 22, unmarried, a Servant.

The next incident of note in the life of the Bridewell was another escape, although this time it made national news – in The Times under the headline "DARING ESCAPE" – as well as a meriting a comprehensive report in the Reading Mercury.[48]

On Wednesday 14th July 1858 there was a muscular Irishman named McQuhae (or McQuaid) locked up in the Bridewell, remanded on a charge of theft from his lodging house. About 7pm Mr. Readings (by this date aged 74 and described in the reports as elderly, infirm and feeble) went into the Bridewell yard to tell McQuhae to enter his cell and be locked in for the night.

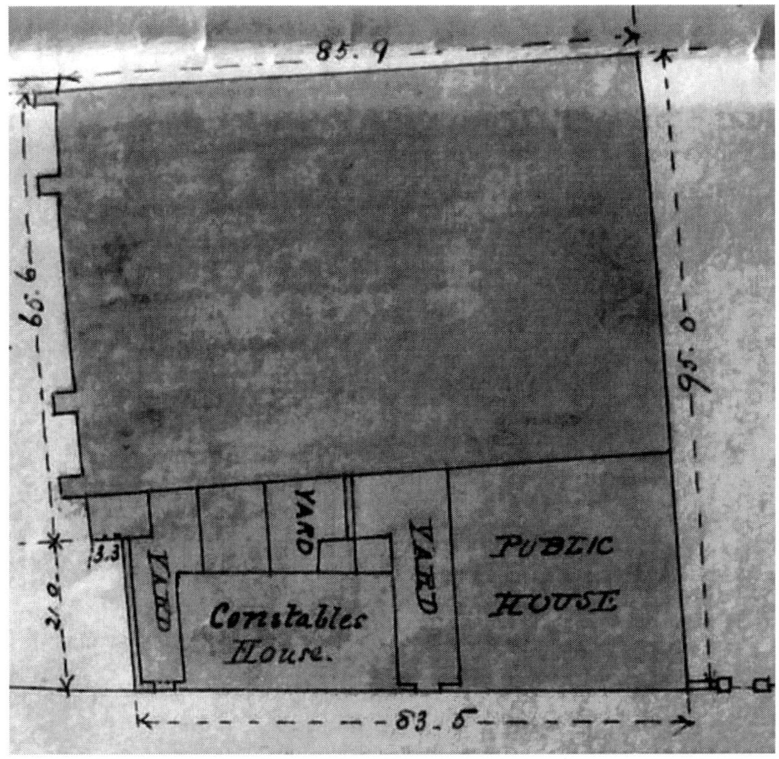

1861 Plan of the Bridewell and Public House[49]
By this time the Keeper was a Police Constable.

McQuhae decided to try to get the keys off the gaoler but John Readings did not part with them easily. The Reading Mercury wrote: "a struggle ensued, and, considering the infirm and feeble state of Mr. Readings, he gallantly resisted his antagonist." However, McQuhae managed to throw the gaoler down onto his back and thus overpowered him. The prisoner then took the keys and shut and locked the yard door, leaving Readings imprisoned in his own Bridewell.

McQuhae walked through into the Keeper's house and there he was met "by a female named Davis who, in consequence of the Governor having been absent longer than usual, suspected something had happened." McQuhae picked her up and put her over his shoulder, cast her into the Debtor's ward and bolted the door on her.

Back in the house, he put on some shoes and a cap for his head and calmly left by the front door on Friar Street. At the front door he was seen by several local people, but, cleverly, McQuhae did not exit quickly, but turned round in the doorway and bowed two or three times as if talking to someone. He then walked quietly away in the direction of "Welldale-street."

Meanwhile, Davis started shouting for help, which eventually arrived in the shape of a young girl from across the other side of Friar Street. Davis was let out of the Debtor's ward easily enough, but John Readings was locked in the Bridewell and McQuhae had taken the keys. The Times said that a locksmith had to be called in to rescue the old man, while the Reading Mercury said that the door had to be forced open. By whatever means, John Readings was rescued and was promptly removed to his bed and attended by a doctor as he had been considerably injured by being thrown down on his back.

Police officers were called to the scene straightaway. They discovered that McQuhae had been seen heading from Bedford Gardens towards the railway. However, the trail went cold from that point and nothing was seen or heard of the prisoner again.

Following this incident, the Council decided that something of an overhaul was needed at the Bridewell. New cells were fitted, furnished with bedding "and other necessary articles." The Council deliberated on the management of the Bridewell and decided, in May 1860, that it was "essential to place it under the control of the police." The chief superintendent of the Reading Police Force recommended Inspector Charles Hardiman as the next Keeper, who would have to be reduced in rank to Sergeant, but would gain a salary of £1 2s per week, have accommodation provided with allowance for coal and gas, and his wife would be appointed Matron at a salary of £5 per annum.[50]

This resolution entailed, of course, the removal of John Readings from his post. The Council awarded him a generous annuity of £35 for life, which was also to cover compensation for his daughter in her role as Matron. In the 1861 census, he is shown living with his son Henry, by now a police constable, at 73 Marshall Place and is described as "Formerly Bridewell Keeper, now superannuated."[51]

Meanwhile, the Borough Bridewell was in the care of its new Governor, Charles Hardiman, aged 44 in 1861.[52] In later censuses he is described as a "Sergeant at Mace." Charles lived in the Bridewell Keeper's house with his wife Ann, five children and a 16 year old nurse maid.

There were just two prisoners in the Bridewell on the night of 7th April 1861:

John Comb, aged 20, unmarried, a Farm Labourer;
Frederick Simpson, aged 23, married, a Bricklayer.

Frederick Simpson had been committed to the Bridewell at least twice before. In a report of July 1858 in the Reading Mercury, carried in the next column to the story of McQuhae's escape, it says:

> Frederick Simpson, a young man, a bricklayer by trade, living in Wynford Street, was brought up in custody, and pleaded guilty to the charge of having been found drunk and disorderly in Kings Road on Monday evening. He also pleaded guilty to the charge of having assaulted police constable Spinks.
>
> The Bench remarked that having been previously in custody for being drunk, they must punish him with some degree of severity, and should therefore fine him in the penalty of 20s. In default of payment in a week, to be committed to the Bridewell for 14 days.[53]

By 1861, 64 Friar Street had changed hands, being now owned by Charles Andrewes, Justice of the Peace and Member of the Town Council. The "Pigeons" public house, at number 66 (changed from the number 65 of ten years before), was in the hands of 40 year old Charles Turton.

Although only having a small capacity – or perhaps because of it – the Bridewell was in constant use. So much so, that when it was empty it was a newsworthy story. The Reading Mercury reported in June 1861 that "There is not a single prisoner in our Bridewell at present, and the keeper has consequently a sinecure." The article goes on to say that it has been some time since this situation occurred and took heart from the lack of prisoners, saying "that it does occur occasionally in a town of 25,000 inhabitants proves a great absence of crime, which is no doubt attributable, in a great measure, to the vigilance and efficiency of our police force."[54]

The 'sinecure' was not to last. In the following week's paper under the headline "A VIOLENT CHARACTER," the Reading Mercury reported: "Catherine Ball was charged with being drunk and disorderly in Queen's Road and for assaulting PC Poynter... She was led to the police station and, on feigning inability to walk to the Bridewell, a truck was procured upon which she was conveyed there, supported on either side by a policeman and accompanied by a crowd of boys, who were intensely amused at the spectacle."[55]

Although the Bridewell was continuing in use, its future had been up for discussion from time to time. In the early 1830s, James Wheble, a local landowner and Justice of the Peace, had approached the Council with a view to purchasing the Greyfriars site and converting it to a Roman Catholic Church. [56] However, at that time, the Council were not willing to sell the Bridewell and Mr. Wheble instead financed the building, from designs by A. W. Pugin, of the Church of St. James & St. William of York on land next to the Abbey ruins. This Church was built over the years 1837 – 1840. Sadly, James Wheble did not live to see the opening of the new church, dying just a fortnight before it opened.

In 1843 the question of the Bridewell's future had arisen again in the Council, but had been dropped in light of the perceived expense of a new Bridewell.[57] Two years later, after a visit from the Architectural Section of the Archaeological Association, the Reading Mercury said that it "still cherished a hope that a future day may see it appropriated to some more seemly usage than the Borough Bridewell."[58] Later that year, the Council decided that, even though it was much cheaper to keep prisoners in the Bridewell than in the County Gaol, the Bridewell was "altogether unfit for the purpose." It did, however, continue to serve that purpose![59]

At a Council meeting in May 1849, the Mayor, Mr. T. Harris, stated that immediate repairs were needed to the Bridewell, costing £5 or so in total. This was a catalyst for several councillors to propose more detailed consideration of the situation. Alderman Blandy argued that, what with the cost of the salaries for the Keeper and Matron, together with all its other expenditure, the Bridewell was not the cheap option the Council tended to believe. His suggestion was to use the Compter premises and do away with the Bridewell altogether and as it was "also one of the most interesting remains of ecclesiastical architecture" which they had in the town, he thought "it was highly desirable that it should be restored to something more nearly approaching its original uses." After further discussion, the Mayor proposed, and it was agreed, that it would be desirable that "the Bridewell should be done away with."[60]

The cost of the Bridewell to the Council in 1855 was a little under £20 a quarter: John Readings' salary was £10 10s a quarter; his daughter as Matron received £2 12s 6d; and in the quarter to September that year, for example, £4 16s 9d covered the remaining cost of “Bread and incidentals.”[61]

However, it took several more years before plans began to crystallize into firm ideas. In 1858, the Council proposed to erect a new Police Building that would bring together all the scattered accommodation to one purpose-built centre including a police station, detention cells, dormitories for the police officers, magistrates’ rooms and fire engine house. As cells would be provided in the police buildings, the Greyfriars site would not then be needed as a Bridewell. The preferred site was identified as High Bridge House, between the river Kennet and Star Lane, on what is now London Street, though there were dissenting voices who thought the site was not appropriate. The Council then voted for sending the issue back to the appointed committee to consider alternative sites.[62]

In spite of this, plans were completed for new Police Buildings at High Bridge by Mr. Woodman, the Borough Surveyor. He presented them to the Council and displayed them to the public in the following month.[63] However, the Council decided not to proceed with High Bridge, but suggested that a site at the Forbury be considered.[64]

The next scheme proposed for the Greyfriars site was following the visit on Friday 16th September 1859 of the Berkshire Congress of the British Archaeological Society. The local gathering at Newbury took a day’s excursion by rail to Reading. Following a civic reception, they toured and inspected in turn St. Laurence’s Church, the Abbey ruins, St. Mary’s Church and then Greyfriars. Following their tour, the chairman, Mr. Pettigrew, read a paper to a large gathering describing the history of Reading. Unfortunately, the tour had taken so long that the report had to be cut short so that the visiting dignitaries could catch their train back to Newbury. During their visit, the members of the Congress expressed dismay at the use to which Greyfriars was being put and the suggestion was made in their report, carried in The Builder the following week, that the Council could turn the building into a town museum.[65]

Instead, the Council were to get their new Police Building at High Bridge and the ruined Church was to be restored and re-consecrated as a place of worship. However, in order to follow the story of these last days of the Bridewell and the first days of the new Church, we first have to meet a new name in the Greyfriars story: Rev. William Whitmarsh Phelps. He is such an important person in the history of Greyfriars that it is worth dwelling for a short while on his life and background before coming back to the sequence of events.

The Rev. William Whitmarsh Phelps M.A. in 1852
From an Engraving by W. Walker from a Painting by T. A. Woolnoth

Chapter 8

Rev. W. W. Phelps: The Restorer of Greyfriars Church

William Whitmarsh Phelps was born on 1st October 1797 in Wilton, Wiltshire, the son of the Master of the Free School there. William went up to Corpus Christi College, Oxford, graduating in classical honours and becoming a Fellow by 1822. Ordained Deacon in Salisbury Cathedral, he became the Curate at Hindon, 12 miles from Wilton. During his four year stay there he married Octavia and over subsequent years they had four sons and a daughter.

Mr. Phelps then became an assistant master at Harrow School, which he enjoyed so much that he stayed on until June 1839, by which time he was 42 years old. Among the many notable students he met there were the two sons of Sir Robert Peel, who were in his care during their school days.

His next move brought him to Reading. Through the offices of his good friend the Rev. John Ball, Vicar of St. Laurence's Church, Reading, he gained the Curacy at St. Laurence's in February 1840. He was soon on the move again, becoming Curate at Sonning in September 1841 and then at Sulhamstead in May 1842.

Mr. Phelps then moved to the heart of Church life at Reading. On Whit Sunday 22nd May 1845 he became Vicar of Trinity Church (now Holy Trinity, Oxford Road), which was then a "proprietary chapel" – that is, one built by a private person. It became a "Chapel-of-Ease in the parish of St. Mary the Virgin" in 1864, after Mr. Phelps had moved on. One of the first things that Mr. Phelps did upon his arrival in his new Church was to invite all the local clergy to a monthly meeting, with a talk, meal and prayer, all focused on Reading and its needs.

In 1860, a year after his wife had died, Mr. Phelps received an invitation from the Rt. Rev. Samuel Waldegrave, who had just been appointed Bishop of Carlisle. The Bishop offered him the post of Examining Chaplain in the Carlisle diocese, with the expectation that he took up parish duties at some later point. On 10th August 1860, the same day that he wrote to Bishop Waldegrave accepting the position, Mr. Phelps wrote in his journal: "Thought out a scheme for a new district Church."[1] Thus we can actually date the beginning of the scheme to purchase the Greyfriars' site and convert it back to ecclesiastical use.

For the moment, passing over the story of the purchase and restoration of Greyfriars which was the fulfilment of the scheme he had thought out, we will follow the story of William Phelps' life after he headed north. He divided his time, from late November 1860, between his new diocesan duties in Carlisle and his continuing incumbency at Trinity Church.

In October 1861, at the age of 64, he married Fanny Fisher. Then in February 1863 he was appointed Archdeacon and Canon of Carlisle. It was around this time that a controversy broke out over whether he should serve in two dioceses. It had been his understanding that Trinity Church was a "Benefice without Cure of Souls," and if that were the case there would be no legal problem with holding the two posts in different dioceses. However, after some legal wrangling, it was decided that Trinity Church was in fact "with Cure of Souls" and so in February 1864, Mr. Phelps resigned his position in Reading.

Continuing as Archdeacon of Carlisle, he added the post of Vicar of St. Lawrence's Church, Appleby, in the Carlisle diocese, in January 1865. He held these posts until his death, aged 69, on 22nd June 1867.

The Carlisle Patriot newspaper carried this tribute to the late Archdeacon:

> He was a consistent clergyman, a sensible and earnest preacher. Providence permitted his services here but for a brief space; still, brief as it was, the memory of it will not soon pass away; unassuming in his manners, and, what in these days is no slight merit, and entitled to no little praise, free from offence to all men. His kindly conduct and steady attention to their welfare, have earned for him the grateful recollections of his parishioners both at Reading and at Appleby; at the former place he was the main instrument in the erection of an additional church, and in the latter he has restored the Vicarage house, leaving to his successors a suitable and most commodious dwelling. We heartily wish his widow and children every consolation that can be granted under what must be a heavy bereavement; and no light part of that consolation will be the ability to look back on the course he has passed.[2]

In addition to a memorial in St. Mary's Church, Wilton, William Phelps has three other memorial tablets on display in churches: one in St.

Lawrence's Church, Appleby; one in Carlisle Cathedral; and one in Greyfriars.

In Greyfriars, upon news of Mr. Phelps's death, the pulpit and reading desk were draped in black. A committee under Rev. S. M. Barkworth was formed, advertising in early July 1867 for subscriptions to erect a memorial in the Church.[3] The early plans were to have a mural tablet that included a medallion portrait of the late Archdeacon and if possible to build a Memorial Porch over the south entrance.[4] Over £100 was subscribed, which was enough for the mural tablet (without portrait) but not the porch.

Marble Memorial to William Whitmarsh Phelps
Now on the north wall, Greyfriars Church
Erected August 1868

This memorial, the earliest of the eight on the walls of the Church, was originally mounted on the south wall of the nave and it outlines his life and achievements. Erected in August 1868, it was designed by William H. Woodman, architect, and executed by Messrs. Wheeler, all of whom worked with the Rev. W. W. Phelps on the restoration of the Church. The monument is "a foliated arch, resting on two dark marble columns, and enclosing a panel of white marble bearing the inscription. The spandrils of the arch are filled with tracery, and the whole is surrounded by a moulded band, in the centre of which is carved a running ornament of natural foliage. The monument is erected in red Mansfield stone, and is designed to harmonize in style and character with the architecture of the Church."[5] The text says:

IN MEMORY OF WILLIAM WHITMARSH PHELPS M.A.
SOMETIME FELLOW OF CORPUS CHRISTI COLLEGE, OXFORD
FOR 19 YEARS INCUMBENT OF TRINITY CHURCH, READING
LATE ARCHDEACON AND CANON OF CARLISLE,
AND VICAR OF APPLEBY, WESTMORLAND,
WHO TOWARDS THE CLOSE OF A LIFE DEVOTED
TO THE SERVICE OF CHRIST, CONCEIVED AND
ACCOMPLISHED THE RESTORATION OF THIS CHURCH.
THIS TABLET IS ERECTED IN GRATEFUL
ACKNOWLEDGEMENT OF HIS PRIVATE WORTH, HIS
MINISTERIAL FIDELITY AND HIS SELF-DENYING
EXERTIONS ON BEHALF OF PURE AND UNDEFILED RELIGION.
BORN AT WILTON OCT 1ST 1797
DIED AT APPLEBY JUNE 22ND 1867.

Returning to the story of the restoration of the Church, Mr. Phelps explained in 1861 that the moment for attempting to purchase the Bridewell had come because a piece of land, between the Church and Caversham Road, had come up for sale.[6] This land was vital for the Church restoration, but if he delayed at all then the opportunity would be lost. Mr. Phelps bought the land for £696 from the Executors of the late Mr. Weedon. This land is the area covered now by the West End and the car park around it.

William Whitmarsh Phelps was clearly both a man of action and a man of connections. No sooner had he outlined in his thoughts the scheme for a new district Church on 10th August 1860 than he started to raise money for the task. By 13th August he had the first contribution: £100, from the Rev. Peter French, Perpetual Curate of Burton-on-Trent, but a native of and a land-owner in Reading. Mr. French said he would give the money if nine others could be found to match the gift.[7]

Before taking the scheme any further, Mr. Phelps sought and obtained permission to proceed with his plan from his old friend and colleague, the Rev. John Ball, Vicar of St. Laurence's Church, since the site was within his parish.[8]

By December 1860, Mr. Phelps had contacted the Council, formally asking them if they were willing to sell the Greyfriars site. The deliberations of the Reading Town Council were summarised in the Reading Mercury of Saturday 22nd December:

> DISPOSAL OF THE BRIDEWELL –
> A letter was read from the Rev. W. W. Phelps, asking the Council if they were disposed to negotiate for the sale of the site of the present Bridewell, and of the premises immediately adjoining, for the purpose of erecting a district church, thereby restoring the Old Grey Friars' Church?
>
> The MAYOR said that he was aware that it had long been upon Mr. Phelps' mind to erect a district Church in the neighbourhood of the Bridewell, and he had now decided upon that building as the site if it were at all practical to obtain it. No doubt the suggestion upwards in everyone's mind would be that "It's a pity the offer was not made twelve months ago," but he thought he might say that the material which had been put upon the ground during the last year was all available for another building... If they could get a suitable sum offered, they would no doubt be disposed to entertain the offer.
>
> Mr. W. Blandy... concluded by moving "That this Council do now resolve to enter into treaty with the Rev. W. W. Phelps and those on whose behalf he has addressed the Council for the sale to them (subject to the approbation of the Lords' Commission and Her Majesty's Treasury) of the properties comprising the Bridewell, the Governor's house, and the 'Pigeons' public house, on such conditions and stipulations as shall be determined by the borough surveyor, under the direction of a committee of the whole Council, provided that Mr. Phelps and his friends shall give an undertaking in writing that such building shall be restored and adapted to the Church."
>
> Mr. Andrewes [who lived next door in "Greyfriars House," 64 Friar Street] said the Borough Surveyor did him the kindness to call upon him and give him notice of what was about to take place and in the conversation with him he intimated that it was the intention to restore it thoroughly in the spirit of ecclesiastical architecture... It rather awkwardly happened that, if the chancel were to be restored, it would take down his kitchen offices as well as trench upon his garden; but still, as the surveyor had shown him, if there were any

> difficulty on that point it might stand over for a time, and perhaps circumstances would require him to move, and there would be no difficulty placed in the way. He should be very glad to see the scheme carried out.
>
> Mr. Darter said... it would be for the committee to take care that Greyfriars Church should be restored to its primitive state as nearly as might be, and if so its accommodation would be well fitted for the poorer classes, the most increasing proportion of the population. It would be one of the most interesting buildings in the Borough of Reading, if it were restored to its original state.
>
> The resolution was carried unanimously.[9]

Incidentally, the comments from the Mayor, regretting that the offer had not been made a year earlier, thus saving the Council a significant outlay on laying material down for a new floor, shows that the Council did not have in mind the demolition of the building at this point, as is thought likely in several of the histories. £150 was added to the purchase price to cover the cost of removing these materials to the new cells.[10]

The Council lost no time in seeking the permission of the relevant powers. There was a legal difficulty regarding the use of the money to be received by the Council for the "Pigeons" public house. As a result, the proportion of the cost of the site that covered the purchase of the "Pigeons" could not be used towards the purchase of the new Police Buildings.[11]

The Lords of the Treasury would not give their agreement until a new Bridewell was in place and so in May 1861 the Council purchased, from Mr. W. Blandy, the large house on High Bridge they had for some time been considering whether or not to buy. It took until late June/early July for the purchase finally to be approved by the Court of Chancery.

On the anniversary of the birth of the project, in August 1861, the Reading Mercury reported:

> The Police Buildings Committee presented a letter which had been received by the Mayor, in reply to a memorial by the council to the Lords of the Treasury, for permission to sell the Bridewell Property to the Rev. Mr. Phelps to lay out the purchase money in New Police Buildings at High Bridge House and to borrow such a further sum as might be required on mortgage. The letter expressed the sanction of their lordships to all these proposals, and the report recommended that £800 should be borrowed on mortgage.[12]

Meanwhile Mr. Phelps, having accepted on 31st January 1861 the price of £1250 that had been set upon the buildings by the Council, continued to seek support for the scheme.[13] On 4th June he wrote a letter to the Reading Mercury, addressed to his "Fellow Townsmen," in order to outline his actions so far and to seek financial aid for the project.[14] Regarding expected costs he wrote:

> It is calculated that, for the completion of the work on the scale it deserves, the sum of not less than £5,000 should be expended on the building, and that £3,000 would be required for the endowment, and £2,000 for the site. In explanation of the last named item, it may be observed that the sum of £696 has been paid to the Executors of the late Mr. Weedon, for the piece of land adjoining the ruins on the west side, and forming a frontage on the corner of Caversham Road: and that the sum at which the Corporation have agreed to sell the Site of the Greyfriars' Church, with beautiful and extensive ruins, and other buildings standing thereon, is £1250.

Mr. Phelps announced the arrangements for the patronage of the Church: responsibility was to be vested in five Trustees, who were also given the authority to choose others to fill any vacancy among their number that would occur in the future. This arrangement held until 1988, at which point responsibility was transferred to the Church Trust Fund. The first five Trustees were:

Rev. John Ball, Vicar of St. Laurence's Church, Reading
Rev. Peter French, Perpetual Curate of Holy Trinity, Burton-on-Trent
John Neale, Esq., Solicitor, 12/13 Friar Street, Reading
Rev. William W. Phelps, Vicar of Trinity Church, Reading
John Simonds, Esq., Banker, Reading

The donations received by this point totalled £3,514 18s, being £2,000 from four of the Trustees and the rest from 35 other donors. Mr. Phelps concluded his letter by "earnestly inviting your attention to the object, and your cordial and effectual co-operation and support to the work."

Meanwhile, work progressed well on the new police and fire building, to contain "commodious" sleeping accommodation, a dining room and day room. Part of the building was to be the residence of the Police Superintendent and it also contained rooms for the local magistrate court and a number of "dry, excellent cells," replacing the Bridewell accommodation.

Although the builder, Mr. S. Biggs of Queens Road, worked as fast as possible, the members of the police force were impatient and moved in before the premises were actually complete! This was in late March, reported in the local news on 22nd March 1862.[15] This date therefore almost certainly marks the end date of the Greyfriars' buildings being in use as a

Bridewell as any prisoners would have been transferred at this point. The beautiful three storey white building on London Street that the police moved into, sandwiched between the river Kennet and Star Lane, is still there and is still known as Highbridge House.

About a month later, the Corporation legally made over the Greyfriars site to William Phelps, having received all the necessary legal consents from London. On Monday 21st April 1862, restoration began!

Greyfriars c1860, before restoration
Photograph by S. Victor White
To the right can be seen the Bridewell entrance and the Keeper's House.
The open space in front of the West End was part of the land purchased by Rev. W. W. Phelps from the estate of Mr. Weedon.

In June 1846, just 16 years before, the remains of the Friary had been closely inspected and the details published in the Archaeological Journal (Volume 3). After a historical preamble, the article meticulously describes the ruins.[16] It begins:

> The Church as it now stands consists of a nave, with north and south aisles. Originally there was a chancel and a tower... All that now remains of the

> chancel is the arch, with its mouldings and jamb-shafts, which is partly bricked up in the wall of an adjoining house. There are no remains of a porch, but it is not probable that so large a Church could have been destitute of this essential feature...
>
> The walls are built of flint, with stone quoins, and plastered inside. Externally the flint is laid in regular courses, and the flints split and squared. The skill and management of the old builders, and the ease with which they made the most rugged materials bend to their purpose, was never better displayed than in the construction of these walls; the thin, narrow joints, sharp surface, and beautiful appearance of the flint work, far surpasses the best attempts of modern days... The aisles are separated from the nave by a stone arcade of five compartments, the arch nearest the chancel of each arcade being narrower and more acutely pointed than the others. The mouldings of both pillars and arches are very well worked and in tolerable preservation, and belong, in common with nearly every other part of the Church, to the style of architecture prevailing in the early fourteenth century, now better known as the "Decorated."
>
> The west window is by far the finest part of the whole edifice, and even now, worn and dilapidated as it is, presents a beautiful appearance. The tracery is of a flowing character, simple but elegant, and when the west front was in its original state, with the roof complete, and the tower in the back ground completing the picture, the whole must have formed as perfect a composition as any of its kind.

The description continues with details of the three aisle windows, each with "remarkably plain" mouldings. Then, where the aisles met the east end of the Church, there were two windows, one in each side. However:

> Of what kind we can scarcely tell, one end being so completely covered with ivy, that it defies penetration, and the other bricked up, shows nothing but the mere outline of the window, which differs from the aisles inasmuch as it is longer and more acutely pointed. There do not appear to have been any west windows to the aisles.

The ground showed no trace of the original flooring, even when excavated, and the report commented that the floor was probably taken up when the Church was converted to a Bridewell. All that was left of the roof of the nave was "the moulding upon the wall-plate, and two or three purlin braces and rafters over the aisles." The report then noted that it was said that the roof was used to replace the old one in the nave of St. Mary's, but that this was not known for sure. The report concluded with:

It is to be lamented that this fine relic of ancient art is devoted to no better purpose than that of a prison. The present scanty Church accommodation would be an ample reason for restoring it to a somewhat more decent state, and as the walls and arches are undisturbed, a small expenditure would render it at once fit for worship, and an ornament to the town.

RUINS OF THE GREY FRIARS CHURCH, READING.

Drawing from the letterhead used by
the Rev. William Whitmarsh Phelps
when writing concerning the subscriptions for the restoration

Chapter 9

The Restoration: 1862 to 1863

The Seal of the Corporation was affixed to the deed of sale on Wednesday 16th April 1862, transferring ownership of the Bridewell, the Keeper's House and the "Pigeons" public house to Mr. Phelps.[1]

On Monday 21st April 1862, work began under architects Messrs. Poulton and Woodman. William Woodman, of 1 Greyfriars Road, has already appeared in the Greyfriars story, being the Borough Surveyor. A Londoner by birth, he had been living in Reading for at least the previous six years. He had celebrated his 40th birthday just over a week before the restoration began. The stone-work contract, initially estimated at £1,885, was placed with Messrs. Wheeler: John, the elder, and sons John and Samuel. The carpenters', tilers' and roofing contract was placed with Mr. Sheppard, to the estimated value of £899. The deadline for completion was set at Christmas 1863.[2]

Within a week of starting, the wooden partitions had been removed. The Reading Mercury reported that:

> The old boarding which is being removed bears numerous traces of the character of the individuals who formerly unwillingly occupied it. One prisoner has recorded the fact of his having been incarcerated at the instance of his brother, for stealing money, while another has carved out in capitals an instance of 'Thief rob thief', in these words, 'George Dell robbed a poor prisoner of three pence in this prison, September 4, 1822.' The stone pillars have also been defaced with initials of the residents, *pro tem*, cut deeply with knives or some other sharp instrument, but all traces of these will of course be entirely removed.[3]

Fortunately, not all such traces were removed and several marks are still in evidence, for example on the first column in the north aisle at the west end in the photograph on the next page.

Graffiti made by Bridewell prisoners. On the first pillar of the north aisle from the west end.

The first major task was to find the lines of the original foundations. Mr. Woodman discovered what he believed to be the north transept foundations lying outside the line of the Bridewell and so the plans were adapted to take this unexpected extension into account. Land was purchased at a cost of £300 from Francis Morgan Slocombe on the north side of the Church so that the north transept could be built.[4] By the terms of the Deed, "William Whitmarsh Phelps... will forthwith erect or cause to be erected a good brick or flint wall fair on both sides of the height of six feet at the least... and also that the glass to be used [in the north transept window] shall be Church or non-transparent glass." The land bought also gave a 9 foot 6 inch wide rectangle of land to the north of the Church, giving access to the north door. The north transept was then built into what had been Mr. Slocombe's garden.

Burial remains were found both inside the nave area and also in Mr. Andrewes's garden next door, where the quire or chancel would have been located. In this latter area, several vaults were found, all of which were left undisturbed.[5]

By the beginning of June, the Bridewell Keeper's house had been demolished.[6] Later that month the Reading Mercury reported another find:

> During this week a very curious piece of pavement has been dug up under the north doorway. It consists of the ordinary small encaustic tile ornamented with

figures of dogs, cats, stags, and various other animals. It has been carefully preserved, with the view, we believe, of replacing it when the work is far enough completed for this purpose.[7]

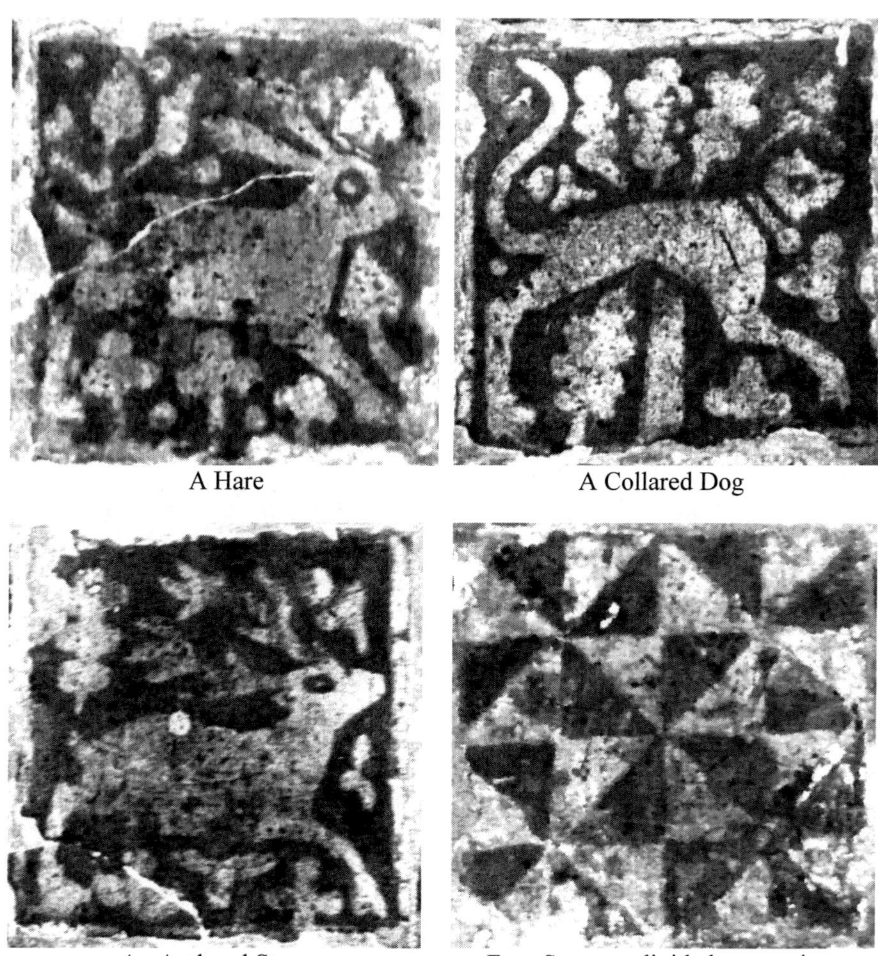

A Hare

A Collared Dog

An Antlered Stag

Four Squares, divided gyronwise

This small piece of paving, about a square yard in all, was in fact the entire original paving that was found in the restoration work. The tiles were indeed, as the Reading Mercury suggested, re-laid in the restored building. The tiles are now in a framed display in the Church on the north wall by the entrance, with this text:

Original Early XIV Century Paving Tiles made of red clay inlaid with white slip and glazed. The designs are neither heraldic nor religious, but show a hare upon a background of trefoil foliage, a dog with a collar and a bell upon a background of oak leaves and acorns, an antlered stag, and a geometrical design of four squares divided gyronwise.

By early August, Messrs. Wheeler had completed the restoration of the west window. The pillars and arches needed "but little work to restore them to their original strength and beauty."[8]

In a letter to the Reading Mercury dated 26th November 1862,[9] Mr. Phelps summarised the cost of purchasing the site:

The Bridewell, Keeper's House and public house adjoining	£1,250
Leasehold interest in the public house	£210
Land contiguous to the ruins on the west side	£696
Land contiguous to the ruins on the north side	£300
Total cost of the site and ruins:	£2,456

He then outlined the expected other expenses of the project: not less than £5,000 to restore and equip the building and £3,000 for the endowment. This latter cost was to provide an annual income for the Incumbent in order to allow a large portion of the seats in the Church to be free for the use of the poor – i.e. not rented by "seat-holders" paying pew-rent. The projected total costs were therefore in the region of £10,500.

Donations to the project were growing slowly. In June 1861, Mr. Phelps had published the first total: £3,514 18s.[10] Seventeen months later, the total had grown by just over £2,500 to £6061 3s 1d (an average of almost exactly £5 per day). The Reading Mercury commented on the appeal indicating its hope that "the Lancashire distress will have ceased to exist" before long and so the benevolence of the people could again be directed to this local cause.

Unfortunately, in December one of Wheeler's men was seriously injured in an accident on the Greyfriars site. John Aust, a stonemason, was working on scaffolding at the chancel arch when he slipped and fell about 15 feet, striking against the wall as he fell and then the stone that he had been attempting to remove fell on his right leg, breaking it "in a fearful manner." He was removed to hospital, where he had to have his leg amputated later that day.[11]

Greyfriars Church being rebuilt 1862-1863
(Photograph courtesy of Reading Library)

By the following May, the east wall had been rebuilt and the building boasted a bell turret, with three bells placed in a row, "which is a peculiar feature," commented the Reading Mercury. The bells were cast at John Warner & Sons of London, who had also cast the original Big Ben in 1856. The tenor bell was E flat, the second F sharp and the third G sharp. The bell turret was built of stone over the chancel arch and was surmounted by a weathercock, rising to a height of 88 feet.[12]

At this time it was realised that it would be necessary for the road to be lowered. The Council undertook this work, with Mr. Phelps contributing £50 and a small piece of land, although it was some time later that the work was actually carried out. The road and footpaths in the immediate area were lowered by 18 inches.[13]

Bell turret
and
weathercock

Erected May 1863

In a letter to the Reading Mercury dated 1st May 1863, Mr. Phelps reported on the progress of the restoration works, the expenses incurred and the donations received. Just over six months had passed since Mr. Phelps's last appeal in November 1862, yet the total donations had only risen by about £500, to £6518 19s 1d (with an average donation rate that had therefore fallen from £5 per day to just under £3 per day).[14]

Mason's mark
for the 1863 restoration.

West window
(Photograph by Mr. F. G. Spriggs)

The next development was the roofing of the nave, which was completed during June 1863. Woodman designed a variety of head-stops, eighteen in all, to go above the tops of each of the columns, where the arches meet. In recent times, one had to be replaced when a television crew's scaffolding brought it down, thankfully not during the recording of the service! Compared with these characterful faces, the six originals which remain at the west end are rather poorly executed.

1863 head-stop

(See page 9 for an original 14th century head-stop)

The builders discovered traces of stained glass in each of the windows. More gruesomely, they also discovered a complete skeleton under the north jamb of the chancel arch in a position that looked as if it had been laid in the foundations when the original Church was being built, with the walls then erected over it.[15]

Inside the completed Church, the pews were made of dark oak and were "extremely comfortable," according to the Reading Mercury reporter. In matching style, the altar rails and reading desk were also of oak, with carvings of foliage. The reading desk was donated by Mr. Sheppard, the contracted carpenter involved in the work. The Church's seating capacity was 750 to 800 persons.

The east end of the Church had the Commandments, the Creed and the Lord's Prayer painted on it. Around the chancel arch was painted the verse: "Why seek ye the living among the dead? He is not here but is risen." In the centre was a mandorla inscribed with IHS. To the left of centre was the pulpit, made of Caen stone, supported on three red marble columns with carved capitals. The pulpit was the gift of "the little daughter of the architect (Mr. Woodman), the result of a collection among friends."

A further donation was a parting gift given to William Phelps in November 1863. The Reading Young Men's Christian Association presented him with a set of service books for Greyfriars: a Bible, the Book of Common Prayer and two Communion Service books "neatly but beautifully printed and bound in morocco, by Eyre and Spottiswood, the Queen's printer, and were stated privately to have cost £15."[16]

The solid silver communion plate was donated by Mr. Neale. At least part of the plate is still in use in the Church, with engraving showing the details of the giver and the date. The communion cloth – of Utrecht velvet with fringes and sacred monograms in gold bullion – was presented by Miss Monck, who had hand embroidered the cloth herself.

The font was placed near the south door at the west end. Like the pulpit, it was made of Caen stone, standing on eight Purbeck marble columns. The font was presented by the stone work contractor, Samuel Wheeler.

The lighting was by "wrought brass standards under each arcade and coronae in the transepts. The elegance of these fittings appears to have attracted as much attention as any part of the edifice." There were eight brass standards in all, each 9 feet tall. The one near the north door was to feature in an accident a few years later. These gas standards were, following the accident, removed by authority of the first Vicar, although I can find no record of the necessary authorisation, or faculty, for it. The coronae in each transept had 15 gas lights in each of them.

Pulpit

Shown in its position by the west window following the reordering in 2000.

Caen stone, supported by three red marble columns, with carved capitals; the body of the pulpit is divided into panels with green marble columns.

Gift of the daughter of Mr. Woodman, architect, and her friends

Font

Shown in its position in the south aisle following the reordering in 2000.

Caen stone, on eight Purbeck marble columns.

Gift of Samuel Wheeler, stone work contractor for the 1863 restoration.

The Cover was the gift of William Ravenscroft, architect, in 1894.

The heating, installed by a company called Haden, of Trowbridge, was a hot air system. The acoustics of the completed building were "very satisfactory," with the harmonium being clearly audible from every part of the Church. The window glazing was undertaken by Mr. Freeman, using a special glass designed to soften the intensity of light from large windows.[17]

The Reading Mercury report concluded its description of the restored Church by considering what the building looked like from the outside: "At present it bears a very unfinished aspect, but when the Board of Health have lowered the roads in the vicinity of the site... it is intended to erect a fence to the street boundary, of wrought iron, on a stone wall, with stone piers at the gateway, supporting wrought iron lamps."[18]

Originally the project was scheduled to finish by Christmas 1863. However, ahead of schedule, all was ready for the celebration of the re-consecration of the Church in early December. When the date was announced in the Reading Mercury in late November, the name of the first

Incumbent was also given for the first time: "We learn that the Rev. S. M. Barkworth, incumbent of Southwold, Suffolk, is appointed to the incumbency of Greyfriars." The writer continued: "One source of regret, however, still remains. No one, after inspecting the varied beauties of the edifice can help lamenting that the obstacles to rebuilding the chancel should at present be insurmountable. The work can never be considered complete until this is done."[19] However, the house and land owned by Mr. Andrewes was either not available for purchase or was too expensive – valued at £1,800 – to be considered by Mr. Phelps with so much cost already being incurred.[20]

For a long time the absence of the chancel saddened many in Reading, whether Church members or not. It remained a hoped-for addition to the Church until well into the twentieth century and was the subject of more than one legal question over legacies, but the chancel (at least to date!) was never built.

Greyfriars Church as it might have been
– original architect's drawing showing a Chancel

Chapter 10

Re-consecration: December 1863

The ceremony of consecration of the new Church of Greyfriars was at 10 o'clock on Wednesday 2nd December 1863.[1] The ceremony began at the south door, where the Rev. John Ball, Vicar of St. Laurence's Church, presented a petition for the consecration of Greyfriars to the Bishop of Oxford, the Right Reverend Samuel Wilberforce.

A congregation of over 700 filled the Church and looked on as the Mayor of Reading and members of the Corporation entered behind mace bearers, followed by the Bishop and a large number of local clergy. The Bishop, the Venerable Archdeacon Randall, the Revs. A. P. Cust (the Rural Dean), T. V. Fosbury (Vicar of St. Giles) and J. R. Woodford all sat within the "altar rail," with the Rev. John Ball at the reading desk. The rest of the clergy, including of course the Rev. W. W. Phelps, sat in a number of front pews.

Mr. Ball read Morning Service, with lessons read by Mr. Fosbury and Mr. Cust, the Ven. Archdeacon Randall (Epistle) and the Rev. J. R. Woodford (Gospel). Choral parts of the service were conducted by Miss Binfield.

The Bishop preached from Matthew chapter 14 verse 16: "And he said unto them they need not depart; give ye them to eat." The Bishop explained his choice of text: "You know that in this great and growing population there has been hitherto very little accommodation for the poor for Christian worship in our churches. This is an attempt, by rebuilding and restoring one in which of old time God has been worshipped, to provide for this necessity. It is the providing for these people the bread of heaven which connects the object today with the passage of scripture which I have selected for our consideration."

After the sermon, the (several hundred word) "sentence of consecration" was read by the Chancellor:

CONSECRATION

OF

Greyfriars' Church, Reading,

WEDNESDAY, DECEMBER 2nd, 1863.

HYMN I.

Come, Holy Ghost, our souls inspire,
And lighten with celestial fire;
Thou the anointing Spirit art,
Who dost Thy seven-fold gifts impart;
Thy blessed unction from above
Is comfort, life, and fire of love.

Enable with perpetual light,
The dulness of our blinded sight:
Anoint and cheer our soiled face
With the abundance of Thy grace:
Keep far our foes, give peace at home;
Where Thou art Guide no ill can come.

2

Teach us to know the Father, Son,
And Thee of both to be but One;
That through the ages all along,
This may be our endless song;
Praise to Thy eternal merit,
Father, Son, and Holy Spirit.

HYMN II.

All people that on earth do dwell,
Sing to the Lord with cheerful voice:
Him serve with fear, His praise forth tell;
Come ye before Him and rejoice.

The Lord ye know is God indeed,
Without our aid He did us make;
We are His flock, He doth us feed,
And for His sheep He doth us take.

O enter then His gates with praise;
Approach with joy His courts unto;
Praise, laud, and bless His name always,
For it is seemly so to do.

For why, the Lord our God is good,
His mercy is for ever sure;
His truth at all times firmly stood,
And shall from age to age endure.

Hymn Sheet from the morning Consecration Service

In the name of God, Amen – Whereas in and by an humble petition [bearing date the Twenty eighth day of November last] presented unto us by the Reverend John Ball, Vicar of the parish of Saint Laurence, Reading, in the County of Berks, within our Diocese, and the Churchwardens and other Inhabitants of the said parish, it is set forth, That from various causes, the population of Saint Laurence, Reading, had greatly increased, thereby rendering it essential that additional Church accommodation should be furnished for the use of such of the Inhabitants who were desirous of joining in the public Worship of Almighty God but had hitherto been improvided (sic) with the requisite means to enable them to do so: - That in order to meet the requirement the said petitioners (aided by the liberality of the Venerable William Whitmarsh Phelps, Archdeacon of Carlisle, and others desirous of promoting the Glory of God) had caused a new Church to be erected, the site of which had been duly conveyed to and vested in the Ecclesiastical Commissioners for England and their Successors as hereinafter mentioned: - That by Deed dated the first of August One thousand eight Hundred and sixty two made under the authority and for the purposes of the several Statutes commonly known as the Church Building Acts, the said Archdeacon of Carlisle (therein described as The Reverend William Whitmarsh Phelps of Reading) being the owner in fee simple, did (without any valuable consideration) give grant and convey unto the said Ecclesiastical Commissioners All that plot of Land containing thirty perches situate in the said parish of Saint Laurence, Reading, bounded on the north and part of the east by Land belonging to Francis Morgan Slocombe Esquire, on part of the south by Friar Street, on the remainder of the south and east by the "Pigeons" Public House, and on the west by other Land of the said William Whitmarsh Phelps, as the same is more particularly delineated on the Plan in the said Deed: To hold (free from Land Tax and Tithe Rent Charge) to the said Ecclesiastical Commissioners and their Successors for the purposes of the said Acts as and for a site for an intended new Church called "Grey Friars Church," with the surrounding Yard and inclosure and to be devoted when consecrated to Ecclesiastical purposes for ever, by virtue and according to the true intent and meaning of the said several and recited Acts; That the said new Church had been appropriately fitted up and adorned, and was ready to be consecrated and that the part of the said thirty perches of Ground which surrounds the said Church was about to be enclosed with a proper and substantial Fence And that the said Petitioners intended to adopt the requisite measures for procuring a separate Ecclesiastical District to be assigned to the said Church: - And the said Petitioners humbly prayed us as in their said petition is set forth: - Now We Samuel by Divine Permission Lord Bishop of Oxford being willing to comply with the reasonable and pious prayer of the said Petitioners Do, by these Presents, by Our Ordinary and Episcopal Authority , separate for the future the said newly erected Church from all common and profane uses, and do consecrate and set apart the same for the Worship of Almighty God, the Administration of the Sacraments, the reading of Prayers, and preaching the Word of God purely and sincerely and for performing all other Religious Ceremonies according to the Liturgy of the United Church of England and Ireland And We do hereby dedicate the said new Church to Almighty God by the name of Grey Friars which said new Church and the Boundaries thereof are more particularly delineated in the Plan drawn on these Presents: Saving nevertheless unto Ourself and Our Successors Our Episcopal rights and privileges herein, and saving likewise unto all Bodies politic and corporate and to all persons whomsoever the respective claims to which they or any of them were entitled before the passing of this Our definitive Sentence and final Decree which We make and promulgate by this present writing.

Signed and published in the new Church called Grey Friars at Reading aforesaid this second day of December in the year of our Lord One thousand eight hundred and sixty three and in the Nineteenth year of our Consecration:-

Samuel Oxon

The Bishop then ordered the signed document to be enrolled and preserved in the Registry of the Diocese. A collection was taken, amounting to £108 14s, and then most of the congregation left, leaving the clergy and a few others to take communion.

At about 1.30pm, the Ven. Archdeacon Phelps presided over a lunch for about thirty guests at the Great Western Hotel, although unfortunately the Bishop had to catch a train to a further engagement in London and so could not stay for the meal. A speech in tribute to the Ven. Archdeacon Phelps was given by the Ven. Archdeacon Randall, referring "to the fact that it was very much owing to [Mr. Phelps] that the great undertaking of restoring the Greyfriars' Church had been carried out." The Ven. Archdeacon Phelps replied, alluding to the "skill of the architect [and] the assiduity, talent and conscientiousness of the builders."

A speech by the Mayor concluded proceedings:

> The MAYOR on behalf of himself and the Corporation thanked the Ven. Archdeacon Phelps for kindly inviting them to the ceremony of opening the new Church, and that handsome spread, and he could assure the Archdeacon that ever since he took the initiative for the restoration of the Church, the Corporation had taken the most lively interest in it. Had it not been for the great efforts and the liberality of the Archdeacon Phelps, Greyfriars' Church would still have been "a den of thieves." (Applause.)
>
> The company shortly after separated.

There was then an evening service at 7 o'clock where the Ven. Archdeacon Phelps was the preacher, taking his text from Isaiah chapter 55, verses 1 and 2: "Ho, every one that thirsteth, come ye to the waters, and he that hath no money; come ye, buy, and eat; yea, come, buy wine and milk without money and without price. Wherefore do ye spend money for that which is not bread? and your labour for that which satisfieth not? hearken diligently unto me, and eat ye that which is good, and let your soul delight itself in fatness." In his sermon, the Venerable Archdeacon sought to remind his hearers of the blessings of the Reformation, pointing out "how much more clearly, in consequence of it, the Church of England now instructs her people in the way of eternal life."[2] There were between 800 and 900 present at this service. A further collection was taken, amounting to £19 9s 1d.

The Ven. Archdeacon Phelps preached at Greyfriars on the two subsequent Sundays – 6th and 13th December. I have been unable to discover the first date on which the new Vicar preached, but it was probably before the new year. Therefore it must be time for us to meet this first incumbent of Greyfriars.

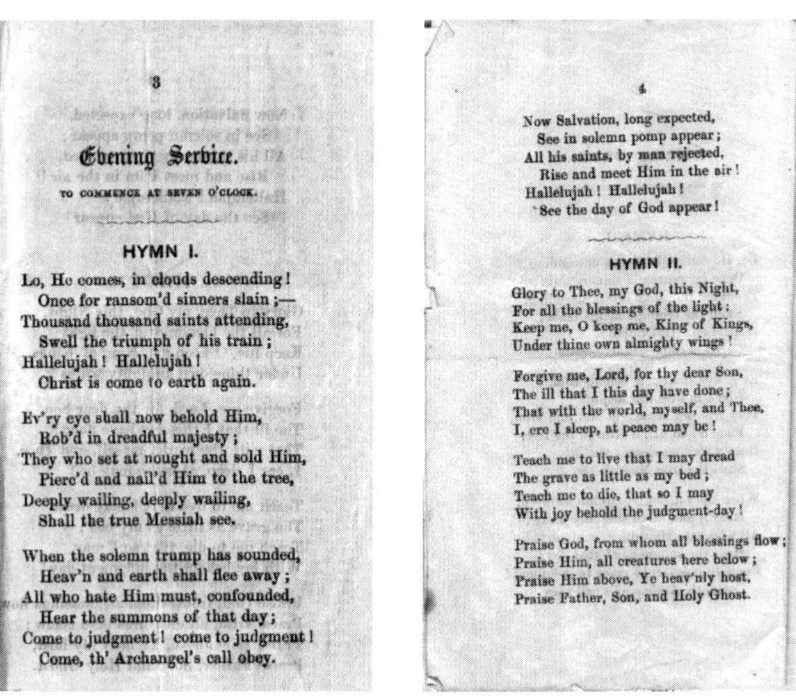

3

Evening Service.

TO COMMENCE AT SEVEN O'CLOCK.

HYMN I.

Lo, He comes, in clouds descending!
Once for ransom'd sinners slain;—
Thousand thousand saints attending,
Swell the triumph of his train;
Hallelujah! Hallelujah!
Christ is come to earth again.

Ev'ry eye shall now behold Him,
Rob'd in dreadful majesty;
They who set at nought and sold Him,
Pierc'd and nail'd Him to the tree,
Deeply wailing, deeply wailing,
Shall the true Messiah see.

When the solemn trump has sounded,
Heav'n and earth shall flee away;
All who hate Him must, confounded,
Hear the summons of that day;
Come to judgment! come to judgment!
Come, th' Archangel's call obey.

4

Now Salvation, long expected,
See in solemn pomp appear;
All his saints, by man rejected,
Rise and meet Him in the air!
Hallelujah! Hallelujah!
See the day of God appear!

HYMN II.

Glory to Thee, my God, this Night,
For all the blessings of the light:
Keep me, O keep me, King of Kings,
Under thine own almighty wings!

Forgive me, Lord, for thy dear Son,
The ill that I this day have done;
That with the world, myself, and Thee,
I, ere I sleep, at peace may be!

Teach me to live that I may dread
The grave as little as my bed;
Teach me to die, that so I may
With joy behold the judgment-day!

Praise God, from whom all blessings flow;
Praise Him, all creatures here below;
Praise Him above, Ye heav'nly host,
Praise Father, Son, and Holy Ghost.

Hymn Sheet from the Evening Service
2nd December 1863

Rev. Shadwell Morley Barkworth D.D.
(Photograph from Greyfriars Annual Report and Accounts for the year ending December 31st, 1906)

Chapter 11

Shadwell Morley Barkworth, the first Vicar: 1863 to 1874

The man chosen by the five Trustees to be the first Vicar of Greyfriars was 44 year old Rev. Shadwell Morley Barkworth. He was born on 5th November 1819, the second son of John Barkworth and Emma (née Boulderson) of Anlaby, Hessle, six miles west of Hull, Yorkshire. Shadwell Barkworth went up to Worcester College, Oxford, at the age of 19. He graduated as a Bachelor of Arts, receiving his degree in May 1842.[1] He was ordained deacon in December 1842[2] and priest the following year by the Archbishop of York at Bishopsthorpe Palace. During 1843 he was the chaplain for Hull General Infirmary.[3]

By April 1844 he had been appointed to his first curacy, which was at Old & New Malton, about 20 miles north east of York.[4] During his time there he received his Master of Arts in Oxford in April 1845.[5]

In September 1846 he left Malton to become Curate at St. Peter-Le-Bailey in Oxford.[6] In the same year he funded a perpetual charity, donating £24 so that the interest would be distributed to the aged men and women of that parish on each 20th August. Money continued to be distributed for one hundred and fifty years until the Charity Commission closed it down in January 1997.[7]

Mr. Barkworth next moved diocese to the curacy at St. Peter & St. Paul, Tonbridge in Kent. In June 1851 he became Perpetual Curate of St. John's Chapel, Walthamstow,[8] where in 1854 he married Ellen Jansen who was, at 23 years old, eleven years his junior.

Just over a year later, husband and wife moved to Chelsea, with Mr. Barkworth becoming Vicar of St. Jude's.[9] He stayed only two years here, but gained a strong reputation as a zealous preacher of gospel truth in the Church and outside, by frequently carrying out open-air preaching in full robes.[10] Mr. Barkworth also took a prominent role in promoting Protestantism and denouncing 'Popery'. This led, on one occasion in March 1857, to him being followed home by a rowdy mob who hurled stones and insults at him after he presided at a lecture entitled "Church of Rome not the Church of Christ."[11]

Mr. Barkworth left St. Jude's, to the deep regret of his congregation, in October 1857.[12] He did not take up another post, however, until 1860, possibly because Shadwell and Ellen lost two children in infancy in those years.

In October 1860, the Barkworths moved to Southwold on the Suffolk coast. Mr. Barkworth became Perpetual Curate at the Church of St. Edmund, King & Martyr.[13] In December 1863 he moved to Greyfriars.

Since there was no Vicarage for Greyfriars, the family moved in to "Trinity Lodge," Trinity Place, off Oxford Road, owned by the Rev. William Whitmarsh Phelps.[14] The house contained 4 reception rooms, 6 bedrooms, a dressing room, bath room, "capital kitchens" and offices, stabling, a tennis lawn, flower garden and an exceedingly large kitchen garden. The property still has a frontage onto Oxford Road next to Holy Trinity Church, with an entrance that was used for carriages from Trinity Place.[15]

Trinity Lodge – now called Carlisle House
Viewed from Oxford Road — Viewed from Trinity Place

Initially, Mr. Barkworth was not in fact the Vicar of Greyfriars but its Perpetual Curate, since all ministers of new parishes and districts established by Acts of Parliament were called Perpetual Curates. The difference was only in funding: a Perpetual Curate was funded by the diocese, whereas a Vicar was funded, at least in part, from tithe income from the parish.

The situation changed in 1868, when the District Church Tithes Amendment Act, presented by Samuel Wilberforce, Bishop of Oxford, was passed by Parliament. This legislation aimed to establish uniformity of designation of incumbents of parishes. In particular, it enabled a parish where the clergyman was authorised to publish banns, solemnize marriages, conduct baptisms and churchings, and received the fees for them, to be called a Vicarage and the incumbent to be styled Vicar. Therefore it is from 1868 that Mr. Barkworth can properly be called Vicar of Greyfriars – a letter to Mr. Barkworth from John Davenport, Notary Public for the Bishop of Oxford, dated 18th August 1868 confirmed the change.

Not long after the new Church opened, a large group from Trinity Church moved to Greyfriars when it changed from being an independent "proprietary chapel" to a "chapel-of-ease" in the parish of St. Mary's.[16]

It was not until 27th August 1864 that the Ecclesiastical Commission assigned a district to Greyfriars. The Commission's proposal had been previously agreed by the Bishop of Oxford and the Vicars of St. Laurence and St. Mary. Greyfriars Church was legally defined as "The Consolidated Chapelry of the Grey Friars, Reading." The district to be attached to the Church was created from "certain extremities of the parish of Saint Laurence, Reading, and of the parish of Saint Mary, Reading... [where] there is collected together a population which is situated at a distance from the several churches of such respective parishes." St. Laurence's parish lay on the east of Caversham Road/Thorn Street, with St. Mary's on the west.

The district's boundaries were defined as: from the point in the middle of the railway bridge (Caversham Road), on the south side, to the corner of the Great Western Railway Station; then along Greyfriars Road to the junction with Friar Street; then along the centre of West Street; then Oxford Street westward to Thorn Street; to the eastern end of Chatham Street, then to York Place; onto Weldale Street, Bedford Gardens, Portland Place and finally Great Knollys Street and thus back to the starting point.[17] The order was ratified by Her Majesty Queen Victoria in Council and took effect on 30th August 1864, the day of publication in the London Gazette.[18]

Just prior to this, on Sunday 24th July 1864, the first Greyfriars' baptism took place: Charles Thomas Marlow, a baker, and his wife Emma, of 6 Caversham Road, brought their son Harry Frank for baptism.[19]

Within six months of taking up his position in Greyfriars, Mr. Barkworth announced a plan to establish schools connected to the Church to cater for the very many poor children in the area. Mr. Barkworth wrote to the Reading Mercury to seek assistance with funding the Schools, in spite of the fact that money was still required for the Restoration Account. He wrote:

> PROPOSED NATIONAL AND INFANT SCHOOLS,
> in connection with GREY FRIARS' CHURCH, READING.
> *To the Inhabitants of Reading and its Vicinity.*
> About six months have elapsed since the opening of Grey Friars' Church. The kind aid which during this period I have received has enabled me to establish Sunday Schools, which now contain upwards of 200 children. As there are no School-rooms in connection with the Church, it has been necessary to secure temporarily a room in West-street, where the children are at present taught on Sundays. It is however, obviously important that an effort should be made as early as possible to supply the large number of poor children who dwell in the immediate vicinity of the Church, with regular religious and secular instruction on week-days. With this object in view, I venture to appeal to those who so generously contributed towards the building of the Church, and to any others who may be willing to help, for such pecuniary aid as may enable me to proceed to the erection of suitable National and Infant School-rooms upon a convenient site which has been secured in close proximity to the Church. From a statement which has been furnished by the Architect, it appears that about £1,100 will be required in order that this undertaking may be brought to a satisfactory conclusion. I would therefore commend the object to the kind consideration of the Christian public, in the earnest hope that (God willing) so important a work may ere long be accomplished.
> S. M. BARKWORTH
> Incumbent of Grey Friars.
> 14th July 1864.[20]

In good weather at 3.30pm on Tuesday 26th July 1864 there was a very well attended "Laying Corner Stone of Schools" ceremony. The Rev. S. M. Barkworth presided, with the Rev. C. J. Goodhart, Minister of Park Street Chapel, Chelsea, as the honoured guest to lay the foundation stone. There was "a singular absence of the local clergy" noted, but several gentlemen were listed as present: "Dr. Cowan, Dr. Moses, and Messrs. Crockett, C. W. Smith, Hoyle, R. C. Dryland, Geo. Ball, Trendall, M. H. Sutton, W. P. Ivey, A. Reed, &c." The choir led the singing of Psalm 118 – Behold the sure foundation stone. Then the Rev. S. M. Barkworth opened in prayer and made a few opening remarks. The Rev. C. J. Goodhart then spoke of his days in Reading and of the proposed schools and the benefits they would confer on the children. The architect, Mr. Woodman, then read out an inscription on vellum:

> In the name of the Father, Son and Holy Ghost. The corner stone of Grey Friars' Church National and Infant Schools was laid by the Rev. C. J. Goodhart, M.A., Minister of Park Street Chapel, Chelsea, formerly Minister of St. Mary's Chapel [Castle Street], Reading, on Tuesday the 26th day of July 1864 in the 27th year of the reign of Queen Victoria.[21]

The inscription was inserted into a bottle, which was then placed into the corner stone. The ceremony ended with a doxology and benediction.

Greyfriars Church c 1880
School buildings to the left[22]

The buildings soon attracted positive notice. The Reading Mercury commented: "The buildings are rapidly progressing, and bid fair to prove not only commodious and well adapted for the purpose for which they are intended, but also in an architectural point of view, a decided ornament to the western extremity of Friar-street and to the Caversham-road."[23] They were described as "in the early decorated style of architecture, and built of flint and stone to harmonise with the Church."

In addition to both the Restoration Fund and the New Schools Fund, efforts were also made to raise funds for a new organ for the Church. On the Sunday following the laying of the schools' foundation stone, Rev. C. J. Goodhart preached at 11am and 6.30pm, with collections especially in aid of this new fund.[24] The Church was completely filled for both services – and in the evening a "large number of people could not gain admission." Up to this time a harmonium had been used to accompany hymns, but on 7th August 1864 the new Church organ was used for the first time. It had been built for Greyfriars by Bevington & Sons of Rose Yard, Soho at a cost of £150 and was installed at the back of the Church by the west window. It contained "nine stops, two octaves of German pedals and three composition pedals, acting on the stops, and there is a general swell, enclosing the greater part of the pipes, which number 421." [25]

The work on the Schools proceeded swiftly. In mid-September, with the school roofs nearly ready for their slates, a new railing, enclosing the Church grounds, was erected.[26] By late October, applications for admission were invited among the poor of the parish, with a capacity of 100 boys and 100 girls in the National School and 129 in the Infant School. The demand was so high that Shadwell Barkworth immediately decided to build an additional Infant School![27]

Although the school buildings were not quite completed, the first "Vestry meeting" of the new Church took place within them on Monday 31st October 1864. At this meeting new Churchwardens of Greyfriars were appointed: Mr. Hodges (nominated by the Incumbent as Vicar's Warden) and Mr. Willson (elected Parish or People's Warden). They took over from Dr. Henry Moses and Mr. William H. Woodman, who had carried out the duties since the re-consecration in the previous December. [28]

Churchwardens during Rev. Dr. S. M. Barkworth's incumbency 1863 – 1874		
December 1863 to November 1864	Dr. Henry Moses	Mr. William Woodman
November 1864 to April 1868	Mr. Charles Willson	Mr. William Hodges
April 1868 to April 1871	Mr. Henry Champ	Mr. William Hodges
April 1871 to April 1874	Mr. Henry Champ	Mr. Charles Willson

In November, Mr. Barkworth wrote a letter to the Reading Mercury with a full update on the school buildings:

> GREY FRIARS' CHURCH, NATIONAL AND INFANT SCHOOLS.
> The sum of £1,027 7s 10d has been collected in aid of the above Schools, and is gratefully acknowledged. Before the completion of the work it has been thought desirable to build another room, which will not only increase the accommodation in the Infant department, but it is hoped will in many ways promote the general welfare of the District. A Soup Kitchen will be added behind the New Room.
>
> The Misses Wilson have kindly headed a fresh Subscription List with a Donation of £100, but as £400 is yet required, an earnest appeal is now made to the liberality of the public. A sale of Fancy Articles and Plain Work is proposed to be held immediately after Easter next, and Contributions in Work or Money will be thankfully received.
>
> S. M. Barkworth, Incumbent of the Grey Friars.[29]

With the first anniversary of the Church restoration, the Ven. Rev. William Whitmarsh Phelps published a summary of the accounts of the Restoration Appeal.[30] Written on 21st December 1864, it appeared in the Reading Mercury on Christmas Eve. The total donations received amounted to £7,618 2s. However, this fell short of the total expenditure of £8,851 11s 3d, which was itemised as follows:

EXPENDITURE	£	s	d
Ruins and Site	1250	0	0
Land of Mr. Slocombe	300	0	0
Ditto Mrs. Weedon	696	0	0
Lease of the "Pigeons" public house	220	0	0
Wheeler, Builder	3250	0	0
Sheppard, Carpenter	2073	3	0
Freeman, Glazing, Staining, &c	191	6	3
Woodman, Architect	296	13	0
Corporation, Lowering Road	50	0	0
Peard and Jackson, Gas Fittings, &c	186	18	3
Haden and Son, Warming Apparatus	72	10	0
Netherclift and Gilbert, Upholsterers	23	6	5
Pecover, Ironmonger	22	10	2
54,800 Gas to Christmas 1863 (sic), at 4s 3d	11	12	10
Laying on Water for Cleaning Church, &c	5	2	4
Barcham, Printing	13	15	11
Welch, Ditto	11	2	0

"Reading Mercury" Advertising (refunded)	15	12	0
Neale, Law Expenses	137	4	10
Sums under £5	24	14	3
	£8851	11	3

The balance – £1233 9s 3d – was therefore owed to Archdeacon Phelps. Elsewhere in its columns, the Reading Mercury encouraged the public to make up the "deficiency," commending the object particularly to those who had not hitherto given it "pecuniary aid."[31]

On Thursday 29th December Mr. Barkworth presided over a gathering of about 300 people at the official opening of the Schools. The Sunday School, which had been meeting in West Street Hall, moved to the new schools from the following Sunday – 1st January 1865. There was a special tea for the 300 or so new pupils from the District on Friday 6th January, which ended with a magic lantern show by a Mr. Bilby of London. The new National Boys', Girls' and Infant Schools opened their doors for the first time for a school session on Monday 9th January 1865. On that day, and at two o'clock on every Monday afternoon, parents could pay money into a "Boot and Shoe Club" saving account to which the Church added 25% to any amount deposited to enable pupils to buy boots or shoes.[32]

Below are the entries made by the Head Mistress in the Infant School Log Book for this first week:

"Jan. 9th: School opened. 92 infants admitted in the morning. 34 more were admitted in the afternoon.
Jan. 10th: Rose Evans, aged 12, came as a temporary monitor.
Jan. 11th: Slates, pencils and books arrived. The children were required to purchase the two former.
Jan. 12th: I commenced classification of the children over 6 years of age. The children appear to know very little.
Jan. 13th: Mr. Barkworth visited the school."[33]

The Head Mistress noted on 24th January that "between 60 and 70 children do not know their alphabet," adding, two days later, "The children have a very great tendency to 'drawl'." In the next week she wrote "Many of the children are much addicted to cruelty to each other. I had occasion to punish a child, 2½ years, for this fault by separating him from his companions."

A variety of lessons are mentioned: reading, writing (for those who had paid for their slates and pencils, at least), sums, singing, needlework (for girls, although a few boys were bold enough to try it too), scripture, catechism and natural history. The staff coped extremely well with so many children in such a small space and with few resources – one blackboard for the whole Infant School at first, for example.

Greyfriars' Schools

Unfortunately, it was not just the children who needed an improved education. The Head Mistress wrote that "I find that Rose Evans and Caroline Gray [a 14 year old trialling as an assistant teacher] remarkably ignorant of common subjects, especially arithmetic: but they are very willing to learn."[34]

On 4th February 1865, the headline in the Reading Mercury was "Explosion of Gas at Greyfriars' Church."[35] The incident had even been reported in The Times the previous day under the headline: "Fearful Gas Explosion."[36] The incident occurred at about half past eight on Wednesday 1st February, soon after the ending of the evening service. About 20 people had stayed behind to practise hymn singing, including the Vicar, Mrs. Barkworth, several other adults and a few children. They were seated in the pews near the organ at the western end of the Church with all the gas lights of the building turned off except those at the organ and the standards close by.

The smell of gas became very evident and one of the choir (a carpenter by trade) lit a candle to try to investigate the cause of the leak. He held it near one of the gas standards and almost immediately there was a huge explosion under the floor. Almost everyone was thrown to the floor, with Mr. Barkworth, who had been seated near the standard, literally blown up from his seat. The force of the explosion was such that several of the pews were broken into fragments and earth and fractured flooring tiles were scattered over a wide area. Several pieces of wood and some books were blown the length of the Church, ending up near the Communion Table at the east end.

The sound of the explosion was heard at quite a distance away and the neighbouring houses were shaken. Mr. Andrewes, from 64 Friar Street next door, rushed round to the Church to see what had happened.

There were many minor injuries, but amazingly nothing of a serious nature. The Reading Mercury reported:

> Mr. Barkworth fell in the aisle near one of the pillars, and his face was bruised, but we are glad to say that beyond this, the respected Incumbent was not injured; Mrs. Barkworth was slightly hurt in the back, and Miss Emery had her foot struck and was the greatest sufferer.

It took the practical mind of Mr. North, the sexton, to run to the gas meter and turn off the gas to prevent a further incident. Shadwell Barkworth was unconscious for a short time. When he had regained consciousness, Mr. Andrewes took him next door to 64 Friar Street to recover.

One of the Churchwardens, Mr. Willson, who lived on West Street, was sent for. After viewing the extent of the damage he locked up the Church for the night and everyone went home.

The next day, workmen dug out the earth around the main gas pipe near the gas standard and discovered that one of the joints had been poorly fitted. There was a space between the pipe and the floor boards and it was in that space that gas had accumulated. In order to prevent any such build up of gas in the future, the Churchwardens directed that holes should be bored in the floor boards. Happily, the building was insured and the repairs speedily carried out and paid for. The Reading Mercury concluded their report by saying that "It is but just to the local gas fitters to state that the pipes were laid down by London contractors." The insurers, Atlas

Assurance Company, promptly settled the payment for repairs costing £35 3s.[37]

By this time Mr. Barkworth had become an admired and esteemed preacher. A series of small booklets began to appear, several of which were later collected in a volume called "Occasional Sermons."[38] The table below shows the titles and dates of five published sermons I have been able to find (all priced 6d and printed, published and sold by T. Barcham, 89 Broad Street, Reading):

Title	Date preached	Date published
"Son, Remember"	21st May 1865	June 1865[39]
"Self-righteousness its own condemnation"	9th July 1865	August 1865[40]
"The Accepted Substitute"	9th September 1866	October 1866[41]
"Grace, and the Knowledge of Jesus Christ: its source, character and obligation"	30th December 1866	January 1867[42]
"Readiness for the Coming of Our Lord"	27th July 1873	August 1873[43]

The sermon on Grace took as its text 2 Peter 3: 18 – "But grow in grace, and in the knowledge of our Lord and Saviour Jesus Christ." Mr. Barkworth then expounded the verse under two headings:

1. To that consideration which engaged the mind of the apostle, "Grace and Knowledge of Jesus Christ."
2. To the duty enjoined by that consideration, "Grow in Grace, and in the Knowledge of our Lord and Saviour Jesus Christ."

My estimation is that the sermon would take between 30 and 35 minutes to read out loud.

As well as for his sermons, Mr. Barkworth was becoming known for composing hymn tunes. His name can be found in several hymn compilations of the last quarter of the nineteenth century. One tune, possibly his first, was named after his childhood home – "Tranby" (shown on the next page). "The Hymnal Companion to the Book of Common Prayer," Third Edition, by Charles Vincent, D. J. Wood & Sir John Stainer, 1890, for example, contained four tunes ascribed to Mr. Barkworth: "Tranby," "Fiat Lux," "Via Crucis" and "Dilexi Decorem."

When the Greyfriars' Organist, John Humphrey Stark, F. C. O., published the lengthily named "Supplement to the Collection of Psalms and Hymns used by the congregations of Greyfriars', St. John's and St.

Mary's Episcopal Chapel" in 1871, several tunes by Mr. Barkworth were included.[44] A year later Mr. Stark and Mr. Barkworth collaborated on another musical venture. This was a book of twenty-one new tunes for favourite hymns, with Mr. Barkworth being the composer of almost all of the "simple and musical" contributions and Mr. Stark scoring them with "good judgment and ability."[45]

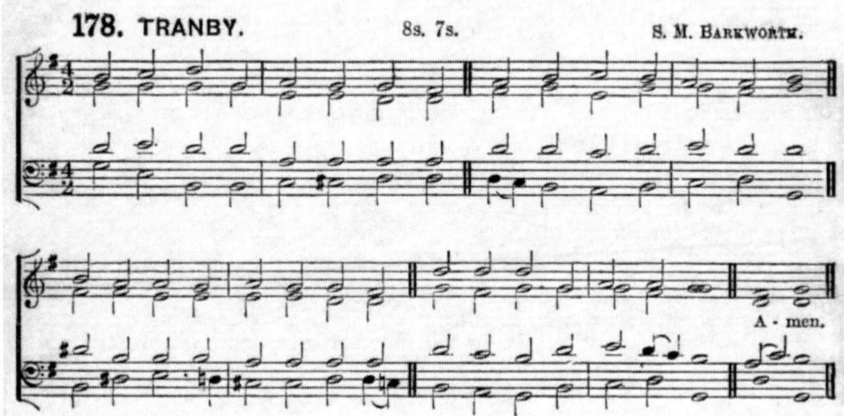

Greyfriars was still making two appeals to the public for funds in 1865: the original subscription fund for the purchase and restoration of the Church and for the expanding needs of the School. However, that did not stop the indomitable Rev. S. M. Barkworth who wished to start up another fund to build a Mission Room on Caversham Road. In order to begin the fund-raising, the Church held a sale from 5pm to 9pm in the new schoolrooms of "useful and ornamental objects" on Thursday 28th December.[46]

On Monday 19th March 1866, Greyfriars celebrated its first wedding: John Allum, a carpenter and widower, married Mary Neal, a farmer's daughter,[47] the necessary permission to publish banns and to solemnize marriages at the Church having been granted by the Bishop on 25th January that year.[48]

In November 1866, plans were formed to erect a porch for the Church and to build a vestry onto the external corner where the north aisle and north transept meet. The cost of these projects was about £300 to £400.[49]

That month Mr. became Dr. Barkworth with the award of both Bachelor and Doctor of Divinity degrees "by accumulation." Agreed at the

Convocation in Oxford on 16th November, the degrees were awarded on 29th November.[50]

The long awaited news that the restoration fund had finally closed was announced on 21st December 1866. The total cost of the purchase and restoration of the Church was £8887 9s 7d. Archdeacon Phelps wrote:

> It only remains that to the ascription of praise to Him, by whose blessing I am thus enabled – within five years and a half from the commencement of the undertaking, and three years from the consecration of the Church, – to record the fact that the subscriptions have overtaken the outlay. I add my grateful thanks to every individual who has contributed to the work: Whilst an especial acknowledgement is due to those latest as well as earliest contributors, who have testified in deed as well as in word, their unwillingness that I should myself bear a larger portion of the expense than I voluntarily incurred at the outset.[51]

The Archdeacon included an analysis of the 390 contributors to the fund:

	£	s	d
28 Contributions of £100 and upwards	6443	0	4
12 Contributions of £50 and under £100	630	0	0
29 Contributions of £20 and under £50	664	0	0
33 Contributions of £10 and under £20	300	7	0
288 Contributions of under £10	790	2	3
	8887	9	7

Therefore almost three quarters of the cost was borne by the 28 contributors who contributed £100 and above. The Rev. Peter French alone contributed a total of £931 3s 6d, being over 10% of the cost. The odd £1 3s and 6d was probably part of the final gift to make the receipts equal the expenses. If so, it would make him the first and the last contributor, as well as the single greatest benefactor of the project. It is a pity that Greyfriars Church does not contain a memorial to this man to whom it certainly owes a debt of remembrance.

It was fitting that Archdeacon Phelps was able to see the conclusion of his great endeavour. Sadly, he died just six months later.

With the continued growth of the poor population in the Greyfriars district, the Schools were full and oversubscribed. The buildings already erected could enable about 450 children to be enrolled and educated at the Day Schools. In March 1867 the Rev. Dr. Barkworth, from his own money, purchased for £275 some land adjoining the Greyfriars site, belonging to

George Simonds Strong of 2 Caversham Road. His aim was to extend the provision by building a new building, containing a large room, next to the Caversham Road. The architect's estimate was that about £350 would be needed for the building.[52] Inevitably, another subscription list opened. Nearly a hundred years later, there would be a legal issue over the ownership of the land that Dr. Barkworth bought, with a claim from one of his grandchildren to ownership of the site.

By July 1867, the new School building by the Caversham Road was completed. The Reading Mercury described it as "a beautiful addition... to the elegant group of buildings adjoining Greyfriars' Church." The finances were almost complete: the total cost of the new building (including the purchase of the land, the erection of the building and the necessary alterations of the existing site) came to about £650. The Rev. Dr. Barkworth had donated £300 and further donations had brought this to a total of £600.[53]

From the May 1868 "Annual Letter Addressed to the Congregation & Parishioners of Grey Friars, Reading, by their Pastor," which was an early form of Annual Report and Accounts, it is possible to obtain a view of the breadth of activities of the Church, just four and a half years after its inception. A list of District Visitors covered the parish in 20 sections. In time, this developed into a major poor relief effort. Mention is also made of Mr. Collins, who "continues to labour faithfully though quietly amongst our poor and that his Mission Room Services are valued by many."

The Day and Sunday Schools' attendances were shown:

DAY SCHOOLS.

School.	No. on Register.	Average Attendance.
Boys	175	156
Girls	148	107
Senior Infants	123	106
Junior Infants	114	102
Total	560	471

SUNDAY SCHOOLS.

School.	No. on Register.	Average Attendance. Morning.	Average Attendance. Afternoon.
Boys	210	122	128
Girls	165	105	122
Infants	168	123	131
Total	543	350	381

Other meetings and activities include:

- Services on Sundays at 11am and 6.30pm, and Wednesdays at 7pm
- Sunday Bible Classes for Young Men in the Mission Room at 9.30am and 2.30pm
- Sunday Bible Class for Servants and Young Women in the Infant School at 3.30pm
- Mothers' Meetings on Mondays, in the Mission Room at 2.30pm and in the Girls' School Room at 7.30pm
- Sunday School Teachers' meetings every other Thursday at 8pm
- Working Party for "our own" Poor on the last Tuesday of the month at 4pm
- Juvenile Missionary Gathering at 2.30pm on the first Thursday and every other Friday afternoon the School Children "work... for Missionary Objects, whilst interesting accounts are read to them."
- Saturday Prayer Meeting at 7.30pm

The Church also ran a Dorcas Society, buying material and making undergarments for poor families to buy cheaply, with a sale every Monday afternoon. The accounts of the Boot Club, mentioned above, record that 198 pairs of boots were bought through the scheme in 1867.

Just over a year after the death of the Ven. Archdeacon Phelps, the memorial tablet (shown on page 67) was erected in Greyfriars. Now on the north wall of the nave, it was originally placed on the opposite side:

> The tablet is fixed to the south wall of the nave, and is supported on stone corbels. The general feature is a foliated arch, resting on two dark marble columns, and enclosing a white marble bearing the inscription. The spandrils of the arch are filled in with tracery, and the whole is surrounded by a moulded band, in the centre of which is carved a running ornament of natural foliage. The monument is executed in red Mansfield stone, and is designed to harmonise in style and character with the architecture of the Church.[54]

Over the next few years, for the remainder of Rev. Dr. Barkworth's incumbency, there was no further building on the Greyfriars' site. The Schools continued to thrive and were funded by voluntary giving by the Church congregation until Local Authority funding was provided for primary education following the Forster Education Act in 1870.

Dr. Barkworth began to suffer deteriorating health. In a "Licence of Non-Residence" dated 30th December 1868, the Bishop of Oxford granted him permission to be absent from his benefice until the end of 1869 "on account of illness and incapacity of body." The Barkworths spent the period of May to October 1869 away from Reading.[55]

Prior to the Vicar's departure, Greyfriars held its Vestry Meeting on Easter Monday 1869, with the Vicar and 5 members being present. William Hodges, an auctioneer and house agent of Oxford Street, who had been one of the first Churchwardens in 1864, was re-appointed to that role, together with Henry Champ, a plumber and painter, of Caversham Road.[56] This was the first Vestry meeting that was recorded, albeit briefly, in writing in a Minute Book.[57]

At the end of February 1870 there was a robbery at the Church. Following the Wednesday evening service the Organist and choir were having their usual practice, with Dr. Barkworth in attendance. Meanwhile a person or persons unknown entered through a window in the Vestry, having removed the pane of glass, and stole two coats, a felt hat (of a style known as a wide-awake) an umbrella and some keys, all belonging to the Vicar, and two tablecloths, two napkins and two brushes. By the end of March three people were in custody and they were brought to the Berkshire Summer Assizes on 9th July.

The three accused were John James, aged 56, his son John, aged 21, a hawker, and Francis Quilter (alias Foster), aged 21, comb-maker. The Assize report gave the circumstances of their arrest:

> On the 1st of March the daughter of the elder James took the two brushes to a man named Chas. Swaine, a brushmaker, residing in Hosier-street, to be repaired. Swaine, curiously enough, from being the bell-ringer at the Church, at once identified the brushes as those belonging to the vestry, and gave information to the police...[58]

The younger John James and Francis Quilter were sentenced to eight months hard labour for the theft.

From time to time over the previous few years, Greyfriars had approached the Council asking for an extra road crossing to be installed near the Church. Consistently this had been refused by the Council Survey Committee, but in May 1870 they agreed to the proposal for a crossing to the principal entrance of the Church – with all the expense to be borne by the Rev. Dr. Barkworth.[59]

Although there was no further building under Dr. Barkworth, the organ was moved and enlarged. It had been installed originally underneath the west end window in August 1864. In May 1870 it was proposed to move it to block the north door and to add another manual. The overall cost was estimated to be at least £200, less the surplus of just over £30 from the Archdeacon Phelps' Memorial Fund.[60]

At 7pm on Wednesday 19th October 1870 the new organ was played for the first time at a special service, where the old friend of Greyfriars, Rev. C. J. Goodhart, was the guest preacher. The final cost of the moving and enlarging of the organ was £250, with the work being carried out by Messrs. Bevington of London. The organ now had both swell and choir manuals and 780 pipes in all. Mr. W. H. Strickland, Organist at Greyfriars, St. Mary's and All Saints, put the organ through its paces that evening with a variety of pieces, including seven voluntaries at the end of the service.[61]

Just a few months later, in March 1871, the organ was again altered. This time Messrs. Bevington carried out the relatively minor work of putting in an additional two stops, the Trumpet and Principal.[62] If that were not enough, in April 1873 the Reading Mercury reported that the "organ has recently undergone considerable alterations, and has been greatly improved by the eminent firm of Robt. Allen and Co., of Bristol. Several new stops have been added, which renders the instrument very effective."[63]

By the end of December 1870, the Rev. Dr. Barkworth had been the incumbent of Greyfriars for seven years. In a touching gesture, the congregation decided to celebrate the anniversary with a presentation of a handsome tea and coffee service, subscribed for in a few days by the members of the congregation.[64]

Greyfriars had expanded its areas of ministry rapidly through those seven years: through the Church services, the work of the Schools and the Mission Room. In October 1870, Dr. Barkworth had introduced an extra service at 3pm on the last Sunday of the month, "with a view to the special benefit of the Young."[65] There were also special one-off services "for the Young": one such was on Sunday 18th June 1871 at 7am! The Reading Mercury reported in its columns on the following Saturday that "an earnest and impressive sermon to the young was preached at Greyfriars' Church on Sunday morning by Rev. Robert Bren. The service commenced at the early hour of 7 o'clock, and every seat was occupied. The text was 'Look unto me and be ye saved'."[66]

Unfortunately, Dr. Barkworth's health was continuing to fail, even though he was only in his mid-fifties. In June 1874 he tendered his resignation to the Bishop. The Reading Mercury reported:

> The resignation of the Vicars of St. Laurence and St. Giles parishes has been rapidly followed by that of the Rev. S. M. Barkworth, D.D., the Incumbent of Greyfriars Church, by which event the town will lose the services of a most useful and zealous clergyman. Dr Barkworth has been associated with Reading for at least ten years, and has heartily devoted himself to his work. The Greyfriars' Schools adjoining the Church, which were erected through his instrumentality, will form a lasting record of his zeal. His congregation will deeply regret his loss, no less than that of Mrs. Barkworth, both of whom were frequent and ever-welcome visitors in the homes of the poor. The friendships formed between pastor and people will long survive their separation and sincere are the regrets of the congregation of Greyfriars', and indeed, of Dr. Barkworth's many friends in Reading, that enfeebled health has led to his resigning the charge of so important a district, wherein he has long and faithfully laboured.[67]

A committee was formed of Church members to decide on a fitting memento of the "affectionate regard" in which the couple were held. The list of the members of the committee provides a roll call of the leading men in Greyfriars at the time: Admiral John Venour Fletcher (treasurer), the Churchwardens (Mr. Willson and Mr. Champ), the Hon. R. Boyle, Dr. Woodhouse, and Messrs. M. H. Sutton, J. Sutton, R. C. Dryland, A. Reed, Hodges, W. Sherwood, Vines, Waller, Weightman, Workman and S. Wheeler.[68]

Shortly after the announcement of his successor, Rev. Dr. Barkworth preached his last sermon as Vicar of Greyfriars at the evening service on 31st October 1874 taking as his text Acts xx., 32:- "And now, brethren, I commend you to God and to the Word of His Grace, which is able to build you up, and to give you an inheritance among all them which are sanctified."[69]

The final farewell to the Vicar took place on the following evening with a very crowded meeting in the School Rooms. Dr. Barkworth was presented with a cheque for £50 and a "handsome clock," supplied by Mr. A. Reed, Jeweller of Duke Street, and a member of the committee that decided what gift to give. It was an evening full of speeches conveying the deep respect and gratitude members of the congregation felt for their Vicar. Dr. Woodhouse, who chaired the meeting, read out a "Testimonial," written on "vellum paper, quarto size, and... richly bound in purple morocco." It had been "beautifully illuminated" by Mr. Edward Dear, a clerk in the office of Mr. Dryland, and had about 200 signatures written on the bottom. The testimonial stated:

To the Reverend Shadwell Morley Barkworth D.D.
Reverend and Dear Sir,- As members of the congregation of Grey Friars' Church, Reading, we feel deeply the severance of the tie which, for the last eleven years, has existed between us and yourself. During this period you have faithfully ministered to us the Word of Life; and we tender to you our hearty thanks for the steadfast adherence to Evangelical and Protestant Truth which you have always manifested. The labours of yourself and Mrs. Barkworth will ever be gratefully remembered here in Reading. Whilst alluding to them, we cannot avoid making special mention of the noble Schools established by you in connection with Grey Friars' Church. These large Schools, in which sound religious and secular instruction is given to about eight hundred children, have greatly flourished under your kind and fostering care; and the beautiful School Buildings which adjoin Grey Friars' Church, and which were erected through your instrumentality, will remain as a monument of your earnestness and munificence. We have deeply sympathised with you in your failing health, and it is our sincere prayer and hope that a temporary relinquishment of your ministerial duties may result in the restoration of your strength, and that you and your beloved wife may long be spared to serve the Lord in His vineyard. In token of our affectionate regard, we beg your acceptance of the accompanying Clock and Cheque, and with our united best wishes for yourself, for Mrs. Barkworth, and for every member of your family,
We are, reverend and Dear Sir,
Affectionately and faithfully yours,
[The many signatures followed][70]

Before the Barkworths left Reading, the ladies of Greyfriars presented Mrs. Barkworth with a gold watch and chain, valued at £51, as a memento of their sincere love and affection.[71] Dr. and Mrs. Barkworth retired to 12 Ferndale Park, Tunbridge Wells, Kent, not far from his second curacy nearly twenty-five years before.[72]

Shadwell Morley Barkworth died on 2nd July 1891, aged 71, leaving a large estate worth just over £12,000.[73] In memory of Dr. Barkworth's incumbency, in 1894 the stone reredos at the east end of the Church was installed with the commandments engraved on it. Later, following his wife's death, a memorial tablet was erected in Greyfriars. The text says:

IN MEMORY OF SHADWELL MORLEY BARKWORTH D.D.
WORCESTER COLLEGE OXFORD
WHO WAS BORN ON THE 5TH NOVEMBER 1819 AND IN
THE YEAR 1863 BECAME THE FIRST INCUMBENT OF THIS
CHURCH IN WHICH HE FAITHFULLY MINISTERED FOR A

PERIOD OF 11 YEARS.
DURING HIS INCUMBENCY THE ADJACENT SCHOOL
BUILDINGS WERE ERECTED BY HIS EFFORTS AND MUNIFICENCE.
HE FELL ASLEEP IN JESUS AT TUNBRIDGE WELLS ON THE
2ND JULY 1891 AGED 71 YEARS.
THE TABLETS FORMING THE CENTRAL PARTS OF THE
REREDOS IN THIS CHURCH WERE ERECTED IN GRATEFUL
REMEMBRANCE OF HIS MINISTRY IN THIS PARISH.
ALSO IN MEMORY OF ELLEN, HIS WIDOW, WHO ENTERED INTO REST
ON THE 6TH FEBRUARY 1895 AGED 63 YEARS.
“I AM NOT ASHAMED OF THE GOSPEL OF CHRIST FOR
IT IS THE POWER OF GOD UNTO SALVATION TO EVERY ONE
THAT BELIEVETH.” ROMANS 1:16
THANKS BE TO GOD WHICH GIVETH THE VICTORY

Memorial tablet in Greyfriars Church, south aisle wall.

In Memory of the Rev. Dr. S. M. Barkworth

Reredos erected in August 1894
in memory of the Rev. Dr. S. M. Barkworth
(Photograph from c1955)

Above: Rev. Seymour Henry Soole M.A.
(Photograph by Sidney Victor White c1892)

Below: Greyfriars in 1875 (Photograph by Henry Taunt)

Chapter 12

Seymour Henry Soole: Vicar 1874 to 1905

The second incumbent of Greyfriars Church was the 33 year old, unmarried, Seymour Henry Soole. He was to remain as Greyfriars' Vicar until he retired from the Ministry 31 years later.

Together with his recently widowed mother, Mr. Soole moved into number 1 Castle Crescent, between Coley Avenue and Coley Hill, off Castle Hill. At some stage in the next twenty years they moved next door to number 3, named 'Sunnyhome', and Mr. Soole lived there until his death in 1912.

Seymour Henry Soole was born in November 1840 in Stanstead Abbots, Hertfordshire. His father, Henry, was a saddler and harness maker, first in Stanstead Abbots and then in nearby Bishop's Stortford. Henry had married Anna Maria Seymour in September 1839 and they combined their names on 25th November 1840 when their only child was baptised Seymour Henry Soole.[1]

Seymour went to Bishop Stortford High School where he was one of four young men who "for distinguished excellence in religious knowledge, and as a testimony to their gentlemanly behaviour and respectful attention to the wishes of their masters during the whole of their career at school, each received from the hands of the Head Master a large and handsomely bound Bible."[2] Then in October 1861 Seymour went up to St. John's College, Cambridge, obtaining his B.A. in 1865 (Second Class in the Theological Tripos and winning a college prize for Hebrew[3]) and his M.A. in 1868.[4]

He was ordained Deacon at Keswick by the Bishop of Carlisle (the Hon. S. Waldegrave we met above) in July 1865,[5] and became the Curate at Christ Church, Carlisle. In May 1866 he was ordained Priest at St. Lawrence, Appleby, where after the ceremony those ordained were entertained at the Vicarage by none other than the Venerable Archdeacon William Whitmarsh Phelps, who, of course, was Vicar in that parish at that date.[6]

Mr. Soole had been Curate of Christ Church, Carlisle for only just over a year when the Trustees of the Church appointed him Vicar there in October 1866.[7] In 1871, his sermon "The census of 1871 and its lessons" was published.[8]

3 Castle Crescent, Reading – "Sunnyhome"
[Awaiting refurbishment in 2012]

Seymour Soole lived here from early in his incumbency until his death in 1912.

In June 1874, in the same week that Dr. Barkworth announced his resignation due to ill health, Mr. Soole was in Reading as a visiting preacher for the Colonial & Continental Church Society, an organisation that Greyfriars had supported over the previous few years. Mr. Soole preached in Greyfriars on 14th June.[9] There is a payment entry dated 27th June 1874 in the "Churchwardens of Greyfriars Church Pew Rent Account" book (1864 to 1876) to "Soole" for the sum of 12 Guineas, no doubt for his expenses.

He must have made a very good impression as before long Seymour Soole was invited to be the new Vicar of Greyfriars.[10]

The Carlisle Patriot newspaper expressed the regret felt by the community to be losing the Rev. S. H. Soole, writing "A more earnest and devoted minister of the Church never laboured in Carlisle. His attention to the various agencies of the parish, particularly its valuable schools, has been exemplary; and his pulpit duties have been admirably discharged."[11]

Mr. Soole officiated for the first time at Greyfriars on Sunday 1st November 1874, taking both the morning and evening services.[12]

In February 1875 the Bishop of Oxford, the Right Rev. Dr. Mackarness, confirmed 11 young men and 32 young women from Greyfriars. This compares favourably with totals before 1874. The table below shows confirmation numbers from Greyfriars for the years around this time: [13]

Year	1868	1871	1872	1875	1879	1881	1883	1886
Total	19	13	16	43	46	40	36	27

If the main legacy of Dr. Barkworth's incumbency was the establishment of the Schools for the children of the parish, Mr. Soole's was mission outreach to the working people of the parish. During March 1875 there was a very successful week-long mission in the parish with addresses by the Rev. W. Haslam of Curzon Chapel, Mayfair:

> The services commenced on Sunday morning. In the afternoon the service was specially for young men. On Monday, an address was delivered in the morning, and there were prayers and sermon in the evening. On Tuesday addresses were delivered to believers, domestic servants and working men. On Wednesday afternoon there was a service for children, and on Thursday and Friday working men and domestic servants were addressed.[14]

The mission continued with a Saturday morning service and an evening prayer meeting. To conclude the special services, the Vicar preached on Sunday morning, with Holy Communion celebrated in the evening. Mr. Haslam came back in July to give two evening Gospel addresses on a Thursday and Friday, both "to large congregations."[15]

In March 1875 Greyfriars said farewell to Charles Collins, who had for several years (at least from 1868[16]) visited the poor of the District and conducted services in the Mission Room in Caversham Road. Greyfriars also used No. 28 Chatham Street as a Mission House rent free from Miss Mary Neale, for about 30 years until 1901.[17]

In the latter part of 1875, Greyfriars gained its first Curate: the Rev. James Fox.[18] Greyfriars has had 40 Curates in total to date and a remarkable proportion (18 out of the 40, or 45%) worked with Mr. Soole between 1875 and 1905 (see the table on the next page). There are two main reasons for this: for much of Mr. Soole's incumbency there were two Curates at the same time whose main role was to run the mission to the parish; the second reason is that, as we shall see, there was a large gap from 1945 to 1969 with no Curate appointed.

The 18 Curates who worked with Mr. Soole	From	To	Next destination
James Fox	1875	1876	Curate: Melcombe Regis, Dorset
Sydenham Lynes Dixon	1876	1878	Curate: St. Mary's Episcopal Chapel, Reading
Gerard Duke Wyatt	1877	1880	Vicar, St. John's, Highbury
John William Merry	1879	1883	Curate: Rimpton, Somerset
Joseph Mitchell	1880	1881	Vicar: St. John's, New Wortley, Leeds, Yorkshire
Arthur Haig	1881	1881	Missionary, Delhi, India
Robert Poynder	1883	1888	Sale, Victoria, Australia
Robert Christopher Oake	1888	1890	Curate: St. Clement's, Oxford
Alfred Babington	1890	1894	Rector: St. Peter's, Wallingford
John Norris Arkell	1890	1892	Curate: St. John's, Wakefield
Frederick Sumner	1892	1897	Curate: St. John's, Folkestone
Walter Atkins	1895	1897	Curate: Great with Little Horkesley, Essex
Clement Arnold Worsfold	1897	1900	Curate: Devizes, Wiltshire
Sidney John Harris	1899	1901	CPAS Secretary, Northern District
Edmund Christopher Hudson	1901	1901	Curate: St. Paul's, Bolton
Edwin Brooshooft Brown	1901	1904	Curate: Staple Fitzpaine with Bickenhall, Taunton
Charles Walter Houlston	1904	1904	Curate: St. Saviour's, Bacup
Warwick Bathurst Soole	1904	1905	Curate: St. Barnabas', Holloway

On Tuesday 2nd May 1876, there was a very special event in the life of Greyfriars Church. Seymour Henry Soole, married Laura Sophia Sutton, the eldest daughter of Martin Hope Sutton and Sophia Woodhead Sutton of Cintra Lodge, Whitley. Seymour was 35 by this date and his young wife just 23.

The marriage ceremony began at 10.30am, with the Church completely full to overflowing. Many people had to remain outside throughout the ceremony and were only able to see the arrivals and departures of the wedding party. Laura, wearing a dress of white Lyons silk, trimmed with orange blossom and myrtle, was accompanied by five bridesmaids – three sisters and two cousins. Seymour's best man was the Rev. Charles David Russell, an old friend from his days at St. John's College, Cambridge, and Associate Secretary of the Church Pastoral Aid Society. There were three officiating clergy: the Rev. Henry Barne (Vicar of Faringdon), the Rev. Gilbert S. Karney (Vicar of Sandown, Isle of Wight) and the Rev. James Fox, Curate. As the bride and groom left the Church, girls from the Greyfriars' Schools, dressed in blue and white dresses, covered the bride's path with flowers.[19]

Mr. Soole welcomed another Curate onto the staff team in June 1876: the Rev. Sydenham Lynes Dixon. Mr. Dixon had graduated that summer as a Theological Associate of Kings College, London and was ordained deacon by the Bishop of Oxford on his taking up this post at Greyfriars.[20]

In July 1876 Martin Hope Sutton bought some land on North Street at a cost of £360 11s 6d and donated it to Greyfriars for the purpose of erecting a large building to be used as a mission hall for the working class of the parish.[21] The building, to be known as the Greyfriars Iron Room, was erected by Messrs. Croggon, of 42 Upper Thames Street, London and took only three months from initial purchase of land to completion.

On Wednesday 4th October 1876, the Greyfriars' Iron Room was opened with a special service. It had a capacity of between 350 and 400 people and on this first evening it was full to overflowing, mostly of the working class people for whom it was built. The Rev. J. Fox read the prayers and the Rev. S. L. Dixon read the lesson. The Vicar preached the sermon, based on Psalm 122. The collection on the night amounted to £30, as a contribution towards the Building Fund. Overall by this time just under £700 had been contributed towards the project. The aim was to hold services at the Iron Room every Sunday and Wednesday and to use the room as much as possible for other purposes during the week.[22]

James Fox had only been the Curate at Greyfriars for a year when, on Sunday 10th December 1876, he preached his last sermons to crowded congregations.[23] He moved on to become the Curate at Weymouth & Melcombe Regis and then three years later, Rector of St. Werburgh, Bristol. He was replaced in 1877 at Greyfriars by the Rev. Gerard Duke Wyatt, who had previously been Curate of Brayton in Yorkshire.

Greyfriars Iron Room
Photograph from Annual Report & Accounts for 1907

Seats in the Iron Room were free, while in Greyfriars 70% of the seats were rented by seat-holders. This meant that any visitor to the Church would need to sit towards the rear of the nave (shown in the plan of Greyfriars opposite). Pew rents, paid for the occupancy of a specific seat, were a (potentially) substantial part of an incumbent's income. Mr. Moore, the Head Master of the Schools since they opened, was the pew rent collector at Greyfriars at this time. The table opposite shows that pew rent made up about 75% of the Rev. S. H. Soole's income.

Six months after its first opening services, the Iron Room celebrated its re-opening on Wednesday 11th April 1877! The services were proving to be so popular that the decision had been taken to enlarge it by lengthening the building and adding side aisles increasing the capacity to almost 800 people.[24]

	Pew Rent Total			Total Income			Pew Rent as
	£	s	d	£	s	d	% of Total
1875	295	5	4	393	15	9	75%
1876	322	13	5	426	3	10	76%
1877	319	5	3	421	10	2	76%
1878	303	8	1	407	2	0	75%
1879	297	7	1	398	6	6	75%
1880	286	12	6	390	12	5	73%
1881	269	2	6	369	7	5	73%

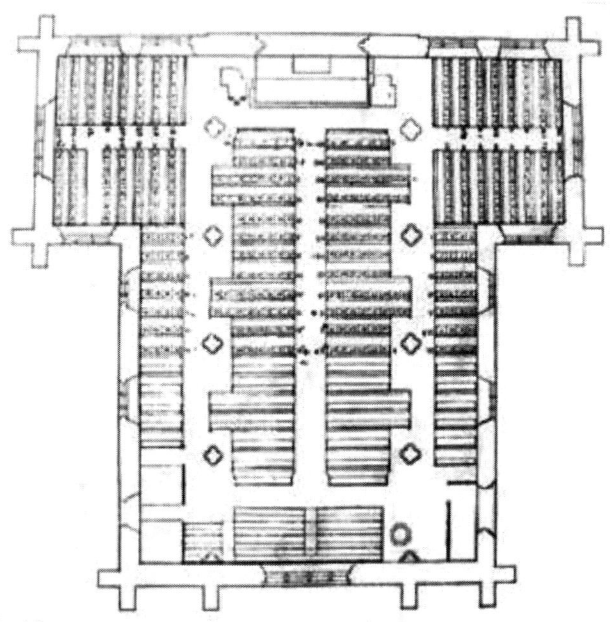

Plan of Greyfriars Church showing the numbered positions of 395 Seat-holders (70% of seats) with an estimated 172 seats ‘free’ (Note that the organ at this time was in front of the north door [bottom left])

The Rev. G. D. Wyatt read the shortened form of the service of Evening Prayer and then there were two short sermons, one from the Rev. S. L. Dixon on Zechariah 4:6 ("Not by might, nor by power, but by my spirit, saith the LORD of hosts.") and the second by the Rev. S.H. Soole on 1 Kings 8:56 ("There hath not failed one word of all his good promise"). The extension cost £530.[25]

The Iron Room's aim was to serve the working people of the parish with a form of Church service that they would find more accessible than the Prayer Book services at Greyfriars. Mr. Soole wrote in 1883:

> A large mission room, seating 780 persons, was erected in 1876, to supply still further the Spiritual wants of the parishioners, most of whom belong to the artizan (sic) or labouring classes. The experiment of providing a *free and open* Church has more than answered the expectation that was formed. This Greyfriars' Iron Room, as it is called, is practically the people's Church, and as the services are somewhat shortened, and bright gospel hymns sung, work of quite a missionary character has been carried on during the past seven years, the congregation at the Parish Church liberally contributing £300 a year for the support of two assistant Curates.[26]

The Iron Room had Sunday services at 11am and 6.30pm, "which are very hearty [and] are well attended, especially on the Sunday evening, when the room is literally filled" according to the report of the First Anniversary Service on 3rd October 1877. Of the Iron Room's overall cost of £1,600 there was still a considerable sum yet to be raised.[27] This did not stop the purchase and installation of an organ, however, which had its inaugural service on Thursday 25th April 1878.[28]

Greyfriars was an integral part of many Church movements in Reading. The Church of England Temperance Society had been established in 1862 to combat the effect of drunkenness, particularly on the poor. The first meeting of the Berkshire Branch was on 26th October 1875, with anyone who was anyone in Reading society present.[29] Mr. Soole seconded a motion recommending parishes to set up their own Parochial Temperance Societies. A total abstainer himself, he said that "He believed half-measures were of little or no use whatever, and if a man wanted to break the habit of drinking, his advice was not to begin by diminishing the quantity, but to make a bold stand and give it up altogether."

It took a little while before the Greyfriars' Branch of the Church Temperance Society was set up. The first meeting was on Tuesday 10th

February 1880 in Forrester's Hall, West Street. Prior to the meeting a circular had been delivered throughout the parish which stated:

> For some time past we have been convinced of the obligation that lies upon us to make some effort against an evil of fearful magnitude, which exists in our midst – intemperance... We are fully persuaded that whatever other forms of evil the Church of Christ has to combat – and these are manifold and grave – the evil alluded to yields in gravity to none. It is accordingly proposed that a Branch of the Church of England Temperance Society be at once established in our parish. We ask you to observe that this society is not a total abstinence society, but temperance, a basis on which all Christian people, whether abstainers or non-abstainers, may meet and join hands, on terms of perfect equality.

Martin Hope Sutton proposed, and Robert Coster Dryland seconded, a motion to establish the Branch under the Vicar, the Rev. S. H. Soole, as President, and the Curate, the Rev. G. D. Wyatt, as Secretary. A committee was established that included the other Curate, the Rev. John William Merry (who had joined Greyfriars in the previous year) and Alfred Callas. During the course of the various speeches, one arresting statistic stands out: Mr. Wyatt stated that in Greyfriars parish, with a population of 4,000, there were 38 public houses and "beershops."[30]

By March, Mr. Soole could announce that a "goodly number [of adults] had already joined, and that their juvenile branch [named the 'Band of Hope'] numbered over 500 members."[31] 430 children assembled for the April 1880 meeting, held in the West Street Hall, where they were entertained by Mr. Toomer's drum and fife band from Twyford.[32]

In the summer of 1880 there was another new venture for the Church: its own Cricket Club. Their first match took place at Martin Hope Sutton's grounds of Cintra Lodge against St. John's. Greyfriars' innings totals of 40 and 14 meant that they suffered an innings' defeat, with St. John's scoring 66.[33]

By the end of August, the Rev. G. D. Wyatt had left Greyfriars after three and a half years' service to take up the living in the new district of St. John's, Highbury, London. At a farewell gathering various testimonials were given, culminating in the presentation of a farewell cheque for £100 together with a study table and chair. Receiving the gifts with grateful thanks, Mr. Wyatt spoke of the Vicar "from whom he had always received the greatest possible kindness and attention, and who had treated him as a brother; he should always regard him as one of the best friends of his life."[34]

In September 1880 the Rev. William Haslam returned, five years after his first mission to the parish, to lead a second mission. Meetings were advertised:

GREYFRIARS' CHURCH, READING.
SPECIAL SERVICES.
THE REV. W. HASLAM, M. A., will preach next week on
SUNDAY, Morning, Afternoon (to the young), and Evening.
EVERY AFTERNOON, at 3.0; Subject – "A Risen Saviour."
EVERY EVENING, at 7.30, Mission Service
WEDNESDAY and FRIDAY mornings, at 11.0 – Address to Workers and Others.
ALL ARE EARNESTLY INVITED.[35]

The mission was a great success, with large numbers attending all of the meetings. The report of the week stated: "The evening addresses were Evangelistic, and much lasting blessing is expected. The services at the Iron Room were specially hearty and earnest."[36]

Another significant feature of the life of Greyfriars under Mr. Soole was the number of musical evenings held. One very special occasion took place in December 1880 in the Boys' Schoolroom: a service of song entitled "The Pilgrim's Progress" given by the Church choir and with connective readings by recently arrived Curate, the Rev. Joseph Mitchell. After prayer by the senior Curate, the Rev. John Merry, Mr. Soole introduced the evening with a short talk about the life of John Bunyan, particularly with reference to a number of narrow escapes that occurred in his life. The Schoolroom was "filled to overflowing with an attentive audience."[37]

In January 1881 Greyfriars published its first Church Magazine. The impetus for the production came from the Curate, Mr. Merry, who continued to edit the Greyfriars' Parochial Magazine until he left in 1883. Thereafter, it fell to the Vicar to be the editor. It retained the same name and style until it was overhauled for the January 1894 edition. It was issued monthly with "Home Words," which consisted of several poems and stories designed for parish magazines.

At the 1881 Vestry meeting both Churchwardens retired. Henry Champ had been Warden for 13 years and Charles Frederick Willson who had been a Warden in 1864 and had served for almost 15 of the years since. They were replaced by two men who remained as Churchwardens for the next twenty years or so: Messrs. Dryland and Callas.[38] Robert Coster

Dryland, aged 52, was a solicitor. The Dryland family name survives in the solicitors' practice Collins, Dryland and Thorowgood of Tilehurst, Sonning Common and Henley. Alfred Callas, aged 34, was an Ironmonger, with a store at 72 & 74 Oxford Street. His family name also lived on for many years in the local firm Callas, Sons & May.

Churchwardens during Rev. S. H. Soole's incumbency 1874 - 1905		
April 1874 to April 1881	Mr. Henry Champ	Mr. Charles Willson
April 1881 to April 1901	Mr. Robert Coster Dryland	Mr. Alfred Callas
April 1901 to April 1905	Mr. George Fuller	Mr. Alfred Callas

In September 1882, two years after the mission led by Rev. W. Haslam, there was a ten day mission led by the Rev. Henry Dening of Bath. Mr. Dening preached two or three times each day to large congregations. The service for men only was crowded, chiefly with working-class men, causing the Reading Mercury to comment: "Seldom, if perhaps ever before, has such a large congregation of men been seen in a Church in Reading on a Sunday afternoon."

On the last three evenings the congregations overflowed the Church and a large number stayed on to "after meetings." The ten day mission then ended with a service of Holy Communion with nearly 300 present.[39]

In 1882 Greyfriars decided to take steps to purchase the property next door at 64 Friar Street. Called Greyfriars House, the 1880 Ordnance Survey map shows the house to have had a large area of land stretching from Friar Street, down to the backs of the gardens at Vachel Road. Much of this land was sold off by the previous owner, enabling the Council to build Sackville Street in about 1881.

The property was occupied at the 1881 census by William Flanagan, a Veterinary Surgeon (and prize-winning pigeon racer), his wife Isabella, their 5 children and two servants.[40] By 1883, Francis W. Sutton, Surgeon at the Royal Berkshire Hospital, was living in the house.[41]

Between these two dates, on 24th October 1882 Mr. R. C. Dryland had written to the Ecclesiastical Commissioners at 10 Whitehall Place, London, to request assistance with funding for the £3000 required to purchase the house.[42]

Unfortunately, the Ecclesiastical Commissioners decided against awarding a grant in the year 1883[43], but as the Commissioners made annual awards, the following year presented another opportunity. Mr. R. C. Dryland therefore submitted the request in due order by 1st December 1883 and a letter dated 6th March 1884 gave the good news that the Commissioners granted £1500 (assuming the Bishop of Oxford's consent) for the purchase of Greyfriars House.[44]

There naturally followed the process of actually purchasing the property which took some time. Following the completion of the purchase, the London Gazette – where all such official Ecclesiastical announcements were given – reported that on 12th June 1884 a grant of £1500 had been paid towards the purchase of the house and premises.[45] Greyfriars had to raise its own £1500, but this was made much easier by one of the Miss Wilsons, sisters who had already been great benefactors of the Church, who donated £1000 towards the sum.[46]

The photograph below shows the Vicarage much later, but it had remained virtually unchanged since the purchase in the nineteenth century.

64 Friar Street
(Photograph by David Page c1960)

Since the intention was for the house to be the Greyfriars Vicarage, it comes as something of a surprise to discover that the first time it actually served as a Vicarage was for the Rev. Hugh Boultbee, the third Vicar, in 1905. It would seem that not even the prospect of living next door to the Church could persuade Seymour Soole to relinquish "Sunnyhome" on

Castle Crescent. Meanwhile, the Church let out the house. From 1885 the tenants were Job Baylis, a grocer and provision merchant, and his family, paying £75 per annum.[47] They are mentioned in both the 1891 and 1901 censuses.[48]

In June 1886 the Church nave lighting was improved by the installation of eight pendants, each with five sets of three gas lights, supported by wrought iron wall brackets fixed in between the nave arches. Originally these fittings were painted in "unobtrusive colours," though with a little gilding. The fittings were designed by Mr. W. Ravenscroft, architect, and were supplied and fitted by Mr. A. Callas (who was also, of course, one of the Churchwardens) at a cost of £155 3s 6d.[49]

These brackets and light fittings are still in use to light the nave of the Church today – although the five sets of three gas lights have given way to five electric lights in each pendant fitting. The colours are brighter now too, being predominantly blue.

1886 fittings, showing five sets of three gas jets

Gas replaced by electrical lights in 1930

Following the reordering in 2000

In November 1887 a meeting of seat-holders resolved to apply to the Bishop of Oxford for a "Faculty" (ie permission) to move the organ from in front of the north door into the north transept. The Faculty was duly agreed and issued in December, allowing the Vicar and Churchwardens to "take down and remove the organ from its present position at the north west end of the Church and to re-construct the same in the north transept of the Church and to remove the fitting consequent thereupon: to re-open the door on the north side of the Church and as a means of entrance exit to and from the Church."[50]

The new three-manual organ, built by Alfred Monk of Holloway Road, London, had its inaugural services on Thursday 26th July 1888. The Vicar preached at the 3pm service that day, taking the text Psalm 108:1 "O God, my heart is fixed; I will sing and give praise." The organ was played by former Greyfriars Organist Mr. F. J. Read, who was by this time Organist at Chichester Cathedral. The total project costs were about £250.[51]

In September 1888 Greyfriars said a fond farewell to the Rev. Robert Poynder who had been Curate for five and a half years. Mr. and Mrs. Poynder were presented with a gift of £70 and some photographs of Reading to take with them as they sailed to Melbourne, Australia. He was replaced by Rev. Robert C. Oake, previously of Clifton, Bristol, at the beginning of October.[52]

Beginning on 16th February 1889, there was a Reading-wide Church Mission, with special missioners and mission services at all fourteen of the Church of England churches in the town. Throughout the town missioners had been appointed and plans drawn up in readiness.[53]

The missioner for Greyfriars was to be the Rev. Sholto D. C. Douglas, formerly rector of All Souls, Langham Place. He visited Greyfriars for a special service ("Missioner's Address to Workers") on Monday 14th January, preaching from Joshua 5:13 ("Art thou for us, or for our adversaries?") with the title "Qualifications for Christian Work."[54] Preparations included a printed address by Mr. Douglas to the parish requesting heads of households to make arrangements so that both they and their servants would be able to attend the special services. The Iron Room had its own Lay Missioner – Mr. W. Spencer Walton.[55] A special Church Mission in Reading handbook was published, containing all the details of services for every church, while Mr. Arthur W. Sutton donated £3 16s 6d for the purchase of 1000 "Hymn Books for Parochial Mission" for use by both the Iron Room and Greyfriars Church.[56]

The Mission began at Greyfriars with a Saturday evening joint prayer meeting for the Church and Iron Room, with both missioners preaching. Over the next eleven days, Rev. Sholto Douglas preached twenty times at Greyfriars. On the first Sunday afternoon a large men-only congregation listened with rapt attention for 65 minutes to lessons from King David's life, entitled "Consequences of Trust & Distrust." That morning, unfortunately, Mr. W. Spencer Walton was unwell – as a result, no doubt, of having just completed a similar mission in the north on the previous Thursday. The Curate, Rev. R. C. Oake, stood in for him both in the morning service and in the afternoon open-air service in Weldale Street.

Services continued throughout the week, usually at 11.30am and 8pm in the Church and at 5.30pm and 8pm in the Iron Room. Special services for women only took place every day at 2.30pm in the Iron Room, taken by Miss E. Thistleton – a crèche was provided so that mothers could attend.

Numbers continued to grow throughout the week and "after-meetings" were held where "many souls appear anxious to be guided and helped in understanding the conditions of acceptance with God, and it is believed that many have commenced the life of faith."[57]

The Rev. Sholto C. Douglas preached his final sermon on Wednesday 27th February at 11.30am, entitled "Comfort to Workers." The evening before, there had been 207 communicants at the last mission meeting (the average at the time being just under 80 at "normal" communion services).[58] Canon Garry, the Chairman of the Reading Mission Committee, said: "The different schools of thought amongst us were ably represented, but the one common object of all was to bring souls to Christ... The unity of effort has made a deep impression on the town."[59]

Hard on the heels of the February Mission, Greyfriars held a series of evangelistic meetings in a tent in Caversham Road, every evening from 29th July to 14th August. The missioner was Mr. J. Brown of the London Evangelization Society. The Tent Mission was blessed by both good weather and high attendances.[60]

The Greyfriars Preachers' Book for the period gives a wonderful record of the week by week life of the Church. Once a month, usually on the first or second Sunday, there were special services, often with a visiting preacher. The focus of these services was split between national Christian Societies and Church financial needs. From the earliest days of the re-consecrated Church, the following Societies formed part of the annual cycle of Greyfriars' special services for most years, many having their own slot at a particular time of year:

Church Missionary Society (CMS)
Church Pastoral Aid Society (CPAS)
Colonial and Continental Church Society
Irish Church Missions to Roman Catholics
Lord's Day Observance Society
The London Society for Promoting Christianity among the Jews
Reading Protestant Association
Reading Young Men's Christian Association (YMCA)

In addition, Greyfriars held an annual "Hospital Sunday," where the collection went to the Royal Berkshire Hospital. Special services and collections were also made in connection with the Assistant Clergy Fund (to provide income for the Curates), for the Day Schools and for various Church or Iron Room improvements or renovations.

In 1890 there were 165 services at Greyfriars, with the normal weekly pattern being services on Sunday at 11am and 6.30pm, and on Wednesday at 7.30pm. There were also daily services in Holy Week. The table below shows the breakdown of preachers and the number of sermons that year:

Preacher	Number	%	Role
Rev. S. H. Soole	88	53%	Vicar
Rev. R. C. Oake	10	6%	Curate to June
Rev. A Babbington	38	23%	Curate from July
Rev J. Arkell	1	<1%	Curate from late December
Others	28	17%	

Mr. Soole managed to preach more than half of the sermons in spite of taking a month off in August/early September. Although it is a sample of just one year, the spread of Mr. Soole's sermons through the Bible is very interesting. He managed a fairly even split between four categories: Old Testament (29%) Gospels (26%), Paul's letters (25%) and the rest of the New Testament (20%). His favourite books that year were: John (8 sermons), Luke and Psalms (7 each), Matthew (6) and 1 Corinthians (5). He preached just once from Mark. In all he preached from 30 different Bible books in 1890.

Holy Communion services were scheduled for the first Sunday at 11am and the third Sunday at 6.30pm and of course at major festivals. In 1890 the average number of communicants fell when compared with the year before and fell again in 1891:

	Average Number of Communicants		
	1st Sunday am	3rd Sunday pm	Festivals
1889	58	117	55
1890	49	87	48
1891	49	80	44

On 2nd July 1891 long-standing Greyfriars' member Mrs. Sophia Fletcher died aged 70. Admiral and Mrs. Fletcher – commemorated by the earliest of the brass plaques in the Church – had been members of Greyfriars since Dr. Barkworth's incumbency. Since retiring from the Royal Navy, John Venour Fletcher had been a Manager of the Reading Savings' Bank from 1863. Born on 14th November 1801 in Chesterfield,

John Fletcher had entered the Royal Navy aged 12 at the tail end of the Napoleonic Wars. In a career spanning almost 50 years he gradually rose in the ranks, becoming Commander (Second in Command to the Captain) of the 74-gun Wellesley in 1839. He saw action in the First Anglo-China War (also known as the First Opium War, 1839 - 1841), with the Wellesley most famously enabling the capture of Hong Kong Island for Britain. The exploits of the Wellesley earned its captain a knighthood and John Fletcher, as the second in command, both his own captaincy and the China Medal. On his retirement in 1861 he was created Rear Admiral, then Vice Admiral in 1866 and Admiral in 1872.

John Venour Fletcher had married Sophia Venour in June 1851. Sophia, almost 20 years younger than her husband, had been born in Cawpore, India, where her father was a Medical Officer in the East India Company. Mrs. Fletcher was, for many years, one of Greyfriars' District Visitors.

Following Mrs. Fletcher's death, her younger daughter Helen Selena (usually known as Selena, or just Lena), moved to Wimbledon. In October 1892 she was back to visit Reading as part of a Church Missionary Society farewell to missionaries – she was going to Hong Kong as an "educational missionary." Since she lived on her own means, Greyfriars was not involved in supporting her financially.

Brass Plaque Memorial in the south transept

Meanwhile, returning to Greyfriars for a third time, the Rev. William Haslam once again led a mission although this time of short duration. It lasted from Sunday 6th December 1891 to Wednesday 9th, with 9 meetings in four days.[61]

In 1892 the long-time Head Master of the Mixed Junior School, William Moore, was the victim of an assault. A boy threw a stone at the School door and William Kirby, a Pupil Teacher (and later Head Master of the School), chased the boy and caught him. Mr. Moore, who had followed, took the boy's name and address. Later, Charles Sealey, a Labourer of 45 Somerset Place and of no relation to the boy, came to the School and "used most filthy and disgusting language in front of the whole School towards Mr. Moore." Sealey refused to leave and continued for some time using bad language. He spat in Mr. Moore's face and then left. A policeman was called and Mr. Moore, on behalf of the Managers of the School, pressed charges. The case came to Magistrates' Court on Monday 7th November, just one week after the incident. Charles Sealey was found guilty and imprisoned for 14 days with hard labour.[62]

In the same month, Reading played host to the great American evangelist, Dwight L. Moody, who led a Mission to Reading from Thursday 10th to Sunday 13th November.[63] At the first mission meeting on the Thursday afternoon, crowds had queued for over two hours to try to gain admittance and many had to be turned away disappointed. The Rev. S. H. Soole had the privilege of opening this first mission meeting in prayer. The Mission was such a success that, although initially due to end on the Saturday, it was extended to the Sunday. After the final meeting it was reported that "several hundred persons assembled in the small Town Hall for prayer and counsel, and for meditation."[64]

To the Mission Hall in North Street was added, in 1893, an adjoining house which became known as the North Street Mission House. Following a subscription the house was renovated and made fit "for Parochial use."[65] This was in addition to No. 28 Chatham Street, loaned for use as a Mission Room free of charge by Miss Neale.

From May to October 1893, open air services led by the Curate, Mr. Sumner, were held three times a week in an effort to reach those in the parish who would not even come to the Mission Hall. On Friday nights in Somerset Place – the poorest of this poor district – and on Sundays and Thursdays in Caversham Road, a group from Greyfriars set up their harmonium, pulpit and banner and held a service.[66]

In February 1894, Laura Soole's mother, Sophia Woodhead Sutton (wife of Martin Hope Sutton), died after a few days' illness, aged 72.[67] Her funeral took place on 20th February.[68] At the same time, Mr. Soole was taken ill and needed several weeks away from Reading for recuperation. He wrote in the Parish Magazine:

> I am pleased to tell you that there is nothing wrong with my throat, but what, we may hope, perfect rest and change of air will, in God's good time set right. I have been working beyond my strength for many years and 'nature is taking her revenge.' I have not taken the one day rest out of the seven, which our merciful Creator has ordained...[69]

Mr. Soole was away from early February, returning in late April. The Reading Mercury reported that he "has returned home much stronger, and hopes at once to resume his ministerial duties."[70] He did indeed resume his duties, preaching at both services from the book of Romans on 29th April, at 11am with the title "Lord of the dead and living," and at 6.30pm "All things for the best." It is hard not to see a connection between their circumstances and the chosen subjects.

In memory of both the Vicar's mother, who had died in 1891, and mother-in-law, the Rev. and Mrs. Soole donated to Greyfriars a beautiful carved and inscribed dark oak and walnut communion table, supplied by Messrs. F. H. & J. Sparrow at a cost of £32[71]. It was used as the Church's communion table from 1894 until the reordering in 2000 and now stands in the south transept.

On Monday 30th July 1894 Greyfriars Church was closed for almost four weeks, reopening on Sunday 26th August, for "necessary repairs and beautifying."[72] Writing in 1906, Mr. Soole briefly described the works as:

> In 1894, important restorations and additions were made, including the completed Reredos, in memory of the first Vicar, and the enlarged Organ with its new oaken case, one of the most effective and beautiful instruments in the town. The total cost reaching £750.[73]

The "important restorations and additions" that Mr. Soole referred to were wide ranging. The walls were dressed with "calcareum, the tint harmonizing admirably with the old stone quoins, arches and pillars, which are of course left untouched." As well as major works to the organ, the organ pipes were decorated. The roof was cleaned and brightened. Radiating stoves were added throughout the building and the curtains in

Communion Table donated in 1894 by Seymour and Laura Soole.
In use until the reordering of the Church in 2000.

Text carved on the front edge:
YEA I HAVE LOVED THEE WITH AN EVERLASTING LOVE

Text carved on the back edge:
GIVEN IN MEMORY OF THEIR MOTHERS:
A. M. SOOLE & S. W. SUTTON
BY S H SOOLE & LAURA HIS WIFE AD 1894

A. M. SOOLE was Anna Maria Soole (née Seymour), who lived with Seymour and Laura until her death aged 86 on 18th June 1891.

S. W. SUTTON was Sophia Woodhead Sutton, (née Warwick), wife of Martin Hope Sutton, who died at Cintra Lodge, Whitley, aged 72 on 16th February 1894.

front of the doors were replaced. Velvet fittings were put in the pulpit and the reading desk and velvet kneelers for the communicants. The font was given a cover (courtesy of Mr. W. Ravenscroft, the architect). The choir seats had "rug-seating and book-rests." The work was "satisfactorily executed under the direction of Mr. W. Ravenscroft, F.S.A., by Messrs. Wheeler Bros., Mr. A. Callas, Messrs. F. H. and J. Sparrow, and Messrs. Sisley and Goodall."[74] During the closure period "united services" were held at the Iron Room at the usual Greyfriars times of 11am and 6.30pm on Sundays and 7.30pm on Wednesdays. Banns of marriage had to be read at St. Mary's Church.

There were several special re-opening services: on Sunday 26th August the Vicar preached to large congregations at both services. On the following Wednesday the Rev. W. Talbot Rice, Rector of St. Peter-le-Bailey, Oxford, "delivered a powerful sermon," and Mr. J. G. Cole, F.R.C.O., Organist of Christ Church, Ealing, gave a short organ recital.[75] The special services continued on the next Sunday when the visiting preacher was the Rev. Sholto Douglas, Vicar of St. Jude's, Glasgow, who had conducted a mission at Greyfriars in February 1889. I would like to have been at the morning service, where the sermon was "a practical unfolding of the law of the 'Red Heifer' in Numbers xix." In the evening Mr. Douglas held the "rapt attention of the congregation for upwards of an hour, as he discoursed upon the hardening of Pharaoh's heart."[76] Just over £40 was collected at the 5 services towards the "Church Renovation and Improvement Fund" – including, according to a marginal note in the Preachers' Book, a £5 note.

On the 31st anniversary of the restoration of the Church, Greyfriars said farewell to its long serving Curate Alfred Babington. He had come to Greyfriars in March 1890 and had preached 240 sermons from Greyfriars' pulpit in the almost five years of his curacy – and no doubt at least as many at the Iron Room. He was appointed to be Rector of St. Peter's Church, Wallingford.[77] At the morning service that day, the Vicar dwelt on the fact that few of the people present on 2nd December 1863 were still alive and he named many who had died, including: "Dr. Barkworth, Archdeacon Phelps, Admiral and Mrs. Fletcher, Adam Read, Dr. Woodhouse, Mrs. Ball, Miss Wilson, Miss Dewe, Miss Boyer, Mrs. Hawkins, Miss Phippen, Dr. Moses, Dr. Vines, the Hon. Robert Boyle, and many other honoured and beloved ones, besides those whose memories were still fresh, who had only that year passed away."[78] In the last category, Mr. Soole would no doubt have included Mrs. S. W. Sutton (his wife's mother), Mr. C. F.

Willson (for many years a Churchwarden), Mr. John Wheeler Jun., and Dr. J. W. Workman (who had been involved in the restoration), all of whom had died in 1894.

In early 1895, Greyfriars appointed the Rev. R. B. Daniel as the new Organist following the retirement after 16 years of Miss Fanny Lyne.[79] Mr. Daniel was not Organist for long, as he was replaced in 1896 by Charles Henry Thackway of 46 Zinzan Street who remained the Church Organist for 25 years.[80]

Sad news reached Greyfriars Vicarage in September 1896: former Curate, Rev. G. D. Wyatt, had died. He had been the third Greyfriars' Curate, serving from 1877 to 1880 before moving on to be Vicar at St. John's, Highbury. The newspaper report stated that he had died after an illness of three years brought on by overwork.[81]

The Curate, the Rev. F. Sumner, upon completion of five years at Greyfriars, was appointed to the Curacy of St. John's, Folkestone. He preached his 203rd and last sermon at Greyfriars at the 11am service on Sunday 29th August 1897: "Last Words" from Matthew 28:18 "And Jesus came and spake unto them, saying, All power is given unto me in heaven and in earth." Mr. Sumner's departure was quickly followed by that of the Rev. Walter Atkins, the other Curate, who had been at Greyfriars since January 1895, living at 5 Coley Hill. Their successor was the Rev. Clement A. Worsfold, fresh out of Corpus Christi College, Cambridge, who moved into 6 Bath Terrace, preaching his first sermon on Wednesday 6th October 1897.[82]

Soon after this there is the first mention that I have found of a Lay Reader working in Greyfriars parish: Mr. C. S. Campbell.[83] His ministry was in the Iron Room, assisting the Curate. He was succeeded in that role within a few years by Mr. G. T. Tredennick.[84]

A special presentation took place in February 1899 to mark the retirement of Thomas North from the post of Greyfriars' Parish Clerk. He had filled this post for the 35 years since the re-consecration of the Church. Mr. North was presented with a clock and an illuminated address (a hand-decorated and framed formal statement, expressing appreciation of the work he had done over such a long time and of the respect and esteem he was held in by all).[85]

Later that year, the Church said farewell to the Rev. C. A. Worsfold. 96 members of the congregation sent him a gift, by banker's draft, of £23 and "an address of loving regard and recognition of three years' faithful work at the Church Iron Room and Schools."[86] Mr. Worsfold preached his last sermon – "Abiding in His love" John 15:9 – at the 7.30pm service on Wednesday 26th September[87], before moving to Devizes. It was not long before Greyfriars' other Curate, Rev. S. J. Harris, was also on the move. In mid-February 1901 Mr. Harris left to take up the post of Association Secretary of the Church Pastoral Aid Society for the Northern District. The newspaper report noted the mixed feelings of the congregation on hearing of Mr. Harris's appointment, for "he is much beloved and highly esteemed as a diligent and devoted worker, and a gifted and faithful preacher. His going will be a great loss to the parish." [88]

Greyfriars Church c1899
In "Mates Illustrated Guides: Reading Illustrated"
Published by W. Mates & Sons, Bournemouth in 1899

Two very notable members of Greyfriars died in 1901. The first was Robert Coster Dryland who died on Easter Monday, two weeks before his 75th birthday.[89] Mr. Dryland was a well-known and respected Reading solicitor, with a particular specialism in conveyancing. His premises were at 165 Friar Street, where in 1898 he had taken into partnership his son Harold C. Dryland and nephew Mr. F. J. Thorowgood. He had been elected Reading Town Clerk in 1873 and had retained the post for three years.

He was also for many years – from 1881 until his death – Vicar's Churchwarden at Greyfriars, becoming one of the five Trustees of the Living. He took a leading role in chairing and speaking at Church meetings.

Two years previously, the Church had held a special presentation ceremony in recognition of Mr. Dryland's long and distinguished service of the Church.[90] The Vicar paid tribute to the whole Dryland family for their services to the Church. The Vicar added that he believed it was due to Mr. Dryland that he had first come to the Church in 1874 – unfortunately not adding any details for us to understand exactly how the circumstances came about! The Church presented Mr. Dryland with a 120 ounce engraved solid silver entrée dish and an illuminated address thanking him for his "diligent, faithful and valuable services" both as Vicar's Warden for 18 years (at that date) but also for his "legal experience and acumen."

Robert Coster Dryland
of Bath Place, Bath Road,
Reading
(21st April 1827 –
8th April 1901)

Photograph from the
Greyfriars Annual Report
for 1906

At the Easter Vestry Meeting on Tuesday 9th April 1901, the day after Mr. Dryland's death, the meeting, in sombre mood, paid tribute to Mr. Dryland and formally adjourned for a fortnight out of respect for his memory.[91] At his funeral at Greyfriars Church, two days later, there was a very large congregation, including the Mayor of Reading, Mr. A. H. Bull.[92]

At the reconvened Vestry Meeting, the Vicar nominated Alfred Callas as his Warden and the meeting chose George F. Fuller for People's Warden. At the same meeting a committee was appointed to consider, with the architect Mr. W. Ravenscroft, how to improve the warming and the paving of the Church.[93]

Following another death, that of Miss Mary Neale (on 18th February 1901), Greyfriars was no longer able to use No. 28 Chatham Street rent-free as a Mission House. The property came up for sale on 13th June 1901. The Estate Agent's notice stated:

> "Dwelling House and Premises, known as No. 28 (formerly No. 84) Chatham Street, Reading... It contains:- Sitting room, kitchen, scullery, large room and 2 bedrooms over, w.c., etc. Neat forecourt and garden in rear. It has a frontage of 15 feet (including half the passage way) and a depth of about 100 feet. The premises are at present in hand but have been used for some years as a Mission Room in connection with Greyfriars Church."

The house was bought by Greyfriars for £100, the relevant documentation being signed by the Rev. S. H. Soole, Mr. A. Callas, Mr. G. F. Fuller and Mr. F. Wheeler.[94] The house was then rented to Thomas Searle and his family for £2 5s 6d a quarter. Mr. Searle had recently become Caretaker of both Church and Schools.[95]

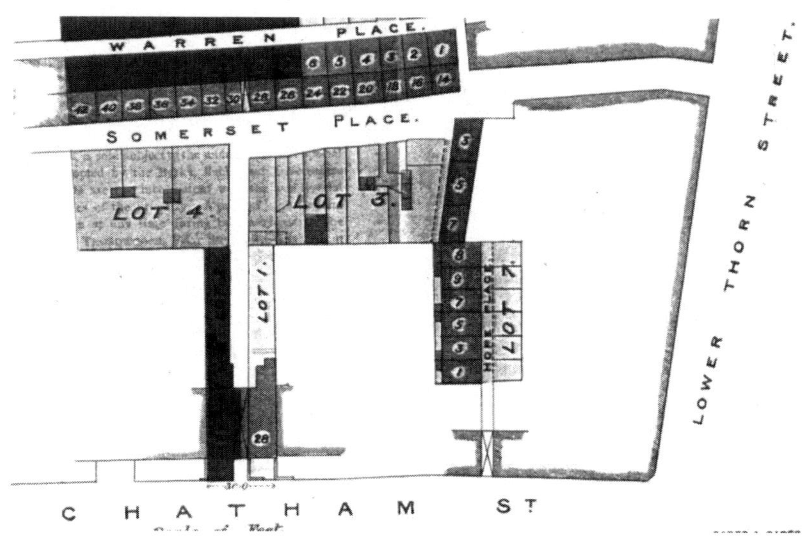

Chatham Street Mission House shown as No. 28, Lot 1.
(Messrs. Oades and Oades, Auctioneers and Surveyors)

On 13th February 1901 Greyfriars welcomed its next Curate: the Rev. Edmund Christopher Hudson. Preaching just 15 times at Greyfriars before his departure in early June, his ministry was somewhat unusual. He left the post suddenly by a mutual agreement with Mr. Soole, when it transpired that Mr. Hudson had not actually been licensed by the Bishop of Oxford to minister in the Diocese. Whether this had been a misunderstanding or a deception is uncertain, but letters written by Mr. Soole to his Wardens seem to imply the latter. It must have been with some relief that the next appointment, the Rev. Edwin Brooshooft Brown in June 1901, proved to be a highly successful one.[96]

Mr. Brown was formally welcomed at a special gathering in the grounds of Greyfriars' Vicarage, Castle Crescent, on a pleasant Wednesday afternoon in early September. 150 gathered, on the invitation of the Vicar to welcome the newcomer and to pay tribute to Alfred Callas, Churchwarden since 1881. The Vicar described how he was struck especially by Mr. Callas's "good common sense, his activity and earnestness in everything he undertook – his loyalty, his many acts of thoughtful kindness and his liberality in helping forward every good work in the parish." Mr. Callas was presented with an engraved solid silver rose bowl "in recognition of his devoted services as Churchwarden for 20 years."[97]

A month later, Martin Hope Sutton died, aged 86. He had been part of the story of the re-consecrated Greyfriars since its early days and had been one of its main benefactors. He had supported his son-in-law, Mr. Soole, financially for many years. His obituary in the Times described how he and his father had set up the now world famous Sutton and Sons firm. It went on to describe his many philanthropic acts, especially connected with several Church and Missionary charities. It credited him with holding the inaugural meeting of the Reading Young Men's Christian Association in his own home in 1846[98] (although it was almost certainly in 1844). The Reading Mercury added that "Mr. Sutton was indeed imbued, nay saturated, with the spirit of true religion – ever seeking the good of his fellow man before his own, ever striving to do good in his generation."[99]

The town flags were flown at half mast on the day of the funeral, with shop shutters down and curtains drawn at private houses. These were visible signs of "a genuine and widely felt sorrow at the decease of one of the founders of Reading's greatness." Thousands silently lined the route to Greyfriars and then later on to the cemetery. The cortège was over a mile long with more than 80 carriages. The Church was decorated throughout with flowers; the pathway to the main door was covered with a red carpet.

Martin Hope Sutton of Cintra Lodge, Whitley (14th March 1815 – 4th October 1901)

Photograph from the Greyfriars Annual Report for 1906

The Churchwardens, Alfred Callas and George Fuller, together with the team of sidesmen – Messrs. F. H. Sparrow, F. Wheeler, J. Gilkes, T. North, W. Mann and T. G. Tredenninck – had the difficult task of co-ordinating the seating in the Church. Meanwhile the Organist, Mr. C. H. Thackway, played Mendelssohn's "O Rest in the Lord," and "I know that My Redeemer Liveth" by Handel. The Rev. S. H. Soole conducted the service for his father-in-law, with the help of the Rev. Canon A. M. W. Christopher, Rector of St. Aldate's, Oxford, who had been for many years a close friend of Mr. Sutton, and the Rev. Claude Hope Sutton, son of the deceased (and Vicar of Southwold where Mr. Barkworth was once incumbent). The choir, composed of employees of Messrs. Sutton and Sons, sang the hymn "Hush! Blessed are the dead, in Jesu's arms who rest" as the coffin was borne out of the Church, beginning the journey to the family vault.

Looking back at the year 1901, when writing his letter to the Parishioners and Congregation for the Annual Report in April 1902, the Vicar wrote:

> We are sadly the poorer through the removal from the Church on Earth of such eminently Christian patterns and examples as Miss Mary Neale, Mr. R. C. Dryland, and Mr. M. H. Sutton. Their prayers, their sympathy, and their practical benevolence were most precious and encouraging. Who will take up their work and do what is possible to strengthen our hands and carry on the service which they can no longer render to the cause of Christ? May *we* have grace to follow Christ as they did.

With Martin Hope Sutton's passing came the desire to mark his life with a memorial. In fact Greyfriars has two memorials to him. One, prominent on the wall in the south transept, was paid for and erected by his nine children. The other, a Memorial Hall, was paid for by many subscriptions.

"Memorial tablet erected to the memory of their father
Martin Hope Sutton
Born March 14, 1815, Entered into Rest Oct. 4, 1901
Who was largely instrumental in the restoration of this Church and with his wife a constant worshipper here for 39 years.
Also to the memory of their mother Sophia Woodhead Sutton who entered into rest
Feb 16, 1894, aged 72 years.
By their loving and grateful children
M.J.S E.W.S L.S.S A.W.S
C.H.S. E.M.S. J.C.S.
L.C.S. & F.R.S."

Memorial in the south transept, south wall

Two parts of the text of the south transept memorial are worthy of comment. Since Mr. Sutton died in October 1901, Greyfriars was yet to reach its 38th anniversary service. However, the tablet states that Mr.

Sutton and his wife had worshipped at Greyfriars for 39 years. They may of course have joined Greyfriars from the first days in December 1863, although the first reference I can find that links Mr. Sutton with Greyfriars is his presence at the opening of the Greyfriars' Schools on 29th December 1864. Since there were many local dignitaries at that meeting, unfortunately even this is not conclusive of their presence Sunday by Sunday.[100] One of the Miss Suttons ran a special Scripture Class at the Schools on Fridays, beginning on 15th November 1867, so it is very likely that the family were part of Greyfriars by that date.[101]

The second point of interest is that Mr. Sutton is described as "largely instrumental in the restoration of this Church," whereas neither in the contemporary press coverage nor in the almost contemporary biography of the Rev. W. W. Phelps does Mr. Sutton merit a mention in the restoration story – except for the generous £100 gift towards the restoration listed in the first subscription list. Mr. Phelps and Mr. Sutton certainly knew each other well. They were both active for many years in the Reading Young Men's Christian Association. Some years later, in 1913, Mr. Sutton's eldest son, Martin John Sutton, remembered "as a boy, even when it was still utilised as the Borough Gaol, how he with his revered father, Mr. Martin Hope Sutton, and Archdeacon Phelps knelt down in prayer in the roofless nave of the Church, seeking God's guidance and help in the work which had come to their minds."[102] Although certainly an evocative, even a romantic, image, I do not think that it is likely that this happened as the young Martin John remembered without Martin Hope Sutton's name being connected with the restoration at the time in 1862–63.

As further evidence against Martin Hope Sutton being instrumental in restoring Greyfriars, on the 70th anniversary Alfred Callas was asked to look back to the years leading up to the restoration. He had been born in 1848 and so had been aged 15 in 1863. He had been a member of Greyfriars Church from the restoration. His article recalls work he did as a bell-hanger in the Bridewell, putting bells in each cell that would ring in Mr. Reading's house. He paid tribute to the work of Archdeacon Phelps and of the architect, Mr. Woodman. However, he made no mention of Mr. Sutton.[103]

Perhaps the solution to the mystery is given in a line from Mr. Phelps's biography, when the first donation of £100 had been pledged by the Rev. P. French on the proviso that nine others each gave the same sum. The biography continues: "Some few other gentlemen of means were consulted, with encouraging results."[104] Since we know that Mr. Sutton also gave £100, perhaps he was one of these "gentlemen of means" who provided such encouragement to Mr. Phelps in his scheme.

The Martin Hope Sutton Memorial Hall subscription list opened in March 1902, aiming to raise £500, [105] although that figure was soon revised upwards. Mrs. Soole wrote to the Reading Mercury that "The Committee find that the total cost of carrying out the scheme in its entirety will be £750... The Committee are at once starting the erection of the Hall... this being rendered possible by the very hearty response which has been made to the scheme and to the kind promises of further assistance if required."[106]

The Martin Hope Sutton Memorial Hall

Sackville Street Entrance

Detail of Inscription

The building, designed by architect Ravenscroft, Son, & Morris of the Forbury, was officially opened at 3.30pm on Thursday 27th November 1902. The room was 34 feet long by 20 feet wide with an entrance lobby on the front, at the Sackville Street entrance, and lavatories at the rear. Its facing of flint and stone was designed to match the Church. The main contractor was Messrs. Wheeler of Caversham Road, and Messrs. Callas, Sons & May installed the electric lighting and the hot water heating system.

Special donations for the interior of the Memorial Hall included "an American organ" from the Churchwardens, a Bible from Mr. & Mrs. Goodhart, an oak table from Mr. F. H. Sparrow, and an armchair from the Misses Callas. The newspaper report named just under a hundred of those present.[107]

Earlier that year, Greyfriars held its longest – and last – mission of Mr. Soole's incumbency. From 20th April to 5th May, the Rev. Dr. Jos. Morris preached 35 sermons to very large congregations over 16 consecutive days.[108] According to the Reading Mercury, the Rev. Dr. Morris's sermons were "remarkably interesting and full of illustrations, and he holds the attention of his hearers from beginning to end." The same report commented that Mrs. Morris was "particularly gifted for addressing women" at her 3 o'clock services in the Iron Room, followed by a 6pm service for children.[109] A more sombre note was struck by the Vicar when writing in March 1903, looking back:

> The Mission, conducted with so much ability and spiritual power by Dr. and Mrs. Morris, proved a time of refreshing to many of God's people; while we can hopefully say that "the Lord added to the Church daily such as were being saved." Would that many more had been brought together to hear the wonderful "words of life." Sometimes it was both humbling and saddening to see the many vacant places, and to think that by more visitors from house to house going into the streets and lanes of the town, so many more might have been lovingly called in to hear the "glad tidings of great joy."[110]

The Church Improvement and Warming Fund had collected just over £330 by the end of April 1902.[111] With costs increasing to over £600, the funds proved difficult to realise – by mid-August, receipts had risen by less than £100. However, the "improvements and renewals" went ahead during August, with the Church re-opening on Sunday 31st.[112] The original heating system had been patched up from time to time, but was now completely replaced by Messrs. Callas, Sons & May. A "powerful wrought welded Climax" boiler was installed, with pipe work feeding a total of nine radiators that had sufficient radiating power to warm the 200,000 cubic feet of air space. Following the heating installation, the aisles were re-paved with "unglazed tiles of a dark red colour, having a plain border of similar tiles in dark red, chocolate and buff colours." [113]

On 31st December 1902 Samuel Wheeler died aged 83, having been ill for some months. The Reading building firm of Messrs. Wheeler had been involved in the original restoration of the Church from 1862 and at every stage of building since then. The Wheeler family, becoming the Williams families, have been members and missionaries of Greyfriars down to the present time.

Samuel Wheeler
1819 – 1902

In October 1903 Greyfriars held a Bazaar in the Large Town Hall. In honour of the occasion a special Souvenir Booklet was produced that included an article by the Rev. Alan Cheales on "The Old Greyfriars 1296 -1863," followed by "The Restored Greyfriars 1863 to 1903" written by the Rev. Seymour H. Soole. The Booklet was well illustrated with drawings and photographs, as well as many advertisements and was on sale for the price of 1 shilling. The Vicar concluded his survey of the Restored Greyfriars with a plea:

> We are now anxious to pay off all our liabilities, as well for these Church Improvements, as for the Warming, Lighting and furnishing of the Hall, together with several extras, such as a strong Safe for the Parish Registers, and certain necessary repairs to the Organ. Having done our best we hope that our friends in the Town and County will come forward and liberally help us at this Sale of Work to raise the remaining sum.

The proceeds of the Sale were an astonishing £339 17s 11d, enabling the Church to pay off its liabilities as the Vicar had hoped. The Vicar wrote: "Again we would set up an Ebenezer – a Memorial Stone of Help – and say 'Hitherto hath the Lord helped us'."[114] The reference is to 1 Samuel 7:12, where the prophet Samuel set up a stone as a memorial of God's help in defeating the Philistines, calling it Ebenezer (literally "stone of help").

Mr. Soole preached 94 sermons at Greyfriars in 1903, but only managed 45 in the following year. By March 1904, he was suffering ill health – the first of two significant illnesses that year. He preached on the day of his Curate Edwin Brown's farewell on 6th March, but not again until 24th April. He preached once on the following Sunday, 1st May, but not again until 5th June. Meanwhile his third son, the Rev. Warwick Bathurst Soole, joined him as his Curate, having been previously Curate of St. Mary's, Doncaster.[115]

By January 1905, Mr. Soole (aged 64) had decided that he had to resign due to his continuing ill health. He wrote to the Bishop of Oxford on 27th January, receiving a reply dated 1st February.[116] At the morning service on Sunday 29th January, following a sermon entitled "The Victories of Prayer" based on Matthew 7:8, he said:

> I have a sorrowful announcement to make, dear friends. I could not make it last Sunday without breaking down, and I can hardly tell it to you now; but I must tell you the truth. You have heard it rumoured that I may have to leave this work, and perhaps leave Reading – although that is another matter – because I do not recover my strength so rapidly as we hoped after the two serious illnesses of last year. So I have to tell you that I have written to the Bishop and that he sees with me that my desire to make way for someone stronger for your sakes and for the sake of the parish, which is increasing, is not altogether a foolish one, and we believe it to have been put into my mind by the Spirit of God. While I should like to continue amongst you as your pastor very, very much I think on the whole that I had better yield, having had 30 years of very hard work here.[117]

Writing shortly before his final Sunday, Mr. Soole addressed a letter to the Parishioners and Congregation in the Annual Report:

> To me you have always been so considerate and kind, that I cannot picture to myself any pastor and flock between whom happier relations could have subsisted, during so many years, than between ourselves.[118]

Both Vicar and Curate, father and son, preached their last sermons at Greyfriars on the same day: Easter Day 23rd April 1905. The Rev. Seymour Henry Soole preached at the 11am service on "That Great Shepherd" from Hebrews 13:20-21,[119] closing his ministry at Greyfriars by saying that he could "leave them in the care of the Great Shepherd Who would never fail them, Who would look after them."[120] The Rev. Warwick Bathurst Soole, who had accepted the curacy of St. Barnabas, Holloway, preached his farewell sermon in the evening.

Mr. Soole's last official duty was to chair the Easter Vestry Meeting on the following Tuesday. Mr. Callas agreed to continue as Vicar's Warden and Mr. Fuller was re-elected People's Warden.[121]

On the next day, in the Iron Room, a great number gathered to say a final farewell. Several speeches of grateful thanks for Mr. Soole's years of service were made, with Alfred Callas, Churchwarden for 24 years, being the main speaker. It was at this meeting that the announcement was made that the five Trustees had made the appointment of a new Vicar: the Rev. Hugh Edmund Boultbee, Vicar of St. Peter's, Clifton Wood, Bristol.[122]

Seymour and Laura Soole continued to live in "Sunnyhome" on Castle Crescent and to attend Greyfriars. Their eldest son, Seymour Waldegrave Soole, lived with them. He had been hoping to follow his father into the ministry, but was prevented by recurrent ill health. Instead, he took up journalism, joining the literary staff of the Reading Standard around the time of his father's retirement.

The Sooles' fourth son, Godfrey Hope Soole, had graduated from Sandhurst Royal Military College in late 1902, receiving a special history prize from Lord Roberts, Commander-in-Chief of the British Army, at his passing out parade. Godfrey was made a Cadet in the India Staff Corps. In January 1903, with the rank Second Lieutenant, he set off to join the Indian Army.[123] Two years later, he was transferred from the 3rd Brahman Regiment to the prestigious 21st Indian Cavalry (Prince Albert Victor's Own) at the instigation of Lord Roberts.[124]

On 20th May 1908 Godfrey Hope Soole, by now a Lieutenant, was killed in action at Umra Killi on the North West Frontier, one of 26 casualties that day.[125] There is a memorial brass plaque to him in the south transept. He was buried in Reading Cemetery (at Cemetery Junction), where his gravestone still stands. Lord Roberts, hearing of Godfrey's death, drove over from Ascot to visit the Sooles to express his sympathy.[126]

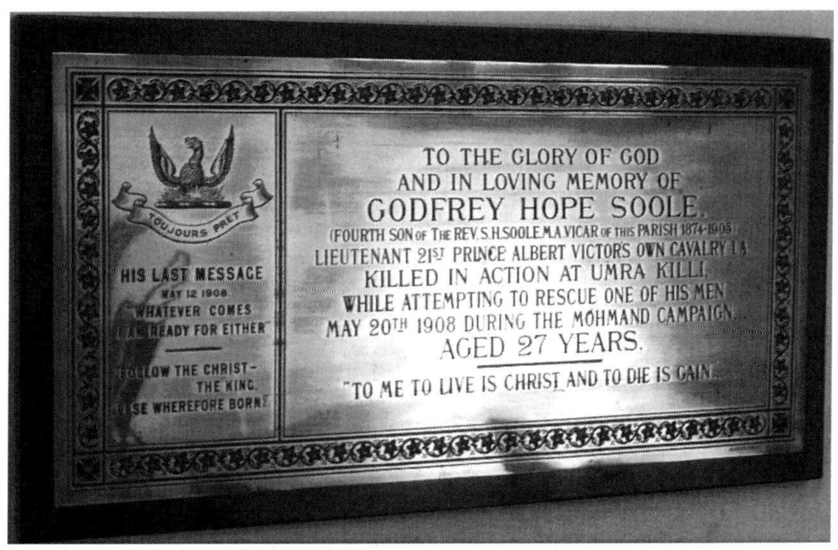

To the Glory of God And in loving memory of
GODFREY HOPE SOOLE
(Fourth son of the Rev. S. H. Soole, M. A., Vicar of this parish 1874 – 1905)
Lieutenant 21st Prince Albert Victor's Own Cavalry I.A. Killed in Action at Umra Killi, While attempting to rescue one of his men May 20th 1908 during the Mohmand Campaign. Aged 27 years.

Brass Memorial, west wall of the south transept

Godfrey's letters home were edited by his mother and were published as a memorial volume: "Ready for Either: Incidents in the Life of a Young Cavalry Officer," which was published in 1911, running to a second edition in 1912. The title came from Godfrey's last letter home, dated 12th May 1908, considering the danger he was in and wondering if he would live through it or not: he wrote "Whatever comes, I am ready for either." This last message is commemorated on the brass plaque.

The Rev. Seymour Henry Soole died from cancer on Saturday 8th June 1912 at home, having been ill for some months.[127] His funeral took place in Greyfriars at 2.30pm on the following Wednesday, with the Rev. H. E. Boultbee officiating.[128] The Church was full, although sadly Mrs. Soole, who had long been an invalid, was unable to be present. On top of the coffin were "two simple wreaths – one of evergreens and the other of lilies of the valley – ... and beside them lay open the deceased's pulpit bible, eloquently symbolical of Mr. Soole's faithful testimony and long ministry."[129] He was buried close to his son Godfrey's grave in Reading Cemetery. Mr. Boultbee wrote of him, in the Annual Parish Report:

> It is impossible to speak, with full justice, of his influence in Reading, of his faithful adherence to Evangelical principles, of his devotion to his Lord and Master, of his prayer life – his prayers were an inspiration – of his loving, gentle character, of all that his ministry has meant to very many of Greyfriars' people – or his triumphant end. Personally I owe him more than I can express – and I feel that in losing him, I have lost one of my best earthly friends.[130]

Memorial to the Rev. S. H. Soole
Now on the north wall

One year later, on Saturday 7th June 1913, a Memorial tablet to Mr. Soole was erected in Greyfriars and placed on the east wall near the reading desk. It was unveiled by Alfred Callas at the conclusion of a special service of prayer and praise. Noting how keen the congregation had been to contribute towards the Memorial, the Vicar said:

> It was not that Mr. Soole's friends needed reminding of his work among them, for his memory was enshrined within their hearts, and his work had laid a foundation that they all could build upon... but it would be of use to future generations who, after those alive were now gone, would come and worship in that Church; they would look on the tablet and learn that it was in memory of one who had done much for the spread of the Christian Church in the town.[131]

The mural tablet was constructed of red and green alabaster, inlaid with a narrow border of mother-of-pearl. The college arms of St. John's, Cambridge, where Mr. Soole had studied, were engraved between the dates of his Vicariate. The design for the Memorial was by Basil Sutton, of Messrs. Webb & Sutton, and the work was carried out by Messrs. Wheeler Bros., masons. The text on the Memorial says:

TO THE GLORY OF GOD AND IN LOVING MEMORY OF
SEYMOUR HENRY SOOLE M.A.
FOR 31 YEARS VICAR OF THIS PARISH
Who Entered Into Rest June 8th 1912 Aged 71 Years
WELL DONE GOOD AND FAITHFUL SERVANT
This tablet has been erected by his Many Friends
1874 – 1905

There is one other Memorial to a member of the Soole family in Greyfriars Church: a brass plaque commemorating Seymour Waldegrave Soole, Seymour and Laura's oldest son. Although deemed unfit for service at the outbreak of the Great War, he was finally enrolled as a Gunner on 12th January 1917. He reported for training at Hilsea Barracks, Cosham, near Portsmouth, but within three weeks had died of cerebro meningitis, contracted while training. In a letter written to Mrs. Soole, Major C. H. Hannington wrote "I shall only be expressing the feeling of all the officers and men of his battery in saying how deeply we sympathize with you in your great sorrow, and it may be some small compensation to know that during the brief time he had been with us your son had made himself liked and respected by all who knew him."[132]

The family were offered a military funeral, but decided against it. The funeral took place at Greyfriars on 6th February, with his coffin draped in a Union Jack. He was buried at Reading Cemetery and shares a headstone with his brother Godfrey.[133] Laura Soole died on 31 July 1927, aged 75.[134]

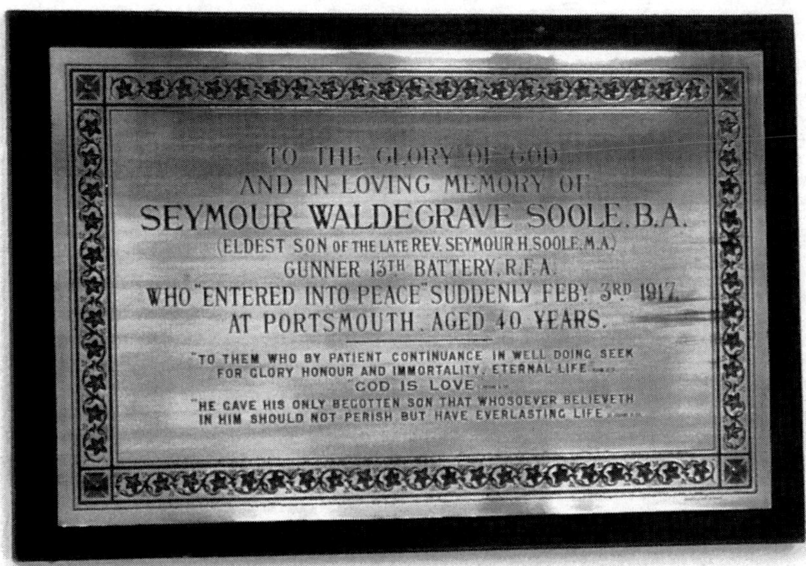

To the Glory of God And in Loving Memory of
SEYMOUR WALDEGRAVE SOOLE, B. A.
(Eldest son of the late Rev. Seymour H. Soole, M. A.)
Gunner 13th Battery R.F.A.
Who "Entered into Peace" suddenly Feb.y 3rd 1917
At Portsmouth, aged 40 years.

Brass Memorial, west wall of the south transept

Interior of Greyfriars Church around 1900[135]
Above: Looking North East
Below Looking South East

Rev. H. E. Boultbee and wife Amy c 1909
Children: Back: Amy, James, Edith; Front: Margaret, Joseph
(Used with permission from "The History of the Boultbee Family")

Chapter 13

Hugh Edmund Boultbee: Vicar 1905 to 1915

Greyfriars' third Vicar – and the first to live in the Vicarage next door – was the Rev. Hugh Edmund Boultbee, who was aged 37 and married with 5 children at the time of his institution in July 1905. [1] Like the first Vicar, he was a Yorkshireman, having been born in Leeds on 23rd June 1868.[2]

Hugh was from a family of clergymen. His father, James, had been Vicar of Wrangthorn near Leeds since 1866, remaining there until his retirement some 42 years later. Hugh's father's brother, the Rev. Thomas P. Boultbee, was the founding Principal of the London College of Divinity in 1863. However, initially, Hugh was not going to add to their number. Following his education at Leeds Grammar School he was apprenticed to Handswell, Clarke & Co. as a railway engineer. Before long he changed direction and went to Durham University, graduating in 1891 as B.A. and L.Th. (Licentiate in Theology).[3] The following year he was ordained Deacon, taking up the post of Curate at St. James, Doncaster.[4] He was ordained Priest in 1893.[5]

In February 1895 Hugh married Amy Lumb of Wrangthorn[6] and in December that year their first child, James, was born. In 1897 Hugh received an M.A. from Durham University.[7] That year, Hugh became Senior Curate at St. Paul's, Southwark, then in 1901 Vicar of St. Peter's, Clifton Wood, Bristol.[8]

Mr. Boultbee later stated that it was largely as a result of the influence of one of the Greyfriars' Trustees, the Rev. George Ferris Whidborne, that he accepted the post at Greyfriars in 1905.[9] This is an interesting indication of the role the five Trustees have played in the life of the Church.

Mr. Boultbee's Institution as Vicar of Greyfriars took place at 12.30pm on Monday 24th July 1905 in the presence of a large congregation that included the Mayor, Martin John Sutton. Former Curate, the Rev. W. B. Soole, and the Rev. James Consterdine of St. Mary's Chapel assisted the Bishop of Oxford.[10]

At the 11am service on his first Sunday as Vicar, Mr. Boultbee, as all new Vicars did, read the "39 Articles of Religion." Mr. Boultbee preached in each of the next twenty-two services – a sequence broken by his father, the Rev. James Boultbee, who preached in the morning of 17th September. Hugh Boultbee went on to preach 68 of the 76 sermons between his Institution and the end of 1905.[11]

Within the first couple of months, the new Vicar changed the Church services, bringing in the use of the Service Book, a shortened form of the Prayer Book. This may have met with some opposition as, later looking back to his first eighteen months as Vicar, Mr. Boultbee wrote: "Where a tendency to criticise our methods seemed to exist, now a beautiful spirit of harmony reigns over the various branches of our organization."[12]

Postcard of Greyfriars Church c1905

In September 1905, Mr. Boultbee was joined by a former colleague from Bristol: Edwin Taylor, a Lay Missioner. Mr. Taylor had been associated with the Church Army for several years before spending four years as Missioner on the Bethel ship in Bristol[13] where he had worked closely with Mr. Boultbee. His role in Greyfriars was to lead the work of the Iron Room, which from this point was re-named as the "Greyfriars Mission Hall," reaching out into the parish. Mr. Taylor continued in this work for the next eight years, until moving on to another lay post at Dunsden,

Oxfordshire, between Caversham and Shiplake.[14]

The parish work was greatly assisted by two Lady Workers, Miss Wells and Miss Pirouet. Miss Anne Wells led Bible classes in the parish, including one at 3pm every Sunday in the Mission Hall. She was also closely involved in various Mothers' Meetings and Open-Air Meetings. Much of her work was among those whom the Vicar called the "Hooligan Class... this most unsatisfactory class of young men."[15] On her death aged 67 on 16th March 1912, the Greyfriars' Parish Magazine noted her "extraordinary will-power and enthusiasm" right to the end of her life and that "she will be greatly missed by Greyfriars' people. Her brightness, her kind sympathy and her love for all for whom she had to do, won for her a very warm place in the hearts of our people."[16]

Since 1901, Miss E. Pirouet had been the main Lady Worker. With a stipend of £73 3s in 1906, hers was a full-time role in the Church. She visited the poor families in the parish, in Mr. Boultbee's words, "grappling with that most difficult problem of poor relief." She also led a Mothers' Meeting in Somerset Place, the most deprived part of the parish – including the notorious district of The Pits, known as Reading's worst slum. On Friday evenings, assisted by Miss Wells and some other ladies, she ran classes in the Memorial Hall educating girls from all parts of Reading for domestic service. The syllabus included sewing, knitting, dressmaking, cookery and "ambulance work." She continued in this work until a combination of her poor health and difficulty in the Church of raising the money for her stipend led to her resignation in November 1914.[17]

Visiting throughout the parish was shared by a system that divided the area into 36 parts, for example "York Road, 1 to 61 (odd numbers only)." In 1906, 21 women and 6 men covered 28 of these, with the remaining being vacant. These visits very often resulted in relief being given from the Greyfriars' "Sick and Poor Fund." In 1906, 662 grants of relief were made. The Annual Report for that year described the application of the fund:

> This fund is distributed chiefly through the medium of our District Visitors. The Clergy, Lay Missioner, and Lady Workers have intimate knowledge of every case to whom relief is granted. Every case is duly sifted and considered at the weekly meetings at the Vicarage, and usually help is given in either bread, meat, coal or groceries... Nine adults were sent to Convalescent Homes or to friends in the country. We have been able to find employment for several women, and would be glad to recommend such for supply, - cooking, cleaning, and needlework by hand or machine. We should be deeply thankful for gifts of old clothes, and boots and shoes, especially the latter for the children.[18]

In February 1906 there was a Mission Hall mission, led by Mr. Goudie of the Evangelization Society: "Many souls found their Saviour under the stirring and persuasive message so earnestly given by the Missioner. It is gratifying to note, that of these converts a large proportion are standing steadfast in their faith."[19]

On the first Sunday of Lent, 4th March 1906, Mr. Boultbee's first Curate arrived, preaching at the 6.30pm service that day. The Rev. Hope Charles Tiarks, aged 35, married and with a young family like the Vicar, moved into "Glendower" on Western Elms Avenue. He had previously been a Curate in Birmingham and in Church Gresley, Derbyshire. In his later career, he became the author of several books, beginning with "Eternal Certainties: or The War, the World and the Future" published in 1918. His son John became the Bishop of Chelmsford in 1962.

Mr. Tiarks had come to Greyfriars having been hand-picked by the Vicar in order to spearhead work among men in the parish. On Sunday 1st April a 3pm (thereafter at 3.30pm) service for men only was inaugurated. Greyfriars had had such special services for men before, but this was the start of a weekly service and of a whole new organisational branch of Greyfriars. 26 were present on the first Sunday, growing to around 50 in the summer and by December membership stood at 176 with weekly attendance being well over 100.

The 4 Curates who worked with Mr. Boultbee	From	To	Next destination
Hope Charles Tiarks	1906	1908	Vicar: Holy Trinity, Kilburn
John Stern	1908	1911	Vicar: St. Peter, Clifton Wood
George Wigram Neatby	1911	1914	Vicar: St. Paul, Devonport
Isaiah Siviter	1914	1917	Vicar: St. John the Baptist, Harborne

The "Greyfriars' Men's Service" chose the aim "Men for Christ" with motto "Others." Its organisation was aided by the formation of a committee (of 21!) by the end of the first month. Numbered membership cards were issued and a Visiting Committee aimed to keep in touch with all who had attended. The Service had its own small orchestra and choir under the leadership of Charles Thackway, Organist, giving the Sunday services a "bright and hearty character." In a great departure for Greyfriars, the services used a special movable pulpit in the centre aisle of the Church. The "message is always the plain simple gospel, but in such a way as to bear on the daily life of men." One Sunday a month was devoted to answering questions submitted in writing.

These highly successful first few months culminated in a "Mass Men's Gathering" on 27th November 1906 at the Abbey Hall with an address from the Chaplain General of the Army, Bishop Taylor Smith D. D., entitled "The Dignity of Manhood," described as "over an hour's straight talk with the audience, and, what was rather novel, [he] drove home his points by the aid of a blackboard and a piece of chalk." [20] He was clearly ahead of his time with visual aids! By the end of 1907 the number of members had risen to 230 on the register, with an average attendance for the year of 111.[21]

Churchwardens George Fuller and Alfred Callas
Photographs from October 1903 Greyfriars' Church Bazaar Booklet

At the Easter Vestry Meeting on 17th April 1906, Mr. Boultbee nominated Alfred Callas as his Warden. George Fuller was re-elected unopposed as People's Warden.[22]

Churchwardens during Mr. Boultbee's incumbency (1905 – 1915)		
April 1905 to April 1915	Mr. Alfred Callas	Mr. George Fuller
April 1915 to April 1916	Mr. Fred Wheeler	Mr. Joseph Gilkes

An exciting development took place in June 1906 with the selection for missionary service of the first person from Greyfriars. There had been previous missionaries supported by the Church and at least one former Curate was involved in the mission field. However, this was Greyfriars' own Miss Elsie Sparrow, who had been a Sunday School teacher and had done much work in the parish. Following her selection for "foreign service" by the Church Missionary Society (CMS), she left for Colombo, Ceylon (now Sri Lanka), in October 1906.

Elsie was the daughter of Frederick and Eleanor Sparrow. The firm of F. H. & J. Sparrow, Cabinet Makers, Upholsterers and Carpet Warehousemen, of 83 & 93 Oxford Road (from 1895 at nos. 128 & 129 Friar Street), had been established in early 1883, following the family's move to Reading from Acton that year. The family soon became prominent Greyfriars' members, with the first reference I can find being the donation of an "admirable platform" for a musical performance in the Iron Room in December 1885.[23] By the following Easter, Mr. F. H. Sparrow had been elected as one of the two sidesmen for the Iron Room.[24]

The family's connection with the Iron Room/Mission Hall continued throughout the ensuing years, with Frederick being the Mission Hall treasurer from 1887 to 1906, and Eleanor being co-leader of the Mission Hall Mothers' Meetings. Frederick had also been a sidesman at Greyfriars from at least 1901 and by 1906 was superintendent of the Greyfriars' Boys' Sunday School.

Greyfriars undertook fully to support Miss Sparrow financially, at an initial cost of £120 per annum.[25] Miss Sparrow's letters home reported that she was able to cope with the intense heat of Ceylon, but found the intricacies of the Sinhalese language problematical.[26] After five years in Ceylon, Miss Sparrow came back to England to marry a fellow CMS missionary, Rev. George A. Purser, on 19th July 1911 in Greyfriars.

Returning to Ceylon in 1912, they lived in Baddegama where Mrs. Purser took charge of a Boarding School of 46 girls while her husband was Missioner-in-Charge of the CMS District. In 1916 they moved to Dodanduwa, on the coast, so that George could superintend the District from there – 21 schools (nearly 1700 pupils in all) and about 650 Christians in the churches throughout the region.

They returned to Reading, with their young daughter Eleanor, for an 18 month furlough in 1919 and during that time George served as Curate to the Rev. William A. Doherty, Greyfriars' fourth Vicar.

MISS ELSIE SPARROW

"Our Own Missionary"
(From "Parish of Greyfriars', Reading, Annual Reports and Accounts for the Year ending December 31st 1906")

Back in Ceylon, in 1921 Elsie became Principal of a different Girls' School while her husband became incumbent of St. Luke's, Colombo, Superintending Missionary for the area and Manager of the English Boys' School! They returned to England permanently in 1923 as CMS had to withdraw its missionaries from the country due to falling financial support. At this point, Mrs. Purser ceased to be Greyfriars' "Own Missionary." George Purser then became Vicar of Barlestone, Leicestershire.

During Mr. Boultbee's incumbency, there was one other almost home grown missionary, Miss Sophy Venour Fletcher, daughter of Admiral John Venour Fletcher, whose memorial plaque is in the south transept (see page 129). Sophy had been born in Reading in 1852 and had lived with her parents, then her widowed mother until she was in her 40s. At some time before 1901, she had moved to Burbage in Leicestershire, where she was described as 'Living on her own means' in the 1901 census. In September 1909 Sophy went out to Hong Kong as a missionary, to join her sister Selena who had gone out in 1892. After her death less than two years later, Mr. Boultbee wrote of Sophy:

> ... we have to allude with sorrow to the death of one of our Greyfriars Missionaries, on whose work of faith and labour of love in our Parish many can look back thankfully – I refer to Miss Sophy Fletcher, Missionary in Hong Kong. She had been for many years a valued Sunday School Teacher and District Visitor in this Parish, and it was while she was Sunday School Superintendent that the call for foreign service came to her. Her life was an especially useful one, for from her earliest days she had devoted herself to the cause of her Saviour.[27]

She is buried in the Old Hong Kong Cemetery, where her headstone states: "In loving memory of Sophy Venour Fletcher beloved daughter of Admiral J V Fletcher born in Reading died in Hong Kong 11th August 1911."[28] Her estate, which passed to her younger sister Selena, was valued at almost £6000 according to the probate record.[29] Selena returned to England the following year, retiring eventually to Llandudno, where she died in 1944.

Miss Sophy Fletcher is also remembered in Greyfriars for a gift that became the Chancel Building Fund. She had put £50 into Reading Savings' Bank, acting according to her mother's wishes following the latter's death in 1888,[30] towards the building of a chancel at Greyfriars. The bank book remained in Sophy's hands and, after her death, was passed by Selena to Mr. Boultbee in 1912, by which time it had grown to £91 14s 1d. The first mention in the Annual Reports of this gift is for 1923, where it stated that with interest it now had reached the total of £132 15s,[31] rising gradually to £249 18s 6d by 31st December 1936.[32] It became a matter of opinion whether the money had to be kept until a chancel was built, or whether it could be used for other Greyfriars' purposes.

At the annual Greyfriars' Social Gathering in the Town Hall on Wednesday 25th March 1908,[33] Mr. Boultbee looked back on much success during his first three years as Vicar. He reported that the total number of communicants per year had almost doubled over the past seven years, from 1446 to 2816. At the Iron Room/Mission Hall there were Sunday evening congregations of 500 to 600 at times, with over 300 attending the Wednesday evening meeting. However, he also had to announce the forthcoming departure of his Curate, Hope Tiarks, who had accepted the living of Holy Trinity, Kilburn. Mr. Tiarks's last day at Greyfriars was on 7th June.[34] The Vicar also announced the forthcoming retirement of the Headmaster of the Greyfriars' Schools – William Moore.

Mr. Moore had become Headmaster when the Schools opened – in fact he was officially appointed on Christmas Day (being a Quarter Day) 1864. Born in 1843 – and therefore just 21 when appointed – he was first a Pupil Teacher at Kington National School, Herefordshire, before completing his 1 year training at Saltley in Birmingham.[35] Mr. Moore completed nearly 44 years as Headmaster, leaving on 2nd April 1908. On the following evening there was a large gathering at the Schools to honour his career and to present him with a "Morocco leather purse containing £52, a framed and illuminated address and a leather album with the names of the subscribers, of whom there were about 120."

> The Vicar, having expressed his great sorrow that Mr. Moore was retiring on so small a pension, said he felt very grateful to the late Headmaster for his work. He had been strikingly able to exercise a good, manly and Christian influence on those who had been brought under the roof of that School (applause). Mr. Moore could not be regarded as a man of namby-pamby instincts, but rather one who believed in the gold old adage that if they spared the rod they spoilt the child (laughter and applause). [36]

Mr. Moore was replaced as Headmaster by William Thomas Kirby, a former pupil at Greyfriars' Schools and a Pupil Teacher there from 1891 to January 1896. Mr. Kirby had gained his Certificate at Birmingham University in 1898 and became Assistant Master at Boxmoor, Hertfordshire. He returned to Greyfriars as Assistant Master in September 1904, becoming Headmaster of Greyfriars' Schools when aged 31. He remained in post until 1925, except for the period from 26th August 1914 until February 1919 when he served on the Western Front.[37]

In July 1908 the Rev. John Stern, senior Curate of All Souls, Langham Place, became Greyfriars' 20th Curate.[38] Like his predecessor, his main task was the Men's Service on Sunday afternoons. The next Curate, the Rev. George Wigram Neatby, arrived in the week following Mr. Stern's departure in February 1911.

In February 1909 there was a mission in the Mission Hall, taken by Wycliffe Pascoe. In a little black notebook, 19 year old Miss Edie Sherwood wrote of one of Mr. Pascoe's talks:

> The older we grow in the Christian life the more we know of the riches of his

> grace, we do not get flooded all at once but bit by bit we have the grace for the need. All things work together for good to them that love God, to them that are called according to his purpose. Then we are to be holy and blameless, God takes us as his adopted children and we become joint heirs with Christ, to all the inheritance of God. We may not be millionaires down here and keep a motor car, but one day we shall be spiritual millionaires...[39]

Edith Sherwood was certainly not a millionaire, since she was at this time a parlourmaid in Goring. Together with her sister Eva Nellie (known as Nellie), the two Miss Sherwoods became great Greyfriars' stalwarts. Nellie played the Mission Hall organ for 43 years from 1923 to 1966. Nellie died aged 74 in 1973 followed by Edith three years later, aged 86.

Mr. Boultbee wrote in his annual letter "To the Congregations of Greyfriars' Parish Church and Mission Hall" in April 1910 of a major concern of the Church's ministry among the young:

> There is, however, one sad feature of our work amongst the young, namely, our inability to keep in touch with young lads of the age of 15 and upwards. The proportion of those who, having passed through our Sunday Schools, continue under Christian influences and under Bible Class Teaching, is alas! very small... Lads now-a-days consider themselves to be men when they leave school and begin to earn a few shillings a week in wages, and seem to recoil from things Christian in their desire to be thought manly. It is a matter of great concern to me and many of my workers that they can roam about the parish in gangs, encouraging each other in that which is unmanly and demoralising...[40]

In order to try to reach these groups, Mr. Boultbee announced the formation of a Greyfriars' Troop of Boy Scouts. Lord Robert Baden-Powell's 'Scouting for Boys' had been published in six fortnightly parts from January 1908 and by the first Scout census in September 1910 there were just over 100,000 Scouts. Greyfriars' Troop was therefore among many early groups. Initially the Troop had 12 members, rising to 27 by July 1912.[41] Their meetings consisted of instruction in "Ambulance, Morse and Semaphore Signalling, Physical Drill and Exercises, Map Reading and Drawing, Pioneering, Knotting and Splicing, and outdoor work such as Tracking, Stalking, Firelighting, Cooking, Dispatch Runs and Scouting Games."

The life of the Church encompassed many areas. This is well illustrated in the list below of accounts in the Annual Report and Accounts for 1911:

Parochial:

- Churchwardens' Account
- Greyfriars' Mothers' Meetings (including Memorial Hall, Mission Hall, Greyfriars' Schoolroom, Somerset Place Mission)
- Lady Worker's Fund
- Greyfriars' Loan Blanket Society
- Congregational Tea Account
- Greyfriars' Parish Magazine
- The Greyfriars' Mission Hall
- Sick and Poor Fund
- Somerset Place Mission
- Assistant Clergy and Lay Missioner's Fund
- General Purposes Fund
- Greyfriars' Infants' Friend Society
- Greyfriars' Mutual Benefit Society
- Greyfriars' Men's Service

Educational:

- Sunday School Fund
- Greyfriars' Sunday School Treat Fund
- Greyfriars' Young Women's Christian Association
- Reading Association Greyfriars' Troop Boy Scouts
- Greyfriars' Day School
- Greyfriars' Temperance Society
- Greyfriars' Band of Hope

Missionary:

- Greyfriars' Church Missionary Association (including Greyfriars' Gleaners' Union, "Our Own Missionary" Fund)
- Church Pastoral Aid Society
- London Society for Promoting Christianity amongst the Jews
- British and Foreign Bible Society

The total receipts for the year were £1929 5s 3d.

At this time there was a growing concern about the future of the Greyfriars' Schools. The local Board of Education condemned the accommodation due to "insufficient lavatory accommodation for the Infants' Department, and also of inadequate playground space."[42] Various plans were proposed but the Board of Education did not approve. Discussions continued until interrupted by the War.

In August 1912 Mr. Boultbee took out a loan with the Governors of

Queen Anne's Bounty. This was a mortgage on the Vicarage for the sum of £100 in order to carry out improvements to the house. The mortgage was drawn up for a term of 18 years, with payment of interest at 4% per annum plus one fifteenth of the principal.[43] In fact Greyfriars paid the sum in less than seven years, as it was reported "extinguished" at the Easter Vestry Meeting in April 1919.[44]

Mr. Boultbee was a great man of prayer. Throughout his letters to the congregation he exhorts everyone to pray and to join in praying together. A good example can be found in his Letter in the October 1912 Parish Magazine:

> My Dear Friends, We are just about to commence our Winter's Work. In preparation for this we shall (D. V.) meet together in Prayer on October 9th. The list of subjects for Prayer is given [below]. I long to see a goodly number of our Congregation gathering together with us and taking a real and Prayerful interest in all that concern's Christ's Kingdom in the Parish. There are many organizations needing our prayers, and without this work of intercession there is always the danger that these various organizations may drift into a mere mechanical effort, capable it may be, of much bustle and semblance of activity but lacking in real results. May God deliver us from mere organization, if it does not lead to souls saved. Hence the need of safeguarding every part of our work by throwing round it a rampart of Prayer and Faith.
>
> Then I am asking you to join with us (till October 19th) in Prayer for the Holy Spirit on the evenings subsequent to the Day of Prayer.

The schedule given for the Day of Prayer in the Mission Hall was:

Hour	Subjects for Prayer	Chairman
7-8	Prayer for the Holy Spirit's Teaching and Guidance throughout the Day.	The Vicar
8-9	Thanksgiving	Mr. E. Taylor
9-10	Our District Visitors	
10-11	Work Amongst Men	Rev. G. W. Neatby
11-12	Foreign Missionary Work	Dr. White
12-1	Home Missions (C.P.A.S. and Work at our Mission Hall)	Mr. E. Taylor
2-3	Work amongst young women (Y.W.C.A.)	Rev. J. Consterdine
3-4	Work amongst women (Mothers' Meetings and Bible Classes)	Mrs. White
4-5	Work amongst young men (Bible Classes, Y.M.C.A. &c)	Rev. G. W. Neatby

5-6	Our Nation and Rulers	
6-7	Temperance Work	Mr. E. Taylor
7-8	Work amongst the Young (Sunday Schools, Band of Hope, Scripture Union)	The Vicar
8-9	Consecration Hour	Dr. White

In the following month's magazine the Vicar wrote that it was a cause of great thankfulness that so many of the congregation gathered for the Day of Prayer and for the following ten days as Dr. White preached on the "Work and Person of the Holy Spirit."

The main focus of the following year – 1913 – was the celebration of Greyfriars' Jubilee, its 50th anniversary. It was decided to hold an "Octave" of services with sermons by former Curates. The Vicar wrote a short Souvenir Booklet "The Church of the Grey Friars, Reading," price 3d, to raise money towards the £500 needed for repairs to the Church. He wrote:

> At the end of the fifty years, we find portions of this fine old edifice showing signs of unmistakable decay. The condition of its west end is serious; the flint work is loose and the stone mouldings are in a crumbling state. Its interior, with its vast roof, urgently cries out for repair and thorough cleansing. But all this lies far beyond the resources of a congregation like that of Greyfriars Church, which though it is a large one, is nevertheless a poor one.
>
> We appeal to our fellow townsmen to give, as God has blessed them, to the prosecution of this work.

While the actual 50th anniversary was on 2nd December 1913, the eight services ran through the following week. Below are the details of the Octave of Services:

Date	Preacher
Monday 8th 7.30pm	Rev. E. B. Brown (Curate 1901 – 1904)
Tuesday 9th 3pm	Rev. G. W. Neatby (Curate at this date)
Tuesday 9th 7.30pm	Rev. C. A. Worsfold (Curate 1895 – 1896)
Wednesday 10th 7.30pm	Rev. W. B. Soole (Curate 1904 – 1905)
Thursday 11th 7.30pm	Rev. S. L. Dixon (Curate 1876 – 1878)
Friday 12th 7.30pm	Rev. J. Stern (Curate 1908 – 1911)
Sunday 14th 11am	Canon E. A. Stuart (Trustee of the Benefice)
Sunday 14th 6.30pm	Canon E. A. Stuart (Trustee of the Benefice)

The Jubilee Services raised over £200 towards the cost of the repairs needed to the Church.[45]

Shortly into the new year, Curate Rev. George Neatby moved to become Vicar of St. Paul's, Devonport, preaching his final sermon at Greyfriars on 18th January 1914.[46] It was not until 16th August that a new Curate started – Rev. Isaiah Siviter – and as a result Mr. Boultbee was under a great deal of strain. He wrote apologetically in the Annual Report for 1913, which appeared in print in the late summer of 1914, that:

> The Annual Report for 1913 has been unduly delayed – but I must crave your indulgence and offer for my excuse for its late appearance a continuance of nerve strain which has been troubling me throughout the year. For seven months I have been working at high pressure without a Curate, and four sermons (sometimes five and six) have been demanded of me each week to say nothing of smaller addresses to Bible classes, &c.

In a period reminiscent of his first few months in charge in 1905, Mr. Boultbee preached 89 sermons in the Church in 27 weeks in 1914.[47]

This was a time of sadness for Mr. Boultbee; his sister Alice died on January 12th. Alice was 13 years Hugh's senior and had remained unmarried. She lived with her parents in 13 Brunswick Hill, Reading, following the move from Wrangthorn on her father's retirement in 1908. The three Boultbees had then attended Greyfriars. Hugh wrote in the February 1914 Parish Magazine: "Nothing has touched me or my aged parents so much as those letters of condolence which have evinced the existence of a close personal friendship between her and so many of our people."

Hard on the heels of losing his Curate, the Mission Hall Lay Missioner, Edwin Taylor, left on 15th February, to take up a similar post in Dunsden. He was replaced by Captain Tibble of the Church Army, who arrived to take over the work of the Mission Hall on 11th March 1914.[48]

In the spring and early summer of 1914, Messrs. Ravenscroft & Morris, architects, produced a plan for the renovation of the Church. The total expense was expected to be in the region of £400 to £500. The Jubilee Service offerings and other collections totalled about £250 by this point. The Church was due to be closed for the last three Sundays in August, with services taking place at the Mission Hall. However, world events intervened when the Great War broke out and the United Kingdom declared war on Germany on 4th August.

The decision was taken by the Vicar and Wardens to postpone the proposed renovation of the Church. Mr. Boultbee wrote:

> ...that in view of the many demands for money which would come to our people during the next few months, and the fact that so many of our supporters have no fixed income but receive a weekly wage, which may be much less in amount during the coming winter, it would hardly be right to make expenditure of money and issue an appeal for the amount needed. Our poorer friends will need every penny they earn for the necessities of life this winter, especially with the increase in prices which must prevail. The work, due for the interior of our Church, can well give place to the more urgent demands of the general situation.[49]

When the Head Master of the Greyfriars' Mixed Junior School, William Kirby, was called to military service on the Western Front on 26th August 1914, he was replaced by Sydney Marsh as Acting Head. Mr. Marsh joined the army on 1st April 1916 and so was replaced in turn by Alfred Briers as Acting Head, seconded from Redlands' Boys' School. He remained Acting Head for nearly two years, moving to become Head Master of Hindley Green School in Lancashire at the end of March 1918. James Piper became the last Acting Head, in post from 9th April 1918 to 4th February 1919, at which point William Kirby returned to his old post.[50]

Intercession Services were set up in the Church at 12 noon each day from Monday to Saturday "for our Country and Soldiers and Sailors," beginning on Monday 17th August 1914 and continuing until almost the end of the war.[51] There were also prayer meetings in the evenings in the Memorial Hall on Mondays and Wednesdays and in the Mission Hall on Saturdays. At each gathering those in action from the parish and from families connected with the Mission Hall and Church were prayed for by name. A list was kept by Ernest Rivers numbering 317 names.[52]

Meanwhile arrangements continued for what was the only Mission at Greyfriars during Mr. Boultbee's incumbency, which took place from 15th to 30th November 1914 with missioner the Rev. Francis Wilmot Eardley. With 20 Services at Greyfriars, 15 Prayer Meetings and 8 Bible Readings, the sixteen days were very busy – especially when the daily Intercession Services from Monday to Saturday were included! Mr. Boultbee wrote:

> We do indeed thank God for sending His servant to us; his knowledge of Bible Truth and the wonderful gift, which he possesses, of being able to expound it so simply and so clearly, have greatly helped our people. The attendances at the services, for some unaccountable reason, have been small. But each service has been characterised by great power. God has been near to us, and I feel sure that 'the Day' will reveal work done for eternity.[53]

1914 proved to be a sad year for Mr. Boultbee. Having lost his sister Alice in January, his father James died aged 87 in December.[54] His memorial service took place at Greyfriars, conducted by a nephew and a grandson, with clergymen sons Hugh and Henry and daughter Agnes as chief mourners.

At the Easter Vestry Meeting in 1915 Alfred Callas retired from being Vicar's Warden after serving as Churchwarden since 1881. The Vicar nominated Fred Wheeler as his Warden in his place. In the election for People's Warden, George Fuller, Churchwarden since 1901, was replaced by Mr. J. C. Gilkes.[55]

This Easter Vestry Meeting was Mr. Boultbee's last, as he resigned his post later in the year to take up the post of Vicar at Christ Church, Surbiton. The members of the Church and Mission Hall gathered in the schoolrooms to pay tribute to the Rev. H. E. and Mrs. Boultbee on Wednesday 1st December 1915. Martin H. F. Sutton, one of the Trustees of the living, said in his speech that "Mr. Boultbee's incumbency at Greyfriars would be remembered by them all for his truly spiritual work and conversion of souls."[56]

The Boultbees were presented with a cheque for £100 and a solid silver tea service from the congregation. On the following Sunday, 5th December, Mr. Boultbee preached his final sermons at Greyfriars at 11am, 3.30pm (the men's service, but on this special occasion women were admitted too!) and 6.30pm.[57]

One way to gauge the success of Mr. Boultbee's time at Greyfriars is to consider the number of communicants per year at the Church. In the two years before Mr. Boultbee started, the numbers were 1751 and 1947. Thereafter, for the pre-war years:[58]

Year	1905	1906	1907	1908	1909	1910	1911	1912	1913
Communicants	2664	2749	2816	2928	3050	3054	3802	3662	4124

Hugh Boultbee remained Vicar of Christ Church, Surbiton, until 1918, at which point he took up what proved to be his final post as Rector of Bebington on the Wirral. He died aged 73 in 1941, a year after his wife Amy.

Several sections of the Church fellowship, upon Mr. Boultbee's resignation, wrote petitions to the Trustees proposing the Curate, Isaiah Siviter, as successor. Petitions were sent by Church Officers and seat-holders, members of the Men's Service congregation, teachers of the

Sunday School and the congregation at the Mission Hall.[59] However, the Trustees' choice fell elsewhere, with William Augustus Doherty being appointed in December 1915[60]. Meanwhile Mr. Siviter remained in charge, conducting 62 of the 65 services between Mr. Boultbee's departure and Mr. Doherty's arrival.

In December 1915 Captain John Tibble died,[61] having been in charge of the work at the Mission Hall for just 9 months. He had impressed all with his hard work throughout the parish. He was succeeded in early February 1916 by Captain J. C. Jones.[62]

Greyfriars Church
(From the 1913 Anniversary Booklet)
The image is criss-crossed with tramwires

Rev. William Augustus Doherty
(Photograph from Berkshire Chronicle 20th June 1924)

Chapter 14

William Augustus Doherty: Vicar 1916 to 1924

William Augustus Doherty was born in Kenilworth, Warwickshire, in May 1873,[1] the youngest of four children. His father, William Butler Doherty, had been born near Dublin and in 1873 was Baptist Minister at Albion Chapel in Kenilworth, although soon after he was ordained into the Anglican ministry and became Curate at Heckmondwike, Yorkshire. All four children were then baptised on the same day, 30th March 1875.[2]

The family moved three more times when William Augustus was young, finally settling in Bristol when his father became Vicar of St. Matthew's, Kingsdown. William Augustus attended Bristol Grammar School then he matriculated at St. John's College, Cambridge in 1892. Following his B.A., he went to Ridley Hall, Cambridge, and became Curate of St. Paul, Southport, Lancashire, in 1896.

In 1898 he married Edith Loesch in Ticehurst, Sussex, moving in the following year to the Chapel Royal in Brighton. In 1903 he became Curate at Horsham. In 1905 he became Vicar of Christ Church, Gorsley, with St. Peter's, Clifford's Mesne, Gloucestershire. His final move before becoming Vicar of Greyfriars was to become Curate of St. Simon's, Southsea, Hampshire, a post he held for 8 years.[3]

The Institution of the Rev. W. A. Doherty as Vicar of Greyfriars took place at 3.30pm on Thursday 10th February 1916, preceded by a welcome at Abbey Hall the previous evening. All the "workers and seat-holders" were invited to the Abbey Hall meeting and People's Warden, Mr. J. C. Gilkes, assured the new Vicar of the congregation's full co-operation with and loyalty to him. The Vicar then addressed the meeting and:

> set the hearts and minds of many at rest by announcing that he meant to uphold the traditions of Greyfriars. The gown would still be used in the pulpit and the psalms read as usual.[4]

It is interesting to note that at this time notices and articles in the Greyfriars' Parish Magazine start to consider that the Lord's return might be very soon. In his first Letter to the Parish in January 1916, Mr. Doherty said: "It may be, our Lord will return before long, and this thought should inspire us to 'run with patience the race that is set before us, looking unto Jesus'." In his second Letter, two months later, he wrote: "... there is unmistakeable evidence that the Lord's return is drawing near." Future meeting dates in the magazine began to be prefaced with "D.V." or "God-willing," which had happened only occasionally before the Great War.

At the Easter services on 23rd April 1916 the offering – of £47 12s 3d – was as usual the congregation's gift to the Vicar. Mr. Doherty started a tradition that it should be shared with the Curate, so he and Mr. Siviter each received just over £23.[5]

Churchwardens during Mr. Doherty's incumbency (1916 – 1924)		
April 1916 to April 1921	Mr. Fred Wheeler	Mr. Joseph Gilkes
April 1921 to April 1924	Mr. William Sparks	Mr. Joseph Gilkes

In late 1916 the Archbishop of Canterbury, Randall Davidson, inaugurated a National Mission of Repentance and Hope, beginning with a special service in Westminster Abbey on Sunday 1st October. He said that "England is fighting a great war for the cause of truth and honour. The greatest victory will not be won if it is our earthly enemies only who are defeated. Among us at home the forces of sin and ignorance are mighty. Through the National Mission of Repentance and Hope we, in Christ's name, call upon every English man and woman to strike a blow at Christ's enemies. This is the victory that overcometh the world."[6] Greyfriars readily embraced the National Mission and preparations had already begun in earnest in late August with the announcement of the Rev. Alvan Birkett, Vicar of St. Paul's, Brixton, as its visiting missioner. Mr. Doherty had worked with Mr. Birkett as a fellow Curate of St. Simon's, Southsea from 1908 to 1910.

By way of preparation, on Sunday 3rd September Rev. Alvan Birkett preached at all three services at Greyfriars (11am, 3.30pm Men's Service, and 6.30pm). He followed this with a meeting the next day in the Memorial Hall and a Week of Prayer from the 18th to 23rd September with daily meetings at 8am, 12 noon, 3pm and 8pm.[7]

The Mission itself lasted from Thursday 26th October to the following Thursday, 2nd November. The services took place in the Church, with the members of the Mission Hall joining the congregations. The two choirs, under Mr. Thackway for the Church and Mr. Harris for the Mission Hall, combined too. On weekdays a meeting for intercession was held at noon in the Church and a "Quiet half-hour of prayer" at 7pm in the Memorial Hall. Then at 7.30pm the Mission Service took place, with Mr. Birkett preaching. The pattern on the Sunday can be seen at the bottom right of the Three Messages circulated (separately) in the parish, shown on the next page.

After this, a Children's Mission ran from Monday 20th November to Sunday 26th. The Rev. Guy King of the Children's Special Service Mission led the meetings, which took place daily at 6pm in the Church. Children were promised that the services would "not last too long."[8]

Possibly as a result of the Mission, by the Easter Vestry Meeting of 1917 the sidesmen reported a difficulty of seating everyone in the Church. With 250 places taken by seat-holders, there were 300 free seats. A notice in the Parish Magazine requested that if seat-holders knew that they would be absent from Church, then by letting a Churchwarden know, their seats could be used for others.[9]

1917 was, like 1914, a year of change. Seymour Waldegrave Soole, son of the second Vicar and a member of Greyfriars all his life, died "Serving the Colours" in February (see pages 149 and 150). At the end of the year, Captain Jones left the Mission Hall in the hands of his wife in order to join the military effort. Between the two events, the long-standing and highly regarded Curate, Isaiah Siviter, took his leave to become the Vicar of St. John's, Harborne, Birmingham, preaching his farewell sermons at the Harvest Thanksgiving Services on Sunday 30th September at 11am, 3.30pm Men's Service and 6.30pm.

Miss Hilda Milward, a longstanding member of the choir, looking back many years later, wrote:

> Great Occasions Remembered: - the most outstanding one to me was the Rev. Isaiah Siviter's farewell service when the congregation was so great the sidesmen were at their wits' end where to put people. Even the choir stalls were used to pack in a few more and there were even people sitting on the pulpit steps! He was greatly loved – many in tears![10]

On the Wednesday prior to that, a large number had gathered in the schoolrooms to bid the Siviters farewell. Presents abounded. To Mr. Siviter: a cheque for £100; an illuminated address; a large framed photograph of the members of the Men's Service and a further "purse of

Parish Notes.

THE MISSION.

GREYFRIARS' CHURCH.

From Thursday, October 26th, to Thursday, November 2nd.

An earnest invitation is given to you to attend this Mission.

A call is going forth throughout the land to

REPENT.

Forsake **SIN** and turn to God.

He is not willing that any should perish, but that all should come to

REPENTANCE.

GOD
OFFERS
SINNERS
PARDON
EVERLASTING
LIFE.

How shall we escape if we neglect so great

SALVATION?

The Gate of Mercy is still open to you,
One day it will close for ever.
"Too late, Too late will be the cry,
Jesus of Nazareth
has passed by."

He calls you through this Mission.

Will you come to Him?

"Him that cometh to ME, I will in no wise cast out."

THE SECOND MESSAGE.

The occasion of this Mission is

A GREAT NEED.

The object is to show clearly how it may be met.

SORROW

has come into our homes.

DEATH

has left many a blank and broken many a heart, but the greatest trouble of all is

SIN.

If sorrow or sin has made you feel your need of

A SAVIOUR

Then know that **JESUS**
EXACTLY
SUITS
US
SINNERS.

HE IS ABLE TO SAVE—TO SUCCOUR—TO KEEP

In this Mission The LORD JESUS CHRIST will be THE PRE-EMINENT ONE.

He will be present at the Mission to supply your need.

Will you come and meet Him?

"Come unto Me all ye that labour and are heavy laden, and I will give you rest."

"My God shall supply all your need."

THE THIRD MESSAGE.

THE WORD OF THE LORD

comes to you again the third time.

ARISE, GO TO THIS MISSION.

God has something to say to you.

May He give you grace to reply,

"Speak, Lord, for Thy servant heareth."

He loves you to the uttermost

And calls you to

"FOLLOW THE CHRIST, THE KING."

He can give you faith to say

FORSAKING
ALL
I
TAKE
HIM.

Many for whom The Saviour died are turning away from Him.

He pleads with you and asks

Will you ALSO go AWAY?

He listens for the answer:—

"LORD, to whom shall I go? Thou hast THE WORDS of ETERNAL LIFE."

MISSION SERVICES.

Sunday (October 29th).

8.0 a.m.—Prayer (Memorial Hall).
11.0 a.m.—Morning Prayer, Sermon, and Holy Communion.
3.0 p.m.—For Men and Friends.
6.30 p.m.—Evening Prayer and Sermon *(After Meeting)*.

Three Messages for Circulation in the parish for the National Mission
Greyfriars' Parish Magazine October 1916 p2

money." To Mrs. Siviter: a "very useful and pretty" cabinet; an afternoon tea table; a Japanese tea tray.[11] Mr. Siviter was instituted into his new parish on Sunday 14th October.

The 4 Curates who worked with Mr. Doherty	Curate From	To	Next destination
Isaiah Siviter	1914	1917	Vicar: St. John the Baptist, Harborne
Robert Phippen Carroll	1918	1919	Vicar: Weybread, Suffolk
George Arthur Purser	1919	1920	Returned to Colombo as CMS Missionary
Wilfred Guy Bidgood Middleton	1921	1923	Curate: St. John's, Deptford

For the first time at an Easter Vestry Meeting, in April 1918 there were ladies present! Among the 20 named persons, along with "several others," Mrs. J. C. Gilkes "and another lady" were recorded.[12]

In October 1918, after a year without a Curate, Greyfriars welcomed the Rev. Robert P. Carroll[13], previously Vicar of Hemswell, Lincolnshire.

"All Praise and Glory be to God for Victory and Peace!" wrote the Vicar in his letter in the Parish Magazine for December 1918, "As suddenly as many expected it, the end of the War came." On the day of the Armistice there was a special service of thanksgiving and praise at Greyfriars at 7.30pm. From the Front in France, Captain Jones wrote both of his feelings upon the peace and also of his narrow escape not many days before:

> Words almost fail me as I commence this note to you. During this past week we have experienced delightful relief by the "cessation of hostilities," and are realising a foretaste of that time for which we have earnestly prayed and so long waited – Peace... Before closing I must ask you to join me in thanksgiving for complete deliverance from special danger, through shell fire, on the night of October 24th. This is another instance of your prayers for me being definitely answered.[14]

Following the departure of Curate Rev. R. P. Carroll in May 1919, the Rev. George Purser, husband of Greyfriars' "Own Missionary," acted as Curate while the Purser family were back on furlough from 1st June 1919 to 18th July the following year.[15] The next Curate, Rev. Wilfred G. B.

Middleton, was welcomed at the Congregational Tea at the Town Hall on 5th January 1921.[16]

At the Easter Vestry Meeting 1920 there was a detailed explanation given by William Sparks of the "Enabling Bill" which had been passed by Parliament in order to give the Anglican Church powers of self-government. This entailed the formation of "Ruri-Decanal Conferences," which met to consider area issues of Church governance, and of the local Church's Parochial Church Council (PCC).[17]

The first ever Greyfriars' PCC meeting therefore took place on Wednesday 14th April 1920, in the Memorial Hall. The membership of this first PCC was:

Ex Officio:

Rev. W. A. Doherty, Vicar	Rev. G. A. Purser, Curate

Elected onto the Ruri-Decanal Conference and thus members of the PCC:

Mr. R. Arnold	Mrs. Doherty
Mr. H. Earles	Mr. J. C. Gilkes, Churchwarden
Mrs. J. C. Gilkes	Mr. J. Gillo
Mr. Greenaway	Mr. E. J. Horsman
Mr. W. Kirby	Mr. W. H. Lawrance
Mr. H. F. Lindars	Mr. J. M. Millar
Mr. W. Moore	Mr. H. J. Rohrbach
Mr. W. Sparks	Mr. F. H. Sparrow
Mr. F. Wheeler, Churchwarden	Miss L. Wheeler
Mr. J. White	Mr. G. E. Wise

Elected onto the PCC:

Mr. A. L. R. Fowler	Mrs. H. Gilkes
Mr. Holdwas (Mission Hall rep.)	Miss Phippen
Mrs. Stainton	Mr. C. Thackway
Miss Weldon	

The Vicar was Chairman of the PCC and Mr. Sparks was elected Vice-Chairman. Mr. Kirby, the Head Master of the Greyfriars' Schools, was elected Honorary Secretary. There were three vacancies for the Ruri-Decanal Conference and so the meeting agreed to add the names of Capt. J. C. Jones, Mr. E. Green and Mr. J. H. Hearn. These three also therefore became members of the PCC.

The minutes gave a summary of the purpose of the committee:

The work and idea of the Church Parochial Council was read from the "Parsons Guide."
They were briefly as follows:
1. To elect a Vice-Chairman
2. To revise Electoral Roll and present a copy to the Council Meeting
3. To present a report of the Council and a statement of finances of the parish
4. That the Council act under orders from the Bishop
5. Special meetings can be convened by special application to the Archdeacon
6. That the Council stands for 1 year.[18]

This first meeting set in place a small committee to "carry out some methods of increasing the Electoral Roll" and agreed the members of the Finance Committee – a group that had started a few years previously. Mr. Sparrow resigned the office of Missionary Secretary and Mr. Rohrbach agreed to succeed him. A small Missionary Committee was created to assist Mr. Rohrbach.

At this time the greatest difficulty facing Greyfriars Church was financial. The table below shows the Churchwardens' Account total income and balance in hand over the early years of Mr. Doherty's incumbency.[19]

	Annual Income	Balance at year end	Balance as % of annual income
1916 – 1917	£181 8s 5d	– £4 5s 2d	– 2%
1917 – 1918	£191 1s 4d	– £9 7s 7d	– 5%
1918 – 1919	£203 17s 4d	+ £2 1s 3d	+ 1%
1919 – 1920	£192 8s 6d	– £18 4s 9d	– 10%
1920 – 1921	£226 13s 4d	– £33 10s 9d	– 15%

With a deficit of 15% of the annual income at Easter 1921, action needed to be taken. Yet the total giving in the Church was much greater than just the Churchwardens' Account shows. In 1920, the total collected as Offertories in the Church was £564 17s, although only 33% of this amount was for Church Expenses (individual gifts brought the figure up from £186 16s 4d to the £226 13s 4d quoted above). Other difficulties over totals were created by the Churchwarden's Account being Easter to Easter, while others were for the calendar year.

In fact, a full analysis of the amount donated through the various accounts shows an astonishing annual sum of £1624 13s 8½d, with the main items shown in the table below:

		% of total
Churchwarden's Account	£226 13s 4d	14%
Mission and Missionary Societies	£484 6s 2d	30%
Assistant Ministry Fund	£385 18s 2d	24%
Sunday Schools and Day Schools	£133 9s 2d	8%
Mission Hall Account	£127 2s 1d	8%

The Assistant Ministry Fund paid for the salary of the Curate (Mr. Purser at this time) and the Lay Missioner (Capt. Jones) at the Mission Hall. It also paid the expenses of visiting clergy throughout the year. This fund was showing a healthy balance of about £120 since Mr. Purser did not take a full Curate's salary. That balance aside, the Church's accounts in total were about £90 in debt.

In order to increase giving, especially to the Churchwarden's Account and for expected expenditure on repairs to the Church, the PCC decided to adopt a scheme called the Free-Will Offering Fund, proposed by Mr. H. J. Rohrbach, adapting a model that had worked well elsewhere.[20] The Secretary of the Finance Committee, Mr. F. H. Sparrow, wrote to the members of the Church in the January 1921 Parish Magazine:

Important about Church Finance.-
The Committee of Church Finance, in going through the accounts of the various necessary expenses, have found during the past year, that the usual offertory and subscription contributions have not been sufficient to meet the increased cost of maintenance. They therefore have been considering how further income may be obtained to avoid running into debt. The matter was brought before the Church Council and explained. They resolved that a scheme should be prepared to obtain additional funds.

The Finance Committee, after very careful consideration of various plans, have come to the decision that it is needful. *In addition* to the ordinary collections and subscriptions, as hitherto, for the Church Expenses Account, Alms Fund, Assistant Ministry Fund, General Purposes Fund, that every worshipper at the Church and Mission Hall be desired to fill in a paper, stating what they are able to give weekly for every week in the year as FREE WILL OFFERINGS, the sums may be from one penny per week to 5/- per week – **as a definite act of worship to God.** That the money promised may be placed in an envelope, which will be supplied to each subscriber (52 for the year), and to be put in the boxes placed in the Church (each envelope will have a number printed, which number will be allocated to each subscriber, and a list of the contributions of each of the numbers will be placed every month in the Church).

It will be seen how very needful that this effort should be energetically made and perseveringly carried out, by comparing the following figures of present income and what is required.

Church Expenses	£190 *a*	£300 *b* *
Alms Fund	£49 *a*	£75 *b*
Assistant Ministry	£275 *a*	£410 *b*
General Purposes Fund	£17 *a*	£25 *b*
Total	£531	£810

a Total offertories and subscriptions for 1919.

b Estimated to be required in the future.

* To include any necessary repairs to the Church Fabric etc.

It is hoped that the Congregation and Parish will heartily and generously support the needs of the Church.

F. H. SPARROW, *Secretary, Finance Committee, Greyfriars' Church*

These estimated future costs would certainly have been enough to shock the congregation and parish, being an increase of more than 50% from the 1919 figures! The Fund was administered by Mr. H. G. Rohrbach as Secretary and Mr. A. W. Milward as Treasurer. The first monthly list that appeared, in March 1921 for the month of January, showed 50 contributors from the Church, totalling £5 11s 7d and 11 from the Mission Hall, with a total of 8s 2d. This first list stated that promised amounts from 92 people in the Church (at an average of £1 17s per head) and 27 in the Mission Hall (average £1) would see £198 collected in the year, falling short of the £400 hoped for.[21]

Greyfriars finally decided to move its year end to 31st December for its Churchwarden's Account, as for all the other accounts, at the Easter Vestry Meeting of 31st March 1921. [22] Therefore the first full year of accounts for the Free-Will Offering Fund was the calendar year 1922. In that year the Fund realised £169 from the Church and £34 from the Mission Hall. This was, however, more than enough to balance the Churchwarden's Accounts which otherwise would have seen a £94 deficit.[23]

On 20th January 1922, the Vicar's mother, Mrs. Elizabeth Doherty, died aged 88. She had been living with William and Edith since at least 1911, as the census that year for 24 Nettlecombe Avenue, Southsea, records. At the time of her death both the Vicar and his wife were ill. Having buried his mother on 24th January, Mr. Doherty then faced a second tragedy: his wife died on the 29th.[24] In the Greyfriars Parish Magazine for March 1922, Mr. Doherty wrote:

> My dear wife and I were both ill with influenza, when my mother was called home. But it seemed to me, at the time, likely that my wife would recover, and this softened the bereavement, for I thought she would be left to comfort me, as nobody else could possibly do. Nevertheless, this was not God's will; he has shown me that when wife and mother leave me, He is able to bind up the stricken heart, and to give grace sufficient for the deepest trial. Needless to say there are moments when the flood would seem to overwhelm me utterly, but always at such times I am conscious, very really conscious, of the near presence of The Lord Jesus Christ. Again and again He has spoken to the deep of my heart, saying, more clearly than any other voice could utter it, 'My grace is sufficient for thee, for My strength is made perfect in weakness.' It is in the valley that you discover the love and tenderness of The Lord Jesus.

In the same magazine, Mr. Doherty also noted the death of the Greyfriars' Organist and Choirmaster, Charles Henry Thackway, who had died two weeks after Edith Doherty. Mr. Thackway had been Greyfriars' Organist for 25 years, having been appointed in May 1896. Latterly, Mr. Thackway had played the organ at four services a week: Thursdays at 7.30pm; Sundays at 11am, 3.30pm (Men's Service) and 6.30pm. The Choir sang at the Sunday 11am and 6.30pm services. At the Men's Service, Mr. Thackway led an orchestra and men's choir, which "added considerably to the brightness of the services," according to the 1910 Men's Services Annual Report.[25]

In November 1911 Greyfriars had presented Mr. Thackway with a "handsomely upholstered easy chair" at a special gathering to commemorate his (then) 16 years as Organist and Choirmaster. The Vicar (Mr. Boultbee) said that Mr. Thackway "had brought the choir to such excellence that at present the congregational singing at Greyfriars was a feature of the services."[26]

Charles Henry Thackway died on Monday 13th February 1922 aged 53 and was buried on the following Saturday. The Vicar (Mr. Doherty) wrote of him: "We have lost a kind and loyal friend and Organist in the late Mr. C. H. Thackway. He was a gentleman of rare musical talent, which he devoted to the service of His Master. Mrs. Thackway, with whom we deeply sympathise, has the joy of knowing that her husband was very much beloved by us all, and that he will have an abiding place in our memory, nor do we think he will miss the 'well done' of his Lord."[27] Friends at

Greyfriars subscribed to a gift for his widow, amounting to £75 – equivalent to a year and a half of the Organist's salary.[28]

At the PCC meeting in June 1923 it was "proposed by Mr. Wheeler, seconded by Mr. Wise: That the necessary permission of the Council be given for the erection of a Memorial Tablet to the late Mr. Thackway. Carried unanimously."[29] The brass plaque, shown below, is the most recent of the 8 memorials on the walls of the Church.

"To the Glory of God and in loving remembrance of
Charles Henry Thackway
Organist and Choirmaster of this Church for 25 years.
Died Feb. 13. 1922. Aged 53 years.
Let everything that has breath praise the Lord. Psalm CL.6"

Brass plaque on the east wall

In these difficult days for Mr. Doherty following his double bereavement, his Curate, Wilfred Middleton, took over, taking and preaching at 23 of the next 29 services until the Vicar returned on 26th February.[30] Mr. G. Cox took over as Organist, first temporarily and then as a permanent appointment from April.[31]

The next change to come upon Greyfriars was the departure for Roxeth near Harrow of Capt. and Mrs. Jones from the Mission Hall. At a farewell gathering at the Mission Hall on 14th November 1922 they were presented with a variety of gifts as tokens of appreciation for their almost seven years' service: £30 cash, a silver watch and various books – including a Moffat Translation of the New Testament.[32] Capt. W. J. Mace, his wife and daughter, arrived in the same month *from* Roxeth as replacements.[33]

On 6th August 1923 there was another farewell gathering: this time for Rev. & Mrs. W. G. B. Middleton. Wilfred Middleton had been Curate from January 1921 and so had served over two and a half years. He preached his last sermon in the Church on Thursday 9th August.[34]

In October 1923, the Vicar re-married. He wrote in the Parish Magazine for November 1923:

> Miss Daisy Sherwood and I were united together in Holy Matrimony, in Greyfriars' Church, on Monday, October 1st, soon after 8.30am. Both Churchwardens were present, and their most kind wishes and congratulations were much appreciated by my wife and myself. The service was very quiet, and we think all must have been impressed with a sense of the nearness of Christ and the favour of His divine blessing.

Daisy Sherwood had also suffered a recent bereavement; her mother had died just a few weeks before the wedding. Daisy was aged 33 and her husband 50. They left, with Daisy's older sister Edith (aged 51) accompanying them, for a honeymoon in Folkestone then Edinburgh.

It was not many months more before the Vicar decided to resign in order to seek a different challenge. The Times reported: "The Rev. W. A. Doherty, Vicar of Greyfriars, Reading, has resigned the living in order to take up mission and convention work."[35]

The Berkshire Chronicle printed extracts of an appreciation of Mr. Doherty from "The English Churchman," stating:

> It is with much sorrow and real regret, which is being freely expressed by many of his people that the ministry of the Rev. W. A. Doherty M.A., Vicar of Greyfriars' Church, Reading, is drawing to a close. For more than eight years he has been faithfully preaching the Gospel truths in that Church. Mr. Doherty is a great Bible student. As a preacher he is exceptionally gifted, and never will his eloquent and powerful preaching, his rich and choice language, his tender and gentle appeals, be forgotten. They will remain fresh in the memories and hearts of the many loyal friends and faithful members of Greyfriars' who love their pastor...
>
> In spite of the fact that Mr. Doherty has been without a Curate since August last year, and that for some months has been suffering from a malady which

> has been most painful, and largely taken away the use of his hand for the time being, the many organisations are being continued and enlarged. ...
>
> Mr. Doherty is essentially a man of prayer, and his work for the Master is one of love, carried on in faith and based on simple and direct prayer. The members of Greyfriars' will suffer a great loss when their Vicar has left them. He has, at times, as far as it has been possible with a large town parish on his hands, taken part in conventions and missions, in which he is especially successful.[36]

The Rev. William A. Doherty preached his final sermons at Greyfriars on Sunday 6th July 1924 at 11am, 3.30pm and 6.30pm – and managed to fit in a baptismal service at 2.40pm for six candidates. He wrote in the Parish Magazine for July: "I shall leave behind me many affectionate and loyal friends. This I know full well, from all the warm-hearted expressions of regret which have reached me, either by letter or word of mouth, from so many. I did not expect that my leaving would call forth so much kind comment as it has done!" With part of the cheque that was presented to him as a farewell gift, Mr. Doherty purchased a "Compactum wardrobe." The Men's Service congregation presented him with a garden seat.

William and Daisy Doherty moved to Folkestone, accompanied by Miss Sherwood (Daisy's older sister). Mr. Doherty was pleased to report that his first two invitations to speak at Conventions arrived in July.[37] He pursued this career until 1928 when he became Vicar of St. Saviour's, Herne Hill Road, Lambeth. Two years later he moved to St. James's Church, Ryde, and then to Christ Church, Worthing in 1934.

William Augustus Doherty died aged 72 in Worthing on 16th January 1946. The Greyfriars Monthly Newsletter of February 1946 noted: "Have just heard of the death of the Rev. W. A. Doherty, who was Vicar of Greyfriars from 1916-1924. He suffered much at the end, so, for him, it would be a blessed release to be absent from the body that he might be present with the Lord whom he loved and served." His widow survived him by 13 years, dying aged 69 in 1959.

Rev. John Clifford Rundle

(Photograph from Berkshire Chronicle 25th April 1924)

Chapter 15

John Clifford Rundle: Vicar 1924 to 1947

As on previous changes of incumbent, it fell to the Trustees to seek for a replacement. The initial 5 Trustees had changed many times since 1862, with those who had died or who were in some way unable to fulfil the role being replaced as soon as possible. A document from 1925 (see next page) shows the lists of Trustees from the first five until that date. Former Vicar Hugh Boultbee had been invited to become a Trustee in 1917 and it was through him that the next Vicar was found.

Hugh's son, James, whom we last met as a child in Greyfriars Vicarage in 1905, was, in 1924, a Curate at St. Clement's, Toxteth – not too far from Bebington where Hugh was then Vicar. The Vicar at St. Clement's was the Rev. John Clifford Rundle. The Chairman of the Trustees, Martin Hope Fouquet Sutton, wrote to Mr. J. C. Gilkes, Churchwarden, saying:

> It is now my privilege to inform you that the Living of Greyfriars has been offered to and accepted by the Rev. Clifford Rundle, Vicar of St. Clement's, Toxteth, Liverpool... Mr. Rundle is a warm supporter of B.C.M.S., and in his present Church he is accustomed to preach in a black gown. He is intimately known to Mr. [H. E.] Boultbee, and I do not think that I am in any way betraying his confidence in saying that he warmly recommended him to the other Trustees for this Living. We feel that Mr. Rundle will worthily uphold the traditions of Greyfriars and it is our earnest prayer that the appointment may prove a very great blessing to the parish.[1]

Hugh Boultbee added in a further letter that Mr. Rundle had "done splendid work in Liverpool – a crowded Church – and he is especially good with young men and women."[2]

John Clifford Rundle was born in Swansea, Glamorgan, on Boxing Day 1878, the sixth of seven children (not counting two who died in infancy). His father, a Cornishman, worked at the Copper Mills, becoming a Foreman. His older sisters became teachers and his brother a Mechanical Engineer.

Graduating from St. David's College, Lampeter, Clifford (as he preferred to be known) was ordained Deacon in 1902 in Liverpool.[3] He remained in that city for the next 22 years, first as Curate of St. Catherine's, Edge Hill (1902 – 1907), then Curate at St. Benedict's, Everton (1907 – 1916) and finally Vicar of St. Clement's, Toxteth (1916 – 1924).[4]

Trustees of Greyfriars (from "Declaration of Trust," dated 25th August 1925):					
8th Aug. 1862	John Ball	Peter French	John Neale	William W Phelps	John Simonds
6th Mar. 1866	Peter French	Edmund Hollond	William W Phelps	John Simonds	James M Strachan
11th May 1875	Robert C Dryland	Peter French	Edmund Hollond	John G Sheppard	Henry Wright
4th Feb. 1881	Charles D Bell	Robert C Dryland	Edmund Hollond	William N Ripley	John G Sheppard
20th Jan. 1887	William H Barlow	Francis A Bevan	Charles D Bell	Robert C Dryland	William N Ripley
12th Feb. 1900	William H Barlow	Francis A Bevan	Robert C Dryland	Edward A Stuart	George F Whidbourne
10th Jun. 1902	William H Barlow	Francis A Bevan	Edward A Stuart	Martin H F Sutton	George F Whidbourne
26th May 1910	Francis A Bevan	Charles J Procter	Edward A Stuart	Martin H F Sutton	John E Watts-Ditchfield
25th Jun. 1917	Hugh E Boultbee	Samuel H Gladstone	Charles J Procter	Martin H F Sutton	John E Watts-Ditchfield
19th Jan. 1924	Hugh E Boultbee	Samuel H Gladstone	Earle L Langston	Martin H F Sutton	Alfred St.J Thorpe

There is an interesting letter written by Liverpool resident J. J. Booker to Mr. Fowler at Greyfriars giving testimony to Mr. Rundle's character and work in the city. He wrote:

> Now about Mr. Rundle, first of all he is miles in front of the average Parson, ... and will not only be a great loss to St. Clement's but to the whole of Liverpool... Before he came to St. Clement's he was for ten years Curate at St. Benedict's, Everton, where he had a Bible Class of over 100 average attendance... He [came] to St. Clement's, congregation small... the Church seats 1100, it is now full on Sunday evenings and more than half full in the

morning; there are 1200 to 1400 in the Sunday School, his own Bible Class 150... Only Scriptural methods are adopted for raising money... he will not have sales of work for anything or whist drives or bazaars... He is a leader and when you get to know him you will love him. There may be many things that you won't at first understand, suspend judgement and wait.

The Thursday evening service when he came had about 20 now over 300 – 95% with own Bibles, and the Church teems with young life...[5]

From the full Church of the later days of Mr. Boultbee, Greyfriars congregation had fallen by 1924. The number of communicants per year below illustrates this, comparing the last years of Mr. Boultbee's time (1910 – 1913) with those of Mr. Doherty (war years not included):[6]

	Mr. Boultbee				Mr. Doherty				
Year	1910	1911	1912	1913	1919	1920	1921	1922	1923
Communicants	3054	3802	3662	4124	2509	2643	2569	2453	2193

Hugh Boultbee wrote of Mr. Rundle: "He is a splendid organizer and I rejoice that he is coming to you. I feel assured that under God he will restore the parish to its former position in the town."[7]

Mr. Rundle, having accepted the position of Vicar of Greyfriars in April 1924, intended to leave his current post at the end of August and to start his new role on 7th September. Meanwhile, he proposed that his Curate, Rev. James Boultbee, should move temporarily to Reading and take care of Greyfriars. This proved acceptable to both Bishops (Liverpool and Oxford) and the younger Mr. Boultbee arrived in Reading on Thursday 10th July,[8] preaching at 36 out of the next 38 services until the end of August.[9]

Mr. Rundle had visited Reading at the very end of April, staying with Mr. M. H. F. Sutton at Erlegh Park and meeting the Churchwardens on 1st May. Mr. Rundle wrote later to Mr. J. C. Gilkes, one of the Wardens:

When I was in Reading the day I met you, the only thing that weighed on my spirit was the Vicarage. It seemed to me to be so gloomy and dingy after the dear little house where I am now living. Am I asking too much, or would it be possible to have it cleaned and some new wall paper put on some of the rooms before I come? If it isn't possible – please do not think anything more about it, but it would be a weight off my mind to think that I was going into a nice brightened house.[10]

The PCC, meeting on 1st August, readily authorised the expenditure of £25 to decorate the Vicarage before Mr. Rundle's arrival in September.[11]

The Bishop of Oxford instituted the Rev. J. C. Rundle to be Vicar of Greyfriars in a private ceremony at Lambeth Palace at 10am on Thursday 24th July. The Bishop suggested this early private ceremony as he was to be away on holiday until the end of September and unable to institute Mr. Rundle otherwise until October.[12] The Induction to the Living took place at 8pm on Friday 5th September, with the Archdeacon of Berkshire, the Venerable R. Wickham Legg, presiding.[13] Within a few weeks the new Vicar was feeling quite settled. He wrote in his first Letter to the Parish, in the October 1924 Parish Magazine:

> My Dear Friends,
> I must at the very outset, thank you all for the very kind way in which you have received me. You can imagine that it was not exactly an easy matter to leave a city where all my ministerial life has been spent and where I have worked for 22 years. I am no stoic, and it was only the clear call of God which made it possible for me to leave behind many who have loved me and whom I have loved in the Lord. The warmth and kindness of your welcome, however, and the encouragement I have already received, have been real balm and consolation, and an added assurance that I am in the place of His will for me. Although the place is strange and I am an entire stranger to most of you, yet I have been wonderfully happy since coming among you, and in fact, I feel every day that I am getting, if I may coin a word, more and more "Greyfriarish."

To complete the welcome of the new Vicar, there was a Parochial Tea and Social Meeting at the Town Hall on Wednesday 1st October. Following the tea, Mr. M. H. F. Sutton presided over the welcome speeches. The evening concluded with a musical entertainment, arranged by Organist Mr. S. E. Marsh.[14]

In the autumn, Greyfriars launched a Special Appeal to raise £300. Mr. Rundle believed that money should only be raised according to Scriptural methods so that funds should be sought from giving rather than, for example, the Sales of Work that Greyfriars had been holding over the years. One result of this was the Special Appeal which, like the Free-Will Offering Fund, required donations to the Church above the normal collections. Before long the Parish Magazine was reporting the totals collected, together with the names of all donors: £124 7s 6d (November 1924); £142 11s by the following month; £147 17s 6d by the end of the year. However, in the final four months of the scheme to April 1925 it only gained a further £20 10s, to end at £168 7s 6d.

The two main purchases with the Special Appeal money were a new set of hymn books – The Church Hymnal – and overhauling and cleaning the organ.[15] Meanwhile, with the last of its money-raising Sales behind it in October 1924, the Mission Hall launched two Special Appeals, for external roof repairs (£35) and a new harmonium for open-air services (£10).

At Mr. Rundle's first Vestry meeting, held in the Memorial Hall on Wednesday 18th February 1925, the Vicar nominated William Sparks to continue as his Warden. Joseph Gilkes was unanimously re-elected People's Warden.[16]

Churchwardens during Mr. Rundle's incumbency (1924 – 1947)		
1924 to 1929	Mr. William Sparks	Mr. Joseph Gilkes
1929 to 1933	Mr. Alfred Milward	Mr. Joseph Gilkes
1933 to 1935	Mr. Alfred Milward	Dr. Jason Bird
1935 to 1946	Mr. Stanley Milward	Dr. Jason Bird
1946 to 1947	Mr. Stanley Dunster	Dr. Jason Bird

Greyfriars held a Children's Mission from 29th March to 6th April 1925, led by Mr. W. J. Graham Hobson. Meetings were held in the Mission Hall at 6pm, with a service for adults at 7.30pm. Mr. Rundle wrote: "Judging from the letters received and from personal observation, quite a number of boys and girls received definite help and blessing."[17]

By the summer of 1925, Mr. Rundle was in need of a break. He had preached at 193 of the 217 services in the first 42 weeks of his incumbency, which represents about 4.6 sermons a week! However, he could say "The ten months I have spent amongst you have been the happiest that I have ever spent in the Lord's service."[18] The Rev. James Boultbee, now Curate at St. Mary's, Cheadle, deputised for three weeks in July while Mr. Rundle recuperated at Swansea.

On 30th July 1925 the longstanding Head Master of the Greyfriars' School left, to take up a promotion to Grovelands Council School in west Reading. William Kirby had been Head Master since the retirement of William Moore in April 1908, except for his war service on the Western Front. He had also taken in his stride becoming Head Master of the reorganised Mixed Junior and Infant Schools when they became a single School in 1923 (with the Head Teacher of the Infant School, Miss Wicks, becoming the new "First Assistant" of the joint School). Mr. Kirby remained a member of the Church, however, and continued as Honorary Secretary of the PCC. Mr. Kirby's last School Log entry was: "I take this opportunity to put on record my deep appreciation of the loyalty and enthusiasm of the staff. Their devotion to the School and its work has borne good fruit. I part from them and the children with real sorrow." [19] On Monday 14th September the Vicar, as Chairman of the School Managers, presented Mr. Kirby with a gift of £14, from 27 subscribers, as a mark of appreciation.[20]

Mr. Kirby was replaced by Sydney E. Marsh as Acting Head, as in 1914 to 1916. Mr. Marsh had also become the Church Organist and Choirmaster in 1923. When a permanent appointment was made in January 1926, Miss Emma Wicks was promoted from First Assistant to become Head of the Mixed School.

In January 1926, Mr. Rundle was joined by his first Curate, the Rev. T. E. Benson, son of the Rev. E. M. Benson, who had been Mr. Rundle's Vicar when he was a Curate at St. Benedict's, Everton[21]. As can be seen from the table below, Mr. Rundle was more often without a Curate than with one.

The 3 Curates who worked with Mr. Rundle	Curate From	To	Next destination
Theodore Ernest Benson	1926	1928	Curate: All Saints, Preston, Lancashire
Richard James Hunt	1933	1934	Rector: Hardington Mandeville, Yeovil, Somerset
George Malcolm	1939	1945	Rector: Swepstone with Snarestone, Leicestershire

A feature of Mr. Rundle's incumbency became clear by 1926. Greyfriars had always supported missionary societies, usually by a collection at a service with a visiting speaker from the society. Mr. Rundle still invited a few such visitors: China Inland Mission, London Jews Society, Bible Churchmen's Missionary Society, Scripture Gift Mission, London City Mission and Church Pastoral Aid Society in 1926, for example. However, in June 1926, the Vicar proposed to the congregation a different method of collecting gifts for missionary work:

> I am wondering, therefore, whether you would not be willing to set apart one Sunday, say in September, as a day in which we could bring some gift of money to God – such money to be distributed after amongst Evangelical Societies known to be perfectly sound. Knowing that I prefer such a gift day to

> a Sale of Work, the ladies of the Missionary Working Party have loyally co-operated with me and are giving up the Sale of Work. I am very grateful to them for this. I propose, therefore, that envelopes in which we could place our offerings, should be given to us some time before the day decided upon, but that as we give them in, no names should be given. We will each settle with the Lord as to our respective gifts.[22]

Not only was the idea of a single gift day an innovation, but also that the donors be anonymous. Previously, Annual Report Accounts abounded with lists by name, stating the amount donated. The exception to this had always been the Sunday collections, which had been recorded simply as totals.

The gift day in September was preceded by a Missionary Meeting at the Mission Hall in North Street, with speakers from the Nile Mission Press and the China Inland Missionary Society. The gift day on 19th September was called "Free-Will Offering Day for God's Work in Other Lands," and the offerings that day totalled £374 12s 5d.[23] In the Annual Report for 1926, Mr. Rundle reflected on how the congregation's giving had increased over the last three years, from £1545 in 1924 (the year Mr. Rundle became Vicar) to £2031 in 1926. A total of £676 18s of the latter total was sent to 12 Overseas and Home Missions – almost exactly a third.[24] The Vicar decided how to distribute the special gift day money, choosing to give:

The Nile Mission Press	£104
The Bible Churchmen's Missionary Society	£100
The China Inland Missionary Society	£100
The Mildmay Mission to Jews	£50
The South American Mission Society	£10 12s 5d
The Africa Inland Mission	£10[25]

With such an emphasis on foreign mission, it was not long before Greyfriars was sending out its own missionary again – the first to be named "Our Own Missionary" since Elsie Sparrow (Mrs. Purser, as she became) left for Ceylon in 1906. After a Farewell Gathering in the Mission Hall on 25th April, John Savage sailed on 2nd May 1929 on the S. S. Orbita, bound for Lima, Peru.[26] He had been accepted by the Evangelical Union of South America Missionary Society (EUSA), an interdenominational mission which had been founded in 1911 to carry out Church planting, medical and educational work, and Bible and Christian literature distribution.

Like the Sparrow family before them, the Savages – father, mother and two sons – were a Greyfriars family. John's brother Frank ran the Bible Class for Young Men on a Sunday afternoon in the Vicarage Classroom and was the PCC's second Honorary Secretary from 1928, succeeding William Kirby.

John Savage became a consistent correspondent in the Greyfriars Parish Magazine from soon after his departure until the late 1940s when he ceased to be financially supported by Greyfriars, rarely missing a month. In the June 1931 magazine he shared the good news of his marriage to nurse Dorothy Franks in Lima. He went on to become the General Secretary of EUSA in the early 1950s.

Greyfriars added a second "Own Missionary" in 1930. Mr. Rundle reported in his Letter in the Parish Magazine: "I am glad to say that Miss Florrie Peaston, one of our Sunday School Teachers, has been accepted by the South African General Mission Society, so we shall have another missionary now, in addition to John Savage, to pray for and help to support."[27] In the same Letter, the Vicar added that former Curate Mr. Benson had also been accepted by the China Inland Missionary Society.

It took Florence Peaston several months to reach her destination – Chididi Mission Station near Port Herald in Nyasaland (now Nsanje, Malawi). Her brother Alfred was already working at the Mission. He had been one of Mr. Rundle's "old boys" back in Liverpool days and so Chididi had become known to Greyfriars' members, with the Sunday School having supported a girl and a boy at the Mission for some time.

Not long after Miss Peaston had arrived at Chididi, Miss Edith Holmes was due to leave for Burma to work for the Bible Churchmen's Missionary Society, with a valedictory meeting planned for October 1st, eight days before her ship sailed. Unfortunately, she was taken so badly ill that her doctor ordered her to take complete rest and she was unable to go. Quite possibly her name had already been enrolled on the Roll of Our Own Missionaries in the Memorial Hall.[28]

A major refurbishment of the Church took place in 1930. This had been originally planned for the summer of 1914, but the outbreak of war had postponed the work on the interior and it had not been put in hand since. Until this time, the interior of the Church had been illuminated by gas light – by eight corona pendants in the nave and a gas lamp standard in each transept, with no lighting in the aisles. It was decided to light the Church by electricity, using the same coronae and wall brackets. The total project cost was estimated to be in the region of £450 to £500.[29] A gift day was announced for Sunday 29th June 1930 and the Church was closed for the whole of July for the work to be carried out. The gift day raised an astonishing £417 4s 10d.[30]

Interior of Greyfriars Church decorated for Christmas
(Photograph earliest 1930 – after gas lights were replaced by electric and latest 1938 – before the organ console was moved to the east wall)

The architect who oversaw the work, Mr. W. Rowland Howell, of Blagrave Street, Reading, did a very thorough job, especially concerning the Church windows. He discovered that the windows were in a very poor state, particularly the west window. He wrote to the Wardens on 1st July 1930:

> When those panes of the west window which were obviously bad, were taken out, I found the lead in such a deplorable state that it was imperative to deal with the whole of the window. This will involve an extra cost of £20.0.0 and I have given Mr. Earthy instructions to proceed.

There began a long correspondence between Mr. Rowland Howell and the firm of Chas. J. Earthy, Artists in Stained Glass, of 80 London St, Reading.

For example, on 22nd August, the architect wrote to Mr. Earthy: "I have had another look at the north window and have been up to some of the lower panes on the outside. I feel sure that this window can be got a good deal cleaner than it is now..." Mr. Earthy managed to obtain a further £15 to cover extra labour and materials to achieve the desired result.

In addition to the electrical supply and glazing, the scope of the 1930 refurbishment ranged from polishing the pews and the marble columns of the pulpit to vacuuming the roof rafters. The total bill came to £713 4s 6d, thus requiring over £300 more than had already been collected. The Church held a second gift day on 30th November, at which £122 3s was raised. There were then some additional donations, plus money received from selling the gas standards from the transepts (£1 8s from G. R. Jackson Ltd., Rag, Skin and Metal Merchants). An anonymous single donation of £141 9s completed the total.[31] This was at a time when the congregation also gave £909 at the Harvest Festival on 12th October, for the annual gift day "For God's Work in Other Lands."[32] In all, in 1930, the congregation gave a total sum of £3209 5s 8d to the various aspects of the Church's work, compared to £2573 1s 0d the year before and £2651 3s 4d in 1931.[33]

In 1932 the Greyfriars' Junior Mixed and Infant School closed. Having opened their doors in January 1865, the Schools had been an integral part of the Church life since almost its first days. There had been many troubled times in the past when it had seemed unlikely that the Schools could continue, but somehow money was found for repairs and the Education Committee allowed the institution to continue. In 1932 Miss Emma Wicks was Head Mistress, having been associated with the Schools first as a Pupil Teacher from 1891 to 1896 and then later as Head of the Infant School until the reorganisation of 1923. She stayed on as First Assistant of the new Greyfriars Mixed Junior & Infant School and was then promoted to overall Head Mistress when Mr. Kirby moved on in 1926.

Although the School had been in danger of closing previously, the actual closure happened very swiftly. The first real intimation of closure that Miss Wicks knew of was a visit from Mr. Rundle and Mr. A. W. Milward, both of whom were Managers of the School. The log entries for the period chronicle the sequence of events:

> July 1st: The Vicar and Mr. Milward visited the School this morning. The Managers have received a letter from the Education Committee urging the closure of the School on account of expense. The matter was brought before a meeting of the Parochial Church Council, but no decision was made.

> July 8th: Repairs to the outside roofing have been carried out this week. The work is being done under the orders of the Managers.
> July 18th: The Vicar visited the School this afternoon to inform us that the Managers have decided to close the School on 28th July 1932, owing to economy in expenditure necessary at a critical time.[34]

The Managers of the School were under significant pressure from the Education Department, who wanted to save the expense of running the Greyfriars' School and place children in nearby schools with surplus places. All children over the age of 5 were placed at other schools, but those younger than 5 were not placed due to insufficient room. All four teaching staff were re-deployed, Miss Wicks being transferred to be Head Mistress of Coley Infants.

The School closed on 28th July 1932. To mark the occasion there was a large farewell meeting involving pupils, staff and parents. The Log Book entry stated "A very large number of gifts were presented to the staff, and gifts were made to each scholar. Owing to the removal of the whole of the stock, the lessons according to the Timetable have been suspended." By the next day all the furniture had been removed.

The Times [35]noted:

> One of the oldest Church schools in Reading, Greyfriars, which stands on the site of an ancient monastery, is to be closed, with the result that an annual saving of £600 will be effected to public funds.

The School's Log Book ended with the statement, for August 29th, "Greyfriars' School now ceases to be used for purposes of Elementary Education, and will now be used for Parochial Purposes only." The buildings became a much used resource for the Church until the 1940s, finally being demolished in 1971.[36]

Within a year the School buildings had been transformed: "bright and clean in their new coats of paint and illumined by electric light, with the old desks vanished and new chairs substituted," wrote the Vicar.[37] Naturally, all this came at a cost and so Sunday 19th February 1933 was set aside as a gift day to raise the money needed. In the following month's magazine, Mr. Rundle was pleased to be able to announce that the sum of £101 7s 3d had been raised, exceeding the expenditure by some £14.

Head Masters and Mistresses of the Greyfriars' Day Schools (where known):

Infant School - January 1864 to May 1923:

c1869	Miss Moody
1874 to ...	Miss A. F. Hickmott
... to Dec 1882	Miss E. Coo
Jan 1883 to Jul 1892	Miss Eliza Yarlett
Aug 1892 to Aug 1896	Mrs Elizabeth Huntley
Sep 1896 to Jun 1918	Miss Florence Chandler
Jun 1918 to Dec 1921	Miss Mabel Edwards
Jan 1922 to May 1923	Miss Emma Wicks

Girls' Junior School – January 1864 to December 1895:

1873 to ...	Miss Marianne Spillard
c1891 to Dec 1895	Miss Gibson

Boys' Junior School - January 1864 to December 1895:

Jan 1864 to Dec 1895	Mr. William Moore

Mixed Junior School – January 1896 to May 1923:

Jan 1896 to Apr 1908	Mr. William Moore
Apr 1908 to Aug 1914	Mr. William Kirby
Aug 1914 to Mar 1916	Mr. Sydney Marsh
Apr 1916 to Mar 1918	Mr. Alfred Briers
Apr 1918 to Feb 1919	Mr. James Piper
Feb 1919 to May 1923	Mr. William Kirby

Mixed Junior and Infant School – May 1923 to August 1932

May 1923 to Aug 1925	Mr. William Kirby
Sep 1925 to Dec 1925	Mr. Sydney Marsh
Jan 1926 to Aug 1932	Miss Emma Wicks

At the Annual Vestry Meeting in 1933, Joseph Gilkes, aged 78, stepped down as Churchwarden. The Vicar:

> remarked that no words of his could express the appreciation due from the congregation for the many years of faithful and loyal service given to the Lord's work in Greyfriars; he hoped, however, at a later date, that the unspoken appreciation would be expressed in a more tangible way. It was a wonderful record that Mr. Gilkes had, 19 years as a sidesman and 20 years as a Warden; a record that deserved the heartfelt thanks of every member of the congregation.[38]

In fact, the figures given by Mr. Rundle were not accurate. Mr. J. C. Gilkes had first been elected as a sidesman in the Annual Vestry Meeting on 2nd May 1895.[39] He was then elected Churchwarden on 6th April 1915[40], resigning on 27th January 1933. He was thus a sidesman for 20 years and then a Churchwarden for 18 (give or take a month or two).

Mr. Gilkes was replaced as Warden by Dr. Jason G. Bird, who began a very long period of office spanning the next 23 years. Dr. Bird became Vicar's Warden and Mr. A. W. Milward, who had been Vicar's Warden since 1929, became People's Warden, the role Mr. Gilkes had held.

Later that year there was a gathering and presentation to Mr. Gilkes of an inscribed rose bowl, a cheque and a "Compactum" wardrobe to commemorate his many years of service:

> A very pleasant event in the annals of Greyfriars took place on Wednesday, July 5th, when a representative gathering from the congregation journeyed by char-a-banc to Woodcote, on the occasion of a presentation to Mr. J. C. Gilkes, who recently retired from the office of People's Warden. This enjoyable outing was due to the great kindness of Mr. & Mrs. Hay Walker, who had extended an invitation to members of the congregation to visit "Wayside" for the event.[41]

A further change to the Wardens was necessary in the following year, due to the death of Alfred W. Milward, aged 63, who died in November 1934. The PCC, who met on 16th November, passed the resolution:

> The Council wishes to place on record its very real sorrow in the loss of our much beloved Warden, Mr. A. W. Milward, and feels that it is impossible adequately to express what this will mean both to the Council and congregation as a whole. We thank the Lord for every remembrance of him; his wonderful life, quiet humility, his great charm, his unostentatious giving in many spheres of the Lord's work, and especially for his realization of the value of prayer and love of God's work. He was one of the Lord's noblemen.
>
> The Council desires to express its Christian sympathy with Mrs. Milward and family.[42]

Mr. A. W. Milward's son, Stanley Joseph Milward, replaced his late father as People's Warden at the Annual Vestry Meeting two months later.[43] Like Dr. Bird, he was also destined to be Warden for 23 years, but in two blocks, of eleven and twelve years.

A great change occurred at the end of 1934. The Parish Magazine, which had been losing money for a number of years, was replaced by the much smaller Greyfriars Monthly Bulletin. The Parish Magazine had contained a calendar of the month's events and four, slightly smaller than A4, pages of news. It also came with a 16-page insert "Home Words" (replaced by "The British Messenger" from April 1930) and many advertisements, including several from members of the congregation. For example, among the 29 advertisers in the September 1926 Magazine were: George Phippen, Florist; H. Frank Dunster & Sons, Bootmakers & Repairers; Milwards, the Shoe Store ("Scientific Shoe Fitting by X Ray"); J. Gillo, Builder, Plumber & Decorator; Gilkes & Son, Engravers.

Monthly Bulletin design used from January 1935 to January 1942

The new Monthly Bulletin was slightly smaller than an A4 sheet, folded into 4. Its usual format was:

Vicar's Letter on the front,
Parish Notes, a letter from "Our Own Missionary" and Mission Hall notes on pages 2 and 3,
Entries from the Parish Baptism/Marriage/Burial record, Offertories and Sidesman rota on page 4

Below is a table of the various designations of the Greyfriars' Monthly Magazine/ Newsletter since it began in 1881.

From	To	Name
January 1881	December 1893	Greyfriars' Parochial Magazine
January 1894	December 1934	Greyfriars' Parish Magazine
January 1935	January 1942	Greyfriars Monthly Bulletin
February 1942	June 1970	Greyfriars Church Monthly Newsletter
July 1970	September 2007	Greyfriars News
October 2007	Present	Greyfriars and New Hope News

By 1937 the Church organ was showing significant signs of age. In a leaflet produced in April 1937, it called the early history of the instrument "obscure," with its year of installation uncertain, believing it to be installed soon after the restoration. However, as we have seen above, the organ was made by A. Monk of London and installed in the north transept in 1888, with its oak case being added in 1894. Some repair works had been carried out from time to time, notably to the pipes in April 1918,[44] but the organ was basically irreparable by this date. The decision was taken therefore at the PCC on 4th December 1936 to launch an appeal to raise approximately £1800 to replace the old organ, while keeping the oak case.

On the special gift day on 23rd May 1937 just over £250 was given[45], quickly rising to £1000, as reported in the July 1937 Monthly Bulletin. However, a further gift day was needed on 5th June 1938 to try to finish the task, raising a further £385. [46] Meanwhile, "about two-thirds of the instrument's resources have become totally unusable,"[47] reported Mr. A. E. Sheppard, Chairman of the Organ Committee. The Organ Fund was completed in late September – with the old organ now entirely unusable – by three generous anonymous donors, two totalling £55 and one a single gift of £500.[48]

The new organ, costing £1972 10s, was duly purchased and installed by the end of February 1939 following the grant of a Faculty by the Bishop in November 1938.[49] This organ, made by John Compton of London, was a three-manual instrument with twelve ranks of pipes.[50] The console, previously underneath the pipes and facing the organ, was moved to a position between the pulpit and choir stalls by the east wall. Apart from the console, which was replaced in 2001, this organ is still in place in the Church – long outliving its 20 year warranty![51]

The Dedication and Opening of the New Organ took place at 7.30pm on Wednesday 8th March 1939. Combined choirs from the Church and Mission Hall led the congregational singing under the Greyfriars' Organist and Choirmaster Stuart Allen. There followed an organ recital given by Allan Brown, Organist of Kingsway Hall, London.[52]

A few months previously, Miss Florence Peaston, "Our Own Missionary," married the Superintendent of the South Africa General Mission, Mr. P. V. Watson.[53] This entailed her leaving her work at Chididi and so she ceased to be financially supported by Greyfriars. In September 1938 she was replaced as "Our Own Missionary" by Miss Mary Quelch,[54] a former member of the Mission Hall congregation, who had first gone out as a missionary to Arua, Uganda, with Africa Inland Mission around 1923.[55]

In early January 1939, Captain W. J. Mace left after 16 years leading the work at the Mission Hall, moving to Derbyshire. At a Congregational Tea in the Schools on 29th March, where missionary John Savage was the main speaker, a presentation was made to Capt. Mace (£47 10s), his wife (an umbrella) and his daughter (a writing case).[56]

Mr. Rundle had been without a Curate since the Rev. R. J. Hunt had left after a short tenure in 1934. In June 1939, George Malcolm – a former missionary with Bible Churchmen's Missionary Society in Persia and India – was ordained, remaining as Greyfriars' Curate until October 1945.[57]

To add to the changes at this time, the longstanding Verger/Caretaker, Mr. Thomas Searle, retired. He was described in the 1901 Census as Caretaker of Greyfriars Church and School and was generally called Sexton from about 1906 to 1915 and thereafter Verger. He lived with his wife Esther and family in the Mission House, 24 North Street, from about 1905 to his retirement. An article in the Reading Gazette, accompanied by a photograph of Mr. Searle, said:

> After almost 40 years' unbroken service as verger at Greyfriars Church, Reading, Mr. Thomas Searle... is retiring. Seventy-two years old, Mr. Searle is giving up the work, which is combined with that of Caretaker, for health reasons... Only once, and that recently, has illness prevented Mr. Searle from attending to his duties. With his wife, who is 74, he will be celebrating his golden wedding next March.[58]

The PCC met in special session on 12th May 1939 to discuss the resignation and to begin the process of appointing a successor and repairing the Mission House for its next occupant. The 36 applicants for the job were whittled down to a final two, who were interviewed by the Vicar, Mr. S. J. Milward and Dr. J. G. Bird, resulting in Mr. Young being appointed to the post.[59] On 19th July, at a large gathering in the Schools, Mr. Searle learnt that the PCC had voted him a £13 per annum pension and presented him with a cheque for £47 10s from donations made by the congregations of the Church and Mission Hall.[60]

The appointment of Mr. Young as Caretaker was not a successful one. After "several serious incidents" he abruptly resigned in early 1943.[61] However, the next Caretaker, Mr. Kent, proved to be worse. After his performance was reviewed and found to be wanting, he asked for a month to prove himself. At the end of that period he was given a month's notice, but found another job after a fortnight and so resigned. He did not, however, vacate the Mission House. After three months the Church took steps to gain rent from him at a rate of 10/6 per week.[62] After a brief tenure of a Mr. Amor, Greyfriars finally appointed a reliable Verger in George Walters in July 1945.[63]

When Britain declared war on Germany on 3rd September 1939 there were some immediate consequences for Greyfriars. The Schools buildings were commandeered by the Army as a Decontamination Centre – although the Church was able to charge a rent of £180 per annum.[64] With blackout coming into force, the Sunday 6.30pm service was moved to 3.30pm from 17th September.[65] After the clocks went back on 19th November, the afternoon service at the Church was stopped altogether for the winter and the congregation joined the Mission Hall service at 6.30pm – it being much easier to black the Mission Hall's windows.[66] The evening service moved back into the Church on 3rd March 1940 at 6pm, moving to its normal 6.30pm on 7th April.[67]

Work was put in hand in the summer of 1940 to achieve a blackout in the Church so that services could continue there. With so many windows and several of them being very large, this was no small undertaking. The PCC agreed in June to carry out the following:

"South Transept:	3 small windows to be permanently blacked out [using paper] and the large south window to be curtained [Blind]
North Transept:	Large window and west window permanently blacked out [using paper] and two east windows curtained
Aisles:	North & south 4 small windows curtained
West Window:	Curtained [Blind]
South Doorway:	Rearrange existing curtains and blinds
North Doorway:	Curtains to be sewn together."[68]

Earlier that year, Mr. Rundle had a shock upon his arrival at Church for morning worship: his Black Preaching Gown had been stolen. He took the occasion to explain the significance of the Black Gown in his monthly

Letter. He concluded his historical survey, which began at the Reformation, with:

> For me, the wearing of a distinctive dress in the pulpit has a special significance and I have always understood that the Reformers had this in mind too. When I wear the Surplice I am a Minister of the Church of England and am bound to use the set form of service as found in our Prayer Book, but when I wear the Black Gown I am the servant of The Lord who has bought me with His blood and have liberty to give out his messages.[69]

The practice of wearing the black Geneva gown continued into and throughout Mr. Page's incumbency.

By the 1940s Greyfriars was associated with a growing number of missionaries, although it counted just two in the category of "Our Own Missionary." The difference was that the congregation provided funds for "Our Own" – £250 p.a. to support John Savage in Peru and £100 for Mary Quelch in Arua, West Nile.[70] The list below shows the other missionaries who had a connection with Greyfriars at this time.[71]

	Location
Rev. Theodore Benson	Szechwan, West China
Jessie Hay-Walker	Dohnavur, South India
Rev. John Hay-Walker	Alexandria, Egypt
Jessie Wade	Pucheng, Fukien, China
Monica Sutton	Nilgiri Medical Mission, South India

In 1941 Greyfriars added a third "Our Own Missionary": Dr. & Mrs. E. H. Williams. Ted (or sometimes Teddy) Williams was the great grandson of Samuel Wheeler, the stone mason and builder who carried out much of the Restoration of the Church in 1862 to 1863. From the opening service of dedication to the present day, members of Samuel Wheeler's family have worshipped at Greyfriars – as far as I know, they are the only family to span the whole 150 years to date.

Ted Williams and his fiancée Muriel Francis were accepted by Africa Inland Mission in April 1940 for service overseas.[72] Having married in summer 1940, they set sail in mid-April 1941 for Africa. They arrived at Arua, where they were to join Mary Quelch, on 22nd July, 14 weeks later.[73] Thus began almost forty years of service, including the building and establishing of Kuluva Hospital in the Arua district.

Meanwhile, in spite of the war, life at Greyfriars continued – which in the case of an old building usually means repairs. The west wall needed serious attention: a special gift day on 5th May 1940 brought in £78 14s 11d of the £100 needed.[74] Then in February 1941 the Church boiler broke down and services had to be held in the Mission Hall for 4 weeks until it was replaced.[75]

No Annual Report was published for 1941 due to the "present conditions (paper shortage, cost of printing, etc)." It was agreed at the PCC just to circulate some sheets of accounts to seat-holders.[76] It is likely that no Annual Reports were published for at least the duration of the War.

Greyfriars lost its iron railings and gates in 1942. They were requisitioned in June by the Directorate of Demolition & Recovery. The PCC "realised that it was helpless in the matter, having no good reasons for appeal, and it was decided to let matters take their own course."[77] For several years the Church had no boundary fence.

At about 2pm on Wednesday 10th February 1943, Reading town centre was bombed by a lone German aircraft. A bomb hit St. Laurence's Church, blowing out its glass and rendering parts of the tower unsafe. In all four bombs were dropped and streets were subjected to machine gun fire, leading to 41 fatalities and a further 49 seriously injured. Mr. Rundle invited the Vicar and congregation of St. Laurence's to use Greyfriars until such time as their Church could be repaired. St. Laurence's held their services at 8am, 9.30am and 2.45pm, with Greyfriars at 11am and 6.30pm.[78]

1943 ended badly for Mr. Rundle. From just before Christmas, he was taken ill, although the record does not specify in what way. He had been troubled by difficulties with his voice and throat for some time and so this is a possibility. On New Year's Day he underwent an operation and then went back to Swansea to his family home to convalesce. He returned to work in March, reporting that the Doctor had told him to "go slow" for a few months.[79]

It was next the turn of "Our Own Missionary" Mary Quelch to be taken ill. She returned to Reading on furlough in early 1944, but remained unfit to return to Africa. She finally ceased being Greyfriars' supported missionary in November 1945.[80]

The final days of the Second World War coincided with a Mission to Children, with missioner, Mr. Mount, which took place from Monday 7th to Friday 18th May 1945. Mr. Rundle reported that, in spite of "a steady stream of interruptions and difficulties to contend with," Mr. Mount and his team soldiered on and "quite a number of boys and girls gave in their names as having given themselves definitely to the Lord."[81]

The Curate, the Rev. George Malcolm, left in October 1945. At a presentation on 24th October,[82] a grateful congregation presented him with a wardrobe, electric cooker, mahogany sideboard and a gilt striking clock for his new Vicarage in the wonderfully named parish of Swepstone with Snarestone, in the Diocese of Leicester, together with a cheque for £57. Following Mr. Malcolm there was a very long gap until the next Curate – Roderick Thorp in 1969.

At the Annual Parochial Church Meeting on 15th March 1946, Stanley Milward retired as People's Warden, standing down due to pressure of business.[83] He was replaced by Stanley Dunster, with Dr. Bird remaining as Vicar's Warden.

In late 1946, Gordon Spriggs produced an "Illuminated History of Greyfriars" which has been displayed at the Church ever since. Individual prints could be purchased for 2/6 (large copy) or 1/- for a smaller version.[84]

The Vicar was again unwell in 1947. He wrote in the March Newsletter that his Doctor had prescribed a complete change and rest. In spite of resting for the months of April and May, by early June he had decided that he needed to resign the Living and take retirement.[85] A special PCC meeting was convened on 20th June to consider the situation. They moved the following resolution:

> On the occasion of his retirement after 23 years ministry in this Parish, the Parochial Church Council desire to place on record their very sincere appreciation of the long and devoted service rendered by the Vicar, the Rev. J. C. Rundle, B.A. They recognise his great ability as a teacher and his utter faithfulness in the preaching of the Word, and wish to convey to him their grateful thanks for all that he has been enabled to do in the Church and Parish. They will miss his presence greatly, but join together in the hope that he will be given restored health, and that God's richest blessing may rest upon him in the days to come.[86]

Mr. Rundle was at this time aged 68. He had been Vicar of Greyfriars for 23 years and in the Ministry for a total of 45 years. He retired back to his beloved Swansea, where he died on 21st January 1967.[87] Stanley J. Milward wrote:

> I, like many others, owed a great deal to Mr. Rundle, for it was he who led me to a saving faith in the Lord Jesus Christ, and therefore I write out of a sense of

> deep gratitude to him. For all the years he was with us Mr. Rundle exercised a truly spiritual ministry, which was a means of blessing to many people. He was indeed a man of the Book, and his Thursday evening Bible Readings were both instructive and helpful... Beneath a rugged and perhaps rather dour exterior there dwelt a lovable and warm-hearted personality, full of humour and good fun! This was marked especially in his way with children, who seemed particularly, and perhaps surprisingly, attracted to him.[88]

The PCC agreed a fitting tribute that reflected Mr. Rundle's love of God's Word. There would be a "modernisation" of the pulpit to install a stand with space for the preacher's Bible and notes and also the purchase of some Bibles for the pews. [89] A commemorative plaque was affixed to the inside of the pulpit that said "In grateful memory of John Clifford Rundle B.A. Vicar of Greyfriars 1924 – 1947 This desk was renovated and Bibles were placed in the pews."

Rev. J. C. Rundle

(Photograph courtesy of Mrs. S. Launders, daughter of Dr. J. G. Bird)

Rev. J. K. Page MBE
(Photograph in the Berkshire Chronicle
15th August 1947)

Chapter 16

John Knott Page: Vicar 1947 to 1968

Greyfriars' sixth Vicar was a Londoner, having been born in Islington on 29th September 1912. John Page attended St. Mary's Church, Islington, where he sang in the choir. His Vicar there, the Rev. H. W. Hinde, became founding Principal of Oak Hill Theological College in 1932.

John left school and went straight into employment. At 20 years of age he left to attend Oak Hill as one of its first students. The College was an Evangelical foundation that allowed men without degrees to study for ordination. He was ordained on his 23rd birthday in 1935 and took up his first curacy at St. Paul's, Hyson Green, Nottingham. He remained there until moving to St. Peter & St. Paul, Felixstowe in October 1939.

Meanwhile, John had married Katherine Held in Islington in September 1937 and in due course they had three children: David, Michael and Kathleen Elizabeth (known as Betty).

In 1940, the Pages moved to Slough, with a curacy at St. Paul's. From there, in 1942, Mr. Page joined the RAF Volunteer Reserve as a Chaplain. Following an initial posting to Morecambe, Mr. Page spent 1944 stationed in Sierra Leone. For his work there he was Mentioned in Dispatches and after the war's end was awarded the MBE. He was demobbed in 1947, spending the summer as Locum at St. Mary's, Weymouth.[1]

Following Mr. Rundle's resignation at the beginning of June 1947, Dr. Bird, as Churchwarden, had written to the secretary of the Trustees:

> Dear Mr. Mohan, Thanks for your letter and for giving me an opportunity of telling you the kind of man I think suitable for Greyfriars. Although Greyfriars is a large parish, very few parishioners attend the Church, and only a few go to the Mission Hall. The congregation, which is a good one, is made up for the most part of Christians from the town and district round about, Greyfriars being the only definite, scriptural, Evangelical parish Church in the neighbourhood. During Mr. Rundle's ministry we have had a profound Bible teaching, and the traditions of Greyfriars have been faithfully maintained.

> I would like our new Vicar to be a real man of God, with a knowledge of the Word which he could pass on. This, I am sure, is the first essential in these days of such great need of "thus saith the Lord." Our traditions are very Low Church and Evangelical. We still have the black gown. There is a fertile field for pastoral work, and the scope amongst youth is unlimited. Also, as you know, we have a University in Reading, and I am sure a great work could be done with students. We are very missionary minded, and support BCMS and several other Evangelical societies. Before the war we had flourishing Campaigner Clans, but now we have Boy's clans only.
>
> It is not a parish for an old man, and I feel it would be helpful to have a married man this time. He would find a wonderful sphere of service here.[2]

The Trustees were the Rev. St. John Thorpe of Watford, the Rev. E. L. Langston of Weymouth, Mr. Phil Sutton of Reading, Mr. F W Carter of Reigate and one other unknown to the PCC. It is interesting that one was from Weymouth, where Mr. Page was spending the summer as Locum! Within a few weeks, the Trustees' choice had fallen on the Rev. J. K. Page. He visited the Greyfriars' PCC on 8th August 1947. He described himself under three headings: history, theology and policy. Having outlined his background he told the PCC:

> Theology: The Bible is the Word of God without any reservations whatsoever. Christ and His blood are the only means of Salvation.
>
> Policy: I desire to do only that which is in the line of His Will, after prayer and the certain conviction that it is His Will. Church work & ministry will be continued.[3]

The PCC minutes continued:

> Dr. Bird then laid before Mr. Page our "peculiarities," the use of the black gown, the reading of the Psalms, the method of taking out the collection. Mr. Page stated that he was in favour of a congregational service and thought ours was a well balanced one. He would continue to say the Psalms as he thought a certain proportion of the Congregation would be ruled out by singing them. He did not expect the Council to sign on the dotted line. The Disposal of the Collection is to continue as now as there may be a sincere feeling that to put it on the Holy Table would signify "laying it on the Altar" to some. He did not intend to make any changes for the present. He promised to support wholeheartedly the missionary character of the Church.

The PCC were unanimous in their decision to approve his appointment.

Mr. Page's Institution took place on Thursday 11th September 1947 at 7.30pm, by the Bishop of Reading, the Rev. A. Parham. There was a large congregation present for the event. The Church was decorated with flowers and greenery.[4] A month later Mr. Page described his initial aims for development: work among girls (there already being groups available for boys) and teenagers; new Bible Classes in the Memorial Hall and Vicarage Classroom; and more District Visitors – with only 7 visitors at this date spread over the 28 streets of the parish.[5]

In March 1948, the long-standing Organist and Choirmaster, Stuart Allen, retired. Having taken up the post in September 1928, he had completed almost 20 years. The choir presented him with an illuminated address and a "Gold Wristlet Watch."

Mr. Allen was succeeded by Mr. F. Gordon Spriggs, who took up the post of Organist and Choirmaster at Easter 1948, although the post was officially recognised at the PCC in July that year.[6] Mr. Spriggs remained as Greyfriars' Organist for 40 years, retiring on 17th April 1988. This makes Mr. Spriggs the longest serving Organist, followed by Mr. Thackway (25 years), Mr. Allen (20 years) and Miss Fanny Lyne (almost 16 years). Since 1988 Greyfriars has not had a paid Organist but several volunteers.

Organists of Greyfriars' Church	From	To
Mr. W. H. Strickland	October 1869	January 1870
Mr. H. J. Stark	October 1871	February 1875
Mr. F. J. Read	April 1875	October 1877
Mr. Biddles	October 1877	March 1879
Miss F. Lyne	July 1879	March 1895
Rev. R. B. Daniel	March 1895	April 1896
Mr. C. H. Thackway	May 1896	February 1922
Mr. G. S. Cox	April 1922	September 1923
Mr. S. E. Marsh	November 1923	August 1928
Mr. S. Allen	September 1928	March 1948
Mr. F. G. Spriggs	March 1948	April 1988

In 1949 the long tradition of Pew Rents was abolished in Greyfriars. At the PCC meeting of 22nd July, Dr. Bird presented three reasons for abolition: it was not bringing in much money; there was a basic inequality with some paying for seats and others not doing so; and there was a difficulty seating the growing congregation. After a brief discussion, where several extolled the benefits of a family pew, the Vicar asked all to pray and consider the issue for a decision next meeting.[7]

At the subsequent meeting Mr. Page made clear his objection to the practice continuing – for which, it was minuted, he was prepared to go to serious lengths. In the resulting vote there was just one vote against, by Mr. Sheppard, although several abstained.[8] I imagine that it was hard to give up one's rights to the family pew that might have been in that family for more than one generation. However, the family pew, although not now paid for, was still a possibility. In the PCC meeting in May the following year the following minute was taken: "Seating of visitors by Sidesmen: A slight misunderstanding had arisen since the abolition of pew rents. We are still under the obligation to ensure that those who were regular seatholders still have the opportunity of keeping their regular pew."[9] Sidesmen did not have an easy life!

The Mission Hall in North Street held its 75th Anniversary Service on 17th October 1951. For over a year, the work there had been led by Mr. W. J. Lammas. Mr. Page wrote "under the gracious ministry and leadership of Mr. & Mrs. Lammas a wonderful work of soul-saving has been experienced, and many have rejoiced over blessings there."[10] The Mission Hall itself had undergone repairs to its roof and both internal and external decoration. However, with only 11 years left on the Leasehold, its future was looking uncertain until, after some wrangling, the owner agreed to sell the Freehold to the PCC for £650. At a gift day on 4th November 1951, over £490 was raised towards the purchase.[11]

Lay Leaders of the Iron Room/ Mission Hall

1897	Mr. C. S. Campbell
1901	Mr. T. G. Tredinnick
1901 – 1914	Miss E. Pirouet
1905 – 1914	Mr. E. Taylor
1914 – 1915	Capt. J. Tibble C.A.
1916 – 1922	Capt. J. C. Jones C.A.
1922 – 1939	Capt. W. J. Mace C.A.
1950 – 1953	Mr. W. J. Lammas
1954 – 1959	Mr. C. Lambourn
1959 – 1961	Capt. G. N. Usher C.A.
1961 – 1962	Mr. C. Lambourn
1963 – 1969	Capt. J. Etheridge C.A.
1969 – 1972	Mr. M. N. Winch
1972 – 1980	Mr. C. Greaves

Iron Room/Mission Hall Wardens

1904	Mr. F. H. Sparrow
1906 – 1931	Mr. J. White
1931 – 1950	Mr. R. White
1950 – 1952	Vacant
1952 – 1953	Mr. R. Allen
1953 – 1980	Vacant

The Mission Hall congregation had all but disappeared due to the gap between the Rev. G. Malcolm's departure in late 1945 and William Lammas's arrival in 1950, but before long it was up to 60 to 80.[12] However, Mr. & Mrs. Lammas did not stay long, relinquishing the work at the end of December 1953. Mr. C. Lambourn, a long-standing member of the Church and Mission Hall and Secretary of the PCC, took over the running of the Hall, which at this time began to hold just an evening service on Sundays.[13]

Having spent money on renovating the Mission Hall, attention shifted to the needs of the Greyfriars' site: the Schools, the Church, the Church grounds, the Memorial Hall and the Vicarage. Over the next ten years, until the Church's celebration of the centenary of the restoration, much time, energy and above all money needed to be spent on each of these.

A leaflet – Finances and Fabric 1954 – was produced by the PCC and circulated to the congregation. It itemised recent expenses: redecorating the Schools after Army use; re-tiling the Church roof and renewing all the guttering (£1088); vacuum cleaning the interior of the roof (£46); re-making the Church footpaths (£47); new Church notice board (£59); treating the pews against woodworm (£66); purchasing the Mission Hall Freehold (£650); redecorating the Mission Hall inside and out (£932); overhauling the Mission Hall organ (£100).

It then went on to present a list of needs not yet addressed:

- clean and protect the Church stonework, redecoration inside and out (between £3500 and £4000)
- repair the bell turret and restore to working order (£500)
- renew Schools' gables, dormers, stacks, gutters, roof timbers, porches and outbuildings (£2000)
- repave the Schools' uneven playground (£600)
- Repairs and interior decoration for the Memorial Hall (£860)

The Vicar and PCC called a Day of Prayer on Friday 3rd December 1954, followed by a Day of Gifts on Sunday 5th. The result of the Appeal for £7,500 can best be told by a quote from the Reading Standard of 7th January 1955:

Record "Plate"

What must surely be a record collection – in Reading at least – was achieved by Greyfriars' Church the other Sunday. The amount was £7,026. No great fuss was made about the collection before or afterwards. The Vicar (the Rev. J. K. Page) merely told his people that £7,500 was needed for the repair and redecoration of the Church. First came a "day of prayer." Following it came the "day of gifts," a Sunday, and the gifts amounted to £7,026.

Greyfriars is not in the least "puffed up" about it. After all, the congregation there is fairly well used to big collections. Not very long ago a missionary fund collection realized £1,700. I can well imagine certain other organizations in the town now trying to raise money wishing they had Greyfriars' secret.

The Vicar's report of the Day of Gifts was from an altogether different angle:

"At our four sessions of prayer on December 3rd, we waited on God with quiet confidence, and truly the Lord was in our midst. And what an abundant answer was given on the Sunday! We were given a lovely day, a warm, full Church, and a very real sense of His Presence, and we record with thanksgiving three souls saved at the Evening Service. And the giving? It was to the Lord, and to Him we give all the glory."[14]

Interior View of Greyfriars Church c1955

The bell turret was already being repaired. The PCC had considered removing the turret entirely, but the combination of the cost of doing so and the unlikelihood of a Faculty being granted by the Bishop led them to repair and renew. Up to this point, the bells had been rung up in the roof-space of the north transept, following what can only be described as a precarious climb outside the north aisle/transept roof exterior (the ladder is still in place). A small hut was built immediately behind the chancel wall in the Vicarage garden from which the bells could be rung without the climb.[15] The stonework and repair to the bells was completed by late June 1955.

Bell-ringer's hut built against the Church's east end, in the Vicarage garden.
Note that the Vicarage had a block built against the east end too.
Photograph by David Page c1960

By May 1955 Mr. Metcalfe, the PCC's Clerk of Works, reported that the external repairs to the Church were nearing completion. Additionally, it was decided that the whole of the Church and Schools needed electrical re-wiring.[16] From 22nd August to the end of September the Church was closed for all the internal works and services transferred to the Mission Hall.[17] The Church held a Day of Thanksgiving and Praise for the completion of the work of redecoration on 1st January 1956.[18]

The Vicarage, by this date about 150 years old, was a major cause for concern. At the emergency PCC meeting earlier in 1955, a report:

> ...dealt with the unsuitability of the Vicarage for present day need and thought the Council might consider disposing of the site and the purchase or building of a more modern house. A long discussion followed dealing with many points of interest as to type of business on the site, effectiveness and duration of restrictive covenants, space to be reserved for a possible chancel, wisdom of having a vicarage far from the parish, possibility of an office for the Vicar near the Church...[19]

The PCC contacted the Ecclesiastical Commissioners in March to ask approval to sell the Vicarage and the Commissioners referred the question to the Oxford Diocesan Dilapidations Board. The application was initially refused, but upon hearing that a purchaser had come forward with an offer of £20,000 for the property the Board changed its mind and strongly recommended that the possibility be explored further.[20] The PCC considered that if they were to sell the plot, they should keep 15 feet from the east wall, in order for an apse, in lieu of a chancel, to be built at some time in the future.

In December 1955 the Bishop of Oxford gave approval for the sale of the Vicarage and permission for the Vicar to reside out of the parish, if required. By a vote of 24 to 2, the PCC agreed formally to proceed to the sale in February 1956.[21] Messrs. Hillier Parker May & Rowden of 77 Grosvenor Street, London W1, inspected the Vicarage and valued it at £35,000 with a likely actual sale price of about £27,500.[22]

In September 1955, there was a two week Parish Mission, led by former Greyfriars' member, now Oak Hill Theological College student, John Dobson. The team visited the approximately 1000 houses in the Parish, conducted open-air services and held short services in a number of pubs.[23]

At the Annual Meeting in March 1956, Dr. Bird retired from being Churchwarden. He had been People's Warden from 1933 to 1946 and Vicar's Warden from 1946, a total of 23 years, exceeded at the time only by Alfred Callas (31 years) and since only by Stanley Dunster (24 years). The Vicar "told of his great regret at Dr. Bird's resignation of this office. Only God knew what Dr. Bird meant to him and what a wonderful ministry he has given Greyfriars Sunday by Sunday."[24] Mr. S. J. Milward agreed to be Vicar's Warden, a post he had previously held until 1946.

Churchwardens during Mr. Page's incumbency (1947 – 1968)		
1947 to 1956	Dr. Jason G. Bird	Mr. Stanley Dunster
1956 to 1968	Mr. Stanley J. Milward	Mr. Stanley Dunster
1968	Mr. John S. Milward	Mr. Stanley Dunster

Greyfriars' Vicarage in the late 1950s

The parish boundary was changed on 1st January 1957 to include the rectangle bounded by Chatham Street, Oxford Road, Thorn Street and Alfred Street – at the time this was mostly a residential area.[25]

On 22nd March 1957 Greyfriars Church became a Grade I Listed Building.[26] By this time, Reading Town Planning had refused permission for shops to be erected on the Vicarage site and the PCC had appealed. The Town Planning Committee then gave its approval in June 1958 for a scheme to build shops and offices on the Greyfriars' Vicarage site, but subject to the approval of the Minister of Housing and Local Government as the Vicarage had been placed on the list of Buildings of Architectural or Historic Interest.[27] The PCC was divided over the plan, some feeling that a commercial development so close to the Church would be out of place.

A Public Inquiry was held on Wednesday 7th January 1959 by Mr. W. A. Devereux, an Inspector of the Ministry of Town and Country Planning. The PCC appointed Mr. Sebag Shaw as Counsel to represent them. Among the briefing papers for Mr. Shaw, Mr. Page gave his view of the Vicarage as a family home:

> It is an extremely large and difficult building to run as a Family House and quite unsuited to the present day needs, when it is not practicable to have permanent assistance in the home. The building as a home cannot be adequately warmed and in winter months, apart from my Study which I personally use, we have found that the domestic quarters are the only practicable part of the building in which to live...
>
> The main reception room on the ground floor is so large that it is not practicable to sit in it in cold weather in spite of such warmth as is given by the only fire in the room. The first floor completely defies any reasonable attempts to make it warm.[28]

The chief architect of Hillier Parker May & Rowden, Mr. E. H. Davies, addressed the issue of whether the building was actually designed by Soane, as that looked to be a major issue in whether the building needed to be preserved. His statement to the Inquiry included:

> I am aware that certain authorities have indicated that the house was designed by Sir John Soane and, while this may be true, I am not convinced that it is one of his best efforts and that it embodies features which are characteristic of that eminent Architect's work.
>
> Indeed it might well be argued that the work, though bearing his name, may have been the effort of his office and not necessarily his own individual design."[29]

As seen earlier (pages 53 and 54), the designs produced by Soane for Laurence Austwick were not used directly for the house, but the research that brought this to light was not carried out until 1962.

The Minister of Housing and Local Government, Henry Brooke, refused the application by the PCC to redevelop the Vicarage land by erecting shops and offices. He did, however, add that the PCC should discuss the matter further with the Diocesan Dilapidations Board with a view to seeing if any renovation or adaptation were possible. If that proved impossible, the Minister added that "a further application for development may be made and the present decision is without prejudice to that possibility."[30]

The missionary life of the Church had undergone several important developments in the years following the Second World War. In Kuluva, Uganda, Dr. Ted and Mrs. Muriel Williams had been joined by Ted's younger brother Dr. Peter Williams in March 1948 and then by Peter's wife Elsie after their marriage in late 1950. They were joined by Ted and Peter's parents, Mr. & Mrs. J. H. Williams, in 1948, not long after Peter's arrival.

Ted and Muriel Williams

Peter and Elsie Williams

In 1953 Ted was awarded the Coronation Medal in recognition of the medical work done in the West Nile District of Uganda.[31] A few years later he summarised the success of Kuluva Hospital. In 1956:

> The outpatient attendances were up by nearly 20%, giving a figure of 76,000 [which is an average of over 200 a day for the 366 days of the year]; patients admitted to the wards totalled over 900, again a substantial rise; and major operations increased by 40% to 250... Everyone attending, for whatever disease, heard the Word of God read and expounded and many received portions of the Word, and through it some have found eternal salvation and many Christian blessings.[32]

Missionaries from Greyfriars Church (Departing up to 1968)			
	From To	Where served	Mission Society
Miss Selena Fletcher	1892 1912	Hong Kong	Church Missionary Society
Miss Elsie Sparrow (Mrs Elsie Purser)	1906 1923	Colombo, Ceylon	Church Missionary Society
Miss Sophy Fletcher	1909 1911	Hong Kong	Church Missionary Society
Miss Ruth Laurence	1928 1972	Beersheba, Palestine/ Israel	
Mr. John Savage	1929 1952	Lima, Peru	Evangelical Union of South America
Miss Florence Peaston	1930 1938	Chididi, Nyasaland, South Africa	South Africa General Mission
Rev. Theodore Benson	1930 1949	Szechwan, West China	China Inland Mission
Rev. John Hay-Walker	1930s 1964	Alexandria, Egypt; Beirut	
Miss Jessie Hay-Walker	1930s 1964	Dohnavur, South India	Dohnavur Fellowship
Miss Jocelyn Cobb	1930s 1930s	Ismailia, Egypt	
Miss Jessie Wade	1930s 1940s	Pucheng, Fukien, China	
Miss Monica Sutton	1930s 1947	Nilgiri Medical Mission, South India	
Miss Mary Quelch	1938 1944	Arua, Uganda	Africa Inland Mission
Miss Ina Lucia	1930s 1940s	Chefoo School, China	China Inland Mission
Dr. Ted & Muriel Williams	1941 1980	Kuluva, Uganda; Kijabe Kenya	Africa Inland Mission
Dr. Peter & Elsie Williams	1947 1974	Kuluva, Uganda	Africa Inland Mission
Mr. & Mrs. John H. Williams	1948 N/A	Kuluva, Uganda	
Rev. Stephen & Rosina Levenson	1952 1967	Sousse, Tunisia; then Jerusalem	Barbican Mission to Jews
Miss Margaret Heale (Mrs M Collard)	1952 1975	Malaysia	China Inland Mission

Missionaries from Greyfriars Church (Departing up to 1968) - Continued			
	From To	Where served	Mission Society
Miss Mary Cundy	1957 1989	Nepal	Bible and Medical Missionary Fellowsip
Miss Daphne Ash (Mrs Daphne Carver)	1957 1963	India	Church Missionary Society
Miss Mary Lewin	1957 1987	Thailand	Worldwide Evangelism for Christ
Miss Shirley Palmer	1959 1969	Nigeria	Sudan United Mission
Miss Mary Hamilton (Mrs Mary Forsyth)	1959 1964	South America	Evangelical Union of South America
Miss Elizabeth Hoyte (Mrs Elizabeth Goldsmith)	1960 1970	Sumatra, then Singapore	China Inland Mission/ Overseas Missionary Fellowship
Rev. John & Jo Dobson	1960 1972	Arua, Uganda, then Bishop Tucker College	Africa Inland Mission
Miss Mollie Clark MBE	1961 1994	Bhutan and India	Leprosy Mission
Miss Ann Sayers (Mrs Ann Long)	1961 1968	Eire	Irish Church Mission
Miss Gillian Hunt	1962 1984	Malaysia, then Philippines	China Inland Mission/ Overseas Missionary Fellowship
Miss Ann Hall	1963 1972	India	Bible and Medical Missionary Fellowsip
Miss Marion Williamson	1964 1974	India	Bible and Medical Missionary Fellowsip
Miss Pauline Halls	1967 1974	Rwanda	Rwanda Mission
Mrs. Catherine Russell	1967 1978	Gindiri, North Nigeria; then Southern France	Sudan United Mission; North Africa Mission
Rev. Peter & Janet Dominy	1967 1982	North Nigeria	Sudan United Mission
Colin & Joy Densham	1967 2004	Kijabe, Kenya	Africa Inland Mission
Paul Mayes	1968 1972	Leeds, then Brighton	Barbican Mission to Jews

While still considering what should be done about the Vicarage, the next Church project was a refurbishment of the Memorial Hall. The PCC decided upon "the repair and redecoration of the Hall, the provision of additional toilet facilities, the installation of a modern heating system, and an alteration to the entrance."[33] The works aimed to make the Hall usable throughout the winter months. The estimated cost was £1,243. A Day of Gifts was held on Sunday 10th January 1960, preceded by four one hour prayer meetings in the "Schoolroom" throughout the day on the Tuesday before – "For the Memorial Hall, and other needs in the Mission Field, our Town and Parish." £997 12s 5d was collected on the day.[34]

During 1960 the PCC, led by its Clerk of Works, Michael Metcalfe, considered and proposed a scheme for the repair and modernisation of the Vicarage. However, the high cost of the scheme was uneconomic and so the only real alternative was to demolish the old Vicarage and build a new one on the same site. By October 1960, the Borough Planning Officer had given the Church the good news that the Town Planning and Buildings Committee had agreed to the project and that the Minister of Housing and Local Government did not propose to intervene further.[35] The PCC appointed as the project's architect Mr. E. J. Lassetter L.R.I.B.A., of Messrs. Lassetter & Judd, Blagrave Street, Reading. A "Vicarage Committee" was formed with membership: Rev. J. K. Page, Mr. S. J. Milward, Mr. S. Dunster, Mrs. C. J. Bird, Mr. W. H. K. Dyer, Mr. J. R. Jeffrey, Mr. C. Lambourn, Mr. W. R. Lawrence, Mr. J. S. Milward (Secretary), Mr. A. E. Sheppard, Mr. G. C. Skinner and Miss S. Yarnold.

However, the next major expenditure was not on the Vicarage, but on the Church organ. By this time the organ was just over twenty years old and was in need of a major clean and overhaul. The work included:

> ...careful cleaning of every pipe; dismantling and cleaning the bellows, reservoirs, windchests and valves; overhauling the wind-trunks, swell-shutters and their action; also detailed attention to the thousands of contacts, solenoids, reversers and other electrical components constituting the key, stop, canceller, and piston actions. A much needed improvement to one of the Pedal organ stops will be included... The organ will be out of commission for six or eight weeks, and much of it will have to be stacked in various corners of the Church and Memorial Hall.[36]

In addition to the money that had been accumulating in the Organ Fund, following a £200 bequest by Miss Harman in 1944, a further £830 was needed. The Gift Day on 4th December 1960 yielded almost £650 towards the cost.[37]

In October 1961, the Mission Hall said farewell to Church Army Captain G. N. Usher who, having worked there for almost three years, left for a new sphere of work in Lowestoft.[38] Mr. C. Lambourn took over again at the Mission Hall, as he had in the past. In December the PCC agreed to a much needed scheme to replace the old stoves that heated the Mission Hall with ten electric heaters at a cost of £251.[39] The new heaters were installed in the following summer.[40] In early 1963 James Etheridge, a 24 year old Church Army Captain, took charge of the work at the Mission Hall. Although young, he was experienced, having already worked in a parish in Leeds.[41]

At the same December 1961 PCC meeting, the first costing of the new Vicarage was discussed:

Building	£9,850
Surface Water Drains	£600
Alterations to front boundary	£300
Old basement alterations	£250
Demolition	£500
Total Estimated Cost	£11,500

There was some financial help available from the Church Commissioners, finally being agreed to be in the region of £3000.[42] By the time the appeal was put to the Church in a leaflet in October 1962, the amount needed from Greyfriars' members was estimated to be £9,500.

The Vicarage Committee continued to meet frequently to discuss and agree the detail of the new building, its walls and garden. Its Secretary, John Milward, reported in detail to the PCC on 26th October on the approved plans. John R. Jeffery, who had recently become PCC Secretary, was appointed Treasurer of the Vicarage Appeal. A Day of Prayer was held on Friday 30th November, followed by a Day of Gifts on the Church's 99th anniversary – Sunday 2nd December 1962. The Gift Day raised £5801 5s.[43]

At a special meeting of the PCC on 13th December 1962, Mr. W. K. H. Dyer, Mr. J. S. Milward and Mr. G. C. Skinner were appointed to be responsible for the oversight of the building work throughout the project. At a further meeting one week later, it was agreed to accept the tender of local firm Collier & Catley at a cost of £11,726. The PCC agreed to the rental for £375 p.a. of 136 Westwood Road, Tilehurst, as a temporary

Vicarage[44] and the Vicar and his family moved there early in the New Year, 1963.

Demolition of the old Vicarage started on 8th February,[45] in the middle of the continuing exceptionally cold winter, with an original estimate of 52 weeks before completion. However, well ahead of this schedule, the work was completed on 8th November, exactly nine months later, and the Page family moved into their new home one week later.[46]

While digging the footings for the new Vicarage, on the west side – and so nearest the Church's east wall – workmen discovered two human skeletons in graves from the old Friary. The graves had been partially disturbed by previous building work, almost certainly that of 1806 when Austwick's house was built.[47]

The new Vicarage looked quite similar to the old one from the outside, as shown by the photographs below. The frontage width of the building remained the same, with the new building being built upon the old one's footings. The depth of the new building was about two thirds of the former one, covering the cellars rather than projecting beyond them as the old building had.

To add to the similarity of appearance, the facing bricks from the original building had been saved and used. The curved walls and iron railings were also retained – these "Quadrant Walls and Railings" had been Grade II listed in 1957.[48]

Old Vicarage
Photo taken in 1942

New Vicarage
Photo taken in 2011

Meanwhile, arrangements for the Centenary weekend were discussed and agreed. A committee with Mr. F. G. Spriggs as Chairman and Mr. J. S. Milward as Secretary met monthly from February.[49] A programme card was issued with the October edition of the Greyfriars' Monthly Newsletter that members of the congregation could send to friends and relatives living elsewhere. The card had a tear off section that could be returned to Mr. W. R. Lawrance, who was co-ordinating the list of those attending.

Centenary Celebration: 30th November 1963 in the Reading Town Hall

At the microphone: Rev. J. K. Page MBE
Front row: (Left to Right) Mr. E. P. F. Sutton (Trustee of the Living), Mr. J. Butcher (Mayor of Reading), the Rt. Rev. E. Knell (Bishop of Reading), Mrs. Mohan and the Rev. T. G. Mohan (Secretary to the Trustees)
Second Row: Mr. S. Milward (Churchwarden), Mrs. V. Milward, Rev. J. Boultbee, Mrs. Boultbee, Mrs. K. Page, Mrs. Dunster, Mr. S. Dunster (Churchwarden)
Third Row: Mrs. Wells, Rev. E. Wells, Mrs Hayward, Rev. Hayward, Mrs. Green. Rev. E. Green, Rev. T. Benson, Rev. L. Persson
Top right: Mr. F. G. Spriggs at the organ and Mr. S. Allen sitting nearby

The four day celebration began with a “Praise and Prayer Meeting” at 7.30pm in the Schools on Friday 29th November. Next day there was a Centenary Celebration and Tea in the Town Hall from 2.30 to 5pm. This was a memorable event celebrating the work of God in the Church, through its history and its activities. It opened with four pieces played on the organ by Stuart Allen (Organist at Greyfriars from 1928 to 1948). After the hymn “Praise to the Lord, the Almighty, the King of Creation,” Mr. Page welcomed members of Greyfriars, past and present, and many distinguished visitors, including the Bishop of Reading and the Member of Parliament for Reading, Peter Emery.
The main part of the afternoon was a “Review of the Goodness of God in the Life and Work of Greyfriars”, led by Capt. Alan Stockbridge, an Army Chaplain and former Chaplain of Reading School. Interleaved with short reports given by members of the congregation, taped contributions from Greyfriars’ missionaries were played, all accompanied by slides. The full programme is shown below:

God’s Goodness to Greyfriars in Years Gone By:

Early History	Capt. Alan Stockbridge
Message from Missionaries	Mr. & Mrs. John H. Williams (Uganda)
The Jubilee of 1913	Mr. Reginald White
Tribute to the Rev. J. C. Rundle	Rev. J. K. Page
Day School and Campaigners	Mr. Len Wicks
Girl Campaigners	Mrs. Margaret Moss
Message from Missionaries	Miss Ruth Laurence (Israel)
Men’s service	Mr. Charles Lambourn
Band of Hope	Mr. Charley Greaves
Young Men’s Bible Class	Mr. A. Edgar Milward, including a taped message from the Bishop of Buckingham
Message from Missionaries	Rev. John Savage (South America)

God’s Goodness to Greyfriars Today:

The Church today	Capt. Alan Stockbridge
Women’s Fellowship	Miss Freda Wheeler
Message from Missionaries	Dr. & Mrs. E. Williams and family, and Dr. & Mrs. P. Williams and family (Uganda)
Cradle Roll Fellowship	Miss Joan Buss
Sunday School	Mr. Arthur Sheppard
Young People’s Fellowship	Miss Cynthia Toms & Mr. Michael Archer

Message from Missionaries	Rev. David Brooke (Canada)
Wednesday Fellowship	Mrs. Joyce Gledhill
Friday Friendship	Mr. Bob Masters
Mission Hall	Capt. James Etheridge and a taped message from Capt. W. J. Mace
Message from Missionaries	Miss Mollie Clarke (North India) Miss Mary Cundy (Nepal)

The tape recordings of Missionaries were organised and edited by Wilfred Dyer and Ron Lowe.

An augmented choir then sang Stanford's "Te Deum Laudamus," followed by a closing prayer by the Bishop of Reading. The formal proceedings closed with the hymn "Now thank we all our God." At 4pm the buffet tea was served by Miss D. Phippen, Mrs. C. Bird, Miss C. Toms and others, until the meeting's end at 5.15pm. The finishing time had to be adhered to closely as the Town Hall needed to be set up for another booking!

On the next day there were four services and a social gathering:

8am	Holy Communion
11am	Morning Prayer – Preacher: The Bishop of Reading
3pm	Family Service – Speaker: Rev. George Malcolm (Curate 1939 – 45)
6.30pm	Evening Prayer – Preacher: Rev. James Boultbee
8pm	Congregational Gathering – in the Schools

The 8 o'clock Congregational Gathering was held through much of Mr. Page's time. It was usually a well attended event where people would call out hymns to sing from the book "Golden Bells." Mr. Page would finish the gathering at 9pm promptly with a "thumbnail thought" lasting 2 or 3 minutes.[50]

The Centenary Service was held on the following day, Monday 2nd December – the exact anniversary of the re-consecration – at 7.30pm. The preacher was Canon T. G. Mohan, General Secretary of the Church Pastoral Aid Society and also Secretary to the Trustees of the Greyfriars' Benefice. In a fitting link with the past the hymn "All people that on earth do dwell" was sung, as it had been in the re-consecration service 100 years before.

A well-edited vinyl record was produced of the weekend as a lasting memorial. Copies on tape were sent to Greyfriars' Missionaries.[51]

Centenary Record and tape

"Every winter the vexed question of Church heating – and draughts – raises its ugly head... Heating problems do not appear to have unduly worried the old friars, but the Parochial Church Council of the present time has long been concerned about them." Thus began an insert that went to the congregation with the July 1964 monthly Newsletter. The PCC had called in architect Mr. E. J. Lassetter, and a church heating expert, to advise them on how best to improve the situation at Greyfriars.[52] The heating system had been installed in 1902 – although the boiler had been replaced in 1941 – and ran on solid fuel that needed George Waters, the Verger, to stoke it on Saturday evening and again at 6am on Sunday. It was decided to replace the boiler with an oil-fired automatic system, retaining the distribution pipes and radiators, and adding a further six radiators in the side aisles.

The heating would then be run through the week, not just at the weekend, from 1st October to 30th April, at an estimated cost of £480 per year. This compared with 18 tons of coke costing £200 plus a £113 gas bill for the burners in the transepts. The installation itself, by Messrs. John Wilder Ltd, was expected to cost £1300, for which a Day of Prayer was called on 28th July and a Day of Gifts on Sunday 2nd August 1964. Work was quickly started so that the new system would be in place before the winter.

In the following month, Greyfriars agreed, with permission from the relevant Church authorities, to sell a strip of land 15 feet wide and just over 120 feet long from the east edge of the Vicarage garden. This was as a result of a Compulsory Purchase Scheme by Reading Corporation in order for Greyfriars Road to be widened and improved.[53] The Corporation paid Greyfriars £100 for the land and also built the replacement brick wall for the Vicarage garden.

Earlier in the year the PCC had discussed a proposal to start Home Bible Study Groups.[54] In October eight members of the congregation had "expressed their willingness to open their homes either once or twice a month for this purpose." Details were given of where, when and what would be studied in the October 1964 Newsletter. Now almost 50 years later, it would be hard to imagine the fellowship without these "small groups."

In April 1966 Stanley Dunster resigned as Treasurer. He had been carrying out these duties since 1949, as well as being Churchwarden throughout the period. He was replaced by Arthur D'Arcy, who remained Treasurer for the next 18 years.[55]

On 23rd October 1966 from 7.25pm, congregational hymns were relayed live by the Reading Hospital Broadcasting Service to the Royal Berkshire, Battle, Blagrave and Park Hospitals. There had been recorded hymns the year before, but this was the first occasion of a live broadcast. There was a rehearsal of the hymn singing after Evening Prayer on the previous Sunday, led of course by Organist and Choirmaster, Gordon Spriggs.[56]

Model of Greyfriars Church, Memorial Hall and Vicarage
Made by David Page
(Photograph from Reading Evening Post 11th June 1971)

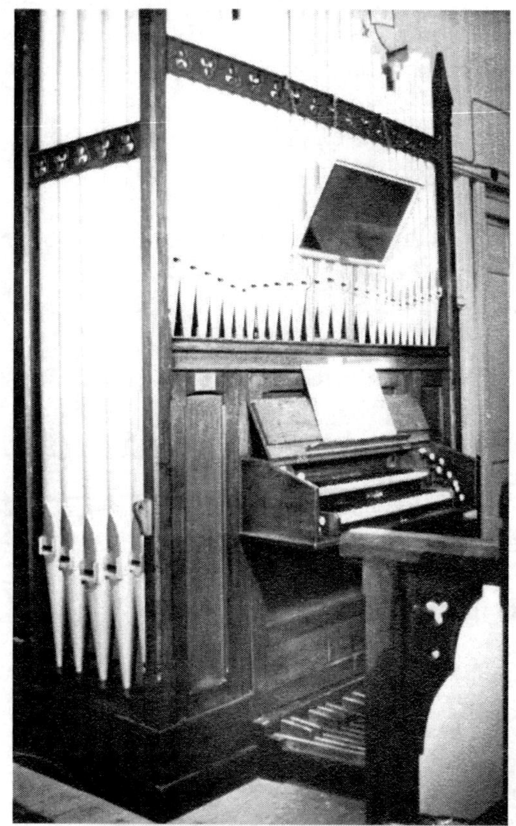

Mission Hall Organ

Below:
Plaque on the organ commemorating Miss Nellie Sherwood

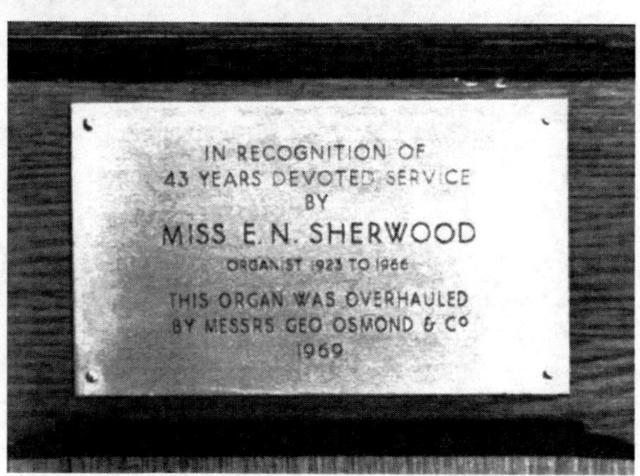

In 1967 a marvellous scale model of the Church, Memorial Hall and Vicarage was made by the Vicar's son David Page.[57] He donated it to the Church and it was on display for many years in the Memorial Hall and then the Church foyer.

The Church gained its first amplification system in April 1967. It is difficult to imagine the sermon being given to a packed Church without any amplification, but that was the situation up until this point. A special meeting of the PCC in February had considered the options researched on its behalf by Wilfred Dyer and Dr. L. J. Herbst. A "Magneta" system, costing about £400, was chosen.[58]

Following various repairs and redecoration to the Mission Hall, it was agreed that the Mission Hall organ needed attention.[59] The organ was the original one installed in 1878, two years after the Mission Hall (then of course known as the Iron Room) was opened; it was possibly second hand when bought, but this is uncertain. The only record of any repair work prior to this date was that of the overhaul in 1954. It had been hand-pumped until 1959, at which point an electric blower was installed at a cost of £70 11s.

The PCC approved an estimate of £439, which included moving the console to a more central position in the Mission Hall. The money was raised at a Gift Day in May 1968. The work was carried out by Geo. Oswald & Co. of Taunton through June and July of 1969. Due to the delay between the estimate and works, the final cost rose to £481.[60] A ceremony on 29th September officially opened the restored organ.

At the Annual Parochial Church Meeting on 1st March 1968, Stanley J. Milward stepped down as Churchwarden. Over two periods (1935 – 1946, 1956 – 1968) he had been Warden for a total of 23 years. He was replaced as Vicar's Warden by his son, John S. Milward. Stanley Dunster was again elected as People's Warden.[61]

On 31st May 1968, at a Special PCC meeting, Mr. Page announced that he had decided, after much thought and prayer, to accept an invitation to become the incumbent of St. John's Church, Weymouth. He told the congregation on the following Sunday. An insert in the Monthly Newsletter for July 1968 stated:

> What joy has been ours over the past twenty-one years to have had the Rev. J. K. Page MBE as our Vicar and as our friend, and how faithfully he has ministered to us the Word of God. Consequently it was with a real sense of loss that the Parochial Church Council heard at the Meeting held on May 31st that

he would be leaving Greyfriars at the beginning of September... We are naturally sad at the prospect of losing one whom we have loved and respected as our leader, but we know that the Lord makes no mistakes, and so we take this as His perfect will. God alone knows the true extent of the blessing which He has given through our beloved Vicar, and we give Him all the praise.

A Farewell Gathering took place at the Town Hall at 6pm on Saturday 31st August 1968, with over 500 present. John Milward, Vicar's Warden, was Chairman. Many tributes were paid to Mr. Page:

Introduction	Mr. S. Dunster, People's Warden
Recollections	Rev. E. A. Wells
Recorded Message	The Williams Family, Kuluva, Uganda
The Parish – An Appreciation	Capt. J. Etheridge
Recorded Message	Miss Pauline Halls, Kabale, Uganda
Outreach from Greyfriars	Mr. David Stillman
The Congregation – An Appreciation	Mr. A. E. Sheppard
Presentation	Mr. S. J. Milward JP

The Page Family
Left to right: Michael, Betty, David, Rev. John K., Mrs. Kathleen
Farewell Gathering in Reading Town Hall
(Photograph from Insert in the Greyfriars' Monthly Newsletter October 1968)

Mr. Page was presented with a cheque and a tape recorder that bore the inscription: “Presented to the Revd. J. K. Page, in appreciation of 21 years faithful ministry at Greyfriars Church, Reading. 31st August 1968.” Mrs. Page was presented with a record player and their daughter Betty was presented with an electric blanket. In reply, Mr. Page thanked everyone for their gifts and continued:

> Now, much has been said this evening about your Vicar and as I sat and listened I wondered who this man was. But seriously (and I mean this) if anything has been experienced of blessing in Greyfriars over these twenty-one years it is due solely to the faithfulness of God and the loyalty of Greyfriars' congregation.

On Sunday 1st September, the Church was full for Mr. Page's final services. In the morning he dedicated the enlarged pulpit desk in memory of the late Rev. J. C. Rundle. In the evening his sermon's theme was “How shall we escape if we neglect so great a salvation?” Hebrews 2:3.[62]

Mr. Page was inducted to the Living at St. John's, Weymouth, on Monday 9th September 1968 at 7pm. He ministered there until his retirement on 31st October 1977,[63] aged 65. He continued to preach and to lead Bible Studies and mid-week meetings, enjoying the variety of types of Church and location. He died in Weymouth in September 1989, aged 77.

Rev. John Knott Page
MBE

Photograph from 1963

Rev. J. K. Spence
(Photograph from Greyfriars' Monthly Newsletter October 1968)

Chapter 17

James Knox Spence: Vicar 1968 to 1978

James (generally known as Jim) Spence was born in India in August 1930 and educated at Charterhouse School and Worcester College, Oxford. He then trained for the ministry at Ridley Hall, Cambridge, and was ordained Deacon in London in 1957. His first Curacy was at Holy Trinity, West Hampstead.

In the summer of 1961 he married Hilary Hacking and they had two daughters, Rowena and Rachel. From 1961 to 1964 Mr. Spence was Curate at St. Ebbes in Oxford and then Candidates Secretary for the Church Pastoral Aid Society. He was in this role when, aged 38, he became Vicar of Greyfriars.

The Trustees, under the auspices of the Church Trust Fund Trust, at this time were: Canon T. G. Mahon, Mr. E. P. Sutton, Mr. M. Birch (Keswick Council), Rev. R. C. Lucas (St. Helen's, Bishopsgate) and Mr. C. W. Robbins. On behalf of the PCC, Churchwarden John Milward sent a description of the parish, its needs and of the qualities desired in the new Vicar for the Trustees to consider at their meeting on 26th June 1968.

> ...The traditions of Greyfriars have long included emphasis upon the conversion of souls, the power of prayer, the preaching and study of the Word of God, the support of Missionary work, and the principle of direct giving...
>
> It would seem that a man with gifts of leadership, well supported by an able Curate, would have unlimited scope in furthering the building up of a team of people fully committed to Jesus Christ and ready to serve Him in fellowship together, and as individuals...[1]

During the interregnum, services were taken by the Rev. W. J. Graham Hobson, who had first been associated with Greyfriars when he was the children's missioner in April 1925.

The Trustees offered the Living to Rev. J. K. Spence on 11th July. Following a visit to the parish, he accepted the post on 25th July, although it took until 12th August for the official notice to come from the Bishop of

Oxford. Mr. Page was therefore able to announce the news in Church on Sunday 18th August.[2]

The Trustees' Secretary, Rev. V. N. Cooper, described what the Trustees knew of Mr. Spence:

> ...An outstanding man, amongst our younger clergy, he differs from many of them in his conservatism, not only in Scripture, but also in the kind of traditional Evangelical Church usage which is so appreciated at Greyfriars. He is a most able expositor of the Word.[3]

The Licensing and Installation of the Rev. J. K. Spence M.A. took place at 7.30pm on Wednesday 27th November 1968, with the Lord Bishop of Oxford, The Rt. Rev. H. J. Carpenter, officiating before a full Church.[4] There was a gathering afterwards in the schoolrooms, with catering organised by Joyce Mundy. On the following Sunday Mr. Spence read the 39 Articles in the morning service.

At the Licensing and Installation of Rev. J. K. Spence M.A.
(Left to right) Rev. J. K. Spence, Dr. H. J. Carpenter (Bishop of Oxford),
Ven. E. Wild (Archdeacon of Berkshire)
and Rev. P. Beresford-Peirse (Rural Dean of Reading)

The Spences were "At Home" on Saturday morning 7th December and invited any of the congregation who were able to visit.[5] Mr. Spence concluded the invitation with: "We cannot claim Mr. Page's wonderful memory of names and faces, but we do look forward to getting to know you." In the January 1969 Newsletter, Mr. Spence set out his initial aims:

> We start now not merely a new year but also what is inevitably in some respects a new chapter in the history of Greyfriars... I have discovered already that there is a widespread desire for a more effective expression of our fellowship as a Church and a company of believers, with opportunities to get to know each other better. We want to build up the work among the young people who will form the congregation and leaders of the next generation, and the young people themselves wish to take their full part in the life of the Church. And there is the constant need of greater outreach in the Parish itself.

Mr. Spence's first Annual Meeting took place on 28th February 1969. He proposed John Milward to continue as Vicar's Warden and Stanley Dunster was re-elected People's Warden. Stanley J. Milward was elected as "Warden Emeritus" in recognition of his past services, especially as Churchwarden.

Churchwardens during Mr. Spence's incumbency (1968 – 1978)		
1968 to 1970	Mr. John S. Milward	Mr. Stanley Dunster
1970 to 1973	Mr. John S. Milward	Mr. Wilfred H. K. Dyer
1973 to 1974	Mr. Jack H. Stemp	Mr. Wilfred H. K. Dyer
1974 to 1976	Mr. Christopher R. Hilliard	Mr. Wilfred H. K. Dyer
1976 to 1977	Mr. Derek Winslow	Mr. Wilfred H. K. Dyer
1977 to 1978	Mr. Derek Winslow	Mr. Christopher Leslie
1978 to 1979	Mr. Wilfred H. K. Dyer	Mr. Christopher Leslie

At the March 1969 PCC meeting, Mr. Spence instituted a structure consisting of six committees.[6] Although changes to the list of committees would occur in the future, this structure has stood the test of time to date.

Committee	First Chairman	First Secretary
Standing & Finance	Vicar	Mr. C. J. Beard
Worship	Vicar	Miss M. Challis
Evangelism & Publicity	Mr. J. M. Lewis	Mr. J. H. Stemp
Missionary	Mr. J. S. Milward	Miss J. Hope
Children & Young People	Mr. C. Greaves	Miss B. Foster
Buildings	Mr. W. H. K. Dyer	Mr. J. J. Clarke[7]

In July 1969, Mr. John H. Williams died in Kuluva, West Nile, Uganda.[8] Since his retirement aged 65 in 1948, he and his wife had gone out to join their sons Drs. Ted and Peter Williams and their families at Kuluva Hospital. Mrs. Williams remained at Kuluva with her family until just before her death in late 1977.[9]

The Mission Hall and Church bade farewell to James and Margaret Etheridge on Sunday 14th September 1969.[10] Capt. Etheridge had led the Mission Hall since January 1963. He had also led the Open Air Witness every summer (Sundays at 8pm), taken a boys' Bible Class on Sunday afternoons, led the Young People's Fellowship (for 20s and 30s) on Thursdays at 7.30pm and the Friday Friendship for 7s-11s at 6pm and 12s-17s at 7.30pm on Fridays. Michael Winch took on the leadership of the Mission Hall, fitting it in with his full-time job as an electrical engineering draughtsman.

Two weeks later, Greyfriars gained its first Curate for almost 24 years. Roderick Cheyne Thorp was ordained in Christ Church, Oxford, on 28th September 1969.

The 3 Curates who worked with Mr. Spence	Curate From	To	Next destination
Roderick Cheyne Thorp	1969	1973	Curate: St. Martin's, Hull
Peter Russell Brown	1973	1974	Vicar: Jesus Church, Enfield
John Spencer Halstaff Coles	1975	1979	Curate: Christ Church, Clifton

In January 1970 the Worship Committee successfully brought forward to the PCC the proposal to trial the "Alternative Services Series 2" Baptism and Confirmation services.[11] The first baptism in a morning service (rather than in a special afternoon service) was on 8th February. There were two babies baptised that day: Michael and Jean Winch's baby Claire and Tracy Evans.[12]

At the Annual Parochial Church Meeting on 6th March 1970, Stanley Dunster stood down after 24 years as People's Churchwarden, a total only surpassed by Alfred Callas's 34 years from 1881 to 1915. He was promptly elected as Warden Emeritus. Wilfred Dyer was elected to replace Mr.

Dunster, with John Milward being proposed again by the Vicar as his Warden.[13]

A printing revolution took place at Greyfriars in the spring of 1970 – a duplicating machine was purchased. This meant that the Church could produce its own service sheets and other items, rather than having to have them printed on its behalf. At the PCC meeting in April, Mr. Thorp proposed that the Monthly Newsletter be replaced with a larger duplicated magazine. He estimated that the move from a 4 page card to a 12 page duplicated magazine would actually save about £12 per month. The PCC approved and from July 1970 the Greyfriars News appeared.[14]

Greyfriars Church in 1971

The old Schools buildings had deteriorated to a very poor state. Back in 1956 there had been a claim from Sir Andrew Wright, a grandson of Rev. S. M. Barkworth, to part of the land on which the Schools were built – that bought by Mr. Barkworth in 1867 for the final extension of the Schools. It took until October 1969 for this claim finally to be laid to rest. However, between the Diocesan Council of Education and Board of Finance in Oxford, the Department of Education and Science in London, and the local Education Board and Planning Department, the overall ownership of the land on which the Schools were built continued to be in dispute.

Demolition of the Schools
Above: Photograph from the Evening Post (24th August 1971)
Below: Photograph from Mr. F. G. Spriggs

Greyfriars, though, owned the buildings. At the PCC meeting on 15th July 1971 it was agreed that, due to their dangerous condition, the Schools should be demolished, at a cost of £475.

With the Schools demolished, there was nowhere for the Sunday School to meet. The problem was solved by Mr. & Mrs. Bardsley, parents of three Sunday School children, who were proprietors of the Mitre pub (now Thai Corner) on the corner of West Street, just opposite Greyfriars. They offered the Church the use of their downstairs "Tippet Bar" on Sunday mornings.

Meanwhile plans were being drawn up by architect Ken White for an extension to the Church. The Parish Buildings Committee had agreed to invite Mr. White to inspect the site and have preliminary conversations in May 1970,[15] and appointed him as architect of the project on 3rd June.[16] In order to begin to form a view of what the Church needed, Mr. White circulated a confidential questionnaire "to people who have any sort of responsibility for activities in the life of Greyfriars."

Mr. White presented a proposal for a semi-circular extension at the western end of the Church at a special PCC meeting in February 1971. The project would also include a kitchen, circulation area and toilets. At this stage, it also included building a new vestry behind the east wall, accessed through a door in the north transept, but this aspect of the plan was dropped. The PCC welcomed the plans, which were then put to the wider Church community at a General Church Meeting on 19th March 1971. The report of the meeting stated:

> A crowded meeting of some 140 people of all ages received with enthusiasm and unanimity the plans for our new building set out on 19 March by Mr. K. C. White, the Architect. The plans envisage a semi-circular annexe to be built onto the west end of the Church. The annexe will have a low level flat roof so that the great west window is not in any way interfered with; the semi-circular shape picks up the curve of the pavement around that end of the Church land. The building will be in materials to blend with the Church itself. Linked to this annexe will also be a development along the north side of the Church, where the cycle shed now stands; this area will be roofed and will contain kitchen, circulating area, toilets and caretaker's room; it will also link with the existing vestry.[17]

The initial estimate of the project's cost was £52,000 – which was remarkably accurate as the actual sum came to £51,813.[18] An Evening of Prayer was held on 15th May, with a Day of Commitment on the next day and a Day of Gifts on 20th June. The Vicar also decided that the Easter

Offering, traditionally part of his income, should go to the New Building Fund. At the PCC on 15th July 1971 it was reported that the fund (including amounts by Deeds of Covenant) stood at £39,427.28. Shillings and pence had been replaced by decimalisation earlier that year.

The first Greyfriars' Membership List was produced in the summer of 1971, with Mike & Jane Page as the co-ordinators. Monthly additions and amendments began to appear in Greyfriars News from October, as people arrived and left the fellowship.

Another innovation that year was a Church Day at Aston Tirrold, near Didcot, on Saturday 18th September. The day included services in the morning and Communion at the end. There was a talk by the Vicar and a session that split into various groups for discussion: Sunday services; young people; work in the New Building; students; and Missionary work.[19]

The first development from Aston Tirrold was a new group for 11 – 14 year olds in late October 1971. On Sunday mornings the young people attended the first part of Morning Prayer and then went to the Mission Hall for a group study with Stan Bolton. On Saturday evenings a club night started in the Memorial Hall with Ray Bennett for games, talks and the opportunity to make things. There was also a new group for those over this age, meeting fortnightly on Saturday evenings led by Bob Palmer at the home of Derek and Dinah Winslow.[20]

One Day Church Conferences during Mr. Spence's incumbency		
September 1971	Church Day	Aston Tirrold
September 1972	Parish Conference	Bradfield College
September 1973	Parish Conference	Cranford House School, Moulsford
November 1975	Church Houseparty	Easthamstead Park
October 1977	Day Conference	Crosfields School

With the Schools demolished and the work on the West End Extension not yet started, it had been decided that the Church should seek to buy a temporary building for various parish purposes, not least the youth work, until the Extension was built. As early as May 1971, architect Ken White had proposed to investigate this possibility.[21] Planning permission was granted by Reading Borough on 10th August 1971, but a suitable Hut was not found until the end of the year. John Milward, Harry Hogg and Derek Winslow visited Deepcut Barracks, near Aldershot, and selected one to buy.[22] The Hut was approximately 60 feet by 20 feet in size and cost £200 including dismantling and delivery to Greyfriars. To have it erected on site cost extra![23] Although the plan was for the Hut to be used only until the West End was ready, it remained in situ for over ten years.

Part of the West End Extension was to be sited on land belonging to the Schools. Therefore building could not start until the Church owned the Schools' land. After much hard work, especially by Arthur Sheppard, the situation was resolved. The Department of Education and Science instructed Greyfriars to advertise the land for sale at £2,000 in the local press, noting that the land was designated for Church use. If no buyer came forward and outbid Greyfriars' £2,000 within a two week period then Greyfriars was free to buy it from the Oxford Diocese. An advertisement was duly placed in the Reading Chronicle on Friday 14th January 1972.[24]

The deadline passed with no other interest shown and so the purchase could finally go ahead. As John Milward, Churchwarden and Secretary of the Parish Buildings Committee at the time, put it: "In effect the Vicar and Churchwardens of Greyfriars bought the site from themselves [the Trustees of the land], paid the Diocesan Council of Education £2,000 and then vested the property in the Diocese." [25] Work began on the West End (although the name had yet to be settled upon) in February 1972.

In the following month, Miss E. Freda Wheeler's booklet "The Great West Window – The Symbol of Light" was printed and went on sale for 30p. This was a re-telling of the history of the Church, weaving historically known dates and facts with a fictional storyline. The Vicar wrote that it was "a delightfully vivid reconstruction of the history of Greyfriars which will be read with enjoyment by people of all ages."[26]

At the Annual Meeting in March, two long-time members of the PCC stood down: Stanley Dunster and Charles Lambourn.[27] The latter had been a member of the PCC since 1930 and its Secretary until 1962, in addition to his two stints in charge of the Mission Hall.

The Mission Hall had one final change of leadership in late 1972: Michael Winch, who had taken over in late 1969, announced on 16th July that he and his wife felt that they were being called to work and witness in the Whitley area. His last Sunday in charge was on 5th November. Charley Greaves accepted the leadership of the Mission Hall, although in the view of the PCC the Mission Hall's days seemed to be numbered. A committee was set up at the PCC meeting of 19th October 1972 to consider the future of the Hall, bearing in mind the redevelopment of the area to house small businesses rather than be residential.

Above: Sketch of Greyfriars with its new West End Extension by B. Morrell
Below: West End interior

Above: Greyfriars West End – illuminated January 1973
Below: The Lord Bishop of Oxford, Rt. Rev. Kenneth Woollcombe (Centre) and Vicar, Rev. Jim Spence (Right)

The building work on the Church extension was completed in time for opening in January 1973. On Friday 5th, the congregation gathered for refreshments, singing, slides and short talks, followed by praise and prayer. On the following weekend, there were two official functions: a Thanksgiving Service on Saturday 13th for friends of Greyfriars, then the Formal Dedication by the Bishop of Reading on Sunday 14th January at 11am, followed by Morning Prayer.[28]

After a little over three years, the Curate, Roderick Thorp, moved to a second Curacy at St. Martin's, Hull. He was given a "grand Farewell" on 28th January in the new West End.[29] The new style Greyfriars News had been Mr. Thorp's idea and he had been the main editor since the first edition in July 1970. From January 1973 the new editor was Mrs. Heather Dyer – a role she continued until the production of the December 2000 edition.

At the Annual Meeting in March 1973, John Milward stepped down as Vicar's Warden following 5 years' service. Until this point there had always been a Vicar's Warden, nominated by the Incumbent, and a People's Warden elected by the fellowship. From this point on, both posts became elected, thus ending the distinction between the Churchwardens. Wilfred Dyer, Warden since 1970, and Jack Stemp were elected.[30] The report of the Annual Meeting in Greyfriars News contained a tribute to Mr. Milward:

> It is impossible to say how much we owe to John Milward for his warmth and friendliness in welcoming and getting to know people, for his encouragement of a raw new Vicar, for his vision and enthusiasm in so many fields, which have stirred and encouraged so many of us, especially on the Church Council.[31]

A new Curate arrived in June 1973: the Rev. Peter Brown, together with his wife Margaret and two young children. Mr. Brown moved from a Curacy at Faringdon, having been ordained two years previously. In order to provide accommodation for the Brown family, the Church bought a house at 18a Berkeley Avenue, at a cost of £12,500.[32]

Since its opening in January 1973, the West End swiftly proved its value on Sunday mornings for the Sunday School (re-named at this point as Climbers, Explorers and Pathfinders) and during the week for meetings – for example the new Business Lunchtime meeting. There were, however, some difficulties with the ceiling sagging and the folding room-partitions jamming. Repairs had to be carried out before final payment was made for the works.[33] The new corridor to the Vestry was connected to the Memorial Hall by a covered walkway area, constructed by Mr. Howick and team.[34]

In August 1973, Churchwarden Jack Stemp tragically died. Mr. Spence wrote that "we have all wept with Olive Stemp over the sad death of Jack in the sea on holiday." Fellow Warden, Wilfred Dyer, wrote a tribute to him, noting Mr. Stemp's time teaching in the Sunday School, as Deputy Churchwarden and then Churchwarden, and his service to the elderly, house-bound and sick by taking them tape recordings of the Church services. He concluded with: "He leaves a gap in our midst that will not easily be filled."[35]

In October 1973, Greyfriars' parish boundaries were extended.[36] The PCC's agreement had been secured in January,[37] but the legal processes involved took time. The additional area meant that the whole of Cardiff Road now belonged to Greyfriars' parish, rather than just the nearer half. This did not include any residential property, but rather industrial units and depots. The parish boundary then ran along Cow Lane going due north from the point under the railway line to Tilehurst and on to the Thames – Richfield Avenue had not yet been built.

The mid-1970s saw some changes to services. Psalm Praise, which was published in 1973, was first used at the Sunday Evening Youth Service on 10th February 1974, with a Congregational Practice at 6.05pm before the 6.30pm service.[38] In all, five items from Psalm Praise were sung that evening:

69 "Forgotten for Eternity" by Michael Saward
151 "Bring to the Lord a Glad New Song" by Michael Perry (Tune: Jerusalem)
43 "Then I saw a New Heaven and Earth" by Christopher Idle
94 "How Great is God Almighty" by Richard Bewes
91 "God is our Strength and Refuge" by Richard Bewes (Tune: Dambusters March)

In the previous month the Organist and Choirmaster, Gordon Spriggs, wrote a review of Psalm Praise in Greyfriars News. In an interestingly worded article (where it is hard to decide if he exactly liked the book or not) he wrote:

> This book provides a fresh approach to the Psalms. Not quite what the Royal School of Church Music would produce, but aimed at more informal gatherings, it offers something deeper than the cheerful ditties and religious Pop wherewith its predecessors Youth Praise I and II have brightened up things

> for the young people; it should, by attractively opening up the great treasure-house of the Psalms, lead beginners on from trivialities towards more disciplined and exalted worship. It introduces 76 Psalms, the Gospel Canticles, and other Bible poetry, in new translation – often in verse, and very good verse too – for those not yet fully able to appreciate Coverdale's matchless prose in the Prayer Book.[39]

Although Psalm Praise was not used often over the following couple of years, its music became a regular feature from early 1976 onwards at both morning and evening services. From late 1973, Series III Holy Communions were trialled – at first only in the unconsecrated West End, but for the first time in the Church by March 1975.[40] The motivation for change was expressed by Mr. Spence at a PCC Day Conference at Stokenchurch on 1st June 1974:

> [The Vicar] pointed out the difference in outlook between those who have attended the Church for years and those who are comparative newcomers, and the need to retain and strengthen the unity between them. He suggested a flexible approach was needed and outlined some practical proposals...

In September 1974 the Curate, the Rev. Peter Brown, moved on to become Vicar of Jesus Church, Forty Hill near Enfield, having only been Greyfriars' Curate for just over a year. He was given a special farewell organised by Contact, the "late teens and 20s" group at this time, who presented a "This is Your Life" – following the pattern of a popular television show compèred by Eamonn Andrews – in the West End.[41]

At the Annual Parochial Meeting in March 1975, Wardens Wilfred Dyer and Chris Hilliard were re-elected and two long-term members of the PCC stood down. Mr. A. Edgar Milward (known by all as "Uncle Edgar") had been a member for 40 years, while his brother Stanley J. Milward had served for 47, and for 6 years before that on the Finance Committee.[42] At the same meeting the Vicar "showed a new font which had been made by Mr. Howard for use at the front of the Church in our baptism services. Mr. Winslow moved and Mr. Boxwell seconded a vote of thanks to Mr. Howard, which was carried with acclamation." This portable font is still in use in the Church and use of the stone font – now in the south aisle – is very rare.

The ordination of the new Curate, John Coles, took place on Sunday 28th September 1975.[43] He took up his duties at Greyfriars that evening and was welcomed at the Harvest Supper on the following Saturday. John married

Anne Grobecker at Greyfriars on 23rd July 1977. John and Anne Coles then remained at Greyfriars until after Mr. Spence had left, leaving on 1st July 1979 for Christ Church, Clifton.[44]

Portable Font
Donated by
N. E. & E. T.
Howard
Easter 1975

At the PCC meeting on 8th October 1975 it was reported that the Greyfriars Missionary Trust had been set up. This Trust, still in operation today, enables Church members to give money to the various Missionaries and Missionary Societies connected with Greyfriars. Initially, and until the advent of Gift Aid, members took out a Deed of Covenant to enable tax to be claimed back by the Church. The first Trustees were: the Vicar, the Churchwardens (Wilfred Dyer and Chris Hilliard), Stanley J. Milward, David Crayford (Secretary) and Miss Marjorie Challis (Treasurer).

At the same meeting John Milward, on behalf of the Membership Committee, submitted a plan to divide the town into 24 areas, each with approximately 10 to 15 Greyfriars households and under the leadership of a PCC member.[45] These "Area Groups" did not initially replace the Home Study groups, 5 or 6 of which still happened each month.

In early 1976 the PCC considered a further extension of the parish boundaries. Due to a proposed union of benefices ("St. Mary the Virgin with St. Laurence, Reading"), the Oxford Diocesan Pastoral Committee aimed to add a large area to Greyfriars' parish from Caversham Road

Greyfriars East Wall
Before June 1976 (above)
After June 1976 (below)

railway bridge to a point near Caversham Bridge, and then along the river Thames to Kennetmouth, and then back along the railway lines. This added Kings Meadow and the residential properties off Vastern Road and Caversham Road to the parish. The PCC agreed to the proposal.[46] The changes took effect on 18th February 1977.

Chris Hilliard retired from the post of Churchwarden in March 1976, to be replaced by Derek Winslow. The minutes recorded: "in view of the pressures on the Wardens it was suggested that the scheme of Deputy Wardens be developed so that there was a team of six or seven to share the overall burden of responsibility."[47] There had occasionally been Deputy Wardens previously, but from this time they became an annual appointment. Mike Page and Chris Leslie were duly chosen at the next meeting of the PCC. At that meeting, the first group of Elders, to share lay leadership with the Wardens, was appointed: Marjorie Challis, John Milward, Peter Williams and Christopher Hilliard.

Over the very hot summer of 1976 the Church was redecorated and various electrical works carried out. The most notable part of the whole was that the east wall texts were painted over and not replaced. This was initially for a trial period, but the east wall has remained blank to date.

At the end of September 1976 the Parish Clerk, Mr. W. R. Lawrance, tried to retire, after almost 40 years in the post. Mr. Spence called him "our unobtrusive but utterly reliable and faithful Parish Clerk," before going on to detail the duties he had faithfully carried out: "Laying and clearing the Holy Table for Communion Services, cleaning the Church silver and arranging the laundering of the linen; opening up the Church for many services; attending weddings and funerals and keeping accounts of all the Church Fees received; writing up the Marriage Registers, Services Register and List of Notices; attending the Clergy in the Vestry at Services to assist them with gowns and punctuality!"[48] In fact, Mr. Lawrance continued many of these services, as no replacement was forthcoming. He finally retired at the end of September 1979.[49]

Parish Clerks at Greyfriars Church		
From	To	
December 1863	February 1899	Mr. Thomas North
March 1899	Easter 1903	Mr. W. Willis
Easter 1903	Easter 1916	Mr. A. J. Darling
Easter 1916	1937	Mr. G. E. Wise
1937	September 1979	Mr. W. Rupert Lawrance

On 10th October 1976 the Mission Hall held its Centenary Service, conducted by Capt. J. Etheridge who had led the work there from 1963 to 1969. Charles Lambourn (Leader 1954–1959, 1961–1962) read the lesson and the Vicar preached. Reginald White, who had been Warden of the Mission Hall from 1931 to 1950, at 86 years old was the oldest member present.[50]

Interior of the Mission Hall
(Photograph c 1970, courtesy of Michael Winch)

In the following year, a committee of local people in the area bounded by the Inner Distribution Road, Battle Hospital, Oxford Road and the Railway, concerned about the lack of facilities for the young people roaming their streets, successfully sought the agreement of the Mission Hall congregation to partition the Hall. Part of the building remained a worship area for the Sunday evening service and the remainder was converted to a Youth Club.[51] By 1979 the Mission Hall was home to a Club (for ages 9 to 21) on Monday evenings and Thursday evenings, Judo Club on Wednesdays and a Disco for 12s – 17s on Fridays.[52]

At the April 1977 Annual Meeting, Wilfred Dyer retired as Warden after 7 years' service. Chris Leslie joined Derek Winslow as Warden for the ensuing year.[53] Much of the PCC's time was taken up with consideration of the need to replace the Hut. The pressing need was for the right spaces for youth work. The Vicar wrote in July 1977:

The biggest decision that confronts us, as it has been for some time, is the development of the site where the Hut at present stands. This is a decision not simply about a building but about the sort of work which we wish to see develop in it. Linked with this is our understanding of the mission which we believe God has given us in Reading and in particular in the central position in the town where we stand.[54]

Missionaries from Greyfriars Church (Departing during Mr. Spence's incumbency)			
	From To	Where served	Mission Society
Ken & Sylvia Cavanagh	1970 1983	Paraguay	South American Missionary Society
Miss Kay McHugh	1970 1972	Yemen	Red Sea Mission Trust
Robert & Liz Dungey	1972 1974	Kuluva, Uganda	Africa Inland Mission
Miss Suzanne Prescott	1972 1978	Yemen, then Ethiopia	Red Sea Mission Trust
Brian & Liz Welters	1973 1975	Addis Ababa, Ethiopia	Sudan Interior Mission
Miss Margaret Readdy	1973 1975	Lebanon	
Mr. Chris Pouncey	1974 1975	Central African Republic	
Miss Pat Morgan	1974 2007	1974-1976 Ethiopia, 1980-2007 Niger	Sudan Interior Mission
Miss Anne Watts	1974 1974	Kenya	Church Mission Society
Miss Gill Budgen	1974 1976	Uganda	
Dr. John & Gill Malcolm	1974 1977	Kenya	
Peter & Frances Tyson	1975 1986	Argentina, then Paraguay	South American Missionary Society
Richard & Jane Gill	1975 1982	Vom Hospital, Nigeria	
Jenny Howick, then Phil & Jenny Bushell	1976 Current	India, then Bangladesh	Operation Mobilisation then Bangladesh Partnership
Mike & Lois Clark	1977 1988	Brazil	South American Missionary Society

An evening of "special prayer" on Saturday 9th July 1977 was followed by a Gift Day the next day. On the following Thursday Mr. K. C. White (who had been the architect for the West End extension) was at a PCC meeting to share some of his ideas for a possible building. However, consensus could not be reached over the proposals. There was also considerable ill-feeling from residents in Sackville Street over the proposed opening of a way into the Church from that side. The PCC, upon the Elders' advice, decided not to proceed with the plans at this time.[55]

In February 1978, Mr. Spence wrote confidentially to the Wardens to tell them that he had decided to accept an invitation from the Rev. Dick Lucas to join the team at St. Helen's, Bishopsgate.[56] This new role involved responsibility for the Sunday morning congregation and for the lunch-hour work on Tuesdays and Thursdays. In addition, the plan was for Mr. Spence to be able to have time put aside for writing.

At the Annual Meeting on 16th March 1978, Mr. Spence announced the move to the fellowship. The minutes record the Vicar's summary of the last ten years in the life of Greyfriars:

> He looked back to 1968 when he first came to Greyfriars and stated that at that time it was clear to him that the Church needed to stand on its own two feet rather than continually look for authoritarian rule from its Vicar. He mentioned the development of the committee system of the Parochial Church Council and of the appointment of Elders within the Church, neither of which developments had achieved their full potential... The West End especially facilitated the work of the Church and had increased the number of young families, since there were now facilities to cater for all age groups. Steps had recently been taken to hold evangelistic services on Sunday evenings each month and this work needed to be developed in various ways...[57]

About 400 attended the farewell gathering for the Spences, at 6pm on Saturday 2nd September 1978 at the Town Hall. Peter Spriggs introduced the programme, which covered the work and developments of the last ten years. The three Curates who had worked with Mr. Spence were present: Roderick Thorp, Peter Brown and John Coles. Wilfred Dyer brought a varied evening to a close with an appreciation of the Vicar's ministry.[58]

Jim Spence stayed at St. Helen's, Bishopsgate, from 1978 to 1982. He then moved to become Priest-in-Charge at Great Baddow, near Chelmsford. Subsequently he became Vicar and then Team Rector there.[59] He retired at the end of September 1995. Jim and Hilary now live in Wallingford.

Chapter 18

Peter Norwell Downham: Vicar 1979 to 1995

Greyfriars' eighth Vicar was a Lancastrian. Peter Downham was born in Liverpool in 1931, Norwell being his mother's maiden name. He graduated in Economics, Politics and Modern History from Manchester University and then completed National Service. He was commissioned in the Sherwood Foresters and seconded to the West African Force in Sierra Leone. Returning from Service, he trained for the ministry at Ridley Hall, Cambridge, in the year above Jim Spence. He was ordained Deacon in 1956, becoming Curate of St. Mary's Church, Cheadle.

The next change in his life was heralded in the Times of 16th July 1957: "The engagement is announced between Peter Norwell, only son of Mr. & Mrs. R. T. Downham, of Chesterfield, Derbyshire, and Joan Garrod, younger daughter of the late Colonel G. Bennett, O.B.E, T.D., D.L. and Mrs. A. G. Bennett, of Bramhall, Cheshire."[1] Following the birth of their sons Mark and Simon, the family moved just over 20 miles north to Rawtenstall, where Mr. Downham was Vicar of another St. Mary's from 1962 to 1968. During this time, he was also Chaplain at Rossendale Hospital. Mr. Downham's final move before coming to Reading was to become Vicar of St. James, Carlisle, in 1968.

During the interregnum, the Curate (John Coles) and the Churchwardens (Wilfred Dyer and Chris Leslie) led the Church. The Secretary of the Church Trust Fund Trust, Rev. David Bubbers, visited the PCC on 20th April 1978 to explain the procedures to appoint the next Vicar. On behalf of the PCC, Wilfred Dyer wrote the Representation to the Trustees, describing the Church and the recent ministry of Mr. Spence. He continued:

> The PCC endorses the continuance of the evangelical churchmanship hitherto enjoyed and prayerfully commend to the Trustees their views as to the needs for our Church and parish. We consider the new incumbent's particular gifts should be in the teaching of the Word and the ability to prepare and train

members for personal and corporate service. He should be a good preacher and have an outgoing personality to continue the motivation of members to active participation.

The Congregation comprises a good proportion of members in the 20/35 year age range and wisdom will be required in the arrangement of Sunday services to reflect the needs of this generation and the unchurched visitors as well as to respect the tradition of the past with its emphasis on the Book of Common Prayer...[2]

Rev. P. N. Downham in 1988

On 7th November 1978 David Bubbers wrote to Wilfred Dyer that he had invited Peter Downham to consider the nomination to Greyfriars. Peter and Joan Downham then visited Reading on 17th and 18th November, staying with Heather and Wilfred Dyer. Following the visit, Wilfred wrote to Mr. Downham: "on behalf of the congregation, Chris Leslie and I would be very happy if you felt called to accept the invitation extended by the Trustees to the living of Greyfriars."[3] On the same day Wilfred wrote to David Bubbers that Mr. Downham was "a forthright man who will inspire others in service for the Lord and we felt very much that with his gifts he would be an excellent successor to Jim."

By early March 1979 all was settled and the announcement was made at the Annual Meeting on 22nd March that Peter Downham was to be the new Vicar.[4] At the same meeting, Greyfriars finally allowed women to become sidesmen – a proposal first made by Harry Hogg five years previously, but then defeated in a vote.[5] The first female sidesmen, joining a list of 41 men, were: Marjorie Challis, Enid Gilkes, Judith Hogg, Hazel Kisiala, Ann Nice and Susan Weston.

The Institution of the Reverend Peter N. Downham B.A. by the Bishop of Reading and the Induction by the Archdeacon of Berkshire took place at 8pm on Tuesday 10th July 1979. In his first Vicar's Letter, Mr. Downham likened an Induction service to a wedding – "everyone else enjoys it except the people involved; they are often too bemused to notice."[6]

Churchwardens during Mr. Downham's incumbency (1979 – 1995)		
1979 to 1980	Wilfred Dyer	Christopher Leslie
1980 to 1985	Peter Spriggs	Christopher Leslie
1985 to 1988	Peter Spriggs	Harry Hogg
1988 to 1996	Dennis Parker	Harry Hogg

Mr. Downham was convinced that Greyfriars needed to continue to modernise its worship. He told the PCC "that in a post-Christian culture we need to have services that can be understood by those who have no Christian culture from home, school or Church. The principle of the reformers was that worship should be in the language of the day. What is understood by us may not be understood by the outsider, and whilst we should not produce services merely for outsiders, we cannot ignore them."[7] The PCC agreed to a six month trial of only authorised alternative services for both the morning and evening worship. This was later amended, by a proposal by Dr. Philip Giddings, to allow 1662 services twice a month both to "acknowledge the feelings of those who are averse to the new services and to refresh our minds of the 1662 services with which we will be making a comparison."[8]

During 1977, the wooden Hut that had been erected in late 1971 was sold and removed to the Dee Road Estate. It was replaced by a Portakabin – although confusingly referred to as the Hut as well![9] A new working committee was set up in May 1979 by the PCC to consider afresh what building should replace the Hut permanently.[10] This "New Building Committee" comprised the Vicar, Wilfred Dyer (Chairman), Stanley Milward (Treasurer), Robin Gambles (Secretary), Enid Gilkes, Simon Dimmick, Janet King, Norman Fisher and Tony Lowman. Peter Spriggs and Chris Leslie (in their capacity as Wardens) also joined the Committee at times. John Bale replaced Stanley Milward as Treasurer in early January 1981.

In late 1979 the New Building Committee appointed Mr. J. Alan Bristow of Charlbury, Oxfordshire, as architect for the project.[11] At a Special PCC meeting in March 1980, Mr. Bristow presented 8 feasibility studies that had variations on the given brief for the PCC to decide between. The PCC chose Study F:

> Study F was in effect a tightening up of Study D – where the Hall would be smaller and turned through 90 degrees so that it occupied the further end of the site from the Church. Various economies had been effected and the seating in the meeting hall and balcony was 300. The building contract figure was £190,000 and the gross figure £226,000.[12]

At the Annual Meeting in April 1980 the building was described and the Vicar asked the meeting to vote on whether they would say "yes" to the project. The votes were: In favour – over 160; Against – 28; Abstentions – 10. There was some concern that with 20% not voting in favour there was not sufficient support.[13] A booklet showing a slightly amended plan was issued in July, stating the purpose of Greyfriars Centre as "a 7 days a week centre housing a variety of activities for both members and non-members of Greyfriars where the love of Christ can be demonstrated in action." The booklet contained both a sketch of the new Centre and a list of the elements of the "well designed and spacious building":

1. A multi-purpose hall and balcony seating 300 and suitable for easy conversion from one use to another
2. An attractive foyer leading to a carpeted lounge

3. A utility room for children and youth activities
4. A well-fitted kitchen with serving access to the hall and coffee lounge
5. A Church office
6. Two additional small meeting rooms
7. Cloakroom and toilet facilities including provision for the disabled
8. Storage facilities for chairs and equipment

The plans then went to Reading Borough Council Planning Committee and were passed on 14th November 1980 for the "Erection of Church Hall/Games Room and meeting rooms."[14] Greyfriars held a Special General Meeting at 7.30pm on 25th November 1980, preceded by prayer from 7.30am to 8am. This was followed by a Day of Commitment in December for both financial support and offers of service in the new building.

At this time, the experimental period with alternative services came to an end. Worship questionnaires were sent out to all on the Church Membership List. Peter Downham recalled that of the 420 sent out, around 340 had been returned, and with these results:[15]

Those who considered that the alternative form of service should always be used	95
Those who considered that the Prayer Book should always be used	85
Those who considered that the Prayer Book and alternative services should always be used	c160

Of the last category, the majority wanted the alternatives to be used more frequently than the Prayer Book. At the subsequent PCC it was resolved to use the Prayer Book service once a month for each of Morning Prayer and Evening Prayer.[16]

Greyfriars' Mission Hall closed with a Carol Service at 3pm on Sunday 21st December 1980,[17] having served the parish for 104 years. The decision to close it had been taken at the PCC on 13th November due both to the poor condition of the Hall and the feeling of uncertainty the small Mission Hall congregation felt over the building's future. The Hall was in due course sold for £65,000[18] with the proceeds going to the New Building Fund towards the cost of Greyfriars Centre.

In January 1981, Stanley Milward died. In a tribute in Greyfriars News in February 1981, Arthur Sheppard wrote of him:

> ... His very walk of life, his serenity, his genuine interest in others, and indeed his whole motivation were the outcome of his deeply rooted faith in his Lord and Master whom he worshipped and served so faithfully and so humbly, for so many years amongst us at Greyfriars. His valued service to successive Vicars as their Warden, and upon the Parochial Church Council and the Standing and Finance Committees, and his deep concern for every aspect of the Lord's work at Greyfriars, and in the wider sphere of Missionary endeavour, have set for us all an outstanding example of devotion in and to the service of his Lord in whom he rejoiced.

At a Special Church Meeting held on 20th July 1981, the various bids for building Greyfriars Centre were considered. After much discussion, it was agreed that the tender from Messrs. Clark & Stone of Kentwood Hill, Tilehurst, would be accepted for the "Complete building with certain reductions and excluding classroom superstructure - £267,000." The cost including the classrooms would have been a further £45,000.

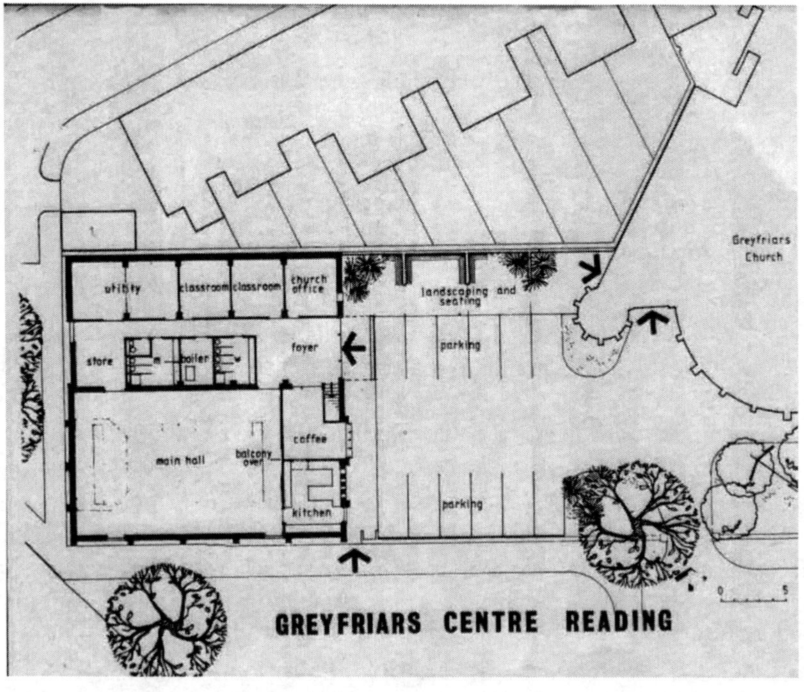

Plan of the Proposed Greyfriars Centre
From the July 1980 Brochure

Contracts were signed on 19th August and work began on the Centre on 1st September 1981.[19] At the PCC meeting on 10th September, Wilfred Dyer reported on the state of the financing of the project: 119 families or individuals, representing about 60% of the active membership of the Church, were contributing, mostly through covenant. £40,000 more was needed in direct giving, together with about £60,000 in interest-free loans. The Church held a Day of Prayer for the New Building Plans on Tuesday 12th January 1982 and a Day of Gifts and Pledges on the Sunday following.[20] As a result the project's finances moved from deficit to a small surplus (£2,185), thus covering the costs for "phase 1" – the Centre without the classroom block.[21] At the PCC meeting in the following month it was agreed to instruct the architect to include the classroom block in faith that the remainder of the funds would be given.[22]

At the Church Day Conference at Crosfields School in September 1981 (the first for four years) the issue of worship and forms of service was a major talking point.[23] This theme resurfaced at the Annual General Meeting in April, with some speakers supporting a greater proportion of Prayer Book services.[24] The PCC decided to hold a Day Conference on 12th June 1982 to give full consideration to the views expressed at the AGM and in writing since. The PCC, following its extensive discussions, produced and circulated the following statement. This Council:

i re-affirms its acceptance of the Doctrines of the Church of England, as grounded in the Scriptures and expressed in the Book of Common Prayer and the 39 Articles of Religion;

ii strongly believes that, as a general policy, the Church should continue to use forms of worship expressed in contemporary language and adhering to these doctrines;

iii notes that the request of the Prayer Book Society that the traditional forms of worship be used at least once per month at main services is being more than met at Greyfriars at present;

iv wishes to continue to maintain a flexibility in patterns of worship such that the variety of the needs of our fellowship can be met, with Gospel Guest Services, Youth Services and Family Services accepted as part of our pattern of worship and used at appropriate intervals in addition to the regular liturgical forms;

v calls on all members of the fellowship, as an act of Christian love, to support the pattern of worship that has evolved at Greyfriars as a reflection of the varied needs and sensitivities of the whole congregation and to endeavour to improve upon the quality of our worship rather than worrying about its form.[25]

Day Conferences during Mr. Downham's incumbency		
September 1981	Day Conference	Crosfields School
September 1982	Day Conference	Crosfields School
September 1983	Day Conference	Crosfields School
September 1984	Day Conference	St. Andrew's Hall
September 1985	Day Conference	St. Andrew's Hall
September 1986	Day Conference	Blue Room Suite, University of Reading
September 1987	Day Conference	Blue Room Suite, University of Reading
September 1988	Day Conference	Crosfields School
September 1989	Day Conference	Crosfields School
September 1990	Day Conference	Crosfields School
September 1991	Day Conference	Crosfields School
September 1992	Day Conference	St. Joseph's School
September 1993	Autumn Focus	Crosfields School

In July 1982 Peter Downham was joined by his first Curate. Giles Williams was ordained in Milton Keynes on 4th July and, as is customary, was at Greyfriars for the evening service that day. Giles and Christine lived at 18a Berkeley Avenue, Coley.

The 4 Curates who worked with Mr. Downham	Curate From	To	Next destination
Giles Williams	1982	1985	Rwanda Mission
Timothy Dougal Mullins	1985	1989	Curate: Haughton Le Skerne, Durham
Leonard Joseph Browne	1989	1991	Vicar: St. Barnabas, Cambridge
Jeffrey Richard Wattley	1992	1996	Vicar: St. John the Baptist, Wonersh

As the Greyfriars Centre neared completion, Joyce Mundy was appointed acting Administrator and Judy Lowman as Receptionist and Office co-ordinator.[26] Although the Practical Completion was not until 14th March, a Service of Thanksgiving and Dedication of the Centre was held at 8pm on Friday 4th February 1983, with the Bishop of Oxford performing the opening ceremony.

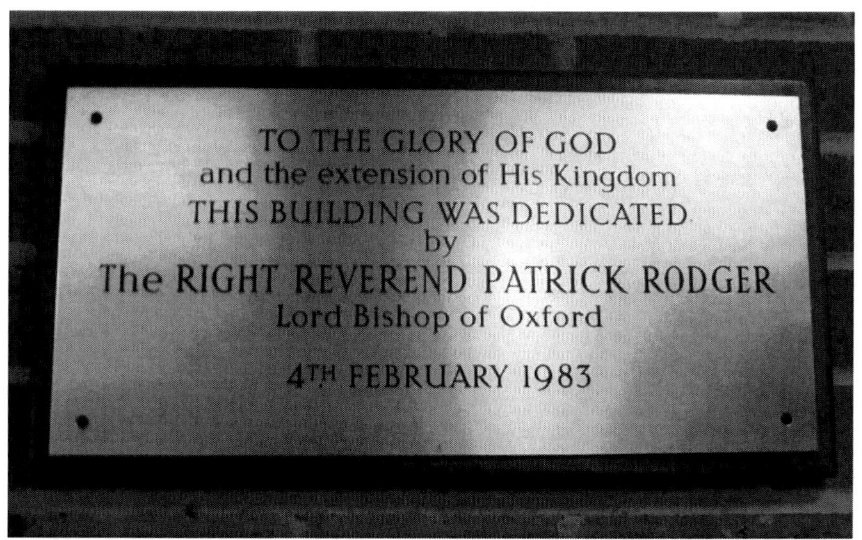

Brass Plaque in Greyfriars Centre

The Centre opened for business on Monday 11th March and at the end of the first year it was reported that "From a modest start of 4 coffees per day we now serve about 70 cups of coffee, 30 teas, plus 3 dozen rolls and 2 dozen pies/pizzas each day." About 30 volunteers helped in the kitchen or serving food, 11 in the office and 9 in the bookshop.[27]

Parking soon became a major issue and so it was decided to install a padlock on the car park gate so that only members would be able to use the car park. The initial cost was £5 plus £3 for a key.[28] For some time, the Church had been attempting either to be permitted to use or to buy the land between the IDR and the Church wall for car parking, believing that as much as a third of the land was owned by Greyfriars anyway.[29] However, the Council disputed this and refused to allow the Church to extend its car parking onto this area or to annexe it as an amenity area.

There were 24 applicants for the post of Greyfriars Centre Administrator, of whom 4 were shortlisted for interview. At the PCC in April 1983, it was announced that John Brown, an Elder at Carey Baptist Church, was the unanimous choice of the interview panel. He took up the post officially on 9th May, with Joyce Mundy becoming Deputy Administrator.[30] Joyce took responsibility for managing the catering arrangements until the first appointment of a Centre Catering Manager – Janet Chambers in June 1984.[31]

Greyfriars Centre
(Photograph taken in 2011)

The total cost of the Centre was £321,242, with a further £14,900 for equipment and fittings.[32] The Centre Management Committee, chaired by Wilfred Dyer, held back £15,700 from the contractor to cover several defects. The major rectification needed was a complete lift and replacement of the hall floor. The contractor, Clark & Stone, went into liquidation in autumn 1983, but the money held back covered the necessary repairs.[33]

In the summer of 1983 the Memorial Hall was redecorated and opened as a Drop-in coffee-bar centre for young unemployed people. Known as The Daybreak Centre, this was run by Bill Anderson and several helpers, opening each afternoon from Tuesday to Saturday. Curate Giles Williams wrote of the venture:

> It's mainly skinheads and punks who come in and they've nearly all been in trouble with the Law (I sometimes think that we've turned the Memorial Hall

> from a house of prayer to a den of thieves!!). But by God's power, and in answer to prayer, there hasn't been any trouble at Daybreak. There is a Christian atmosphere about the place. A great deal of love and practical help is given. People with drug problems have been linked up with Yeldall Manor. Many come to Bill or others to share worries and problems. Gently, we're seeing people's hardness to the Gospel disappear. One or two have made a commitment to Christ in the last month.[34]

In late 1983 a Hearing Loop was installed in the Church, the costs being paid for by Vi Milward in memory of her late husband Stanley, and a cycle rack was erected behind the West End kitchen tower.[35]

In July 1984, the PCC considered purchasing 14 Sackville Street, which was for sale but under offer, to provide a base for missionary families when on furlough. Pending prayer and further discussion, it was agreed that an offer would be made on the house if it again became free and a sub-committee consisting of Marjorie Challis, Simon Dimmick and Robin Gambles be set up to handle the business on behalf of the PCC.[36]

The prospective buyer of 14 Sackville Street withdrew at the end of August, opening the way for Greyfriars to make their offer. At a Special Meeting of the PCC on 6th September it was decided to go ahead with an offer of £29,500. The purchase was completed in October 1984.[37] Loans enabled the purchase to be made and giving gradually paid these back, helped by a successful Gift Day in February 1985.[38] The priorities for the house's use were agreed to be: "our own missionaries; special needs within the Church (e.g. those with pastoral or housing needs or part-time caretakers for the Centre); and missionaries from other Churches in the town."[39] Gillian Hunt was the first missionary on furlough to stay in the house, arriving on 3rd January 1985.[40]

Meanwhile a report on the condition of the organ by Rushworth & Dreaper showed that £25,366 of work needed to be done. After thoroughly considering other options, it was decided that the best option was to carry this work out. With a little over £4,000 in the Organ Fund and £8,000 in the Capital Fund, about half the cost was already provided for.[41] Following successful receipt of a Faculty from the Diocese, the work was carried out in 1986, completed in time for Easter Day.[42]

Chris Leslie retired as Churchwarden in March 1985 after 8 years' service. Harry Hogg was elected as his replacement, joining Peter Spriggs who continued in the role.[43] In July, the Church held a farewell gathering for Giles and Christine Williams who left to prepare for their move to Kigali, Rwanda, and Bible translation work.[44]

The morning Communion service on Sunday 1st September 1985 was televised live on ITV (TV South). Beginning with a rehearsal the day before, everyone had to be in place by 9.15am for a 10am start. The only hitch happened when the scaffolding that held the lighting rigs was erected – one of the head-stops from 1863 was knocked off. Peter Spriggs provided the commentary on the television sound track. Peter Downham's sermon, aided by the use of an overhead projector (an innovation brought in by Giles Williams), was a clear statement of the Gospel and resulted in over 300 letters of enquiry.[45]

On 29th September, Tim Mullins was ordained at 10am in Sunningdale, becoming Greyfriars' 33rd Curate.[46] Tim and Lucy, who had been recently married, moved into 18a Berkeley Avenue. They soon involved themselves in the Church's student ministry, visiting on campus and hosting a Students' Tea on 13th October.[47]

In March 1986 architect Alan Bristow, who had carried out the work for the Centre, produced plans for possible reordering of the east end of the Church. The overall aims of the reordering were to provide greater visibility and flexibility and so the designs aimed to remove the fixed furniture (including the pulpit) and raise the floor level. One design included a short chancel, going out about 3m from the east wall.[48] It was subsequently decided that, since the flooring of the south transept was in need of substantial repair, the first phase of the reordering would be to address that area.[49] By June 1987, the PCC agreed to seek a Faculty from the Diocese "to carry out the following works in the south transept (1) dispose of pews (2) [lay a] new wooden floor (3) [covered by] carpet squares (4) re-site radiators (5) [install] additional lights [and] (6) additional amplifier sockets (7) [and make] provision of chairs."[50] The works, costing £21,665, were completed by March 1989.[51]

Two effective evangelistic events were organised at Greyfriars at this time. In early December 1986, the Centre was converted for a few days into a cinema. About 1,800 people in total over the five days' showings came to see the "Jesus" film, based on the Gospel of Luke.[52] The second was a "Mini-mission" led by the Rev. Denis Shepheard, an evangelist with the Church Pastoral Aid Society in October 1987.[53]

Denis and his wife Sheila had worshipped at Greyfriars since 1983, making Denis one of the Church's Associate Clergy. He was described in a letter to the Times (which was positioned bottom right on the page and hence not to be taken seriously) quoted in Greyfriars News as follows:

Sir,
What is the Church of England coming to? Our local church [in St Leonards-on-Sea] is advertising a guest preacher, an Evangelist with the Church Pastoral Aid Society. He is described as "not a typical Church of England minister" with the following credentials: his father was a window cleaner, he was brought up in a council house, served in the navy and has taught in a girls' school. But the most horrifying revelation of them all is that he has a "cockney accent." I am still reeling from the shock.
Signed D.V.[54]

The table below shows the Associate Clergy at Greyfriars. David Harris and Douglas Benson may have been at Greyfriars from an earlier date, but the one given is the first recorded in Greyfriars News.

Associate Clergy		
Rev.	From	To
David R Harris	July 1980	January 1983
Douglas Benson	July 1980	May 1991
Denis Shepheard	April 1983	June 1992
Robert McKemey	June 1991	January 2005
David W. Vail	May 1997	Current

Arising from the 1985 report "Faith in the City," which raised awareness about the growing gaps in society and particularly in inner city areas, Greyfriars formed a link with St. Augustine's Church, Bradford. An Urban Priority Area Church, it had been on the point of closure four years before but had now become an active centre for its parish's needs. The Vicar, the Rev. Robin Gamble (not to be confused with Greyfriars' own Robin Gambles), visited the PCC in July 1987.[55] The main need identified was funding for a Church Administrator – Greyfriars gave its Christmas 1987 offerings to St. Augustine's, amounting to almost £2,000.[56] Greyfriars hosted a visit by Robin Gamble and four of his parishioners in March 1988, with a return visit to Bradford by Peter Downham and team in October 1989.[57] Articles in Greyfriars News helped the congregation to get to know the Church and its needs.[58]

In November 1987 James Russell was appointed as a "Lay Assistant," with duties that included being Verger.[59] The table below shows those appointed to similar roles during Peter Downham's incumbency.

James Russell	Lay Assistant	1987 – 1988
Penny Russell	Lay Assistant	1988 – 1990
Nikki Atherton	Lay Assistant	1991
Clare Jenkins	Lay Worker	1991 – 1992
Jonathan Piesse	Pastoral Worker	1991 – 1994
Steve Smith	Lay Assistant	1992 – 1993
Tim Vinall	Lay Worker	1993 – 1994
Sid Marshall	Pastoral Worker	1994 – 1996
Linda Giffin	Verger	1994 – 1997

At the Annual Meeting in March 1988 Peter Spriggs retired as Warden, having served for eight years. Dennis Parker joined Harry Hogg as Warden; they remained as Wardens for the remainder of Peter Downham's incumbency.[60]

On 17th April 1988, Gordon Spriggs played the organ as Greyfriars' Organist and Choirmaster for the final time, with 1662 Prayer Book Morning Prayer and Songs of Praise in the evening. At a tea in the afternoon there was a marvellous cake shaped like the organ console and about 150 people present to say farewell. Gordon Spriggs wrote "No words can express my gratitude for that unbelievably generous cheque, with which I shall get music recording and reproduction equipment as a tangible and appropriate reminder of the love and goodwill enjoyed throughout almost 60 years of membership of this noble old Church, where it has indeed been a privilege to take a leading part in the worship of the Transcendent Majesty on High."[61] His final hymn was "Now thank we all our God", number 22 in the Anglican Hymn Book.

In May, about 180 of the fellowship attended the first Parish Weekend Away, where "we had some heartwarming worship and the ministry of Keith Weston really inspired and encouraged," in the words of Peter Downham.[62]

Church Weekends Away during Mr. Downham's incumbency		
	Location	Speaker
20th -22nd May 1988	Annan Court, Sussex	Keith Weston
19th -21st May 1989	Annan Court, Sussex	Geoffrey Shaw
1st-3rd June 1990	Ashburnham Place, Sussex	Monty Barker
17th-19th May 1991	Ashburnham Place, Sussex	Norman Sinclair

Early in 1988 the Elders had proposed that the Church should launch an appeal to fund restoration of the external stonework, it being the 125th year since the re-consecration of the Church. The PCC approved of the idea and resolved that the 125 Jubilee Appeal should have an initial target of £125,000 and aim to give a third of the money to the Lord's work elsewhere. The Appeal Committee was formed with John Milward as Chairman[63] and the Appeal itself was launched with an article in Greyfriars News in March and at the Annual Parochial Church Meeting on 24th March. By the end of the year there had been 115 pledges totalling just over £91,000; by December 1989 the revised target of £100,000 was reached.

The projects that were funded by the one third were: the Nairobi Evangelical School of Theology, the Church in Bangladesh, the Chapel Fund for Mildmay Aids Hospice, and the Crusader Development Worker Appeal.[64]

To celebrate the 125th anniversary on 2nd December 1988, two days of events were planned. On Saturday 3rd December, there was an open day from 10am until 5pm in the Church and Centre with an exhibition both of the history of the Church and of its present day work, with guided tours of the Church – and especially the stonework restoration. This was followed at 7.30pm by an Informal Reunion for past and present members in the West End. On the Sunday Greyfriars' old boy, now Bishop of Doncaster, Bill Persson preached at the morning service at 11am. There was then a fellowship tea at 4.30pm, followed by the evening service at 6.30pm, at which former Vicar Jim Spence preached. Heather Dyer wrote "The Story of Greyfriars Church and Centre", bringing the history of Greyfriars up to date, ready for the weekend; in honour of the 125th anniversary it sold for £1.25.[65]

Following the "Mini-mission" of October 1987, Greyfriars held "Mission 89," entitled "Which Way?," from 13th to 18th March 1989, led by Philip Hacking, Vicar of Christ Church, Fulwood, Sheffield. The programme included:

A Ladies' night on Monday
A Men's dinner on Tuesday
A Mums & Tots coffee morning on Wednesday
Business Lunches on Wednesday, Thursday and Friday
A Contact [20s/30s group] progressive supper on Thursday
A Concert on Friday with Martyn Joseph
A Men's breakfast on Saturday
A Skittles' evening on Saturday
Special Services for all ages on Sunday[66]

The Curate, Tim Mullins, was able to report to the PCC that as a result of the mission, 4 beginners' groups and 1 enquirers' group had been set up. Plans were also under way for the next mission, to take place in November 1990.[67]

Tim and Lucy Mullins left in June 1989, to be replaced by Northern Irishman Leonard Browne, his wife Alison and two young children in July.[68] The Curate's house at 18a Berkeley Avenue was too small for a young family and so the PCC took steps to replace it, selling 18a for £65,000 and buying 26 Prospect Street, a four-bedroomed older terraced house, for £95,000.[69] The Brownes had to move into 18a when they first came as the purchase had not yet been finalised.

Alterations had been carried out by this time in Greyfriars Centre. A glazed screen had been installed in the balcony and the office had been moved up to this rather larger space. The work was completed by June 1988 by Francis Brothers at a cost of £6,546 plus VAT, overseen by Alan Bristow, architect.[70] Then in 1989 the dividing wall between what was the office (which had become the book room) and Room 1 was knocked out, creating a larger Bookroom.[71]

In early 1990 the PCC decided, after consultation with the rest of the fellowship, to appoint a full-time Musical Director.[72] In the consultation booklet "Music in Greyfriars," the role was described as:

> To take up leadership responsibility for all aspects of the music at Greyfriars with a view to providing:
> - a high standard of musical contribution to match our high standard of teaching
> - a greater variety of material
> - a deeper insight into worship.
>
> The Musical Director would take responsibility for the organ, piano, orchestra, vocalists and instrumentalists and would be directly responsible to the Vicar.

Sara Brown was appointed as the first Greyfriars' Musical Director, effective from September 1990. She had been previously in a similar role in St. Luke's Church, Upper Norwood.[73]

Under the heading "Ecclesiastical O.B.E." in Greyfriars News, the announcement was made that Peter Downham was to be made an Honorary Canon of Christ Church, Oxford at evensong in the Cathedral on Saturday 28th April 1990.[74]

Greyfriars held its first Bible Convention in May 1990 with Michael Wilcock as the guest speaker. The event was held in the Centre over two evenings, with Reading Churches invited to attend. Subsequent speakers were: David Jackman (1991), Alastair McGrath (1992), Roy Clements (1993) and Mark Ashton (1995).[75]

In November 1990 the Parish Mission "Somebody Loves You" was preceded by house to house visiting throughout the Greyfriars' parish. Denis and Sheila Shepheard led the mission, with events of many kinds to give an opportunity for parishioners to join in. Many people came back to several events, with events for children, Mums and Toddlers and for "older folk" being especially well attended.[76] As a result of the Mission, EP Club was started on Friday evenings in E. P. Collier School in the parish for Primary School aged children. By the summer of 1992 it had about 30 children regularly attending and they had their first weekend away, going to Weymouth in July 1992.[77] A second initiative was the Wednesday Welcome Club, a weekly meeting for retired people which started in April 1991.[78]

The Church carried out a remarkable survey of the congregation in 1990. With 400 responses to the Survey (and an electoral roll of 422 – although 26% of respondents were not on the electoral roll), the results could be considered a very reliable snapshot of the Greyfriars' fellowship.[79] The age distribution (shown below) showed a higher proportion of those in their 20s, but generally a fairly even spread.

Age	Under 19	19-29	30-39	40-49	50-64	65+
%	8.4	23.8	18.7	14.6	18.4	15.9

In terms of geographical distribution, almost half of the congregation came from central and west Reading (RG3 is now split into RG30 and RG31).

Area	RG1	RG2	RG3	RG4	RG5	RG6	RG7	RG8	Other
%	22.8	8.2	26.1	16.1	1.3	6.1	1.5	5.1	11.8

57% of respondents were female; 40% were single, 52% married and 8% widowed, separated or divorced. 33% came to Church twice on Sunday and 55% once; a surprising 2.6% attended less frequently than monthly (not counting visitors). Perhaps the most striking statistics were those detailing how long people had been worshipping at Greyfriars:

Years	<1	1-2	2-3	4-5	6-10	11-20	20+	Visiting
%	13.8	10.5	12.8	9.5	16.1	14.8	18.7	3.6

This shows that about a quarter of the congregation had been at Greyfriars for less than two years. At the Annual Meeting earlier in the year, Peter Downham had highlighted this mobility by informing the meeting that over the two and a half years between Church Membership Lists there had been a 40% change in the people listed.[80]

61% belonged to a Home Group and 79% read the Greyfriars News. 95% identified themselves as committed Christians. 74% read the Bible most days. 92% prayed on most days, however the prayer pointers were only used by 28%. 22% had brought someone to one of the Guest Services. The Covenant Schemes (the forerunner of Gift Aid) did not fare well: 62% did not covenant their giving to the Church and 77% did not covenant to the Missionary Covenant Scheme.

What do you find the most helpful part of the service?	%
Sermons	37.3
Worship	23.5
Music	11.3
Fellowship	9.7
Prayers	5.1
No answer given	13.1

Asked about types of service, there was a split about Family Services (48% wanted more, 42% did not); 51% wanted Greyfriars to continue with the 1662 services compared with 37% who wanted them to stop. Overall, in presenting the data, the Curate Len Browne wrote: “In summary, we have a good age spread, a rather transient congregation, and varying ‘needs’ when it comes to worship!”

In 1991 Peter and Joan Downham exchanged “pulpits” with Allan and Pamela Blanch. The Blanches arrived on 22nd April, with the Downhams leaving for St. John’s Church, Beecroft in the western suburbs of Sydney, Australia.[81] The exchange was for just four months, with each couple returning to their own home in late August.[82]

Following the successful alterations to the south transept, it was agreed to develop the north transept by removing the pews and making the area into a much more flexible space for musicians.[83] The work to remove pews, re-lay the floor and carpet the area was carried out following the necessary approvals in early 1992.[84]

In the summer of 1991 Greyfriars appointed Valerie Worsley to be its first full-time Church Secretary,[85] although Sue Weston had been in a similar role as a full-time Church Administrator for a year in 1980.[86] By October 1991, the staff team consisted of:

Peter Downham, Vicar
Len Browne, Curate
John Brown, Centre Administrator
Sara Brown, Musical Director
Mabel Boyd, Centre Caterer
Valerie Worsley, Church Secretary
Clare Jenkins, Lay Worker
Jonathan Piesse, Pastoral Worker

In December 1991, Len Browne left to become Vicar at St. Barnabas Church, Cambridge.[87] The next Curate was Jeff Wattley, who was ordained at Christ Church, Oxford, on 28th June 1992.[88] Between these two dates, Peter Downham was seriously ill leading to his absence throughout the period from April to the end of June, although he returned to work in time for Jeff Wattley's ordination service.[89]

A further staff change became necessary when Sara Brown stepped down from being Musical Director in late 1993. The PCC stated that "Sara had caused tremendous steps forward, with a definite growth in standards, and with significant development and extension of the place of music in the life and worship of Greyfriars."[90] Rachel Lee-Johnson took over the post in a temporary capacity and then she was appointed (part-time) Music Team Leader in July 1993.[91]

Dr. Ted Williams had died in late September 1992, aged 76.[92] He had been a Greyfriars missionary from 1941 to 1980 (see page 202) and had been instrumental in building Kuluva Hospital in Uganda. The Dr. Ted Williams Memorial Library was created to provide the Kuluva Hospital staff with both medical literature and Christian books.[93]

The Memorial Library was an unexpected beneficiary of a fire in the Greyfriars Centre in January 1994. This had been started deliberately in several places following a break in. Thankfully a passer-by saw flames and phoned 999 – the Fire Officer thought that half an hour more and the building would have been totally lost. Smoke damaged much of the Centre, including all the book room stock. The Insurance Loss Adjuster told Peter Downham to give the books to the Third World, so after a clean the books were sent to Kuluva.[94]

Missionaries from Greyfriars Church (Departing during Mr. Downham's incumbency)			
	From To	Where served	Mission Society
Sheila Williams	1979 2000	Rift Valley Academy, Kenya	Africa Inland Mission
Derek Winslow	1981 1982	India	
Lynne Pulvermacher	1983 1987	Birmingham	Church Mission among the Jews
Annette Smith	1984 1986	Kenya	Church Mission Society
Darius Campbell	1984 1985	India	Church Mission Society
Phil Hilman	1984 1985	Kenya	Africa Inland Mission
Ruth Williams	1985 Current	France	Christian Literature Crusade
Richard & Christine Viney	1985 1989	India	Bible and Medical Missionary Fellowship
Mark Bolton then Mark & Jane Bolton	1985 to 1988 1995 to 2000	Portugal	A Rocha
Peter Goodright	1985 1988	Nairobi, Kenya	Church Mission Society
Rev. Giles & Christine Williams	1986 1994	Kigali, Rwanda	Rwanda Mission
John Jolliffe	1986 1987	Jos, Nigeria	
Helena Wilkinson	1986 1986	South Africa	
Simon Vaney	1986 1987	Njeleni, Kenya	Africa Inland Mission
David Baldwin	1986 1987	Ethiopia	Sudan Interior Mission
Craig & Ruth Hampton	1987 1995	Sudan then Uganda	Church Mission Society
Ian Hogg	1987 1988	Asuncion, Paraguay	South American Missionary Society
Sarah Shepheard	1989 1990	Papua New Guinea	Wycliffe Bible Translators

Missionaries from Greyfriars Church (Departing during Mr. Downham's incumbency) continued			
	From To	Where served	Mission Society
Claire Hepburn	1989 1993	Zimbabwe	Bible Churchmen's Missionary Society
Roger & Jos Sharland	1990 Current	Kenya	Rural Extension with Africa's Poor
Andrew Howe	1992 1992	Kenya	
Matthew Leigh-Hunt	1992 1992	Kenya	
David & Georgina Gray	1993 Current	Central Asia, then based in the UK	Wycliffe Bible Translators
Peter & Debbie Thompson	1993 2007	Trujillo, Peru	Navigators
Steve Smith	1994 1994	Nairobi, Kenya	Church Army
Chris & Louise MacClay	1995 1999	Abuja, Nigeria	Church Mission Society

At the end of Peter Downham's incumbency, the list of missionaries then currently being supported was:

Mark & Jane Bolton in Portugal (A Rocha) – from July 1995
Phil & Jenny Bushell in UK and Bangladesh (Operation Mobilisation)
Colin & Joy Densham in Kenya (Africa Inland Mission)
David & Georgina Gray in Central Asia (Wycliffe Bible Translators)
Craig & Ruth Hampton in Uganda (Church Mission Society) – to April 1995
Chris & Louise MacClay in Nigeria (Church Mission Society)
Pat Morgan in Niger (Sudan Interior Mission)
Roger & Jos Sharland in Kenya (Rural Extension with Africa's Poor)
Peter & Debbie Thompson in Peru (Navigators)
Ruth Williams in France (Christian Literature Crusade)
Sheila Williams in UK (Africa Inland Mission)

Two major works were carried out on the Church buildings at this time. In October/November 1993 the Church was re-wired and the lighting was completely renewed – although the 1863 coronae hanging fittings were retained. The work was carried out by Anthony J. Smith (Gloucester) Ltd at a cost of £18,710 + VAT.[95] The second of the works was a complete replacement of the flat roof above the West End lounge and Vestry, which was now 20 years old. This project cost £23,000 and was completed by early October 1993.[96]

Meanwhile the discussions about the reordering of the east end continued, with the Working Party (Vicar, Wardens, Arthur Burrows, Simon Cuthbert, Philip Giddings, Chris Greaves, Rachel Lee-Johnson, Philip Rees, J Shaw and Wendy Stormont) liaising with the architect, Alan Bristow. Mr. Bristow attended the PCC in February 1994 to put forward his plans:

> The essentials of the proposals are: remove 5 rows of pews, rails, desk, and holy table; pulpit remains; extend permanent raised area, approached by 3 steps, and have available further platform extensions; pew space filled with chairs, or extension platform as relevant. A new, lower, holy table to be installed, being of such a height as not to obscure the Tablets of the Ten Commandments. The order of cost estimate for all work and furniture is £25,000.[97]

The PCC agreed to pass the plans to the Diocesan Advisory Committee for approval. By the end of June 1994, the DAC had given their approval providing that the changes were made in such a way that they could be reversed in future, and that the plans for the new Communion Table and rail were submitted to them.[98] However, the project did not proceed further as by this time Peter Downham had given notice that he was going to leave Greyfriars and so the Elders felt that the project should be put on hold.[99]

Throughout 1993 and 1994 there had been continuing preparations for a major mission: Thames Valley Alive. Greyfriars' own Wilfred Dyer was Chairman of TVA, with Curate Jeff Wattley co-ordinating the Reading Central area events. There had been many training events, study courses for Home Groups and special prayer meetings, all leading up to the Mission from 25th September to 9th October 1994. The main events were led by "the two Michaels," Marshall and Green, at the Rivermead Centre for four nights 5th – 8th October.[100] In the week before the mission 120,000 leaflets entitled "Whose Life is it Anyway?" were delivered to houses in the area.[101]

In all over 100 Churches took part in TVA. With hundreds of events organised, an estimated 10,000 attended. Hundreds responded to the call to commitment to Christ, either as new believers or as enquirers, and as a result many small follow-up groups were set up.[102]

Just after the Thames Valley Alive Mission, Peter Downham announced that he and Joan would be moving on to the parish of Cotehill, just south east of Carlisle. On Saturday 14th January 1995 there was a farewell gathering in the Centre, hosted by Peter Spriggs. Peter Downham then preached his final Greyfriars' sermons at the 11am and 6.30pm services on the following day.[103] At his final service, the Rev. Canon P. N. Downham preached from Philippians 3: 8 – 14 under the title "Your Ambitions." His final message to the fellowship was "Press on towards the goal to win the prize for which God has called you heavenward in Christ Jesus."[104]

Peter was a member of the General Synod from 1995 to 2005. He retired from Parish Ministry at the end of October 1998. He and Joan moved to Dalston near Carlisle, then later to Goring in Oxfordshire.

64 Friar Street,
Reading. RG1 1EH

Tel: 0734 573822

Drawing of Greyfriars Church and Centre

– Occasionally used as the letterhead for the Vicar's Letter

This particular image was used for Peter Downham's last letter to the fellowship in Greyfriars News, January 1995

THE REVD. JONATHAN AND MRS. SUSAN WILMOT WITH THEIR SONS, THOMAS AND MICHAEL

From Greyfriars News August 1995 p1
(Their third son Christopher was born in September 1995)

Chapter 19

Jonathan Anthony de Burgh Wilmot: Vicar from 1995

The next Vicar of Greyfriars was – and still is – the Rev. Jonathan Wilmot. He is the second Vicar to be born abroad: in Jonathan's case in January 1948 in Accra, Gold Coast, West Africa, where his father Tony (Anthony) held an important Colonial Administration post until the country's independence as Ghana. Tony became the first Chairman of the Pan-African Fellowship of Evangelical Students and began what became the Nairobi Evangelical Graduate School of Theology. In 2000 the Tony Wilmot Memorial Library was named there in his honour.

One of Jonathan's great grandfathers on his mother's side, Stanley Peregrine Smith, was a member of the Cambridge Seven, a group who went as missionaries to China in 1885. Stanley married Sophie Reuter, a Norwegian missionary in China, and they had one son, Algernon, before Sophie's untimely death three years after their marriage. Algernon became a missionary Doctor with the Church Missionary Society, a co-founder of the Rwanda Mission and later a Bible translator in Rwanda.

Jonathan studied at St. John's College, Nottingham, and the University of Nottingham, gaining both a Licentiate and Bachelor of Theology. In 1974 he was ordained Deacon in Ely Cathedral and for the next three years worked as Curate at St. Martin's Church, Cambridge. For his next role, he moved to France where he became Chaplain in Chantilly from 1977 and assistant Chaplain at St. Michael's, Paris, as well as War Graves Commission Chaplain in Arras, Northern France.

In January 1982 he married Susan Lovett and later that year moved to become the Chaplain in Versailles at St. Mark's (succeeding David and Sue Vail there).[1] In 1988 they moved back to the UK as Jonathan became Vicar of St. John the Evangelist, Blackheath, London SE3.[2]

Soon after Peter Downham had resigned, the PCC had put in place a Drafting Group for the Parish Profile, under the chairmanship of John

Kent.[3] The Draft Parish Profile was agreed at a PCC meeting in January 1995, including the following as key points:

- The fact that the Church members are largely middle class people and that very few of the fellowship live in the parish
- The important role of the Greyfriars Centre
- The role of Music Team Leader
- The fact that the reordering of the east end awaits full consultation with the fellowship
- The desire to begin to explore new patterns for effective evangelism
- The best way to reflect the relationships between those holding differing views on Worship and the ministry of the Holy Spirit[4]

As previously, during the interregnum, the Curate (Jeff Wattley) and the Churchwardens (Harry Hogg and Dennis Parker) led the Church. The Patronage Secretary of the Church Pastoral Aid Society (who administered the Church Trust Fund Trust), the Rev. David Field, visited the PCC on 2nd February 1995 to describe the process of appointing a new Vicar and to discuss the Parish Profile.

By June 1995, the interview process was complete and the post of Vicar of Greyfriars was offered to and accepted by Jonathan Wilmot. Harry Hogg wrote: "We chose him for his godly character, biblical commitment, preaching skills, simple direct leadership skills and overall, his love of the Lord Jesus."[5]

Jonathan Wilmot was inducted to Greyfriars on Wednesday 4th October 1995 at 8pm. In the Vicar's Letter for the following month, Jonathan wrote:

> Dear Friends,
> Thank you so much for your warm welcome to us as a family. You have taken us to your hearts and made us feel instantly and completely at home. It is an enormous privilege for us to be working with you here in Reading. There is such a wealth of talent in the congregation and we look forward to developing friendships with you in the job of making Christ known in our town.

In November the PCC agreed unanimously to Sue Wilmot being Licensed as a Reader in Greyfriars.[6] She had been admitted as a Lay Reader in the Diocese of Southwark the previous month, having completed the requisite training there. At the 11am service on 4th January 1996 she was duly Licensed, joining Wilfred Dyer, Philip Giddings and Bill Jolliffe as Readers at Greyfriars.[7]

In a move reminiscent of the Rev. William Whitmarsh Phelps when he became Vicar of Trinity Church in 1845 (see page 65), one of Jonathan's first acts as Incumbent was to institute a weekly prayer meeting for Reading Clergy to pray for the town. This continues to the time of writing.

In early 1996 Wendy Bowie retired from being the organiser of the Flower Rota. Flowers were first acceptable in Greyfriars (apart from at Festivals) following agreement by the PCC in January 1969 – "only in the most suitable and acceptable position."[8] Within a couple of weeks, Wendy had become the Flower organiser, no doubt not suspecting that she would continue in that role for the next 27 years! She was succeeded as organiser by Wendy Stormont.[9]

In February 1996, Jeff and Sheila Wattley left, their last day being Sunday 11th. Jeff preached at the morning service and then there was a farewell tea at 4pm in the Centre. Jeff became Vicar of St. John the Baptist, Wonersh.[10]

VISION

"We want to see Jesus"

VALUES

- We value a wholehearted submission to the Lordship of Jesus
- We value a wholehearted submission to the direction of His Holy Spirit.
- We value being challenged to allow Greyfriars to be His Church rather than ours.
- We value a shared vision for the mission of the Church.
- We value a hunger for greater spiritual maturity.
- We value a deeper concern for effective evangelism and outreach.
- We value a sense of being an interdependent community of love.
- We value depth and joy in worship.

Greyfriars' Statement of "Vision and Values"

From the Parish Profile. Published in March 1996.[11]

"Our Purpose" was subsequently added: "To know Christ Jesus and to make Him known."

At the Annual Meeting in April 1996, Dennis Parker stood down as Churchwarden, a post he had held since 1988. He received a standing ovation for his work over those eight years and especially through the interregnum. Harry Hogg continued as Warden and was joined by Rosemary Gambles, the first ever female Churchwarden at Greyfriars.[12]

Churchwardens during Mr. Wilmot's incumbency (From 1995 to present)			
1995 to 1996	Dennis Parker	Harry Hogg	
1996 to 1997	Rosemary Gambles	Harry Hogg	
1997 to 2001	Rosemary Gambles	Steve Smith	
2001 to 2002	Jonathan Thatcher	Steve Smith	
2002 to 2004	Jonathan Thatcher	Jenny Roper	
2004 to 2007	Jonathan Thatcher	Alan Smith	
2007 to 2009	Jonathan Thatcher	Alan Smith	Mark Hinckley
2009 to 2013	Jonathan Thatcher	Mark Hinckley	Dave Elliott
2013 to date	Jonathan Thatcher	Mark Hinckley	

Interestingly, it took even longer before Greyfriars had its first female PCC Secretary: Ruth Hampton took up the post in September 2011. To date, the Church has not had a female PCC Vice Chairman or Treasurer.

From	To	PCC Secretary
1920	1928	William T. Kirby
1928	1931	Frank Savage
1931	1934	John H. Williams
1934	1962	Charles Lambourn
1962	1967	J. R. Jeffrey
1967	1974	Robert V. Masters
1974	1978	Arthur S. A. Vickerage
1978	1981	David A. Crayford
1981	1984	Anthony W. Lowman
1984	1986	Graeme R. N. Naish
1986	1994	Peter B. Holland
1994	1999	Trevor M. Gill

From	To	PCC Treasurer
1920	1932	Joseph C. Gilkes
1932	1934	Alfred W. Milward
1934	1946	Stanley J. Milward
1946	1966	Stanley Dunster
1966	1984	Arthur C. D'Arcy
1984	1992	Chris Leslie
1992	1995	Simon Porter
1995	1998	Steve Magee
1998	2000	Ian Clark
2000	2002	Steve Magee
2002	2007	Simon Porter
2007	2008	Murray Lewis

From	To	PCC Secretary
1999	2007	Graham Underwood
2007	2011	Stuart Freebody
2011	Present	Ruth Hampton

From	To	PCC Treasurer
2009	Present	Alan Cross

From	To	PCC Vice Chairman
1920	1928	William Sparks
1928	1934	Alfred W. Milward
1934	1956	Dr. Jason G. Bird
1956	1973	Stanley J. Milward
1973	1982	Wilfred Dyer
1982	Present	Peter Spriggs

The first mention of emails in an article in Greyfriars News occurred in April 1996, where Tim Mote suggested compiling a list of people's email addresses to be placed in a directory. Tim's email address was a distinctly unmemorable 100634.631@compuserve.com!

There were several personnel appointments and changes around this time. Prue Magee became the Vicar's PA in March 1996.[13] Sid Marshall resigned as Pastoral Worker at the end of July[14] and Mark Wibberley was appointed as the first Greyfriars Youth Worker, starting in September 1996 on a one year contract.[15] Rachel Lee-Johnson stood down as Music Team Leader in the autumn of 1996 and was replaced in the following March by Ruth Courtney as Music Co-ordinator.[16]

The first Greyfriars Alpha course took place on Wednesdays starting on 9th October 1996, led by the Vicar and supported by the first Alpha team:

Administration	Helen Wilkinson
Baby-sitting	Deirdre Underwood
Catering	Ros Johnson
Transport	Helen Boyer

The reordering of the east end of the Church was again firmly on the agenda. Jonathan invited Robert Maguire OBE, of High Street, Thame, an architect he had worked with previously, to speak to the PCC in May 1996.[17] It was agreed at that meeting that Mr. Maguire would carry out a feasibility study by September and so be able to propose some reordering options.

The study, named the "Report on the Possibilities for Rearrangement of the Interiors of the Church and Entrance Hall,"[18] clearly identified the issues that the Church faced:

- The sanctuary area was too cramped and the communion rail poorly positioned "for the celebration of a modern Eucharist"
- The sanctuary area, being raised by only one step, was therefore not easily visible in a Church with 19 rows of pews and 73ft (23m) to the furthest member of the congregation
- Space for a music group and for drama and dance were needed
- The pulpit was poorly placed, with many seats in the north aisle blocked by pillars. In fact, the architect found that only 344 of the 458 seats (75%) in the Church were "viable," ie able to see without either a pillar or other impediment being in the way
- The pews were "generally found to be uncomfortable and fixed too close together (825mm where the modern norm is 900mm)"

Roof and interior, following the roof project.
August 1997
(Photographs by kind permission of Gullett and Sons Ltd)

A second major strand of the project was to improve the inefficient heating of the Church, which was linked to a need to insulate and repair the roof. This project therefore needed to encompass far more than just a reordering of the east end, but rather be a redesign of the whole interior.

The roof work was agreed to be the first phase. Alan Bristow, the architect who carried out the construction of the Centre, produced a full specification that included inspection and repair of the roof timber, insulation of the roof and redecoration of the walls at high level. Gullett and Sons Ltd, Chesham, Buckinghamshire, were appointed to carry out the work at an initial cost of £86,000. The work began on 7th April 1997, closing the Church building for a little over four months.[19] At the end of the project, Harry Hogg wrote to Gullett and Sons Ltd on behalf of the Church to say "It is fitting to pay tribute to the quality of your work and the dedication of your staff... who worked hard and obligingly and with skill."[20]

Meanwhile, the Vicar proposed that the fellowship consider moving to two morning services, one with Alternative Service Book (ASB) Liturgy and the other a family-oriented service. Jonathan wrote in Greyfriars News: "Church growth surveys show that when a Church is 80% full it ceases to grow."[21] A questionnaire was sent out at the end of May 1996 to the 385 persons on the Electoral Roll and 214 (56%) were returned. The headline figure from the analysis of the questionnaire returns was that 56% believed there were good reasons for introducing a second morning service, but little agreement over when the children's work should take place or the format of the services.[22]

The PCC agreed to a six month experimental period of two morning services, beginning on 6th April 1997, at 9.15am and 11am. The first services were in the Church but, due to the roof project, moved to the Centre from the following Sunday. The 9.15am service was informal and was provided with crèche, Sunday School and Pathfinders. The later service was formal and without any groups for children. When the experimental period was over, the single morning service moved to 10.30am from 2nd November 1997. Following an extensive review, the PCC agreed to retain the single morning service, with 65% of the questionnaires returned being in favour of 1 service.[23]

At the April 1997 Annual Meeting, Harry Hogg stood down as Churchwarden after 12 years' service. Steve Smith was elected to join Ro Gambles as Warden for the following year.[24] David Brown was thanked at the meeting for making and donating a large wooden cross that initially went into the Centre as the Church was closed due to the roof repairs and later went into the reordered Church.

In July 1997 Janet King retired from leading Friday Club, where 5 – 11s gathered at 6pm every week, after 40 years' service. The Church presented her with a blue porcelain vase from Chantilly in gratitude.[25] Another long-time servant of the Church retired at this time: Wilfred Dyer, who had first been elected to the PCC at the Annual Vestry meeting in May 1951 resigned from that body in July 1997.[26] The Vicar wrote: "Included in those years have been stints as Church Warden, Deanery and Diocesan Synod Representative, Lay Chair of Deanery Synod and a host of other responsibilities. Our prayerful good wishes go with him during this second retirement. We are fortunate to have the benefit of the wisdom and grace of such elder statesmen in Greyfriars."[27]

In September 1997 Jonathan Wilmot's first Curate, Nick Lyness, started at Greyfriars. Unfortunately, due to difficult personal circumstances, he had to resign with effect from mid-October.[28] He was replaced by William Olhausen who, with his wife Tanya and their three young girls, moved to Reading at the end of June the following year.[29]

The 5 Curates who worked with Mr. Wilmot (to date)	Curate From	To	Next destination
Nicholas Jonathan Lyness	Sept 1997	Oct 1997	
William P. Olhausen	1998	2001	Associate Vicar: Holy Trinity, Cambridge
Phil Andrew	2002	2006	Vicar: St. Mary's, Reigate
Mark Pads Dolphin	2008	2011	Priest-in-Charge: St. Matthew's, Southcote
Dan Heyward	2011	Present	

In September 1997 Andy Freeman was appointed Youth Worker.[30] He took up the post in January 1998. Greyfriars did not have suitable accommodation for Andy and his family so initially they stayed in the Curate's house. The Church bought 72 York Road, in the parish, for £80,750.[31] A legacy (by Miss E. J. Lawrence) to the Missionary Trust enabled it to buy 14 Sackville Street from the Church for £67,500, as it was used for missionaries on furlough, releasing money towards the purchase of 72 York Road.[32]

From 26th to 28th September, "150 people took part including 25 children and 5 toddlers" in the Greyfriars Weekend away at the Pioneer Centre, near Kidderminster.[33] This was the first weekend away since 1991.

Church Weekends Away during Mr. Wilmot's incumbency		
	Location	Speaker
26th-28th September 1997	Pioneer Centre, Kidderminster	Mark Brown
10th-12th September 1999	Wycliffe Centre, Horsleys Green, High Wycombe	Graham Ingram

In January 1998 there was a surprise 50th birthday party for the Vicar. "Announced in Church on the Sunday after Christmas when Jonathan was away, and the congregation sworn to secrecy, plans went ahead to organise a 'This is Your Life' entertainment... The evening ended with the presentation of a zimmer frame for the ensuing years and a comic song, written and presented by the staff."[34]

In late July 1998 the reordering plans were submitted to the Diocesan Advisory Committee in late July 1998 (see Plan B below). The DAC approved them by December. Meanwhile, the PCC sought the necessary Faculty from the Diocese.[35]

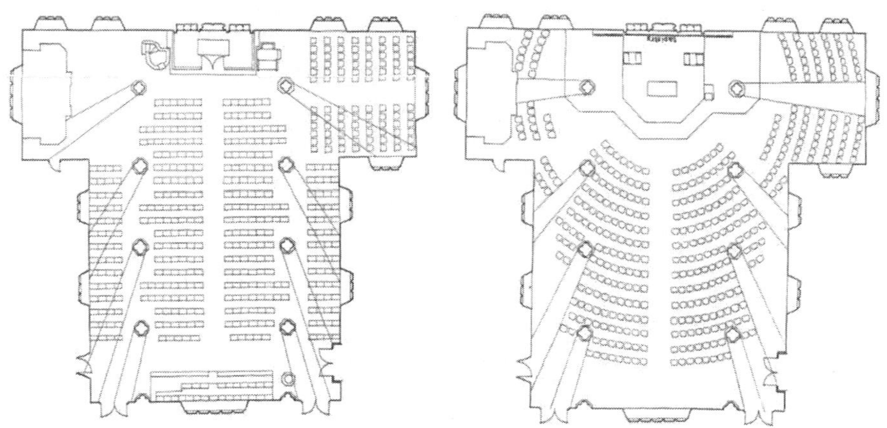

Reordering Plans
Left: "Plan A (as existing)" Right: "Plan B"

In December 1998 the Business Lunch meetings, recently renamed LunchBreak on Thursdays, were discontinued. The Lunches had run for 26 years at Greyfriars, initially led by Wilfred Dyer. Changes to the way people work, especially with fewer people able to take over an hour off at lunch time, meant that reluctantly it was decided that the LunchBreak meetings should cease. Grateful thanks were expressed to Judith Holland, who for the last 10 years had organised the catering team.[36]

On Wednesday 3rd March 1999 Greyfriars received its (to date) only visit from the Head of the Anglican Communion – The Most Rev. & Rt. Hon. the Lord Archbishop of Canterbury. The occasion was a gathering of 150 clergy from the Reading Archdeaconry, hosted by the Rt. Rev. Richard Harries, Bishop of Oxford, with the Rt. Rev. Dominic Walker, Bishop of Reading. Archbishop George Carey hosted a "question and answer" session and then talked about his vision for the next 10 years. Those gathered then joined in a 1662 Evening Prayer service.[37]

Good news arrived via the fax machine on 16th July 1999. The Victorian Society, who had had concerns about the reordering of the east end of the Church, decided not to object to the plans.[38] In October, the Faculty was received from the Oxford Diocese enabling the work to go ahead.[39] The overall projected cost of the reordering project at this point was £550,000 with £260,000 still to be raised. Tuesday 9th November was therefore set apart as a day of fasting and prayer for the project, followed by a Gift Day on Sunday 21st that raised a further £230,000.[40]

Several changes in personnel took place around this time. Sue Giles had become the Church and Centre Secretary in October 1998, taking over from Mark Wibberley who had carried the work out on a temporary basis.[41] A "Youth Team," soon renamed "Reach," consisting of Nathalie Kusicka, Martha Reed and John Snelson, joined Andy Freeman in working with young people both in Greyfriars and in some local schools on a year's contract.[42] The following year the team expanded to four: Jenny Dale, Nathaniel Fisher, Luke Prankard and Erica Woodhouse.[43] In the autumn of 1999, Mabel Boyd resigned as Centre Catering Manager, having almost completed 10 years in the post. She was replaced by Geraldine Mann, who with her husband Dennis had been carrying out the duties of Verger for the previous two years.[44]

Sue Wilmot had been co-ordinating the work of Home Groups for some time. At the PCC in April 1999 she proposed an additional staff post to develop this work.[45] After much consideration, the post of Pastoral Director was advertised in early 2000. Following interviews, Phil Cole was appointed with effect from 1st July 2000 and he and Shirley moved into 39 Newport Road in the parish.[46]

The reordering project began to pick up pace. The proposals included extending and raising the east end, and removing the pulpit (which now sits at the west end), the reading desks and the sanctuary rail. Only moveable furniture was to be included so that there would be complete flexibility of use. A ramp was to be installed against the east wall from the south transept, to allow for wheelchair access. The reredos was to be covered by a hanging, initially by a single tapestry with a text and later by curtains.

Looking east, after the reordering in 2000

Under floor heating was installed throughout the Church and the flooring replaced with light-coloured tiles. The fixed pews were replaced by chairs, allowing for complete flexibility of seating plan. The lighting was upgraded, although the original 1863 coronae were retained throughout the nave, with two being moved to the transepts. Extra lighting was installed throughout the building and especially at the east end. The Reordering Working Party, chaired by Jonathan Thatcher, worked closely with architect Bob Maguire throughout the project.

The main contract was placed with Boshers (Cholsey) Ltd to the value of £355,000 in January 2000[47] and the work started on site on Monday 14th February. Sunday morning services moved to the Centre, with two morning services at 9.15am and 11am. Evening services were held in St. Laurence's Church at 6.30pm.[48]

When the flooring had been taken up in the Church, various discoveries were made: "a well, a fireplace, Victorian heating ducts and the occasional bone." However, the Oxford Archaeological Unit decided that these items were not of historical significance.[49]

The various pieces of furniture were made of light-coloured wood, contrasting with the previous dark oak. The table, with the legend *I am the Bread of Life*, cost £1900; the two clergy stools and kneelers £1700 each; the lectern £1450; and the east wall hanging £550.[50]

The 1939 Compton organ was still in good condition and so was kept in its dark oak case (dating from 1894). However, the detached console was in a poor condition, with deteriorating wiring. The best quote for a replacement came from Pels d'Hondt, a Belgian company. Following a visit to inspect their work, David Rance recommended to the PCC that they be awarded the £26,000 contract for a moveable console.[51] The new console was installed in March 2001.[52]

Organ and moveable Organ Console

The reordering was completed by 21st August 2000, just one week after the initial estimate. The Church was ready for occupation not long after, with Sunday services resuming there on 3rd September. The building was re-dedicated by the Bishop of Reading at a special evening service on 17th September. Reflecting on the impact of the reordering on the Church, Heather Dyer wrote:

> The vision for the reordering was that it would facilitate and enhance worship, and would also enable the building to be used more effectively in the ministry and mission of Greyfriars. Experience has fully borne out this expectation. The reordering has facilitated a variety of forms of worship, including adult baptisms by immersion in the font inset into the dais, and has also allowed the building to be used for conferences, Alpha banquets, prayer vigils, and many other events. Moreover, the reordering has revealed in a new way the wonderful lightness, simplicity and elegance of the original Franciscan design of the building.[53]

East end dais
and
Baptistery.

Baptistery first used for a full immersion baptism at the morning service on Sunday 26th November 2000, when Jonathan Wilmot baptised Jonathan Brent[54]

As with previous large projects, the Church committed a tithe of the gifts to a wide variety of projects around the world, complementing the tithing of the general income of the Church, which is given to local Christian organisations.

Before the Church was reordered, the weekly offering had been collected during services by sidesmen. The Vicar proposed that there should be a receptacle for gifts so that those who wished to give would do so on the way into Church. These offerings would then be brought to the table on the dais during the service. It was agreed that there should be one collection box by each door.[55] These boxes were funded from the legacy from Arthur D'Arcy, who died in April 2000. He had been Treasurer from 1966 to 1984 and had continued to count and bank the offerings each week.[56]

One of two offering collection boxes

The label at the base says: "In Memory of Arthur D'Arcy"

When the services resumed in the Church, the morning service was at 10am and the evening service at 6.30pm. The Vicar proposed to the PCC an additional Sunday service at 4.30pm, with a tea served at 4pm.[57] This service was to be "liturgically Anglican but recognisably Greyfriars." The first 4.30pm service took place on 5th November 2000, with former Greyfriars' Vicar Peter Downham speaking on "Protecting the Unity of our Fellowship." Although initially attracting small congregations, this has become a much valued service for many. On the same date, the morning service moved back to 10.30am and the evening service to 7pm.

The reordered Church enabled the use of the Church building for other events. In June 2001, for example, Greyfriars' group CAST (Christian ArtS Trust) performed the Rob Frost/ Sue Pottinger play "Dangerous Journey," based on "The Pilgrim's Progress" by John Bunyan. The play was produced by Wendy Stormont and the actors, dancers, musicians, stage designers, stage and lighting crew were almost all Greyfriars' members.

Poster for the 2001 perfomance of Dangerous Journey
in the reordered Church

Heather Dyer retired as editor of Greyfriars News after being responsible for 336 issues (28 years) with the production of the December 2000 edition. Helen Smith took on the role, with a small team around her to assist. Helen continued as editor until December 2005.

For over a year there had been discussions about the provision of additional office space for the staff team. It was decided that a temporary building (such as provided by the company Portakabin) could be placed on the grassed area between the Centre and the West End kitchen. Finally, with Planning Permission granted, the building was delivered and installed at a cost of about £11,000.[58]

"The Portakabin"
(Photograph taken in 2012)

In January 2001 the demolition of St. Paul's United Reformed Church in York Road started. The building and land had been bought for £940,000 by New Hope, a company (and by September 2001 a charity) founded and funded by Steve and Prue Magee. Their vision was for a church plant and community centre with supported housing as a mission to Greyfriars parish. The redevelopment project cost a further £1.6 million.[59] In January 2001, the New Hope Trustees were Simon Cuthbert, Karen Freeman, Peter Holland, Prue & Steve Magee, Richard Taylor and Jonathan Wilmot.[60]

"To the Glory of God this stone was laid by William McIlroy Esq June 5th 1901"

"We rejoice in the hope of the Glory of God Romans 5:2 Built in 2001"

New Hope Community Church Foundation Stones

Building work, carried out by Cornerstone Construction (Countrywide) Ltd of Baughurst, continued throughout 2001. On 19th January 2002 the foundation stone, cut from the back half of the original foundation stone of St. Paul's Church, was unveiled by the Rt. Rev. Dominic Walker, Bishop of Reading, at a special ceremony.[61] Situated side by side in the new building, both were unveiled in the ceremony.

New Hope Church and Community Centre, York Road

Greyfriars sought an Associate Vicar to lead the ministry at New Hope. After interviews at the end of April 2002, the Rev. Jon Westall was appointed and he, his wife Rachel and their two girls, moved into 93 York Road in July. Mr. Westall was licensed as Associate Vicar at Greyfriars and Priest in Charge of New Hope by the Bishop of Reading at the evening service at Greyfriars on 8th September 2002. After the service the congregation divided into four groups and walked from Greyfriars to New Hope by different routes through the parish, praying as they went. One group, by invitation, attended a blessing service for New Hope in its "Upper Room" (first floor of the community centre).[62]

Associate Vicars of New Hope	
2002 – 2006	Jon Westall
2006 – 2012	Catharine Morris
2013 –	Joy Atkins

The New Hope buildings consist of a community centre (on three floors: community hall on the ground floor; the Church meeting room on the first floor; offices and meeting rooms on the second floor), a home for the Associate Vicar connected to the community centre and five terraced houses.

In March 2003, six months after the commissioning service, Jon Westall reported that the New Hope "team consists of 21 adults, 12 from Greyfriars, 9 from other Churches; 17 live in the parish ([of whom] 12 in the New Hope accommodation)."[63]

There were several personnel changes at this time. In April 2001, Jonathan Thatcher became Churchwarden in place of Ro Gambles, who stood down after 5 years' service. Steve Smith continued as Warden for one more year, at which time he was replaced by Jenny Roper.[64] In May 2001, Ruth Courtney resigned as Music Director, to be replaced in February 2002 by Dr. Phil Cooke.[65] In June 2001, Curate William Olhausen left, moving to Holy Trinity, Cambridge.[66] Then in July, Andy Freeman resigned as Youth Pastor to "pioneer the establishment of, and head up, a new venture called the Boiler Room, a 24/7 prayer venture with youth in mind."[67] Andy's replacement was Derek Attrill, who joined the Greyfriars' staff in August 2002.[68]

In mid-2002, Jonathan was joined by his next Curate, Phil Andrew, who was ordained Deacon at Christ Church, Oxford, on 30th June.[69] Phil had been an engineer before moving to ordained ministry and his wife Sue had worked as a GP. Like Jonathan and Sue Wilmot, Phil and Sue Andrew had a family of three boys.

Dennis Mann retired from being the Verger in April 2003, followed a month later by the resignation of Geraldine Mann as Catering Manager.[70] Paul Kelly took up the post of Verger in June[71] and Jo Law became the new Catering Manager soon after, remaining in post until April 2011.[72]

In 2003, Greyfriars became embroiled in what the Vicar called "extraordinary turmoil."[73] The Bishop of Oxford nominated the Rev. Jeffrey John to be the next Bishop of Reading. Looking back almost ten years later, a Profile of Jeffrey John on Christianity Magazine's website stated:

> Jeffrey John is a Church of England priest, and has been in the same sex relationship (albeit celibate) with his partner, Grant, for more than 35 years. John first came to national attention in 2003 when his nomination as Bishop of Reading was disputed by Anglican evangelicals who objected to an openly gay clergyman, who refused to repent of his homosexual relationship, taking such an office.[74]

There was a great deal of media interest in the controversy, often focused on Greyfriars' Elder, Dr. Philip Giddings. The Vicar wrote in his Annual Report for 2003 that Philip "did an outstanding job as a spokesperson, under huge pressure, often with very little warning, as he represented not only Greyfriars, but also all those who want to live a Biblically obedient lifestyle."[75] Following intervention by the Archbishop of Canterbury, Mr. John's nomination was withdrawn. In January 2004 the Rev. Stephen Cottrell was appointed Bishop of Reading.

From June to August 2003, Jonathan Wilmot was on sabbatical. Following a retreat on the island of Mull, he visited several city churches – in Glasgow, Manchester and Sheffield. Then the Wilmot family went to Florida both for a holiday and as an opportunity to visit Idlewilde Church, a sister church of Saddleback Community Church in California. Jonathan wrote: "The result was that we have all returned home enriched, relaxed and encouraged and with renewed vision. Sue returned to start work for the Bible Society as Development Manager for the South East."[76]

In early 2003 the first discussions about the possible conversion of the Vicarage into a children's Nursery occurred.[77] By June, Kate Fielden had produced a feasibility report, which stated that it was a viable proposition. There was uncertainty as to how the plan might fit into the general redevelopment of Greyfriars, but support for the project gradually grew. By March 2004 the Diocese had agreed that they would buy a new Vicarage – although they wanted the cost of the new one to be matched by the funds received for the old – and that they thought that the plans to open a Nursery fitted their criterion of "cutting edge ministries."[78] In May 2004, Jonathan summarised his vision:

> My long-term vision is to see a complete renewal of the buildings on our site, not so that we can do what we are currently doing out of them, but so that we can do much more than we are currently doing. God wants us to expand our horizons. He wants to see more people influenced for the gospel having their lives turned upside down by the risen returning Christ. God has given us a strategic space in the town of Reading from which that vision can be launched.

> I ask you to join with me in praying, giving and working to that end from this wonderful facility that is Greyfriars that this would be a Church in the heart of Reading with Reading on its heart. May he be praised by all we do.[79]

At a special tea on 29th February 2004, Greyfriars said farewell to Phil and Shirley Cole as they left for Bransgore at the end of almost four years serving as Pastoral Director (Phil) and being in charge of the Sunday School (Shirley).[80] About three months later, Phil was replaced on the staff by Pads Dolphin, who became Small Groups & Alpha Co-ordinator.[81]

The Annual Parochial Church Meeting was postponed in 2004, or more accurately adjourned, while a replacement for Jenny Roper as Warden was sought. A month later, Alan Smith joined Jonathan Thatcher as Churchwarden.[82]

In June 2004 the Church held its first "Fun Day" to bring together its four congregations: New Hope, and Greyfriars 10.30am, 4.30pm and 7pm. It was held at Rushall Farm and started with an informal service in the barn at 10.30am. This was followed by a picnic lunch and then a variety of activities – including various inflatables "for all ages." After afternoon tea and cakes the day ended with a service of praise to God.[83]

At the end of August 2005, Youth Pastor Derek Attrill left, moving to Dorset.[84] After three and a half years as the Vicar's PA, Janet Shury changed role in 2005 to become Office and Finance Manager. At the same time John Brown, who had been Centre Manager since 1983, became Centre Bookshop Manager and Centre Chaplain and the post of Centre Manager lapsed.[85] In January 2006, Rebecca Chapman was appointed as Jonathan's new PA.[86]

The Nursery Project team, led by Kate Fielden and Ian Hunt, had been meeting since September 2004.[87] Jonathan Thatcher took responsibility for steering the project through both the PCC and the Diocese. In September 2005, the PCC resolved to establish a Nursery at 64 Friar Street, seeing the project as the first stage of the development of the whole Greyfriars' site.[88] In February 2006, the PCC decided to form Greyfriars Ministries Limited (GML) as the controlling company to run the Nursery. The first Directors of GML were Jonathan Wilmot, Steve Smith, Graham Underwood (Company Secretary) and Stephen Clague (Finance Director). In mid-2006 Helen Kinch was appointed Nursery Manager, with Donna Overton as her Deputy.[89]

The Vicar wrote, looking back for the Annual Report: "In January we had a day of fasting and prayer towards our having funds to purchase No.

64 from the Diocese for the ministry of Greyfriars in Reading. On 29th January we had the most joyful gift day I have ever known as God encouraged us to give sacrificially. On March 13th we finally owned No. 64..."[90] The gift day raised an astonishing £740,000 towards the Nursery project.[91]

On 2nd March 2006 the Wilmot family moved out of the town centre to a new Vicarage at 28 Westcote Road. Soon after, Kingsmen Builders moved into No. 64 and began to alter virtually every room to create a modern, purpose-built, Nursery for up to 55 children.[92]

Greyfriars Nursery Logo

The December 2005 issue of Greyfriars News was Helen Smith's last as editor. By May 2006, the team of Laurie Anstis and Dave and Ellie Spence had taken on the role, with Laurie becoming sole editor from September 2010.[93] The magazine, which had been A5 size since July 1970, was issued in A4 format from February 2006, initially as one A3 sheet folded and gradually gaining extra sheets.

At the Annual Meeting in April 2006, the existing Churchwardens – Alan Smith and Jonathan Thatcher – were re-elected and were joined by a third Warden, Mark Hinckley.[94]

During the Greyfriars and New Hope Fun Day at Rushall Manor Farm on 25th June 2006, the Church said farewell to Curate Phil Andrew and family, as they moved to St. Mary's, Reigate.[95] Soon after – in mid-August – Jon Westall moved on from New Hope to be Vicar of St. Dunstan's with St. Thomas, East Acton.[96]

The Rev. Catharine Morris joined the staff as Associate Vicar, New Hope, starting in November 2006. Greyfriars also welcomed Carol Atkins as its new Children's Worker from late August and Stan Lyth as Youth Pastor in October. To complete the picture of staff changes, Penny

Cuthbert and Mark Autherson joined the staff in voluntary capacities. Penny became Parish Assistant and Mark Pastoral Assistant.[97]

Greyfriars Day Nursery was officially opened on Thursday 28th September 2006. The Mayor of Reading cut a ribbon at the front door and the Bishop of Reading prayed for God's blessing on the venture. Helen Kinch and her team opened the Nursery doors to the first 8 children on Monday 2nd October.[98] Remarkably, the business reached a break-even point on its operating costs within three months.[99] The Nursery has been used every Sunday morning since for the youngest Trekkers.

At the opening of the Nursery:
Rt. Rev. Stephen Cottrell,
Bishop of Reading,
Cllr Bet Tickner,
Mayor of Reading,
Helen Kinch, Nursery Manager

Photograph from
Greyfriars News October 2006

On 12th January 2009 the Nursery extended into the Memorial Hall, specifically for 3-year-olds as Government funding allowed for all of that age to have 5 sessions paid for each week. In order to prepare the Hall for this use, £20,000 of work was undertaken.[100]

Since early 2003 the Greyfriars' Songwriters' Forum, started by Phil Cooke and led by David Horne, had been meeting and encouraging home grown musical talent. The Forum held a very well-attended "Songwriters' Soirée" at New Hope on 28th April 2006 where many new songs were performed. This was followed three weeks later by the recording of a compilation CD of 23 compositions by 6 different Greyfriars' songwriters. On 7th October 2006 at the Globe, just off Portman Road, the CD "AsOne" was performed and recorded live as the culmination of a collaborative project between Greyfriars, Brookside and The Deliverance Centre Churches. 5 of the 14 tracks were by Greyfriars' songwriters. All proceeds from the sale of the CD went to the local charity Christian Community Action (CCA).

asone

01. **AS ONE** Dionne Williams
02. **JUMP UP!** Tom Pollard
03. **THE CHURCH'S CONFESSION** Marie Thomas
04. **CHRIST BE WITH ME** Cathy Summers
05. **SOMETHING ABOUT JESUS** Immaculate Nansasi
06. **YOU ARE LEADING US** Helen Stephenson
07. **THE WHOLE EARTH SHALL BE FILLED** Chris Mitchell
08. **JUST GIVE ME TIME** Chris Mitchell & Patricia Beall Gavigan
09. **SPIRIT OF GOD** Linda Stevens
10. **WAKE UP!** David Rowland
11. **ONLY YOU CAN SATISFY** Tom Pollard
12. **WE GIVE YOU PRAISE** Junior Bernard
13. **BLESSED IS THE KING** Chris Mitchell
14. **INVITATION** Chris Mitchell & Patricia Beall Gavigan

AsOne CD October 2006
Tracks 2, 4, 6, 10 & 11 by Greyfriars' songwriters

"Saturday Outreach" began in 2006 and was renamed Prayer Café in April 2007. By early 2008 Prayer Stop was added. At the 2009 Annual Meeting, Gill Beard reported that "The Prayer Café is seeing more and more people coming in for prayer during these events, and benefits hugely from the prayer support it receives. Prayer Stop is much smaller, but receives around 30 to 40 requests at each event. In the last two years 2,321 people have been prayed for either through Prayer Café or Prayer Stop."[101]

During 2007 some long-standing Mission Partners returned home. Peter and Debbie Thompson had been in Trujillo, Peru, since 1993 and Pat Morgan had been in Niger since 1980, having been in Ethiopia from 1974 to 1976. At the PCC in January 2007 Craig Hampton reported that there were at that time 22 Mission Partners supported through the Greyfriars Missionary Trust.[102] The GMT had been set up by Trust Deed on 25th September 1975 as the means by which the Greyfriars' fellowship channelled their financial support for Missionaries and Mission Societies. In 2007 the Trust's income was £142,500 and under Chairman of Trustees, John Roper, was responsible for distributing £108,700 to Mission Partners and £37,800 to Mission Societies.[103]

Missionaries from Greyfriars Church (Departing from 1995)			
	From To	Where served	Mission Society
Scopas Elias	1995 Current	Sudan and Kenya	Episcopal Church of the Sudan
Joy Fleming	1995 Current	China	Overseas Missionary Fellowship
Sarah Wallace	1995 1997	UK	Youth With A Mission
Richard & Riekje Wallace	1997 Current	Portugal then Spain	Christian Associates International
Patrick Cordery	1997 2001	South Africa	Scripture Union
Peter Kent	1998 2004	France	Open Air Campaigners
Jimmy & Gemma Solomon	1998 2000	Chad	Action Partners
Judith Tuckey	1998 2000	Kisiizi, Uganda	Africa Inland Mission
Mike & Doro Buckle	1998 Current	South East Asia	Overseas Missionary Fellowship
Victoria Mountain	1999 2001	Portugal	A Rocha
Miguel & Paula Figueiras	2001 2004	Portugal	A Rocha
Jo Watson	2001 Current	UK	Viva Network then Tearfund
Ann Naish	2001 2002	France	Mission to Seafarers
Liz Baron	2002 2003	South Africa	Scripture Union
Carole Jarvis	2003 2009	Mozambique	Hope for Africa
Kevin & Kate Brits	2003 Current	Zimbabwe	OASIS
Tim Giddings	2003 2004	South Africa then Tanzania	Scripture Union
Tom Wilmot	2003	South Africa	Scripture Union
Clare Brown	2004 2005	Bolivia	Youth With A Mission

Missionaries from Greyfriars Church (Departing from 1995) continued			
	From To	Where served	Mission Society
Emmanuel & Grace Sharland	2006 Current	Sudan	Action Partners/Pioneers
Jo Donaldson	2009 2010	Mozambique	OASIS
David & Emma Craig	2010 Current	Kenya then Uganda	Pioneers
Tom & Daiga Ellaby	2011 Current	Latvia	Children Our Future

From 1st to 4th February 2008 the Church celebrated the 25th anniversary of the opening of Greyfriars Centre. The celebrations started with an event for Trekkers (children aged 3 to 11) on Friday, followed by an all-age party in the Centre Hall the next day. On Sunday at 4.30pm there was a special service with former Vicar Peter Downham as guest preacher. There was even a birthday cake, cooked by Fiona Rowlandson. On Monday – the actual anniversary – there was a formal lunch in the Centre Hall, attended by Reading MPs Martin Salter and Rob Wilson, Reading's Mayor, two local Councillors, former Vicars Peter Downham and Jim Spence, and representatives of the various organisations that used the Centre.[104]

Jonathan Wilmot wrote:

> In the first week of February we celebrated the Centre's 25th birthday. We made a list of the number of pints of blood that have been given through the Centre, the number of cups of coffee that have been drunk and how many books have been sold. We didn't try to estimate how many children have learnt

about Jesus, how many young people have experienced activities and teaching that has stayed with them for the rest of their lives, but the hope is that it's quite a few, and maybe you were one of them.

All this adds up to the fruit of a dream to have a seven day a week centre opened in the heart of Reading that was accessible to all. Twenty five years on that dream is still with us. It still burns as brightly as it did, but with those years of experience behind us we are better placed to know what will work, and how our community interfaces with us.

On 27th February I would like to invite you to an evening with architect Jeremy Bell as he presents to us his concept of what the Greyfriars site might look like, and what facilities it might offer as we seek to fulfil our God given vision to make Christ known.[105]

Rev. Jonathan Wilmot

Jonathan became an Honorary Canon of Christ Church, Oxford, in 2008.[106]

[Photograph from Greyfriars News October 2001]

The redevelopment of the Greyfriars site continued to be discussed, especially by the PCC and by the Redevelopment Working Group chaired by Jonathan Thatcher. At the PCC in July 2007 it was agreed to approach architects to "aid thinking about how the Greyfriars site can be redeveloped." Subsequently Jeremy Bell of JBKS Architects, Aston Rowant, Oxfordshire, was chosen to take the project forward.[107]

Initial Concept Design by Jeremy Bell for the Redevelopment
From Greyfriars and New Hope News July/Aug 2008

On 27th February 2008 the Centre Hall was packed to capacity to hear the initial concept presented by Jeremy Bell. This was followed by a round of consultation meetings with Home Groups, Time Out (women's group) and other small groups. In June 2008 the PCC decided to undertake a feasibility study that would:

- clarify the Church's requirements, especially in the light of consulation so far
- initiate discussions with English Heritage, Borough Planners, the Diocese, and any other relevant body
- complete preparatory work for a future Planning Application and Faculty petition
- produce outline building plans
- obtain an initial cost estimate

By the end of 2008 a number of important issues had emerged from the further discussions that the architect needed to consider and to incorporate into a revised concept.[108] By early 2009 Jonathan had spoken with both Bishops, of Oxford and of Reading, and gained their support for the project.[109]

On 29th June 2008 Pads Dolphin, who had been Greyfriars' Small Groups and Alpha Co-ordinator since 2004, was ordained Deacon at Christ Church Cathedral and became Greyfriars' new Curate. He had been accepted onto a four year "Mixed Mode" training in 2006, which combined residential periods at St. John's College, Nottingham, with full-time ministry experience in the parish.[110]

At the Annual Meeting in April 2009 Alan Smith stood down as Warden, having held the post for 5 years. Jonathan Thatcher and Mark Hinckley were re-elected and Dave Elliott was elected to join them. The Electoral Roll stood at 502, the first time it had been above 500 since 1968. As the Roll is periodically completely revised (as for example in 2013), the pattern of the Roll since 1945 shows several sharp dips, followed by recovery.

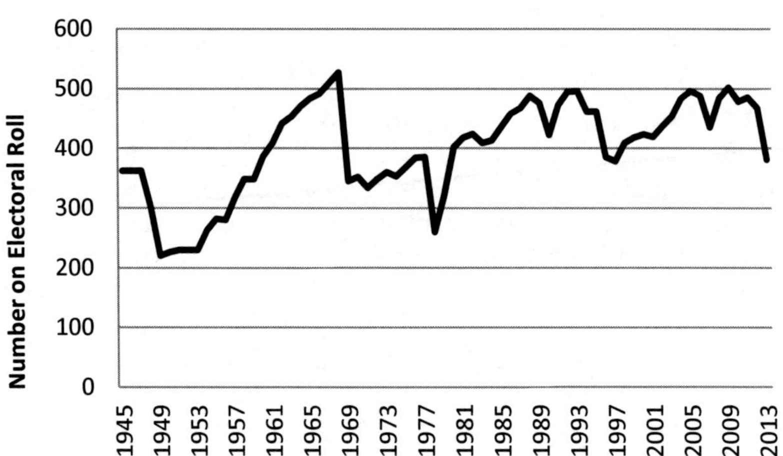

In June 2009, Ann Cogle took on the collation of the monthly Prayer Pointers, soon renamed the Prayer Guide. Before this date, Margaret Readdy (from 2002, Milward) had compiled the list for 33 years.[111]

The Church Weekend conference in January 2009 had been called "Restoring Our Spiritual Foundations." It was followed in February 2010 by a Church Day entitled "Building for the Future." Much of the focus of the latter was to pray as a fellowship about the redevelopment proposals.[112]

After 27 years' service in Greyfriars Centre as Centre Manager then Bookshop Manager, John Brown retired at the end of June 2010. A well-attended Retirement Party was held on Saturday evening 15th May in the Centre, where "supper [was] served at 6.30pm followed by a trip down memory lane!"[113] Debbie Thompson replaced John as Bookshop Manager, with Emma Sanderson becoming Worship and Services Administrator at the same time.[114]

John Brown in the Greyfriars Centre Bookshop
Photograph from Greyfriars and New Hope News December 2009

In 2011, two extensions to the Nursery building were completed, with costs met from the Nursery profit for 2010. The cellars were made fully habitable to provide a staff room and much more storage space, and a single storey extension was built on the Greyfriars Road side to provide more room for the children.[115] The extension was built on the site where the old Vicarage classroom had been, which had had an entrance from Friar Street and from the Vicar's study. This classroom had been demolished at the same time as the old Vicarage in 1963.

In 2011, Greyfriars celebrated 700 years of history. The planning group (Tonia Elliott, Gaynor Burton, Sue Rees, John Ledger, Jonathan Thatcher and the Vicar) had been meeting throughout 2010 and organised several congregational events. The first was a Church Weekend from 21st to 23rd January entitled "Preparing for Kingdom Adventure," led by former Greyfriars Curate, now Director of New Wine, John Coles.[116]

Motto Card
2011

Before the main celebrations in July, Pads and Kirstie Dolphin departed for St. Matthew's Church, Southcote, where Pads became Priest-in-Charge. The Church said farewell at a lunch after the morning service on 12th June. Several families who lived in the Southcote area moved from Greyfriars to St. Matthew's to support Pads' new ministry there.[117] The PCC agreed to "seed fund" a part-time staff member, giving £25,000 to the St. Matthew's PCC in 2011 and again in 2012.[118]

Greyfriars was not without a Curate for long, as Dan Heyward was ordained as Deacon on 2nd July. Dan was no stranger to Greyfriars, having been a member of the Church ten years before. He had married Caroline Leslie at Greyfriars in January 2004.[119]

The main celebration events of the 700th Anniversary were over the weekend of 8th to 10th July 2011. On the Friday there was an Evening Reception for local civic and business leaders, former members of the Church and representatives of organisations linked to Greyfriars. Former Archbishop of Canterbury, Lord Carey of Clifton, spoke at the event.

On Saturday from 11am there was a "Hunt the Monk" treasure hunt, with 10 grey-robed "monks" (friars, of course, really) stationed around the town centre to be located by solving clues. At the Church there were other activities for children – a football cage, craft and dance workshops – and "colours" advice for ladies. Prayer Stop offered prayer for anyone passing by outside the Church throughout the day. A barbecue lunch was provided in the car park.

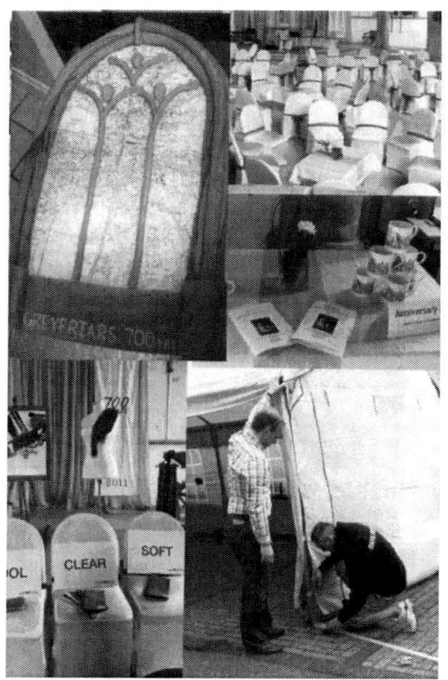

700th Anniversary Celebrations: 8th to 10th July 2011
Photographs from Greyfriars and New Hope News

The main event was in the Church itself at 1.30pm, repeated at 3.15pm: "700 years in words and music." The music, provided by Greyfriars' group Chorum, spanned the whole of Greyfriars' history, from 13th century "Sumer is icumen in" to the 21st century "The Lord is My Shepherd" composed by Greyfriars' member Cathy Summers. Interspersed among the musical items, Peter Spriggs narrated the Church's history, using Heather Dyer's "The Story of Greyfriars Church and Centre."

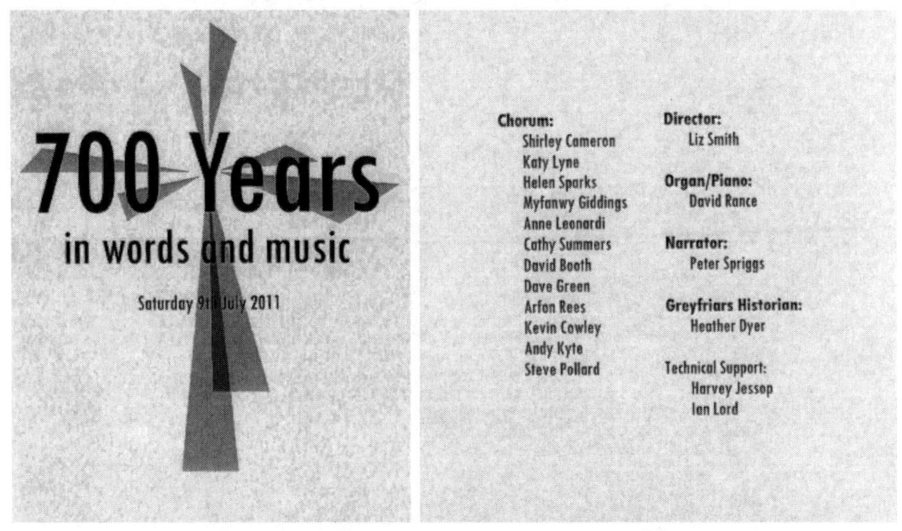

At 4.15pm there was a ceremonial cutting of the cake by Jonathan and his son Christopher. Baked by Angela Bevan and Laura Tucker, the cake was modelled on the west window, with a map of Reading drawn in icing.

On Sunday 10th July there were three special services, all led by Jonathan Wilmot. At 10.30am there was a 700th Anniversary Celebration Communion, with the Bishop of Reading, the Rt. Rev. Andrew Proud, preaching. This service included three songs by Greyfriars' songwriters: "We have been chosen" by Tom Pollard, "You are leading us" by Helen Sparks and "The Lord is My Shepherd" by Cathy Summers.

Afternoon tea was served at 3pm, followed by the 4pm Evening Prayer service. Two former Greyfriars' Vicars took part in this service: Peter Downham led the prayers and Jim Spence preached. At 7pm, the final celebration of the weekend was a service of praise to God for 700 years. At this service, Joel Thomas preached and Vernon Orr led the prayers, both men being local Church leaders. Catharine Morris, Associate Vicar, read the Bible passages at the 10.30am and 7pm services.

At the end of July 2011 Phil Cooke resigned as Worship Pastor in order to continue studying, along with Kath his wife, for ordination. At the same time, Stan Lyth, Youth Pastor, resigned to undertake a Masters in Biblical Interpretation.[120] In August, interviews were held for the post of Worship Pastor and Eileen Shipton was appointed, at first part-time due to her other commitments and from November as full-time.[121] It proved more difficult to locate a suitable Youth Pastor, taking until early in the new year for Heather Lewis to be appointed. She started in the role in August 2012.[122]

From 9th to 16th October 2011 Greyfriars held a Redevelopment Week of Prayer. Earlier in the year Jeremy Bell had shared the revised concept plans for the site with representatives of Reading Borough Council, English Heritage and the Diocesan Advisory Committee. The Council confirmed in principle their agreement to an entrance to an underground car park from Sackville Street and English Heritage approved the scale and footprint of the proposed development.[123] The PCC therefore proposed a Week of Prayer to seek God's will over the move to a full planning application.

A brochure entitled "Redevelopment of the Greyfriars Site: The vision, the story so far and the proposal for the future" was produced, together with a booklet of daily Bible Study and prayer. Presentations were made at services to ensure that the whole congregation was well informed of the proposals.

Redevelopment Concept – 2011

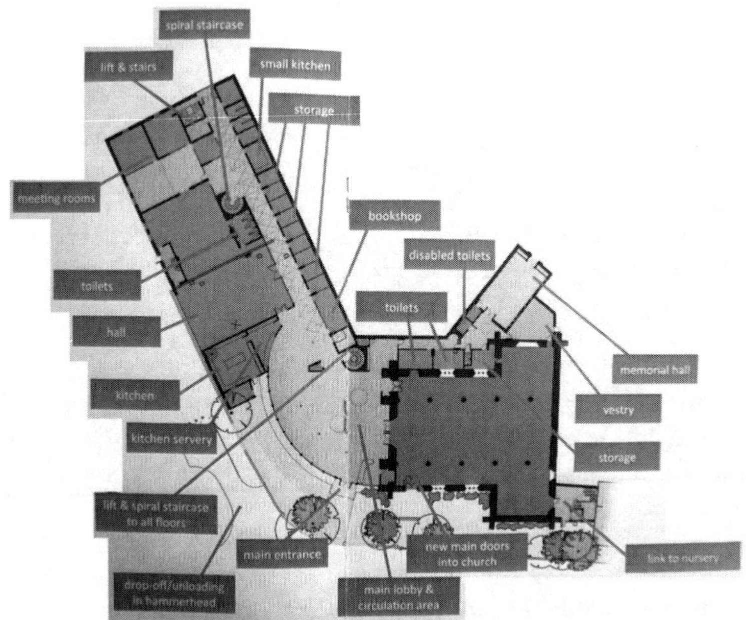

Floor plan: Redevelopment Concept – 2011

Following the Week of Prayer, the fellowship was asked to complete a feedback survey. Nearly 300 responses were received with 78% in favour of going ahead with a full planning application on the basis of the proposals.[124] The PCC put an action plan together to make the necessary progress before the planning application could be made.[125]

On 22nd January 2012 New Hope held a special 10th Anniversary Service, taking the form of Holy Communion with Andrew Proud, the Bishop of Reading. Many guests were invited to the service and lunch with celebration cake to follow. Nine days later, Associate Vicar Catharine Morris left New Hope to become Parish Development Officer for the Berkshire Archdeaconry. She was succeeded as Associate Vicar by the Rev. Joy Atkins in August 2013.[126] In the 2012 Greyfriars and New Hope Annual Report, Jonathan Wilmot praised the interregnum team "Jackie Fountain, Mary Dias-Murtagh and Lesley Brown for the incredible job they have done in the day to day running of New Hope."

The redevelopment proceeded apace, led by the Steering Group that consisted of Mark Hinckley, Janet Shury, Chris Tinker, Jonathan Thatcher and Jonathan Wilmot. An "Archaeological Desk-Based Assessment" was carried out by John Moore Heritage Services who produced their report in March 2012.[127] This report concluded that there was a possibility of a 10th or 11th century enclosure underneath Greyfriars as the construction of the Friary post-dated the road system which goes around the area. Berkshire Archaeology recommended that trial pits should be dug in the car park to ascertain if any significant material was present. These pits were dug in August 2012, with nothing of significance found.

Archaeological Dig
August 2012

Provelio, a Project Management Consultancy, was appointed to work with architect Jeremy Bell. To address significant technical issues in the design, Provelio recommended a period of risk-reduction work, which was carried out in the latter half of 2012. By late November a full design team had been assembled and began the work of room-by-room detailed consideration. The design team produced their report for the PCC in March 2013.[128] At the Annual Parochial Church Meeting in April 2013, Chris Tinker presented the current position of the redevelopment under the headings Fact Finding, Due Diligence and Communication. He reported that the Steering Group had visited other Churches with similar large scale projects to look at vision, project management and fund raising and had then spent a considerable time developing the detailed design. Finally, Chris stated that with a constantly changing congregation at Greyfriars, the redevelopment needed to be continually communicated and to be underpinned by an agreed vision.[129]

At the same meeting, Jonathan Wilmot reflected on the 150th anniversary of the reopening of Greyfriars with its opportunity to celebrate and remember God's goodness and faithfulness to His Church. Reflecting on changes in the previous twelve months he mentioned the appointment of Phil and Kath Cooke as Curates in Oxfordshire, Penny Cuthbert as Curate at St. Agnes in Whitley, Dan Heyward being priested in June and Caroline Obonyo becoming Catering Manager. In this context, Jonathan reminded the meeting of the 2012 verse for the year: "Be joyful always, pray continually, give thanks in all circumstances, for this is God's will for you in Christ Jesus." He concluded his report with the statement: "It seemed right that as we approached 2013 and the 150th anniversary of the reopening of Greyfriars that we should have as our verse for the year "Let us draw near to God."[130]

Motto Card
2013

Greyfriars Church in 2013 is alive and growing:

- Its small group ministry is thriving, with another well-attended Alpha course under way in the Autumn 2013 term and about 20 home groups meeting week by week around the town;
- An emphasis on prayer, on drawing near to God, has led to several initiatives, including a weekly mid-week opening of the Church for all to come to pray during the working day;
- A large number of volunteers help to lead the many children's and young people's groups;
- Its worship, led by a variety of people, encompasses both new and old styles of music, using worship bands and organ;
- Greyfriars Nursery is expanding to take on a site in Caversham;
- Prayer Café and Prayer Stop seek to meet the needs of a growing number of Reading residents;
- New Hope Community Church, with its new Associate Vicar, continues to reach out to its local community;
- Time Out for Women (for many years organised by Pauline Kenyon, now by Carrie Heyward) provides a mutually supportive environment, as well as time for Bible Study and prayer;
- The ministry among men is developing, having had an annual weekend organised by Arfon Rees over recent years;
- Following the sterling work of Margaret and Dennis Parker, and led by Deirdre Underwood, Tuesday Special continues to be, as the name suggests, a special time of worship and teaching for adults with learning difficulties and their carers;
- There is a continuing desire to support Mission Partners financially and in prayer and to send out more to the mission field;
- On Sundays the Church is full of worshippers, from the very young to those who have lived through several chapters of this history!

The next major change for the Greyfriars' site – the redevelopment – is an exciting prospect. The proposed plans fulfil the well-articulated vision of a site that will enable the Church's week by week activities to take place in sufficient accommodation, that will have enough working space for the Greyfriars' staff and most importantly that will make Greyfriars attractive and accessible to the local community.[131]

Epilogue

Jesus Christ – the same yesterday, today and forever

Fifty years ago, the four days' celebration in 1963 ended with the Centenary Service of Holy Communion at 7.30pm on Monday 2nd December. The preacher was the Rev. Canon Talbot Greaves Mohan M.A., General Secretary of the Church Pastoral Aid Society and Secretary to the Trustees of the Benefice of Greyfriars. The Church was full to overflowing with Greyfriars' members past and present – all the men in suits and ties and every woman wearing a hat.

Mr. Mohan drew parallels between the description of the early Church in the Acts of the Apostles and the Church in 1963, asking "How do we measure up today?"

He concluded his sermon by saying:

> "Tonight we have hearts full of thanksgiving for all that this Church has meant down the years... We go forward in confidence in God that the best days of Greyfriars are still yet to be and the secret of success will be the same today, as in the past, for the future.
>
> In this changing world there is one thing that will never change. Jesus Christ is the same yesterday, today and forever, and His truth is unchanging, and the secret of our success will be a common faith, all of us believers in the Lord Jesus Christ as our personal Saviour; a common life, all one in Christ Jesus; and a common purpose, to bring in the outsider, not simply to Church, but to faith in the Lord Jesus Christ, that our Saviour may be theirs."

As Greyfriars Church reaches the 150th Anniversary of its reconsecration on Monday 2nd December 2013 it is this same hope in the unchanging Saviour and the same desire to reach out to others with the Gospel message that fills and motivates the Church on its mission, as it was with the first Grey Friars working among the poor of 13th century Reading.

Acknowledgements

Many people have helped with this history and it would stretch the patience of the reader to mention each one! I will, however, mention just a prominent few who have made a considerable contribution in a variety of ways.

Amongst other valuable material, John Milward provided me with a nearly complete set of over 40 years of issues of the Greyfriars newsletter that he had collected. As important as that was to my research, it pales into insignificance beside the encouragement that he has given me time and time again throughout the two years or so that I have been living with Greyfriars' past.

Peter Spriggs generously allowed me to benefit from the treasures that his father Gordon had amassed over his many years lovingly exploring Greyfriars' history. The list of items is a long one and they greatly helped me to chart the history from late Victorian times to the 1960s. I was absolutely delighted to hear from Peter that his father, in his last days, was enjoying my historical articles in the Greyfriars and New Hope News.

Harry Hogg presented me with a wonderful old metal chest (labelled "Greyfriars Churchwardens") that held documents from as early as 1868, including the earliest minutes of meetings taken at the annual Church Vestry meeting. Harry also let me have many old Greyfriars newsletters from the 1970s onwards, which marvellously managed to fill the few gaps in John Milward's collection!

Mike Page was a great help to me in understanding not only his father's time as Vicar but also something of Mr. Page's character – a man who seems to have left his very positive mark on all who knew him. Mike also put me in touch with his brother David, who proved to be a great authority on the original Vicarage.

I owe a debt of thanks to Janet Shury who provided me with minutes of the meetings of the PCC (from 1961) and of the Church AGMs (from 1954). She tirelessly tracked down missing meeting minutes for me, enabling me to bring my history to the present day. I would also like to thank Laurie Anstis for his encouragement and willingness to print my articles in Greyfriars and New Hope News, and Rebecca Chapman for sharing documents she found in the Church office.

My thanks also to Reading Library Local History department, where I spent many hours reading through their micro-filmed newspaper archive, and to the staff of Berkshire Record Office who were always helpful.

I am hugely grateful to my wife Cathy who painstakingly read through the whole book and removed many typographical and grammatical errors. Any errors that remain are most certainly my own.

Finally, my grateful thanks go to the last three Vicars of Greyfriars. Jim Spence left Greyfriars a few years before I joined the Church and so I was delighted that he gave time to visit us. I enjoyed immensely our conversation about his Greyfriars' years and of something of his own background prior to that.

I joined Greyfriars in 1981 when Peter Downham was Vicar and, like so many others, I benefited hugely from his tireless ministry. It is a great pleasure to be able to look back upon the fact that he married Cathy and me at Greyfriars in August 1984.

For the last 18 years, of course, Jonathan Wilmot has been Vicar of Greyfriars. I would like to thank Jonathan for his encouragement to me in producing this book. Even more importantly I would like to acknowledge here the debt we as a Church fellowship owe him for his wisdom, prayerfulness and leadership as we as a body seek "To know Christ Jesus and to make Him known."

Sunday morning congregation
(Photograph courtesy of Julian Rowlandson)

Endnotes and Sources:

Chapter 1 The Grey Friars: 1233 to 1538

[1] "Collectanea Anglo-minoritica" Volume 1 p5 by Anthony Parkinson, 1726
[2] "Franciscan Martyrology" by Br. Arturus of Rouen, quoted in "Collectanea Anglo-minoritica," Volume 1 p6 by Anthony Parkinson, 1726
[3] "Collectanea" by Leland, quoted in "Collectanea Anglo-minoritica," Volume 1 p7 by Anthony Parkinson, 1726
[4] "Annales Prioratus De Dunstaplia 1233" in "Annales Monastici" Volume 3, Edited by Henry Luard, 1866, p134. With thanks to Eleanor Summers for the translation from Latin.
[5] Calendar of the Charter Rolls 17 Henry III membrane 2d (14th July 1233)
[6] Close Rolls 15 Henry III m. 14 (2nd May 1231)
[7] Ibid. 18 Henry III m. 25 (2nd May 1234)
[8] Ibid. 18 Henry III m. 17 (28th June 1234)
[9] Calendar of Liberate Rolls 21 Henry III m. 3 (29th August 1237)
[10] Close Rolls 22 Henry III m. 15 (29th April 1238)
[11] Calendar of Liberate Rolls 23 Henry III m. 8 (1st August 1239)
[12] Ibid. 24 Henry III m. 18 (10th February 1240)
[13] Ibid. 23 Henry III m. 6 (27th August 1239)
[14] Ibid. 23 Henry III m. 3 (12th October 1239)
[15] Ibid. 26 Henry III m. 15 (6th December 1241)
[16] Ibid. 28 Henry III m. 11 (9th May 1244)
[17] Ibid. 28 Henry III m. 10 (9th May 1244)
[18] Ibid. 28 Henry III m. 7 (5th July 1244)
[19] Ibid. 30 Henry III m. 17 (14th February 1246)
[20] Ibid. 30 Henry III m. 17 (29th [sic] February 1246)
[21] Close Rolls 31 Henry III m. 6 (25th June 1247)
[22] Ibid. 41 Henry III m.5 (30th June 1257)
[23] Ibid. 42 Henry III m. 4 (12th August 1258)
[24] Ibid. 43 Henry III m. 12 (6th March 1259)
[25] Ibid. 44 Henry III m. 3 (23rd September 1260)
[26] Calendar of Close Rolls 8 Edward I m. 5 (27th June 1280)
[27] Reg. Epist. Peckham (Rolls Ser.), iii, 211–12, quoted in "The History and Antiquities of Reading" by Charles Coates, 1802, p301
[28] Calendar of the Close Rolls 14 Edward I m. 2d (7 Kal. June [25th May] 1285)
[29] British Museum Cotton Manuscript, Vespasian, E. v, folio 55
[30] Calendar of the Close Rolls 31 Edward I m. 19 (11th January 1303)
[31] British Museum Cotton Manuscript, Vespasian, E. xxv, folio189, transcription in "Reading Abbey Cartularies," Camden Fourth Series, vol. 33 Ed. by B. R. Kemp (1987), p166-7
[32] "The History and Antiquities of Reading" by Charles Coates, 1802, p300
[33] "History of the Church of Greyfriars, Reading" by F. Gordon Spriggs, 1963, p15, drawing by A. R. Martin, amended.

[34] "On the History and Remains of the Franciscan Friery (sic), Reading," Archaeological Journal, June 1846
[35] "Medieval Sourcebook: The Rule of the Franciscan Order," translated by David Burr, at www.fordham.edu accessed March 2012
[36] Sarum Episcopal Register: Mortival, ii, fol. 186 – Reading was under the authority of Salisbury until transferring to the Oxford Diocese in 1836.
[37] "Collectanea Anglo-minoritica," Volume 1 p30, by Anthony Parkinson, 1726
[38] Leland quoted in "Collectanea Anglo-minoritica," Volume 1 p187f, by Anthony Parkinson, 1726
[39] "Collectanea Anglo-minoritica," Volume 1 p191f, by Anthony Parkinson, 1726
[40] Berkshire Record Office reference R/AT1/202
[41] The Quarterly Journal of the Berkshire Archaeological and Architectural Society Volume ii, No. 7, October 1892, p150. With thanks to Dr. David Peacock for this reference.
[42] Berkshire Record Office reference D/EBz T1/6 (Papers of Alderman F. D. Bazett of Newbury) Dated at "Radyng" in 1492
[43] "The Register of Thomas Langton, Bishop of Salisbury 1485 – 93 Part CXLVII Volume LXXIV" Edited by D. P. Wright f 569
[44] "A History of the Municipal Church of St. Laurence, Reading" by Rev. Charles Kerry, 1883, p168
[45] "The Register of Thomas Langton, Bishop of Salisbury 1485 – 93 Part CXLVII Volume LXXIV" Edited by D. P. Wright f 538, 80 & 185
[46]National Archives Reference PROB11/13; also see The Berkshire Archaeological Journal Volume 5 (1899) p49 – 50
[47] "A History of the Municipal Church of St. Laurence, Reading" by Rev. Charles Kerry, 1883, p116f
[48] "Antiquarii De Rebus Britannicus Collectanea Vol IV" by John Leland, p57
[49] "A History of the Municipal Church of St. Laurence, Reading" by Rev. Charles Kerry, 1883, p175 – 7 The Will was proved at Lambeth on 21st January 1534.
[50] Ibid. p177f
[51] Letters and Papers, Foreign and Domestic, 27 Henry VIII, Volume 10 (22nd April 1536)
[52] Ibid. 28 Henry VIII, Volume 12 Part 1 (15th April 1537)
[53] Ibid. 29 Henry VIII, Volume 12 Part 1 (30th April 1537)

Chapter 2 Dissolution and Disposal: 1538 to 1542

[1] "Bare Ruined Choirs: The Dissolution of the English Monasteries" by Dom David Knowles (Published 1976) p240
[2] Letters and Papers, Foreign and Domestic, 30 Henry VIII, Volume 13 Part 2, (14th September 1538)
[3] British Museum Cotton Manuscript, Cleopatra, E. iv, folio 227; Letters and Papers, Foreign and Domestic, 30 Henry VIII, Volume 13 Part 2 (31st August 1538)
[4] In an uncharacteristic error, "The History and Antiquities of Reading" by Charles Coates, 1802, p303 has 1539 instead of 1538. The Deed was signed in Henry VIII's 30th year, which was from 22nd April 1538 to 21st April 1539: thus 13th September of 30 Henry VIII must be in 1538.

[5] "The History and Antiquities of Reading" by Charles Coates, 1802, p303-4; Lambeth MSS. 594, fol. 129
[6] Letters and Papers, Foreign and Domestic, 30 Henry VIII, Volume 13 Part 2 (14th September 1538)
[7] British Museum Cotton Manuscript, Cleopatra, E. iv, folio 226; Letters and Papers, Foreign and Domestic, 30 Henry VIII, Volume 13 Part 2 (17th September 1538)
[8] British Museum Cotton Manuscript, Cleopatra, E. iv, folio 223; Letters and Papers, Foreign and Domestic, 30 Henry VIII, Volume 13 Part 2 (18th September 1538)
[9] Dictionary of National Biography, 1900, Volume 34
[10] British Museum Cotton Manuscript, Titus, B. i, folio 129; Letters and Papers, Foreign and Domestic, 31 Henry VIII, Volume 14 Part 2 (20th November 1539)
[11] Letters and Papers, Foreign and Domestic, 31 Henry VIII, Volume 14 Part 2 (probably 30th November 1539, but undated)
[12] Calendar of the Charter Rolls 31 Henry VIII (5th February 1540), quoted in 34 Henry VIII (24th April 1542)
[13] Ibid. 34 Henry VIII; Grants in April 34 Henry VIII, Letters and Papers, Foreign and Domestic, Henry VIII, Volume 17 (24th April 1542)

Chapter 3 The Guildhall: 1542 to 1578

[1] "The History and Antiquities of Reading" by Charles Coates, 1802, p307
[2] "Reading Records: The Diary of the Corporation" Edited by Rev. J. M. Guilding 1892 Volume 1 p270f (Articles of Charter 34 Henry VIII)
[3] Ibid. p201 (23rd September 1547)
[4] Ibid. p210 (21st December 1548)
[5] Ibid. p203 (19th December 1547)
[6] Ibid. p226 (1552)
[7] Ibid. p243 (1st October 1554)
[8] Ibid. (p244 1st October 1554)
[9] The National Archives PROB11/59 FF 45-46v. The date of the Will would be January 1577 in 'historical' or 'new' style. The Will was proved on 7th February, showing that Thomas Aldworth died between 4th January and 7th February 1577. With thanks to Dr. David Peacock for this reference.
[10] "The History and Antiquities of Reading" by Charles Coates, 1802, p306
[11] Ibid. p78 fn
[12] "Reading Records: The Diary of the Corporation" Edited by Rev. J. M. Guilding 1895 Volume 2 p64 (3rd March 1615)
[13] Charter of 2 Elizabeth, Clauses 49-50

Chapter 4 The Hospital/Poor House: 1578 to 1614

[1] "The History and Antiquities of Reading" by Charles Coates, 1802, p308
[2] The National Archives Catalogues Reference PROB 11/62 folio 147v. With thanks to Dr. David Peacock for this reference.
[3] "The History and Antiquities of Reading" by Charles Coates, 1802, p307

[4] "Reading Records: The Diary of the Corporation" Edited by Rev. J. M. Guilding 1895 Volume 2 p28 (16th December 1608)
[5] Ibid. 1892 Volume 1 p403 (18th December 1590)
[6] 43 Elizabeth I c. 2
[7] "Reading Records: The Diary of the Corporation" Edited by Rev. J. M. Guilding 1895 Volume 2 p39 (1st September 1610)
[8] Ibid. p38 (1st June 1610)
[9] Ibid. p160 (9th November 1623)
[10] "The History and Antiquities of Reading" by Charles Coates, 1802, p308
[11] "Reading Records: The Diary of the Corporation" Edited by Rev. J. M. Guilding 1895 Volume 2 p59 (1st March 1614)

Chapter 5 The House of Correction: 1614 to 1642

[1] "Reading Records: The Diary of the Corporation" Edited by Rev. J. M. Guilding 1895 Volume 2 p59-60 (22nd April 1614)
[2] Ibid. p62-63 (30th October 1614)
[3] Ibid. p71f
[4] Ibid. p68 and 75
[5] Ibid. 1896 Volume 4 p195 (22nd May 1646)
[6] Ibid. p431 (19th March 1652)
[7] Berkshire Record Office reference R/Z 8/1 (This remarkable document contains 9 sheets, each slightly larger than A4, of flowing 'Secretary Hand' writing)
[8] "Reading Records: The Diary of the Corporation" Edited by Rev. J. M. Guilding 1895 Volume 2 p209 (17th December 1624)
[9] Berkshire Record Office reference R/Z 8/2 (April 1620)
[10] Ibid. R/Z 3/13. Although the document is undated, since William Hill was Constable in 1620 – 1, that date is the most likely. (For William Hill, see "Reading Records: The Diary of the Corporation" Edited by Rev. J. M. Guilding 1895 Volume 2 pages 85 and 209)
[11] "Reading Records: The Diary of the Corporation" Edited by Rev. J. M. Guilding 1895 Volume 2 p110 (15th January 1623)
[12] Ibid. p111 (4th February 1623)
[13] Ibid. p126 (30th April 1623)
[14] Ibid. p95 (4th December 1620, being the accounts for Michaelmas 1619 to Michaelmas 1620)
[15] Ibid. p185 (28th April 1624)
[16] Berkshire Record Office reference D/P 97/1/1 St. Laurence's Church Burials 1605 to 1654 (Burial date 20th August 1621)
[17] "Reading Records: The Diary of the Corporation" Edited by Rev. J. M. Guilding 1895 Volume 2 p221 (2nd March 1625)
[18] Ibid. p201f (1st October 1624)
[19] Ibid. p190 (28th June 1624)
[20] Ibid. p226 (28th March 1625)
[21] Ibid. p188 (23rd June 1624)
[22] Ibid. p444 (6th January 1629)
[23] Ibid. p226f (28th March 1625)

[24] Ibid. page 228f (11th April 1625)
[25] Ibid. p238 (10th June 1625)
[26] Ibid. p273 & 285 (16th January 1626 & 20th March 1626)
[27] Ibid. p287 (3rd and 23rd April 1626)
[28] Ibid. p404f (19th May 1628)
[29] Ibid. p459 (6th March 1629)
[30] Ibid. 1896 Volume 3 p11f (23rd April 1630)
[31] Ibid. p48f (18th February 1631)
[32] Ibid. p163 (7th March 1633)
[33] Ibid. p230f (2nd July 1634)
[34] Ibid. p222 (28th March 1634)
[35] Ibid. p236 (15th August 1634)
[36] Ibid. p239 (10th September 1634)
[37] Berkshire Record Office reference D/P 97/1/1 St. Laurence's Church Baptisms 1605 to 1654 (Baptism date 28th April 1616)
[38] "Reading Records: The Diary of the Corporation" Edited by Rev. J. M. Guilding 1896 Volume 3 p257 (31st December 1634)
[39] Berkshire Record Office reference R/Z 8/5 Dated September 1634. Also see "Reading Records: The Diary of the Corporation" Edited by Rev. J. M. Guilding 1896 Volume 3 page 236 (15th August 1634)
[40] Ibid. R/FZ 2/23/8
[41] Ibid. D/P 97/1/1 St. Laurence's Church Baptisms 1605 to 1654 (Henry's Baptism date 18th July 1642); Burials 1605 to 1654 (Mary wife of Henry Tubb 19th July 1642; Henry son of Henry Tubb 1st August 1642)

Chapter 6 A Soldiers' Barracks: 1642 to 1643

[1] Berkshire Record Office reference R/Z 8/4/2 Payments for the House of Correction from Michaelmas 1641 to Midsummer 1657
[2] "Reading Records: The Diary of the Corporation" Edited by Rev. J. M. Guilding 1896 Volume 4 page viii
[3] Berkshire Record Office reference R/FZ 2/24/4

Chapter 7 The House of Correction, then Bridewell: 1644 to 1862

[1] "Reading Records: The Diary of the Corporation" Edited by Rev. J. M. Guilding 1896 Volume 4 p200 (8th July 1646)
[2] Ibid. p218 (21st October 1646)
[3] Ibid. p246f (12th July 1647)
[4] Berkshire Record Office reference R/Z 8/7
[5] Ibid. R/Z 8/4/1
[6] "Reading Records: The Diary of the Corporation" Edited by Rev. J. M. Guilding 1896 Volume 4 p195 (22nd May 1646)
[7] "Abstract of the Title of Mr. F. M. Slocombe to a Freehold piece of Land, part of the Grey Friars Estate in the parish of Saint Lawrence, Reading" 1862

[8] "The History and Antiquities of Reading" by Charles Coates, 1802, p308f

[9] Ibid. p302

[10] Berkshire Record Office reference D/P 97/1/4 Reading St. Lawrence – Burials 1724 – 1772; D/P 97/1/5 Burials 1772 - 1812

[11] Reading Mercury 19th January 1789 p3

[12] "The Life of John Howard; with comments on his character and philanthropic labours" by Rev. John Field, 1850, p185

[13] 22 George III c. 64

[14] Berkshire Record Office reference D/ELV 017 (16th July 1782)

[15] Reading Mercury 13th May 1782 p2

[16] The Berkshire Archaeological Journal Volume 69 p63

[17] Ibid. p66

[18] Reading Mercury 2nd October 1786 p3

[19] Ibid. 18th December 1786 p3

[20] Ibid. 4th April 1791 p2

[21] Ibid. 24th January 1791 p3

[22] For example in the Newcastle Courant 23rd April 1791 p1

[23] "Statutory Declaration of Mr. J. J. Blandy, the Town Clerk, in proof of the identity of portions of the Bridewell and "Pigeons" properties" (28th April 1862)

[24] "The Gentleman's Magazine and Historical Chronicle," Volume 74 Part 1

[25] Berkshire Record Office reference D/EX 1668/1/1/5 A document pertaining to the Will of John Weedon Esq, from 1835, which also summarises the purchases involving the land from Austwick's purchase.

[26] "Reminiscences of Reading by an Octogenarian" by William Darter, 1888, p50

[27] Information given to the author by David Page, son of Mr. Page, the Vicar at the time, who carried out the exploratory dig.

[28] I am indebted to David Page for the details of this paragraph. The information about the letter from Soane to Austwick is from a letter to David Page from the Sir John Soane Museum, dated 12th June 1962

[29] "The Stranger in Reading in a Series of Letters from a Traveller to his Friend in London" by John Man, 1810, p28 – 30

[30] Reading Mercury 21st January 1811p3

[31] "Reminiscences of Reading by an Octogenarian" by William Darter, 1888, p51f

[32] Ibid. p50f

[33] Reading Mercury 12th May 1838 p3

[34] Ibid. 22nd December 1838 p3

[35] "Statutory Declaration of John Readings in proof of the identity of portions of the Bridewell property" (16th January 1862)

[36] Berkshire Record Office Reading St. Lawrence D/P 97/1/5, 10, 13, 15

[37] 1841 Census Reference: HO107/35/8 St Laurence Berkshire, Borough Bridewell

[38] Reading Mercury 29th January 1842 p3

[39] Ibid. 21st September 1844 p3

[40] Ibid. 5th October 1844 p3

[41] Ibid. 14th March 1846 p3

[42] Ibid. 15th June 1844 p3

[43] Ibid. 2nd August 1845 p3

[44] Ibid. 1st July 1843 p3

[45] Ibid. 16th March 1844 p3
[46] Ibid. 8th November 1845 p3
[47] 1851 Census Reference HO107/1692/307/27
[48] The Times 21st July 1858 p5; Reading Mercury 17th July 1858 p3
[49] Detail from "Release of a Piece of Land Messuage and Hereditament called the Bridewell and Pigeons in Friar Street Reading from Mortgage of 31st March 1854" Dated 3rd August 1861
[50] Reading Mercury 12th May 1860 p5
[51] 1861 Census Reference: RG 9/749/43/5
[52] Ibid. RG 9/747/13/22
[53] Reading Mercury 17th July 1858 p5
[54] Ibid. 8th June 1861 p5
[55] Ibid. 15th June 1861 p5
[56] "Life of the Reverend and Venerable William Whitmarsh Phelps" by Rev. Charles Hole, Volume 1, 1871, p217; also "History of the Church of Greyfriars Reading"by F. G. Spriggs, 1963, p23
[57] Reading Mercury 6th May 1843 p3
[58] Ibid. 20th September 1845 p3
[59] Ibid. 15th November 1845 p3
[60] Ibid. 19th May 1849 p3
[61] Ibid. 8th September 1855 p6
[62] Ibid. 26th June 1858 p2
[63] Ibid. 10th July 1858 p5
[64] Ibid. 7th August 1858 p5
[65] Ibid. 17th September 1859 p5

Chapter 8 Rev. W. W. Phelps: The Restorer of Greyfriars

[1] "The Life of the Reverend and Venerable William Whitmarsh Phelps M.A." by Rev. Charles Hole, 1873, Volume 2 p213
[2] Quoted in Reading Mercury 6th July 1867 p5
[3] Reading Mercury 6th July 1867: black drapes p5, advert p3
[4] Ibid. 26th October 1867 p4
[5] Ibid. 15th August 1868 p5
[6] Ibid. 8th June 1861 p. 6 & 15th June 1861 p7
[7] "The Life of the Reverend and Venerable William Whitmarsh Phelps M.A." by Rev. Charles Hole, 1873, Volume 2 p213
[8] Ibid. p218
[9] Reading Mercury 22nd December 1860 p2
[10] Ibid. 26th January 1861 p2
[11] Ibid. 9th February 1861 p6
[12] Ibid. 10th August 1861 p6
[13] "The Life of the Reverend and Venerable William Whitmarsh Phelps M.A." by Rev. Charles Hole, 1873, Volume 2 p219 footnote 1
[14] Reading Mercury 8th June 1861 p. 6 & 15th June 1861 p7
[15] Ibid. 22nd March 1862 p5

[16] "On the History and Remains of the Franciscan Friery (sic), Reading," Archaeological Journal, June 1846 p143ff

Chapter 9 The Restoration: 1862 to 1863

[1] Reading Mercury 26th April 1862 p5 – letter to the Editor dated 24th April from Rev. W. W. Phelps
[2] Ibid. 24th May 1862 p5
[3] Ibid. 26th April 1862 p5
[4] Deed dated 19th June 1862 between Rev. W. W. Phelps and Mr. F. M. Slocombe; also Reading Mercury 24th May 1862 p5; cost of land 24th December 1864 p3
[5] Berkshire Chronicle 5th December 1863
[6] Reading Mercury 7th June 1862 p5
[7] Ibid. 21st June p5
[8] Ibid. 9th August 1862 p5
[9] Ibid. 29th November 1862 p3
[10] Ibid. 8th June 1861 p6
[11] Ibid. 20th December 1862 p5
[12] Ibid. 9th May 1863 p5
[13] Ibid. 7th November 1863 p6
[14] Ibid. 9th May 1863 p1
[15] Ibid. 5th December 1863 p6; Berkshire Chronicle 5th December 1863
[16] Ibid. 21st November 1863 p5
[17] Berkshire Chronicle 5th December 1863
[18] Reading Mercury 5th December 1863 p6
[19] Ibid. 21st November 1863 p5
[20] 1903 Bazaar Souvenir: Editorial note by Rev. S. H. Soole

Chapter 10 Re-consecration: December 1863

[1] Reading Mercury 5th December 1863 p6; Berkshire Chronicle 5th December 1863
[2] The Life of the Reverend and Venerable William Whitmarsh Phelps M.A." by Rev. Charles Hole, 1873, Volume 2, p235f

Chapter 11 Shadwell Morley Barkworth: Vicar 1863 to 1874

[1] "Alumni Oxoniensis 1715 – 1886" Volume 1, 1968, p61
[2] Morning Post 20th December 1842 p3
[3] Hull Packet 26th May 1843 p3
[4] York Herald 27th April 1844 p7
[5] London Standard 18th April 1845 p2
[6] Reading Mercury 19th September 1846 p3
[7] Charity Commission: Charity 242822 Charity of the Reverend S M Barkworth (available online at www.charitycommission.gov.uk)
[8] Morning Post 23rd June 1851 p3

[9] Ibid. 16th July 1855
[10] West Middlesex Advertiser & Family Journal 16th May 1857 p3
[11] Lincolnshire Chronicle 6th March 1857 p7
[12] West Middlesex Advertiser & Family Journal 24th October 1857 p2
[13] Wells Journal 20th October 1860 p7
[14] 1871 Census Reference RG10/1279/5/3
[15] Reading Mercury 4th September 1897 p5
[16] Article: "The Restoration of Greyfriars Church" by Rev. S. H. Soole in Greyfriars Annual Report & Accounts for the Year ending December 31st 1906
[17] Berkshire Record Office reference D/P 97/28/2 (Map)
[18] London Gazette 30th August 1864 p4221; Berkshire Record Office reference D/P 97/28/8/4
[19] Berkshire Record Office reference D/P 163/1/1 Baptisms 1864 – 1875
[20] Reading Mercury 16th July 1864 p3
[21] Ibid. 30th July 1864 p7
[22] "Strangers Guide to the Town of Reading" by George Hillier, 1882
[23] Reading Mercury 6th August 1864 p5
[24] Ibid. 30th July 1864 p5
[25] Ibid. 6th August 1864 p5
[26] Ibid. 10th September 1864 p5
[27] Ibid. 29th October 1864
[28] Ibid. 5th November 1864 p5
[29] Ibid. 26th November 1864 p3
[30] Ibid. 24th December 1864 p3
[31] Ibid. 24th December 1864 p5
[32] Ibid. 31st December 1864 p5
[33] Berkshire Record Office reference R/ES4/1 Infant School Log Book 1865 to 1887 p1
[34] Ibid. R/ES4/1 Infant School Log Book 1865 to 1887 p3 (22nd February 1865)
[35] Reading Mercury 4th February 1865 p5
[36] The Times 3rd February 1865 p5
[37] Reading Mercury 11th February 1865 p5
[38] "Crockford's Clerical Directory," 1874
[39] Reading Mercury 10th June 1865 p3
[40] Ibid. 12th August 1865. Also published by Hamilton, Adams & Co., London
[41] Ibid. 13th October 1866 p3
[42] Ibid. 5th January 1867 p3. Also published by Hamilton, Adams & Co., London. Copy in Reading Central Library Local Studies Reserve reference R/UH/BAR
[43] Reading Mercury 16th August 1873 p5. Published by Messrs. Barcham & Beecroft. Copy in Reading Central Library Local Studies Reserve reference R/UH/BAR
[44] Ibid. 7th October 1871 p5
[45] Ibid. 18th May 1872 p5
[46] Ibid. 23rd December 1865 p5
[47] Berkshire Record Office reference D/P 163/1/5 Marriages 1866 – 1896
[48] Original document in the author's possession
[49] Reading Mercury 17th November 1866 p5
[50] Morning Post 19th November 1866 p2; London Daily News 30th November 1866 p2

[51] Reading Mercury 29th December 1866 p2
[52] Ibid. 9th March 1867 p5
[53] Ibid. 13th July 1867 p5
[54] Ibid. 15th August 1868 p5
[55] "Licence of Non-Residence Vicarage of Grey Friars Reading Berks" dated 30 December 1868, with effect until 31st December 1869
[56] Ibid. 3rd April 1869 p5; 1871 Census Reference RG10/1281/20/35
[57] Greyfriars Church Minutes of Vestry Meetings from April 1869 to April 1910
[58] Reading Mercury 26th February 1870 p5; 5th March 1870 p5; 12th March 1870 p5; 26th March 1870 p5, 9th July 1870 p5 and 16th July 1870 p2
[59] Ibid. 14th May 1870 p5
[60] Ibid. 7th May 1870 p1
[61] Ibid. 22nd October 1870 p5
[62] Ibid. 18th March 1870 p5
[63] Ibid. 26th April 1873 p5
[64] Ibid. 31st December 1870 p5
[65] Ibid. 15th October 1870 p5
[66] Ibid. 17th June 1871 p5; 24th June 1871 p5
[67] Ibid. 27th June 1874 p5
[68] Ibid. 19th September 1874 p5
[69] Ibid. 31st October 1874 p2
[70] Ibid. 31st October 1874 p2
[71] Ibid. 21st November 1874 p5
[72] 1881 Census Reference RG11/916/17/28
[73] England & Wales, National Probate Calendar (Index of Wills and Administrations), 1861-1941, entry for 1891

Chapter 12 Seymour Henry Soole: Vicar 1874 to 1905

[1] Cambridge University Alumni 1261 – 1900 entry for Soole, Seymour Henry
[2] Chelmsford Chronicle 18th July 1856 p5
[3] Ibid. 5th October 1866 p3; also Reading Mercury 5th February 1905 p7
[4] London Standard 21st May 1868 p3
[5] Westmorland Gazette 17th June 1865 p5
[6] Carlisle Journal 29th May 1866 p2
[7] Pall Mall Gazette 13th October 1866 p6
[8] Crockford's Clerical Directory 1874
[9] Reading Mercury 20th June 1874 p2
[10] Ibid. 17th October 1874 p5
[11] Ibid. 7th November 1874 p5, quoting the Carlisle Patriot
[12] Ibid. 7th November 1874 p5
[13] Ibid. 23rd May 1868 p5; 1st July 1871 p5; 3rd February 1872 p5; 27th February 1875 p5; 14th June 1879 p5; 2nd July 1881 p5; 12th May 1883 p5; 10th July 1886 p5
[14] Ibid. 20th March 1875 p5
[15] Ibid. 24th July 1875 p5

[16] "Annual Letter Addressed to the Congregation and Parishioners of Grey Friars, Reading by their Pastor" p8 states that "Mr. Collins continues to labour faithfully though quietly amongst our poor and that his Mission Room Services are valued by many."
[17] Greyfriars' Annual Report & Accounts for 1900 p1
[18] Reading Mercury 6th November 1875
[19] Ibid. 6th May 1876 p5
[20] Licensed by John Fielder, Bishop of Oxford, on 11th June 1876; Morning Post 12th June 1876 p6
[21] Greyfriars' Annual Report & Accounts for 1906, Article by Rev. S. H. Soole, p4
[22] Reading Mercury 7th October 1876 p5
[23] Ibid. 16th December 1876
[24] Greyfriars News April 1981 Article "The Story of the Iron Room" p15
[25] Reading Mercury 14th April 1877 p5
[26] "An Ecclesiastical History of Reading with a Description of the Churches and a Record of Church Work, By the Clergy of Reading, and other Writers," Edited by P. H. Ditchfield, 1883, p45
[27] Reading Mercury 6th October 1877 p5
[28] Ibid. 20th April 1878 p5
[29] Ibid. 30th October 1875 p5
[30] Ibid. 14th February 1880 p2
[31] Ibid. 18th March 1880 p5
[32] Ibid. 17th April 1880 p5
[33] Ibid. 10th July 1880 p5
[34] Ibid. 28th August 1880 p5; 4th September 1880 p2
[35] Ibid. 18th September 1880 p6
[36] Ibid. 25th September 1880 p5
[37] Ibid. 11th December 1880 p5
[38] Ibid. 23rd April 1881 p5
[39] Ibid. 23rd September 1882 p5; 30th September 1882 p5
[40] 1881 Census Reference Class: RG11; Piece: 1305; Folio: 4; Page: 1; GSU roll: 1341317
[41] Reading Mercury 14th July 1883 p1
[42] Berkshire Record Office reference D/P 163/3/7/1
[43] Ibid. D/P 163/3/7/5
[44] Ibid. D/P 163/3/7/8
[45] London Gazette 20th June 1884 p2693
[46] Reading Mercury 15th September 1888 p6
[47] Entry for 26th April 1901 in "Minutes of Vestry Meetings from April 1896 to April 1910"
[48] 1891 Census Reference Class: RG12; Piece: 997; Folio: 88; Page: 1; GSU roll: 6096107; 1901 Census Reference Class: RG13; Piece: 1152; Folio: 133; Page: 19
[49] Reading Mercury 12th June 1886 p5; Minutes of Special Vestry Meeting 28th December 1886
[50] Berkshire Record Office reference D/P 163/6/1 (12th December 1887)
[51] Greyfriars' Parochial Magazine August 1888 p2; Reading Mercury 28th July 1888 p5; Greyfriars' Service Book 1888 – 1905
[52] Greyfriars' Parochial Magazine October 1888 p2; Reading Mercury 15th September 1888 p6; Greyfriars' Service Book 1888 – 1905

[53] Reading Mercury 19th January 1889 p4
[54] Greyfriars' Service Book 1888 – 1905
[55] Greyfriars' Parochial Magazine February 1889; Reading Mercury 26th January 1889 p6
[56] Greyfriars' Parochial Magazine May 1889 Mission Accounts
[57] Reading Mercury 23rd February 1889 p6, quoting an article in the Guardian
[58] Greyfriars' Preachers' Book 1888 – 1905; Greyfriars' Parochial Magazine March 1889 p2 and 3
[59] Reading Mercury 2nd March 1889 p5
[60] Greyfriars' Parochial Magazine September 1889
[61] Ibid. December 1891 p3
[62] Greyfriars' Boys' and Mixed School Log Book 1891 to 1930 (4th & 11th November 1892) Berkshire Record Office reference R/ES 4/4; Reading Mercury 12th November 1892 p6
[63] Reading Mercury 5th November 1892 p6; 12th November 1892 p5
[64] Ibid. 19th November 1892 p6
[65] Greyfriars' Parochial Magazine April 1893 p2
[66] Ibid. June 1893 p3 and December 1893 p3
[67] Greyfriars' Parish Magazine March 1894 p3
[68] Reading Mercury 24th February 1894 p5
[69] Greyfriars' Parish Magazine April 1894 p3
[70] Reading Mercury 28th April 1894 p5
[71] Invoice dated 10th December 1894, with note of payment by Rev. S. H. Soole on 14th December.
[72] Reading Mercury 4th August 1894 p6
[73] Greyfriars Annual Report and Accounts for the year ending December 31st 1906 – article on the Restoration of Greyfriars Church p5
[74] Greyfriars' Parish Magazine September 1894 p3; Reading Mercury 8th September 1894 p5
[75] Reading Mercury 1st September 1894 p5
[76] Ibid. 8th September 1894 p5
[77] Greyfriars' Parish Magazine October 1894 p3; Oxford Journal 22nd September 1894 p5
[78] Reading Mercury 8th December 1894 p5
[79] Berkshire Record Office reference D/P 163/1C/6/1
[80] Memorial Plaque on East Wall; Reading Mercury 24th April 1897 p7
[81] Reading Mercury 26th September 1896 p5
[82] Greyfriars' Preachers' Book 1888 – 1905; Reading Mercury 2nd October 1897 p7
[83] Reading Mercury 20th November 1897 p7; "Greyfriars' Annual Statement for the year 1897" p1 (report dated 30th March 1898)
[84] "Parish of Greyfriars' Reading Pastoral Letter and Parochial Report for the Year 1901" p3
[85] Reading Mercury 18th February 1899 p7
[86] Ibid. 3rd November 1900 p7
[87] Greyfriars' Service Book 1888 – 1905
[88] Reading Mercury 15th December 1900 p7 and 22nd December 1900 p7; Greyfriars' Service Book 1888 – 1905 (last sermon 11am 17th February 1901)
[89] Ibid. 13th April 1901 p7
[90] Ibid. 28th October 1899
[91] "Minutes of Vestry Meetings from April 1869 to April 1910"

[92] Reading Mercury 13th April 1901 p7
[93] "Minutes of Vestry Meetings from April 1869 to April 1910"; Reading Mercury 27th April 1901 p7
[94] Indenture of Purchase of No. 28 Chatham Street, dated 13th July 1901
[95] Rent Account No. 28 Chatham Street dated 1st Quarter 1902
[96] Greyfriars' Preachers' Book 1888 – 1905
[97] Reading Mercury 7th September 1901 p7
[98] The Times 7th October 1901 p4
[99] Reading Mercury 12th October 1901 p2
[100] Ibid. 31st December 1864 p5
[101] Berkshire Record Office reference R/ES 4/3 Log of the Greyfriars' Junior Infants School 1867 to 1875 p14
[102] "The Church of the Grey Friars, Reading" - a souvenir booklet for the 50th anniversary in 1913, written by Rev. H. E. Boultbee, p12
[103] Greyfriars' Parish Magazine December 1933 p2 and p3
[104] "The Life of the Reverend and Venerable William Whitmarsh Phelps M.A." by Rev. Charles Hole, 1873, Volume 2 p219
[105] Reading Mercury 29th March 1902 p8; Reading Mercury 12th April 1902 p4 & p7
[106] Ibid. 31st May 1902 p7
[107] Ibid. 29th November p8
[108] Greyfriars' Preachers' Book 1888 – 1905
[109] Reading Mercury 26th April 1902 p7
[110] "Parish of Greyfriars', Reading, Pastoral Letter and Parochial Report (for the year 1902)" p1
[111] "Ibid. (for the year 1901)" p2
[112] Reading Mercury 16th August 1902 pp2 & 4
[113] Ibid. 30th August 1902 p7
[114] "Parish of Greyfriars', Reading, Pastoral Letter and Parochial Report (for the year 1903)" p1
[115] Greyfriars' Preachers' Book 1888 – 1905
[116] Letter dated 1st February 1905 from Francis, Lord Bishop of Oxford
[117] Reading Mercury 5th February 1905 p7
[118] "Parish of Greyfriars', Reading, Pastoral Letter and Parochial Report (for the year 1904)" p1, dated 7th April 1905
[119] Greyfriars' Preachers' Book 1888 – 1905
[120] Berkshire Chronicle 29th April 1905 p5
[121] Ibid. 29th April 1905 p5
[122] Reading Mercury 29th April 1905 p7
[123] Ibid. 27th December 1902 p5; 31st January 1903 p7
[124] The Times 4th October 1932 p10 – letter to the Editor from Warwick Bathurst Soole on the occasion of Lord Roberts' death
[125] Ibid. 22nd May 1908 p7; also 1st June 1908 p6
[126] Ibid. 4th October 1932 Letter from Warwick Bathurst Soole
[127] Ibid. 10th June 1912 p12 (Short obituary); Greyfriars' Parish Magazine July 1912 p2 & 3
[128] Reading Standard 12th June 1912 p3; The Times 13th June 1912 p11
[129] Ibid. 15th June 1912 p8

130 "Parish of Greyfriars, Reading, Annual Report and Accounts for the Year Ending December 31st 1911" p9
131 Berkshire Chronicle 13th June 1913 p7
132 "De Revigny's Roll of Honour Volume 3" p253
133 Reading Standard 10th February 1917 p2
134 "England & Wales, National Probate Calendar 1858 – 1966" 1927, p397
135 Photograph from the Annual Report & Accounts for the year ending December 31st 1906

Chapter 13 Hugh Edmund Boultbee: Vicar 1905 to 1915

1 "The History of the Boultbee Family", online at http://www.boultbee.freeserve.co.uk/ accessed 29 March 2013
2 "The History of the Boultbee Family," online at www.boultbee.freeserve.co.uk, for family details in this chapter
3 York Herald 25th June 1891 p3
4 York Herald 14th March 1892 p5; Crockford's Clerical Directory
5 Yorkshire Gazette 23rd December 1893 p6
6 Wrangthorn St. Augustine Parish records; York Herald 23rd February 1895 p4
7 Morning Post 16th December 1897 p3
8 Pall Mall Gazette 6th December 1900 p3
9 "Parish of Greyfriars', Reading, Annual Report and Accounts for the Year ending December 31st 1909" p7 – noting the death of Rev. G. F. Whidborne
10 Berkshire Chronicle 29th July 1905 p3
11 Greyfriars' Service Book 1905 – 1941
12 "Parish of Greyfriars', Reading, Annual Report and Accounts for the Year ending December 31st 1906" p6
13 Berkshire Chronicle 9th September 1905 p5
14 Greyfriars' Parish Magazine February 1914 p3
15 "Parish of Greyfriars', Reading, Annual Report and Accounts for the Year ending December 31st 1907" p8
16 Greyfriars' Parish Magazine April 1912 p2
17 Ibid. November 1914 p2, April 1915 p2
18 "Parish of Greyfriars', Reading, Annual Report and Accounts for the Year ending December 31st 1906" p24
19 Ibid. p17
20 Berkshire Chronicle 1st December 1906 p2; also "Parish of Greyfriars', Reading, Annual Report and Accounts for the Year ending December 31st 1906" p29 & 30
21 Berkshire Chronicle 25th January 1908 p6; also "Parish of Greyfriars', Reading, Annual Report and Accounts for the Year ending December 31st 1907" p30 & 31.
22 "Minutes of Vestry Meetings from April 1869 to April 1910"
23 Reading Mercury 12th December 1885 p5
24 Ibid. 1st May 1886 p5
25 "Parish of Greyfriars', Reading, Annual Report and Accounts for the Year ending December 31st 1906" p46
26 Ibid. 1907" p46
27 Ibid. 1911" p8

---

[28] Online at http://gwulo.com/node/8741 (accessed August 2012)
[29] England & Wales National Probate Calendar for 1912 (Probate awarded 26th July 1912). This record adds that Sophy died in the Peak Hospital, Hong Kong.
[30] "Parish of Greyfriars, Reading, Annual Report and Accounts for the Year ending December 31st 1937" p4
[31] Ibid. 1923" p13
[32] Ibid. 1936" p4
[33] Berkshire Chronicle 28th March 1908 p12
[34] Greyfriars' Service Book 1905 – 1941
[35] Log Book of Greyfriars Boys and Mixed School 1891 to 1930 Berkshire Record Office reference R/ES 4/4
[36] Berkshire Chronicle 8th April 1908 p7
[37] Log Book of Greyfriars Boys and Mixed School 1891 to 1930 Berkshire Record Office reference R/ES 4/4
[38] Berkshire Chronicle 25th April 1908 p5
[39] With thanks to Mrs. Olive Stemp for this "Notebook of Miss Edie Sherwood"
[40] "Parish of Greyfriars, Reading, Annual Report and Accounts for the Year ending December 31st 1909" p8
[41] Greyfriars' Parish Magazine August 1912 p2
[42] Ibid. September 1912 p3
[43] Berkshire Record Office reference D/P 163/3/1/1
[44] "Minutes of Vestry Meetings 1911 – 1953" Berkshire Record Office reference D/P 163/8/1
[45] Greyfriars' Parish Magazine May 1914 p2
[46] Ibid. January 1914; Greyfriars' Service Book 1905 – 1941; Reading Standard 21st January 1914 p3 and 24th January 1914 p8
[47] Greyfriars' Service Book 1905 – 1941
[48] Greyfriars' Parish Magazine March 1914 p2
[49] Ibid. September 1914 p2 to 3
[50] "Log Book of Greyfriars' Boys' and Mixed School 1891 to 1930" Berkshire Record Office reference R/ES 4/4
[51] Greyfriars' Parish Magazine September 1914 p2; Greyfriars' Service Book 1905 – 1941
[52] Handwritten notebook by Ernest Rivers; online, e.g. at http://purley.eu/WM5206.pdf, accessed September 2012
[53] Greyfriars' Parish Magazine December 1914 p1
[54] Ibid. January 1915 p1 and 2; Reading Standard 19th December 1914 p5
[55] "Minutes of Vestry Meetings 1911 – 1953" Berkshire Record Office reference D/P 163/8/1
[56] Berkshire Chronicle 3rd December 1915 p6
[57] Greyfriars' Service Book 1905 – 1941; Reading Standard 11th December 1915 p9
[58] "Parish of Greyfriars, Reading, Annual Report and Statement of Accounts" for the years 1908 (p9) and 1913 (p5)
[59] Petitions from Church Officers and Seat-holders, the Men's Service and Sunday School teachers in my possession. Copy of letter to Trustees mentions the other petition.
[60] The Times 7th December 1915 p4; Reading Standard 11th December 1915 p5
[61] Greyfriars' Parish Magazine January 1916 p2

[62] Ibid. February 1916 p4; Reading Mercury 5th February 1916 p7

Chapter 14 William Augustus Doherty: Vicar 1916 to 1924

[1] Cambridge University Alumni Register
[2] West Yorkshire Archive Service, Yorkshire Parish Records D88/1/2
[3] Crockford's Clerical Directory 1932 p361
[4] Greyfriars' Parish Magazine March 1916 p2
[5] Berkshire Record Office reference D/P 163/8/1 "Minutes of Vestry Meetings 1911 – 1953"
[6] Dover Express 6th October 1916 p5
[7] Greyfriars' Service Book 1905 – 1941
[8] Greyfriars' Parish Magazine November 1916 p2
[9] Ibid. May 1917 p2 – 3
[10] Reminiscences of Greyfriars Choir by Miss H. M. Milward 12th June 1953
[11] Greyfriars' Parish Magazine November 1917 p2; Reading Standard 29th September 1917 p10
[12] Berkshire Record Office reference D/P 163/8/1 "Minutes of Vestry Meetings 1911 – 1953"
[13] Greyfriars' Parish Magazine September 1918 page 1
[14] Ibid. December 1918 page 3
[15] Greyfriars' Service Book 1905 – 1941
[16] Greyfriars' Parish Magazine February 1921 p1 and 2
[17] Berkshire Record Office reference D/P 163/8/1 "Minutes of Vestry Meetings 1911 – 1953"
[18] Ibid. D/P 163/8A/1 "Greyfriars' Church Parochial Council Minutes April 1920 to April 1928"
[19] "Parish of Greyfriars, Reading, Annual Report and Statement of Accounts" for the years 1916 to 1920. The financial year was Easter to Easter.
[20] Berkshire Record Office reference D/P 163/8A/1 "Greyfriars' Church Parochial Council Minutes April 1920 to April 1928": meeting of 1st December 1920
[21] Greyfriars' Parish Magazine March 1921 p4
[22] Berkshire Record Office reference D/P 163/8/1 "Minutes of Vestry Meetings 1911 – 1953"
[23] Parish of Greyfriars, Reading, Annual Report and Accounts for the year ending December 31st 1922 p5
[24] Greyfriars' Parish Magazine March 1922 p3 - burial dates; England & Wales National Probate Calendar for 1922 p111 – death dates
[25] Berkshire Chronicle 29th January 1910 p10
[26] Greyfriars' Parish magazine January 1912 p2
[27] "Parish of Greyfriars, Reading, Annual Report and Statement of Accounts 1921" p6 (Published April 1922)
[28] Greyfriars' Parish Magazine April 1922 p2
[29] Berkshire Record Office reference D/P 163/8A/1 "Greyfriars' Church Parochial Council Minutes April 1920 to April 1928": meeting of 29th June 1923; Greyfriars' Parish Magazine August 1923 p2

[30] Greyfriars Service Book 1905 - 1941
[31] Greyfriars' Parish Magazine May 1922 p1
[32] Ibid. December 1922 p1, 2 and 3
[33] Ibid. November 1922 p3
[34] Ibid. September 1923 p2; Greyfriars Service Book 1905 – 1941
[35] The Times, Monday 17th March 1924 Issue 42882 p10
[36] Berkshire Chronicle 6th June 1924 p11
[37] Greyfriars' Parish Magazine August 1924 p2

Chapter 15 John Clifford Rundle: Vicar 1924 to 1947

[1] Letter dated 10th April 1924 from Martin H. F. Sutton to Mr. J. C. Gilkes
[2] Letter dated 14th April 1924 from the Rev. H. E. Boultbee to Mr. J. C. Gilkes
[3] The Times 25th February 1902 Issue 36700 p14
[4] Crockford's Clerical Directory
[5] Letter dated 4th June 1924 from J. J. Booker to Mr. Fowler
[6] Greyfriars' Service Book 1905 – 1941
[7] Letter dated 14th April 1924 from the Rev. H. E. Boultbee to Mr. J. C. Gilkes
[8] Letter dated 28th May 1924 from the Rev. J. C. Rundle to Mr. J. C. Gilkes
[9] Greyfriars' Service Book 1905 – 1941
[10] Letter dated 28th May 1924 from Rev. J. C. Rundle to Mr. J. C. Gilkes
[11] Berkshire Record Office reference D/P 163/8A/1 "Greyfriars' Church Parochial Council Minutes April 1920 to April 1928": 1st August 1924
[12] Greyfriars' Parish Magazine August 1924 p2
[13] Reading Mercury 30th August 1924 p7 and 13th September 1924 p5; Greyfriars' Parish Magazine September 1924 p2
[14] Greyfriars' Parish Magazine November 1924 p2
[15] Berkshire Record Office reference D/P 163/8A/1 "Greyfriars' Church Parochial Council Minutes April 1920 to April 1928": 11th March 1925; Greyfriars' Parish Magazine April 1925 p2
[16] Berkshire Record Office reference D/P 163/8/1 "Minutes of Vestry Meetings 1911 – 1953"; Greyfriars' Parish Magazine March 1925 p2
[17] Greyfriars' Parish Magazine May 1925 p1
[18] Ibid. July 1925 p1
[19] Berkshire Record Office reference R/ES 4/4 "Log Book of Greyfriars' Boys and Mixed School 1891 to 1930"
[20] Greyfriars' Parish Magazine October 1925 p3
[21] Ibid. February 1927 p1; Crockford's Clerical Directory 1932 p97
[22] Ibid. June 1926 p1
[23] Greyfriars' Service Book 1905 - 1941
[24] "Parish of Greyfriars, Reading, Annual Report and Accounts for the Year ending Dec. 31st 1926" p3 and p15
[25] Greyfriars' Parish Magazine November 1926 p1
[26] Ibid. April 1929 p1; May 1929 p1 and 2
[27] Ibid. October 1930 p1
[28] Ibid. August 1931 p1, October 1931 p1

[29] Notice to Members of Greyfriars Church, Reading, from the Churchwardens A. W. Milward & J. C. Gilkes, June 1930
[30] Greyfriars' Service Book 1905 to 1941
[31] "Parish of Greyfriars Annual Report and Accounts for the Year ending 31st December 1930" p11; receipt from G. R. Jackson dated 16th September 1930
[32] Greyfriars' Parish Magazine November 1930 p1
[33] "Parish of Greyfriars Annual Report and Accounts for the Year ending 31st December 1930" p17; .".. For the Year ending 31st December 1929" p17; .".. For the Year ending 31st December 1931" p15
[34] Berkshire Record Office reference R/ES/ 4/5 "Log Book of the Greyfriars', Reading, Junior Mixed and Infant School 1930 – 1932" p16 and 17
[35] The Times 25th July 1932, Issue 46194, p9
[36] Reading Evening Post 24th August 1971 p7
[37] Greyfriars' Parish Magazine February 1933 p1
[38] Berkshire Record Office reference D/P 163/8/1 "Minutes of Vestry Meetings 1911 – 1953," meeting dated 27th January 1933
[39] "Greyfriars Church Minutes of Vestry Meetings from April 1869 to April 1910"
[40] Berkshire Record Office reference D/P 163/8/1 "Minutes of Vestry Meetings 1911 – 1953," meeting dated 6th April 1915
[41] Greyfriars' Parish Magazine August 1933 p2 to 3;article by Mr. J. H. Williams
[42] Ibid. December 1934 p2
[43] Berkshire Record Office reference D/P 163/8/1 "Minutes of Vestry Meetings 1911 – 1953," meeting dated 25th January 1935
[44] Ibid. D/P 163 8/1 "Minutes of Vestry Meetings 1911 – 1953," meeting of 2nd April 1915
[45] Greyfriars' Service Book 1905 to 1941
[46] Greyfriars' Monthly Bulletin July 1938 p2
[47] Ibid. May 1938 p2
[48] Ibid. November 1938 p2 to 3
[49] Berkshire Record Office reference D/P 163/6/4/1 dated 7th November 1938
[50] "Brief History of the Organ" by David Rance
[51] Berkshire Record Office reference D/P 163/6/4/2
[52] Greyfriars' Monthly Bulletin April 1939 p2
[53] Ibid. September 1938 p2
[54] Berkshire Record Office D/P 163/8A/2 "Parochial Council Minutes February 1928 to May 1939," meeting of 30th September 1938
[55] Greyfriars' Monthly Bulletin March 1939 p1. Her name was added to the "Roll of Honour" following agreement at the PCC on 24th June 1939
[56] Ibid. January 1939 p2; May 1939 p1 and 2
[57] Ibid. March 1939 p3; April 1939 p3; Greyfriars' Monthly Newsletter October 1945 p1
[58] Reading Gazette 16th June 1939
[59] Berkshire Record Office reference D/P 163/8A/3 "Minutes of the PCC June 1939 to October 1960," meeting of 24th June 1939
[60] Greyfriars' Monthly Bulletin August 1939 p2. This amount was increased to £18 at the PCC on 13th April 1945, and then awarded to his widow for her lifetime at the PCC of 22nd October 1948
[61] Berkshire Record Office reference D/P 163 8A/3 "Minutes of the Greyfriars PCC 1939 to 1960," meeting of 30th April 1943

[62] Ibid. meeting of 3rd November 1944
[63] Ibid. meeting of 3rd November 1944 and 29th June 1945
[64] Ibid. meeting of 15th March 1940
[65] Greyfriars' Service Book 1905 to 1941; Greyfriars' Monthly Bulletin October 1939 p1
[66] Greyfriars' Service Book 1905 to 1941; Greyfriars' Monthly Bulletin December 1939 p1
[67] Greyfriars' Monthly Bulletin March 1940 p1, April 1940 p1
[68] Berkshire Record Office reference D/P 163 8A/3 "Minutes of the Greyfriars PCC 1939 to 1960," meeting of 14th June 1940
[69] Greyfriars' Monthly Bulletin April 1940 p1
[70] Ibid. November 1940 p1
[71] Ibid. January 1941 p3
[72] Ibid. May 1940 p1 to 2
[73] Ibid. August 1941 p1
[74] Greyfriars' Service Book 1905 to 1941
[75] ibid.; Greyfriars' Monthly Bulletin March 1941 p1
[76] Berkshire Record Office reference D/P 163 8A/3 "Minutes of the Greyfriars PCC 1939 to 1960," meeting of 27th March 1942
[77] Berkshire Record Office reference D/P 163 8A/3 "Minutes of the Greyfriars PCC 1939 to 1960," meeting of 12th June 1942
[78] Greyfriars' Monthly Newsletter March 1943 p1 and 2
[79] Ibid. January to April 1944
[80] Ibid. February 1944 p1, November 1945 p2
[81] Ibid. June 1945 p1
[82] Ibid. December 1945 p2
[83] Ibid. April 1946 p1
[84] Ibid. November 1946 p2 and December 1946 p1
[85] Berkshire Chronicle 6th June 1947 p16
[86] Berkshire Record Office reference D/P 163 8A/3 "Minutes of the Greyfriars PCC 1939 to 1960," meeting of 20th June 1947
[87] Greyfriars' Monthly Newsletter February 1967 p3
[88] Ibid. March 1967 p1
[89] PCC Minutes 3rd November 1967; Greyfriars' Monthly Newsletter December 1967 p3; PCC Minutes 21st June 1968

Chapter 16 John Knott Page: Vicar 1947 to 1968

[1] Much of the background information here was given by Mr. Page's son, Mike. In addition, see Berkshire Record Office reference D/P 163 8A/3 "Minutes of the Greyfriars PCC 1939 to 1960," meeting of 8th August 1947 and Crockford's Clerical Directory
[2] Berkshire Record Office reference D/P 163 8A/3 "Minutes of the Greyfriars PCC 1939 to 1960," meeting of 20th June 1947
[3] Ibid. meeting of 8th August 1947
[4] Greyfriars' Service Sheets 1948 to 1955, which has an insert of the Institution Order of Service to which Mr. F. Gordon Spriggs has hand-written some (eyewitness) observations

[5] Berkshire Record Office reference D/P 163 8A/3 “Minutes of the Greyfriars PCC 1939 to 1960,” meeting of 17th October 1947
[6] Ibid. meeting of 23rd July 1948
[7] Ibid. meeting of 22nd July 1949
[8] Ibid. meeting of 21st October 1949
[9] Ibid. meeting of 5th May 1950
[10] Greyfriars’ Monthly Newsletter October 1951 p1
[11] Ibid. December 1951 p3
[12] Berkshire Record Office reference D/P 163 8A/3 “Minutes of the Greyfriars’ PCC 1939 to 1960,” meeting of 27th July 1951
[13] Greyfriars’ Monthly Newsletter February 1954 p2
[14] Ibid. January 1955 p1
[15] Berkshire Record Office reference D/P 163 8A/3 “Minutes of the Greyfriars’ PCC 1939 to 1960,” meetings of 1st October 1954 and 6th May 1955
[16] Ibid. meeting of 6th May 1955
[17] Greyfriars’ Monthly Newsletter August 1955 p4 and September 1955 p3
[18] Ibid. December 1955 p2
[19] Berkshire Record Office reference D/P 163 8A/3 “Minutes of the Greyfriars’ PCC 1939 to 1960,” meeting of 25th February 1955
[20] Berkshire Record Office reference D/P 163/8A/19/1
[21] Ibid. D/P 163 8A/3 “Minutes of the Greyfriars’ PCC 1939 to 1960,” meeting of 10th February 1956
[22] Ibid. D/P 163/8A/15 dated 25th November 1955
[23] Greyfriars’ Monthly Newsletter October 1955 p3
[24] “Greyfriars’ Church Minute Book of Annual Parochial Meetings 1954 to 1981” meeting of 2nd March 1956
[25] London Gazette Issue 40966 pages 93 – 94, dated 1st January 1957
[26] English Heritage Building ID: 38955; Listed 22nd March 1957
[27] Berkshire Record Office reference D/P 163 8A/19/1 page 5
[28] Ibid. D/P 163 8A/20/23 and 24
[29] Ibid. D/P 163 8A/20/13
[30] Berkshire Chronicle 12th June 1959
[31] Greyfriars’ Monthly Newsletter September 1952 p2
[32] Ibid. March 1957 p2 to 3
[33] Ibid. September 1959 p2 to 3
[34] Ibid. February 1960 p3
[35] Letter from the PCC Secretary to Sir John Somerson, Sir John Soane’s Museum, London, dated 7th November 1960
[36] Leaflet: “Greyfriars Church, Reading: The Organ” 1960
[37] Greyfriars’ Monthly Newsletter January 1961 p2
[38] Ibid. November 1961 p2 and 4
[39] PCC Minutes 11th December 1961 p1-2
[40] Greyfriars’ Newsletter September 1962 p3
[41] Greyfriars’ Monthly Newsletter December 1962 p2
[42] PCC Minutes 22nd August 1962 p2
[43] Greyfriars’ Newsletter January 1963 p2
[44] PCC Minutes 28th November 1962 p1

[45] Ibid. 19th April 1963
[46] Greyfriars' Monthly Newsletter December 1963 p1
[47] The Berkshire Archaeological Journal Volume 61 (1963-4) p106
[48] English Heritage Building ID 38954; Listed 22nd March 1957
[49] PCC Minutes 1st February 1963; first meeting of the Centenary Committee 22nd February 1963
[50] Information from Mike Page
[51] Minutes of Greyfriars' Centenary Committee 3rd January 1964; PCC Minutes 31st January 1964
[52] Minutes of Special PCC Meeting 5th June 1964
[53] Deed of Conveyance dated 9th September 1964 between the Vicar, Rev. J. K. Page, and Reading Corporation
[54] PCC Minutes 31st January 1964
[55] Ibid. 15th April 1966; Greyfriars' Monthly Newsletter June 1966 p3
[56] Greyfriars' Monthly Newsletter October 1966 p3; Greyfriars' Service Sheets 1962 – 68 for 31st October 1965 and 23rd October 1966. Further broadcasts were made on 22nd October 1967, 3rd November 1968 and 1st February 1970
[57] Minutes of the Annual Parochial Meeting 3rd March 1967
[58] Minutes of a Special Meeting of the PCC on 24th February 1967
[59] Minutes of a Special Meeting of the PCC on 11th August 1967
[60] Greyfriars' Monthly Newsletter July 1968 shows £441 10s raised on 12th May, being the amount needed plus £2 10s; PCC Minutes 24th October 1969
[61] Annual Parochial Church Meeting Minutes 1st March 1968
[62] Greyfriars' Monthly Newsletter October 1968 p1 & 2
[63] The Times 29th August 1977 p10

Chapter 17 James Knox Spence: Vicar 1968 to 1978

[1] Letter from Mr. J. S. Milward to Rev. V. N. Cooper, Secretary to the Trustees, dated 24th June 1968. The letter had been drafted by Mr. A. Sheppard and Mr. F. G. Spriggs
[2] Greyfriars' Monthly Newsletter September 1968 (Insert)
[3] Hand-written letter from Rev. V. N. Cooper to Mr. J. S. Milward, dated 11th July 1968
[4] Greyfriars Service Sheets 1962 – 68; Reading Chronicle 29th November 1968 p31
[5] Greyfriars' Monthly Newsletter December 1968
[6] PCC Minutes 28th March 1969
[7] Ibid. 16th May 1969
[8] Greyfriars' Monthly Newsletter August 1969 and September 1969
[9] Greyfriars News February 1978 p5-6
[10] Greyfriars' Monthly Newsletter August 1969
[11] PCC Minutes 30th January 1970
[12] Greyfriars' Monthly Newsletter March 1970
[13] Minutes of the Annual Parochial Meeting 6th March 1970
[14] PCC Minutes 17th April 1970 and 12th June 1970
[15] Parish Buildings Committee Minutes 6th May 1970
[16] Ibid. 3rd June 1970
[17] Greyfriars News April 1971

[18] PCC Minutes 8th May 1974
[19] Greyfriars News October 1971
[20] Ibid. November 1971; PCC Minutes 15th October 1971
[21] PCC Minutes 6th May 1971
[22] Information from Harry Hogg, April 2013
[23] PCC Minutes 7th December 1971
[24] Ibid. 27th January 1972
[25] "Greyfriars Church, Reading – Key Moments in its History", 2010, by John S. Milward, p23f
[26] Greyfriars News April 1972
[27] PCC Minutes 23rd March 1972
[28] Berkshire Record Office reference D/P 163/1C/7, a 10 page booklet entitled "Dedication of Extension etc; Recommendations for Consideration and Discussion by the PCC"; Greyfriars News December 1972, January 1973
[29] Greyfriars News March 1973
[30] Minutes of the Annual Parochial Meeting 8th March 1973
[31] Greyfriars News April 1973
[32] PCC Minutes of 15th May 1973
[33] Greyfriars News June 1973 and November 1973; PCC Minutes 11th October 1973
[34] Greyfriars News July 1973
[35] Ibid. October 1973
[36] London Gazette 30th October 1973
[37] PCC Minutes 25th January 1973
[38] Greyfriars Service Sheets 1969 – 1975
[39] Greyfriars News January 1974
[40] Minutes of the Annual Parochial Meeting 5th March 1975
[41] Greyfriars News October 1974 p13
[42] Minutes of the Annual Parochial Meeting 5th March 1975
[43] Greyfriars News September 1975 p2
[44] Ibid. June 1979 p7
[45] Ibid. December 1975 p2; PCC Minutes 8th October 1975
[46] PCC Minutes 22nd January 1976
[47] APCM Minutes 25th March 1976
[48] Greyfriars News October 1976 p3 and 4 (also see p12)
[49] Ibid. October 1979 p5
[50] Ibid. October 1976 p20, November 1976 p12, April 1981 p16
[51] Ibid. November 1977 p1
[52] Appendix to PCC Minutes 18th October 1979, report written by Chris Leslie
[53] Minutes of the Annual Parochial Church Meeting 31st March 1977
[54] Greyfriars News July 1977 p1
[55] PCC Minutes 6th October 1977
[56] Letter from Rev. Jim Spence to Mr. Wilfred Dyer dated 21st February 1978
[57] Minutes of the Annual Parochial Church Meeting 16th March 1978
[58] Greyfriars News October 1978 p1 to 4
[59] Crockford's Clerical Directory

Chapter 18 Peter Norwell Downham: Vicar 1979 to 1995

1 The Times 16th July 1957 p12 Column B
2 Representation to the Trustees, dated 30th April 1978
3 Letter from Wilfred Dyer to Rev. P. N. Downham, dated 19th November 1978
4 Annual Parochial Church Meeting Minutes 22nd March 1979
5 Ibid. 14th March 1974
6 Greyfriars News August 1979 p1
7 PCC Minutes 24th January 1980
8 Ibid. 8th May 1980
9 Flyer entitled Hut Site Development dated July 1977
10 PCC Minutes 10th May 1979
11 Ibid. 24th January 1980, referring to the decision taken by the New Building Committee on 8th December 1979
12 Ibid. 27th March 1980
13 Annual Parochial Church Meeting Minutes 17th April 1980
14 Reading Borough Council Plan No. 80/TP/729; Committee meeting 14th November 1980; Letter of Approval issued 18th December 1980
15 Personal memory of Mr. Downham, given to the author on 24th September 2013; see also PCC Minutes 13th November 1980, where the figures are not yet final
16 PCC Minutes 8th January 1981
17 Ibid. 8th January 1981
18 Ibid. 19th November 1981
19 Greyfriars Centre Maintenance Manual
20 Greyfriars News January 1982 inside cover and p3
21 Greyfriars Centre Updated Report 31st January 1982
22 PCC Minutes 25th February 1982
23 Ibid. 25th February 1982
24 Annual Parochial Church Meeting Minutes 1st April 1982
25 PCC Minutes 8th July 1982; Greyfriars News August 1982 p5f
26 PCC Minutes 27th January 1983; Greyfriars News February 1983 p11
27 Greyfriars Centre First Annual Report 1983/1984
28 Greyfriars News April 1983 p4
29 PCC Minutes 27th January 1983
30 Greyfriars News June 1983 p11; PCC Minutes 26th May 1983
31 Greyfriars News June 1984 p13
32 Greyfriars New Building Account at 31st December 1990
33 PCC Minutes 26th January 1984
34 Greyfriars News June 1985 p18
35 PCC Minutes 24th November 1983; Greyfriars News January 1984 p16
36 PCC Minutes 12th July 1984
37 Greyfriars News November 1984 Inside back cover
38 Ibid. April 1985 p3
39 PCC Minutes 6th December 1984
40 Greyfriars News January 1986 p8
41 PCC Minutes 11th July 1985

[42] Greyfriars News November 1985 p4; May 1986 p3
[43] Annual Parochial Church Meeting Minutes 28th March 1985
[44] Greyfriars News July 1985 Inside front cover; August 1985 p3
[45] Greyfriars Prayer Calendar 1st October 1985
[46] Greyfriars News September 1985 Inside cover
[47] PCC Minutes 3rd October 1985
[48] Improvements & Reordering Project at Greyfriars Church, March 1986, by J. Alan Bristow & Partner, Charlbury, Oxon (Ref. 340)
[49] PCC Minutes 25th September 1986
[50] Faculty of the Diocese of Oxford dated 10th December 1987
[51] PCC Minutes 17th January 1988; Certificate of Completion of Works Authorised by Faculty dated 2nd March 1989
[52] PCC Minutes 11th December 1986
[53] Ibid. 16th July 1987; Greyfriars News October 1987 p2
[54] Letter to the Times 31st May 1991 (Issue 64033) p19, quoted in Greyfriars News July 1991 p5
[55] PCC Minutes 29th January 1987 and 16th July 1987
[56] PCC Minutes 28th January 1988
[57] Ibid. 10th March 1988, 21st September 1989
[58] Greyfriars News February 1988 p3, September 1988 p4, February 1989 p3
[59] Ibid. November 1987 p5
[60] Annual Parochial Church Meeting Minutes 24th March 1988
[61] Greyfriars News July 1988 p5
[62] Ibid. January 1989 p1
[63] PCC Minutes 28th January 1988
[64] Greyfriars News January 1989 p6f
[65] Ibid. November 1988 p12
[66] Ibid. March 1989 p3
[67] PCC Minutes 4th May 1989
[68] Greyfriars News June 1989 p; July 1989 inside cover
[69] Minutes of Special PCC Meeting 8th August 1989
[70] Letter from Alan Bristow to John Brown, Greyfriars Centre Manager, dated 19th January 1988; PCC Minutes 30th June 1988
[71] Greyfriars News May 1989 p10
[72] PCC Minutes 4th January 1990; consultation booklet "Music in Greyfriars"; PCC Minutes 8th February 1990, 8th March 1990 and 3rd May 1990
[73] Greyfriars News August 1990 p4
[74] Ibid. March 1990 p4
[75] Ibid. May 1990 p5, May 1991 inside front cover, June 1992 inside cover, May 1993 p1 & 8, May 1995 inside front cover
[76] Ibid. December 1990 p5
[77] Ibid. July 1992 p4, September 1992 p5
[78] Ibid. June 1991 p10
[79] Ibid. November 1990 p6f
[80] Annual Parochial Church Meeting Minutes 5th April 1990
[81] Greyfriars News March 1991 p4, April 1991 p1f, 10
[82] Ibid. August 1991 inside front cover

[83] PCC Minutes 6th December 1990
[84] Greyfriars News February 1992 p9
[85] Ibid. September 1991 p1, February 1992 p8
[86] PCC Minutes 13th November 1980
[87] Greyfriars News October 1991 p5, November 1991 p1 & 10
[88] Ibid. June 1992 inside front cover
[89] Annual Parochial Church Meeting Minutes 2nd April 1992, Greyfriars News May 1992 p1, June 1992 p1, July 1992 p2
[90] PCC Minutes 26th November 1992
[91] Greyfriars News August 1993 p2
[92] Ibid. November 1992 p3f
[93] Ibid. September 1993 p10 – article by Peter Williams
[94] Ibid. March 1994 p1f
[95] PCC Minutes 22nd April 1993
[96] Ibid. 1st July 1993, 7th October 1993
[97] Ibid. 3rd February 1994
[98] Ibid. 30th June 1994
[99] PCC Meeting 24th November 1994
[100] Greyfriars News February 1993 p5; July 1993 p11, December 1993 p11, May 1994 p11
[101] Ibid. November 1994 p4
[102] Ibid. December 1994 p10f
[103] Ibid. January 1995 p10
[104] Ibid. February 1995 p6f

Chapter 19 Jonathan A. de B. Wilmot: Vicar from 1995

[1] "A History of St Marks Versailles" by Peter Milner on www.stmarksversailles.org accessed 12th August 2013
[2] Clerical appointments from Crockford's Clerical Directory
[3] PCC Minutes 24th November 1994
[4] Ibid. 21st January 1995
[5] Greyfriars News July 1995 p5
[6] PCC Minutes 23rd November 1995
[7] Greyfriars News January 1996 p5
[8] PCC Minutes 31st January 1969
[9] Greyfriars News February 1996 p4
[10] Ibid. February 1996 p2
[11] Ibid. March 1996 Inside Back Cover
[12] Annual Parochial Church Meeting minutes 18th April 1996
[13] Greyfriars News March 1996 p9
[14] PCC Minutes 4th July 1996
[15] Ibid. 26th September 1996, Greyfriars News November 1996 p4
[16] Greyfriars News March 1997 p4
[17] PCC Minutes 18th January 1996 and 23rd May 1996
[18] Initially September 1996, then with amendments November 1996. Produced by Robert Maguire OBE AA Dipl(Hons) RIBA of Maguire & Co, 104 High Street, Thame OX9 3DZ

[19] Greyfriars News May 1997 p2, July/August 1997 p2
[20] Letter dated 16th March 1998 to Mr P. J. Reynolds, Director, Gullett and Sons Ltd. With thanks to Gullett and Sons Ltd for a copy of this letter
[21] Greyfriars News July/August 1996 p1
[22] PCC Minutes 17th October 1996, Greyfriars News December 1996 p4
[23] PCC Minutes 30th April 1998
[24] Annual Parochial Church Meeting minutes 17th April 1997
[25] Greyfriars News September 1997 p5
[26] PCC Minutes 12th June 1997
[27] Greyfriars News September 1997 p1
[28] Ibid. November 1997 p1
[29] Ibid. July 1998 p1
[30] PCC Minutes 18th September 1997
[31] Ibid. 12th March 1998
[32] Ibid. 30th April 1998
[33] Greyfriars News November 1997 p4
[34] Ibid. March 1998 p8f
[35] PCC Minutes 17th September 1998, 16th November 1998, 10th December 1998
[36] Greyfriars News December 1998 p2
[37] Ibid. April 1999 p10; PCC Minutes 4th March 1999
[38] Greyfriars News September 1999 p3
[39] Ibid. November 1999 p2
[40] PCC Minutes 28th October 1999, 9th December 1999
[41] Ibid. 17th September 1998, Greyfriars News November 1998 p5
[42] Ibid. 17th September 1998, Greyfriars News November 1998 p12
[43] Greyfriars News November 1999 p12
[44] PCC Minutes 23rd September 1999, 9th December 1999
[45] Ibid. 29th April 1999
[46] Greyfriars News June 2000 p1; biographical details July 2000 p4
[47] PCC Minutes 13th January 2000
[48] Greyfriars News January 2000 p1
[49] Annual Report 2000 for Greyfriars Church, Reading p3, 9
[50] PCC Minutes 17th April 2000, 6th July 2000
[51] "Brief History of the Organ" by David Rance; PCC Minutes 17th April 2000
[52] Annual Report 2000 for Greyfriars Church, Reading p9
[53] "The Story of Greyfriars Church and Centre" by Heather Dyer, Revised August 2006
[54] Greyfriars News January 2001 p16
[55] PCC Minutes 2nd November 2000
[56] Annual Report 2000 for Greyfriars Church, Reading p6
[57] PCC Minutes 21st September 2000
[58] Ibid. 4th March 1999, 21st September 2000 and 2nd November 2000; Annual Report 2000 for Greyfriars Church, Reading p7
[59] Report of the Directors of New Hope 31st December 2002 (Company Registration Number 4096676, Charity registration Number 1088333)
[60] New Hope Trustees Meeting Minutes 8th January 2001
[61] GetReading Newspaper 22nd January 2002; Greyfriars News February 2002 p5
[62] Greyfriars News October 2002 p7

[63] Annual Parochial Church Meeting minutes 31st March 2003
[64] Ibid. 26th April 2001, 1st March 2002
[65] Greyfriars News June 2001 p4; February 2002 p3
[66] Ibid. June 2001 p3, July 2001 p3
[67] Ibid. July 2001 p3
[68] Ibid. August/September 2002 p4; October 2002 p11
[69] Ibid. June 2002 p4 and 38
[70] Annual Report 2003 for Greyfriars Church, Reading, p2 and 3
[71] Greyfriars News July /August 2003 p14f
[72] Ibid. September 2003 p15; PCC Minutes 16th May 2011
[73] Annual Report 2003 for Greyfriars Church, Reading, p3
[74] http://www.christianitymagazine.co.uk - article dated December 2012, accessed 6th September 2013
[75] Annual Report 2003 for Greyfriars Church, Reading, p3
[76] Greyfriars News October 2003 p4
[77] PCC Minutes 27th January 2003
[78] Greyfriars News May 2004 p5
[79] Ibid. May 2004 p6
[80] Greyfriars News February 2004 p10; March 2004 p4
[81] Ibid. June 2004 p3
[82] Annual Parochial Church Meeting minutes 29th March 2004, 26th April 2004
[83] Greyfriars News June 2004 p22; August/September 2004 p34f
[84] Annual Report for 2005 for Greyfriars Church, Reading, p3
[85] PCC Minutes 15th October 2005; Greyfriars News December 2005 p7
[86] Greyfriars News February 2006 p1
[87] PCC Minutes 27th September 2004
[88] Ibid. 5th September 2005
[89] Greyfriars News July/August 2006 p5
[90] Annual Report for 2005 for Greyfriars Church, Reading, p4
[91] Annual Report for 2006 for Greyfriars Church, Reading ,p3
[92] PCC Minutes 27th February 2006, Greyfriars News March 2006 p1, 3; May 2006 p1; Annual Report 2006 for Greyfriars Church, Reading, p3, 27
[93] Greyfriars News December 2005 p2; May 2006 p4; September 2010 p1
[94] Annual Parochial Church Meeting minutes 24th April 2006
[95] Greyfriars News July/August 2006 p2
[96] Ibid. July/August 2006 p3
[97] Ibid. September 2006 p1; December 2006 p2; PCC Minutes 4th September 2006
[98] Ibid. October 2006 p1
[99] Annual Report for 2006 for Greyfriars Church, Reading ,p29
[100] PCC Minutes 6th October 2009
[101] Annual Parochial Church Meeting minutes 20th April 2009
[102] PCC Minutes 15th January 2007
[103] Annual Report for 2007 for Greyfriars Church, Reading, p21f; the Greyfriars Missionary Trust is registered charity No. 270369
[104] Greyfriars and New Hope News November 2007 p8; February 2008 p7
[105] Ibid. February 2008 p1

[106] English Churchman 1st & 8th February 2008 p9
[107] PCC Minutes 3rd December 2007; 14th January 2008
[108] Greyfriars and New Hope News December 2008 p6; Annual Report for 2008 for Greyfriars Church, Reading, p32
[109] PCC Minutes 16th March 2009
[110] Greyfriars and New Hope News May 2008 p3f
[111] Ibid. June 2009 p8
[112] Ibid. January 2010 p2
[113] Ibid. April 2010 p12
[114] Ibid. April 2010 p2
[115] Ibid. November 2010 p3
[116] Ibid. October 2010 p2
[117] Ibid. April 2011 p2
[118] Annual Report for 2011 for Greyfriars Church, Reading, p4
[119] Greyfriars News December 2003 p36; Greyfriars and New Hope News July/August 2011 p8
[120] PCC Minutes 16th May 2011
[121] Ibid. 19th September 2011
[122] Ibid. 20th February 2012
[123] Ibid. 16th May 2011
[124] Annual Report for 2011 for Greyfriars Church, Reading, p35
[125] PCC Minutes 16th January 2012
[126] Greyfriars and New Hope News May 2013 p1, July/August 2013 p3
[127] John Moore Heritage Services, Beckley, OX3 9UZ, Project No. 2587
[128] Annual Report for 2012 for Greyfriars Church, Reading, p39f
[129] Annual Parochial Church Meeting minutes 15th April 2013
[130] Annual Report for 2012 for Greyfriars Church, Reading, p5
[131] Redevelopment of the Greyfriars Site, Autumn 2011 p3